WITHDRAWN

No longer the property of the
Boston Public Library.
Sale of this material benefits the Library.

W9-ATP-442

ALSO BY ILYON WOO

The Great Divorce:
A Nineteenth-Century Mother's
Extraordinary Fight Against Her
Husband, the Shakers, and Her Times

MASTER SLAVE HUSBAND WIFE

An Epic Journey
from Slavery
to Freedom

ILYON WOO

SIMON & SCHUSTER
New York London Sydney Toronto New Delhi

To Joon
and
to Kian, Oan, and Nari

Simon & Schuster
1230 Avenue of the Americas
New York, NY 10020

First Simon & Schuster hardcover edition January 2023

SIMON & SCHUSTER and colophon are registered
trademarks of Simon & Schuster, Inc.

For information about special discounts for bulk purchases,
please contact Simon & Schuster Special Sales at
1-866-506-1949 or business@simonandschuster.com.

The Simon & Schuster Speakers Bureau can bring authors to
your live event. For more information or to book an event,
contact the Simon & Schuster Speakers Bureau at
1-866-248-3049 or visit our website at www.simonspeakers.com.

Interior design by Lewelin Polanco
Map on p. vi by David Lindroth

Manufactured in the United States of America

3   5   7   9   10   8   6   4

Library of Congress Cataloging-in-Publication Data has been applied for.

ISBN 978-1-5011-9105-3
ISBN 978-1-5011-9107-7 (ebook)

Contents

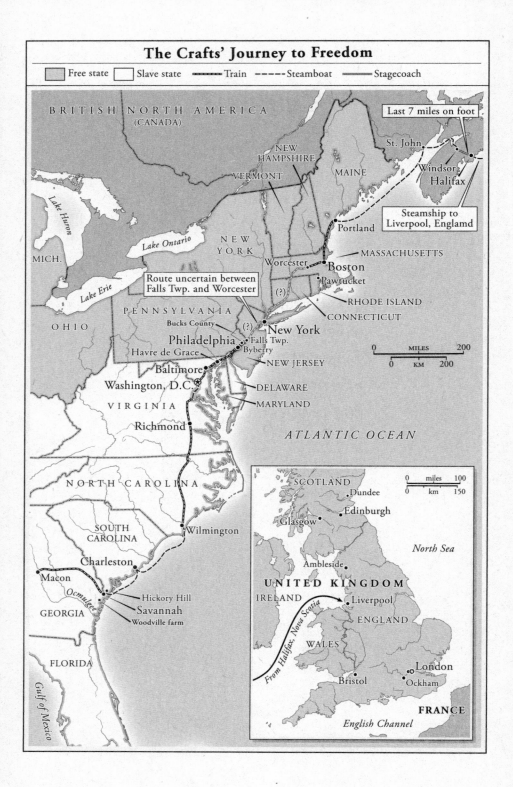

The Crafts' Journey to Freedom

Free state   Slave state   ┅┅┅ Train   ------ Steamboat   ──── Stagecoach

BRITISH NORTH AMERICA
(CANADA)

NEW HAMPSHIRE

VERMONT

MAINE

St. John

Last 7 miles on foot

Windsor
Halifax

Portland

Steamship to
Liverpool, Englamd

NEW YORK

Lake Huron

Lake Ontario

MICH.

Lake Erie

Worcester

Boston

MASSACHUSETTS

Pawtucket

Route uncertain between
Falls Twp. and Worcester

(?)

RHODE ISLAND

CONNECTICUT

OHIO

PENNSYLVANIA

Bucks County

(?)

Philadelphia

Falls Twp.

Byberry

New York

Havre de Grace

NEW JERSEY

Baltimore

DELAWARE

Washington, D.C.

MARYLAND

VIRGINIA

Richmond

ATLANTIC OCEAN

MILES   0   200

KM   0   200

NORTH CAROLINA

SOUTH CAROLINA

Wilmington

Charleston

Macon

Ocmulgee

Hickory Hill

GEORGIA

Savannah

Woodville farm

FLORIDA

Gulf of Mexico

SCOTLAND

Dundee

miles   0   100

km   0   150

Glasgow

Edinburgh

North Sea

Ambleside

UNITED KINGDOM

IRELAND

Liverpool

ENGLAND

From Halifax, Nova Scotia

WALES

London

Bristol

Ockham

FRANCE

English Channel

OVERTURE

REVOLUTIONS
OF 1848

||||||||||||||||||||||||||

In 1848 William and Ellen Craft, an enslaved couple in Georgia, embarked upon a five-thousand-mile journey of mutual self-emancipation across the world. Theirs is a love story that begins in a time of revolution—a revolution unfinished in the American War for Independence, a revolution that endures.

This story opens in that year of global democratic revolt, when, in wave upon wave—Sicily, Paris, Berlin, Vienna, and all across Europe—the people rose up against tyranny, monarchy, the powers that be. News of these uprisings ricocheted, carried across the seas by high-speed clipper ships, overland by rail, and in defiance of time and space by the marvelous Electro-Magnetic Telegraph. From New York down to New Orleans, Americans raised torches in celebration, sure that these revolutions rhymed with their own.

Americans watched Europe, while the ground shifted beneath their own feet.

In 1848 the war with Mexico was over, and the United States laid claim to five hundred thousand square miles of new territory. More than six states would emerge from this gigantic stretch of land, including California, where the discovery of gold would bring a rush of "forty-niners" the next year. The spirit of Manifest Destiny ran high: that will "to overspread and to possess the whole of the continent which Providence has given us for the development of the great experiment of liberty and federated self-government."

But cracks were forming along with this movement. A global pandemic, the cholera, was traveling fast. New immigrants joined the nation from Ireland, Germany, China, and other distant lands, challenging ideas of what an American could be. The two-party political system was breaking down, as voters became polarized over the engine that powered all that national growth: slavery. Politicians came to blows over the future of slavery in the territories, the rights of slavers, the question of who would inhabit the nation's expanded lands.

Meanwhile, those who could not claim the rights of American citizenship demanded the rights denied them.

In July 1848, at the historic first Woman's Rights Convention in Seneca Falls, New York, signers of a "Declaration of Sentiments" proclaimed, "We hold these truths to be self-evident: that all men *and women* are created equal." A leader among them was Frederick Douglass, who connected the revolutions in Europe to America's, and denounced the gulf between American aspirations and realities. As he would declare a few years later, one memorable July Fourth: "There is not a nation on the earth guilty of practices more shocking and bloody than are the people of the United States, at this very hour."

Still, Douglass held out hope. Change was coming: "The arm of commerce has borne away the gates of the strong city. Intelligence is penetrating the darkest corners of the globe. It makes its pathway over and under the sea, as well as on the earth. Wind, steam, and lightning are its chartered agents. Oceans no longer divide, but link nations together. From Boston to London is now a holiday excursion.

"Space," he said, "is comparatively annihilated."

Across space and time, in Macon, Georgia, William and Ellen Craft would also find inspiration in the American Declaration of Independence, whose words they knew, even as they were forbidden to read them—words that were read aloud in celebration every year on the very courthouse steps where William had once been sold.

This line caught their attention: "We hold these truths to be self-evident, that all men are created equal; that they are endowed by their Creator with certain inalienable rights; that from these, are life, liberty, and the pursuit of happiness." So, too, did this biblical verse, spoken by the apostle Paul: "God made of one blood all nations of men" (Acts 17:26). And in these words, William and Ellen Craft found fodder for a revolution of their own.

On their revolutionary travels, they did not swim, run, or hide, navigating by starlight. No Underground Railroad assisted them out of the South. Rather, they moved in full view of the world, harnessing the latest technologies of their day: steamboats, stagecoaches, and, above all, an actual railroad, riding tracks laid by the enslaved, empowered by their disguise as master and slave, by the reality of their love as husband and wife.

They would ride these same technologies to become celebrities on the lecture circuit and then defy a merciless new Fugitive Slave Act that helped draw the nation toward Civil War. In their own time, the Crafts were hailed as emblems of a new American Revolution. One of the most famed orators of their day prophesied that "future historians and poets would tell this story as one of the most thrilling tales in the nation's annals, and millions would read it with admiration." Theirs is a story that now, more than ever, requires retelling and remembering.

The story they lived is not neatly told. It offers no easy dividing lines between North and South, Black and White—no single person or place to blame. It is a story that holds the entire United States accountable and resists the closure of a happily ever after.

The Crafts passed through Washington, DC, at a time when enslaved men, women, and children were marched in shackles past the Capitol; when US congressmen looked out onto the streets to see them, and some wished to avert their eyes. They lived in Boston at a time when not only Southern slavers but also Americans across the country would have sent them back into bondage.

But they also lived in a time when people stood together with them—men and women of many colors, thousands strong in Boston's Fanueil Hall, who put aside political and other differences, if only for a moment. And when Frederick Douglass thundered, "Will you protect, rescue, save these people from being re-enslaved?" the thousands roared, "Yes!" in resounding affirmation, determined to do what was right, even if it meant sacrifice.

This book tells the story of the Crafts' revolt during the combustive years of 1848 to 1852, when the trajectories of the couple and the nation collide most dramatically. Though propelled by narrative, this work is not fictionalized. Every description, quotation, and line of dialogue comes from historic sources, beginning with the Crafts' own 1860 account, *Running a Thousand Miles for Freedom*. The story is also informed by historical materials beyond the scope of the Crafts' presentation, all detailed at the end of this book.

These sources make it possible to tend to questions such as: Why did the Crafts escape when they did? What inspired them? Who were their enslavers? What were the sleights of hand behind the magic they pulled off? Behind these questions, larger ones loom. Why is such an epic American story not better known? Or: What is it about this unforgettable story that makes it so difficult for us, as a nation, to remember?

Here is a picture of a couple and a nation in motion: a moving pan-orama, to reference a medium of the age. At heart, this is an American love story—not in the fairy-tale sense, but an enduring relationship between a man and a woman, a couple and a country. It begins in the earliest hours of a late-December morning.

MACON

Day 1, Morning:
*Wednesday,
December 20, 1848*

THE COTTAGE

|||||||||||||||||||||||||||

It is predawn in Macon, Georgia, and at four o'clock, the city does not move. The air is windless, chill, barely stirring the high, dark pines. Cotton Avenue is quiet, too, the giant weighing scales suspended, for the moment, behind closed warehouse doors. But the Ocmulgee River flows along the eastern shore, and so too, an enslaved couple moves, ready to transform, in a cabin in the shadow of a tall, white mansion.

They have scarcely slept these past few nights, as they rehearsed the moves they now perform. Ellen removes her gown, forgoing a corset, for once, though she needs to reshape her body in other ways, flatten or bind the swell of her breasts. She pulls on a white shirt, with a long vest and loose coat, slim-legged pants, and handsome cloak to cover it all. She does up the buttons, breathing in the late-December cold. Christmas is coming soon.

She dresses by candlelight, which flickers through the cottage, "her" workshop, locked with a key, the least of which she'll lose if she is caught. All around are the tools of her trade—workbaskets stocked with needles and thread, pins, scissors, cloth. Her husband's handiwork is in evidence as well: wood furniture, including a chest of drawers, now unlocked.

Ellen slips her feet into gentleman's boots, thick soled and solid. Though she has practiced, they must feel strange, an inch of leaden weight pulling each sole to the ground, an extra inch she needs. Ellen may have inherited her father's pale complexion, but not his height. Even for a woman, she is small.

William towers beside her, casting long shadows as he moves. They must do something with her hair, which he has just cut—gather it up, pack it. To leave it behind would be to leave a clue for whoever eventually storms down the door.

There are the final touches: a silky black cravat, also the bandages. Ellen wears one around her chin, another around her hand, which she props in a sling. She has more protection for her face, green-tinted glasses and an extra-tall silk hat—a "double-story" hat, William calls it, befitting how high it rises, and the fiction it covers. These additions hide her smoothness, her fear, her scars.

Ellen stands, now, at the center of the floor, transformed. To all appearances, she is a sick, rich, White young man—"a most respectable-looking gentleman," in her husband's words. He is ready too, in his usual pants and shirt, with only one new item, a white, secondhand beaver hat, nicer than anything he has worn before, the marker of a rich man's slave.

To think it had been a matter of days. Four days since they had first agreed to the idea, first called it possible. Four days of stuffing clothing into locked compartments, sewing, shopping, mapping the way. Four days, they would claim, to prepare for the run of a lifetime. Or, a lifetime of preparation, narrowed down to this.

William blows out the light.

They kneel and pray in the sudden dark.

They stand and wait, breath held.

Is that someone listening, watching outside? Just beyond their door is the back of the Collins house, where Master and Mistress should be asleep in bed.

The young couple, holding hands, step to the front of the cottage, as gently as they can. William unlocks the door, pushes it open, peers out. There is just the circle of trees, a whispering of leaves. Such stillness: he thinks of death. Nevertheless, he gives the sign to go.

Spooked, Ellen bursts into tears. They had borne witness to people torn by bloodhounds, beaten and branded, burned alive. They had seen the hunts, the frenzy around a slave chase. All this, they know, might be in store for them. They draw back in, holding each other one more time.

Each will have to begin the journey alone, on a separate path through Macon. William will take the shortest route available and hide aboard the train. It would be a danger for them both if he was recognized. The dangers may be even greater, though, for Ellen, who must travel a longer road. It would be bad enough for her to be caught trying to escape at all. How much worse for Master Collins to awake to learn that his wife's favored lady's maid dared to be a gentleman like him. Collins was a person of careful method, who believed that a punishment should fit a crime, and be instructive. What kind of instruction he would provide in such a case could only be imagined. William's thought: double vengeance.

As for the mistress, if she had ever interceded on behalf of her favorite slave—also her half sister—it is unlikely she would do so here, not if Ellen were found dressed in a man's pants, possibly from the master's own cloth. Ellen might have been spared at previous sales, but not this time. At the very least, she and William would be separated for good, likely after being made to witness one another's pain—if, that is, they remained alive.

Now silent, Ellen centers herself in prayer, in the faith that she will move by as she battles for mastery over every inch of the one thousand miles to come: faith in a power greater than any earthly Master, such as she will pretend to be. Stilled, she owns the moment.

"Come, William," she speaks.

Once more, the door opens. The two step out, their footfalls soft, like light on water. William turns the lock, pockets the key, a drop of metallic weight. They creep across the yard, to the street, near the house of the sleeping slavers. With a touch of hands, they part. When they next meet—or so they hope—they will take their places as master and slave, escaping to reunite as husband and wife.

WILLIAM

||||||||||||||||||||||||

William knew he needed to move fast. The train to Savannah did not leave until seven o'clock, giving him three more hours of darkness. But Macon would have its eyes wide open.

Having worked both as a hotel waiter and, in the early-morning hours, as a cabinetmaker, William was familiar with the city's waking rhythms: the hotel breakfasts, served hot before sunrise; the movement of porters hauling luggage to the curb for an even earlier train to Atlanta; the shuttling of trunks and hatboxes, carpetbags and passengers onto hacks across town. The market would be abuzz before daybreak, while vendors and wagons would crowd the street by city hall. Where the Collins house stood on Mulberry Street was quieter, but one never knew. Opposite the house lived Eugenius Nisbet with his wife and twelve children, including babies who might cause wakings at any hour. William would have to take care not to be observed.

It was a fraction of a mile in total from the Collins mansion to the railroad: roughly fourteen hundred feet down Mulberry, another thousand feet to cross the bridge at Fifth Street, then a final short walk to the station to the eastern side of the city. But of the one thousand miles to come, this first half mile would be among the longest.

William was conspicuous, being more than six feet tall, broad shouldered, and handsome, by all accounts. Even in a crowd, he stood out, a head taller than the average American man. He moved past the mansion with his hat low, its fuzzy white brim casting a shadow over his deep-set eyes, his high cheekbones, the dark skin that marked him as a slave.

In Georgia, any Black person was legally presumed to be enslaved until proven otherwise. William could be questioned at any time, not only by slave patrols but also by any White person, who was authorized to "moderately correct" him if he did not respond. It would be illegal for William to fight back. For an enslaved person to maim or bruise a White person—unless under the command or in the defense of another White person—was a capital crime.

For these reasons and more, William was required to have the pass he carried. Only with this precious slip of paper, which approved travel to a specific destination for a set time, could he travel legally. By law, the punishment for being caught without a pass was "a whipping on the bare back, not exceeding twenty lashes."

The pass had not come from William's official owner (his third enslaver, a young man named Ira Hamilton Taylor, whom he scarcely saw), but from his main employer, the cabinetmaker who had trained him since boyhood. William had made arrangements with his owner to pay for the "privilege" of hiring himself out and wore a special badge that identified him as a skilled laborer. The cost of this arrangement was high, especially since William had to cover all his personal expenses, but it gave him space to earn wages, and some mobility.

William had asked for permission to accompany his wife on a journey about twelve miles away, to see a dying relative. The cabinetmaker had been reluctant, for the holidays were a busy time at the shop. As he issued the pass, he told William that he would have to return by Christmas. But William intended that he and Ellen would be in a free city, Philadelphia, by Christmas Day—even farther north, hopefully, by the time they were discovered missing. They planned three moves:

from Macon, a train to Savannah, Georgia;

from Savannah, a steamboat to Charleston, South Carolina; and

from Charleston, a final steamship to Philadelphia, Pennsylvania, and beyond.

They aimed for Canada, a land without slavery. Not only did William's latest enslaver have roots in the North, but Ellen was held captive by one of the most enterprising middlemen in Macon, with friends and business partners all along the eastern coast. It would be safer to set their sights beyond the nation. But first, there was Macon to cross.

William was intimately acquainted with the city's downtown, where he worked and slept most nights, all except for the one night a week he was allowed to spend with Ellen, sometimes more, if they could sneak in extra meetings, as they had the past several nights. Mulberry led straight down to Fifth Street, by the bridge. But William might have chosen a different route this morning, one that would avoid his usual places, and Court-house square.

It was here that he had seen fugitives handcuffed, bloodied, limping along, their bodies so ravaged from battles with slave hunters and bloodhounds that they could barely make their way to the jailhouse on the southwest corner. Then there was the courthouse. High on the steps of the distinguished edifice where some went for justice, others were sold. Public slave auctions were held on the first Tuesday of every month, with notices posted on the courthouse door, and in the newspapers, where human beings were listed for sale beside furniture, house lots, and livestock. William had once stood here, alongside his younger sister. Now he vowed not to be taken alive.

William moved swiftly in the darkness, venturing toward the light cast by the Fifth Street Bridge, the only place to cross the river for miles around. Directly over the Ocmulgee, along the road pointed toward the state capital, Milledgeville, lay more hotels and stores, including that of a self-emancipated man named Solomon Humphrey, known as "Free Sol," who had purchased freedom himself and his family members, and now bought and sold cotton. It was said that Humphrey hired all White clerks in his shop, and that he had White guests to dinner, though it was also said he was careful to serve his guests himself. For William, Humphrey's rare path to freedom was a road not taken, or denied. Whatever hopes William might once have harbored of pursuing such a path—of buying himself and Ellen, of having some kind of freedom where he now stood—disappeared, he knew, as soon as he defied the law by escaping.

Having successfully crossed the river, William crept past the stores and the hotel by the depot, not knowing what sleepless guest might be up already. He ventured past the lone ticket booth, the warehouses behind it, and toward the sleeping train. He slipped into the designated Negro car.

It was the first successful step in the plan, his passage to the east side of the river—a return. His parents, whose memory he kept, once lived in that direction. As he waited for Ellen, he could only pray that he would not lose her, as he had lost them.

ELLEN

||||||||||||||||||||||||||

Ellen had nearly three hours to spend in the city she had known since she was eleven years old. Macon must have seemed bewildering, outsized, then, when she had been first separated from her mother and disposed of as a wedding present for her half-sister-turned-enslaver. The city was scarcely older than Ellen, carved up from ancient lands once marked as Muscogee or Creek. (Ellen's father, who counted land surveying among his many trades, had helped draw the city lines himself.) But Macon had grown up fast and would grow even faster, fueled by cotton money from the surrounding country and its prime spot on the river.

The gambling and lawlessness that once plagued the town had settled down by the time of Ellen's arrival. Shade trees were planted to block the heat, and houses went up in orderly lines, though cattle, hogs, and other beasts still roamed wild. Among all the grand new homes studding the city grid, there had been none finer than the mansion built for Ellen's young mistress. Three stories high, bright white, with six front pillars and ample wings, the mansion promised empire, if superficially. (The brick house was plastered and painted to evoke marble.)

From the shadow of this building, Ellen emerged, dressed like a man who might inherit such a home—a man for whom Macon was a playground. There were excellent hotels with day rates, hung with sensuous paintings in the style of Titian and Correggio. Eating houses served venison and oysters, imported nightly by railroad. Entertainment included bowling saloons and a theater, scandalously converted from a church. Macon offered most anything that might appeal to a rich young man with a freely spending hand.

Soon the stores would open, and a gentleman of Ellen's appearance might get a shave or have his hair washed and oiled at the Macon Shaving Saloon. Amid debates over the virtues of facial hair, the *Georgia Telegraph* recently quoted one young lady declaring her preference for the clean shaven. In a few years, the popularity of the sweet, boyish look would fully give way to a chunkier, bearded, paternal style. Fortunately for Ellen, this was not yet the case.

But of all the sites where Ellen might have lingered, the one that would have drawn her most powerfully, in spirit if not in body, was the house where her mother remained enslaved by the man who was Ellen's enslaver—and her father.

James Smith was over six feet tall and big bodied, with a ruddy complexion and voice "like a bassoon" when he let it roar. As described by his son Bob's friend, the "old major" was a "rich cotton planter who . . . had high notions of personal honor, who took his 'drams' when he felt like it, used profane language except in the company of women."

Recalled as hot tempered but generous, Smith had been known to dispense a mighty hospitality from his mansion in Clinton, Georgia, where he had lived before moving across the river to Macon. There, from behind the shade of double piazzas that kept his loved ones cool, it was said he "sold his crop and occasionally a negro, thought himself a good citizen, and felt sure that he was sound on politics and fox hunting." There, as further recalled, he "worked many negroes, to whom he was kind in his own imperious way."

More than Smith's voice and personality were outsized. When Ellen was growing up, Smith was one of the most powerful men in Clinton, then the seat of Jones County. Famous for its hospitality and practical jokesters, Clinton was where ladies ventured for dress fabrics, and the devout came to worship. Plantations spread wide, and Samuel Griswold, a Connecticut Yankee, made a fortune in cotton gins—the invention associated with another New Englander, Eli Whitney. But darker profits also flourished. One day, an infamous slave trader, Hope Hull Slatter, would announce his business in Baltimore with a sign reading: "From Clinton, Georgia." No other words were needed to advertise his credentials or what his business was about.

A child of the republic, Smith had arrived in this area as a young man, with his nineteen-year-old bride and little more. He had inherited from his father—a South Carolinian Revolutionary War veteran—not so much money or property as a taste for movement and independence, borne of rebellion, which he would pass on. But the man who would become Ellen Craft's father was a restless spirit who used his imagination, gumption, and geographic sense to shape his world. He became a city planner, merchant, attorney, justice, and elected official. Early on, he laid claim to a little land, his wife, one baby, and one slave. By midcentury, he had more land, houses, and carriages than he could occupy at once. He was also a major enslaver, with 116 souls named among his possessions, among them, Ellen's mother.

Two stories about her father would have been familiar to Ellen from the days of her childhood and just before. The first testified to his extreme wealth. When the Marquis de Lafayette swung through the region, looking younger with his fake hair than his bald-headed son (named Georges Washington de Lafayette), James Smith was among those invited to a feast. He had a seat in Lafayette's orbit, near enough to be noticed when he fainted upon discovering that a thief had emptied his pocketbook of as much as $5,000 in notes.

Smith's second claim to fame came when he served as the defense attorney in a sensational case of identity theft involving the impersonation of a prodigal rich man's son who stood to inherit one of the largest fortunes in the county. The scion in question, Jesse Bunkley (nephew to Clinton's infamous slave trader Hope Hull Slatter), was called "a wild, bad boy." He had been kicked out of college and stolen a horse before being presumed dead in New Orleans. Then, years later, James Smith received mail from a young man claiming to be Bunkley.

There were many reasons for Smith to be skeptical. Jesse was sandy haired and snub nosed, with hazel eyes and a chewed-up middle finger, while this man had dark hair, a hooked nose, blue eyes, and all his fingers intact. When handed a pen, the young man—supposedly trained in the Classics—had trouble writing his own name. But Smith summoned more than one hundred witnesses, transforming the courthouse into a veritable Georgian circus, especially when the testimony turned to the delicate matter of whether the unusual markings on the accused's private parts—mismatched testicles, and a strange "ring of hair"—matched Bunkley's.

In the end, the young man, Elijah Barber, was convicted as a swindler, but some remained adamant that a mistake had been made. The trial was widely debated and no doubt known to every level of Smith's household. It may well have come to the attention of his children—one of whom, Ellen, may have absorbed both the dangers and possibilities of impersonation. Here, after all, was an enterprising, dark-haired nobody who could scarcely hold a pen, but who, with the counsel of her own father, had nearly passed for a son of the highest class.

What Ellen might have felt as she left the Smith house, in body or spirit, can only be imagined. A light might shine on the child who had suffered, on her longing for the mother who taught her to love. But there was this too: now on the run, the child who had once been banished from this household for her physical resemblance to her enslaving father, which his wife could not stand to see, harnessed that likeness as a power. She had command of her ambiguity. In a moment of her own choosing, she had sprung from the lowest rung of the social ladder, to the very top. If only her hold would stay.

As a White man's son, Ellen now had infinite mobility through the streets she had once been forbidden to walk without a pass. But there were streets to avoid. Not far from where her mother lived, on Poplar Avenue, stood the outdoor cotton market. And all along that street, down to Fourth Street, were the businesses of Macon's slave trade.

In some cities, slave sales took place in any alleyway or street corner, but in Macon, the law required traders to keep their business indoors—for even slavers recognized that the business appeared unseemly. Human property had to be stored, or kept off the street, in "slave pens," as these prisons were called. A visitor to one such establishment remembered hearing of the men, women, and children he had glimpsed behind the gate: "You may have them singly or by the lot, just as you wish."

As an alternative route, Ellen might have ventured to the northern part of the city, where a women's college stood upon a hill, its windows dark. Claimed to be the first in the world to grant a degree to a woman, the future Wesleyan College had its roots in Ellen's father's work, too, in a female seminary he had helped found. At the school's first baccalaureate address, its president—a preacher well known to Ellen's enslaving family—was exultant as he exhorted, "Woman can do more! It is her province, her right, her duty. . . .

"Come forth and live!" he urged. "Let your understandings swell out to the fullness of their native dimensions, and walk abroad majestic in thought."

As an enslaved lady's maid, Ellen would have heard none of his exclamations. For her, all doors to learning remained closed. It was against the law for her to acquire literacy, though secretly, she and William had familiarized themselves with the alphabet, if not enough to read. This was one among many reasons Ellen ran now. She yearned to learn, to write her name and decode signs—skills without which she was in ever greater danger.

Even so, the words uttered by the preacher-president had hovered in the ether. And now, disguised as a man, the young woman to whom all education was denied seized upon the creed.

By six in the morning, patchworks of illumination were visible in Macon's hotels, as passengers bound for the earlier train to Atlanta prepared for departure. Wherever she might have wandered before, Ellen eventually needed to head for the bridge and train. The streets were ripe, since sewage and garbage were managed ad hoc, as was standard in these times. Store signs caught the eye, including one featuring a mammoth hat. But there was an even more unusual display, closed at this hour, that people would long remember.

Guests at Washington Hall and others passing near the corner of Mulberry and Second Streets would encounter a Black man appearing to fish for a book in a tub of water. Asked what he was doing, the man would reply that he was fishing for his master, and direct them to a jewelry store. The sign announced the services of William Johnston, "a native Georgian and a self-taught Genius." Witnesses to the fisherman would not forget that name, which meant something to Ellen too, for William Johnston (or Johnson) was the name she would use on this journey.

In unaccustomed clothes, with an unaccustomed status, this young Mr. Johnson now walked toward the station where, as an enslaved lady's maid, she had previously stepped, perhaps carrying parcels or minding children. The outfit was definitely too big on Ellen's small frame, the vest reaching her hips. Indeed, William had worried when she had first tried it on. But as Ellen knew well, the sacque-style coat was meant to hang loosely, and it hid her vest. Most importantly, the pants fit right—guaranteed, since Ellen had sewn them herself.

Under all the outer baggage, freedom from corseting was surely a novel feeling; so, too, were the gentleman's drawers. American ladies typically did not wear underwear, as known today. The closest thing to panties, owned by a wealthy few, were crotchless drawers, open in the middle, so that women could relieve themselves more easily beneath the burden of their skirts and petticoats. Those who could afford such luxuries had access to vessels shaped like gravy boats, called *bordalous*, which they could hold under their skirts, then hand to others to empty.

The absence of skirting, the lightness of her hair, an unencumbered torso, all that bandaging—no matter how much she had practiced, Ellen surely felt strange. As a clothing expert, too, she was aware of her deficiencies: namely, the poor fit of her manufactured clothing. Even if she overheated, she would have to keep on her layers to cover that absurdly proportioned vest. Only from afar, with a squint, might she pass as a man of style.

But Ellen could also take hope in the other signifiers, encoded in her outfit, which displayed her status, including her spurred, calfskin boots, which raised her up and announced her as an equestrian: the kind of man who owned horses that were so fine, fast, or wild that they required her to keep them in line. They advertised her readiness for motion, no matter her disability. And ultimately they showed what kind of master she was, ready to use force, inflict pain upon another body, if need be.

No one noticed or objected as she finally neared Court-house square, edging toward the bridge. Following the flow of the traffic, the wagons, the riders, and travelers on foot, Ellen crossed the Ocmulgee, passing the shops and hotels of East Macon, as William had. To be determined: whether she would pass muster in an actual exchange. With her right arm snugly in her sling, her gaze obscured, she braced herself for the ticket booth, ready to pay.

THE STATION

|||||||||||||||||||||||||

William waited in the Negro car, closest to the tender and engine, with its flying sparks and noxious fumes. The car more resembled a freight carrier than a carriage, transporting luggage alongside enslaved people—some of whom, like William, accompanied their enslavers, others who traveled to be sold.

As dawn began to break, the station filled with travelers bound for Savannah, their bags surely bursting with parcels, gowns to be worn at Christmas, treats to share with loved ones. Ensconced quietly in the only car where a Black man was supposed to sit, William carried the cottage key and a pass. And he, or perhaps Ellen, carried a pistol.

How the Crafts had obtained the weapon, contraband for the enslaved, is a secret neither would disclose. It is also unclear who carried the gun at this time. But decades later, William would testify that they had a pistol in their possession, a final means of defense and escape. On this morning, William had to hope that they would not need to use it. He himself had resolved to kill or be killed, rather than be captured.

Traffic at the station now thinned, as travelers crowded about the train, ready to board. Some checked their bags, their hat boxes, their trunks, in exchange for small brass tags. They said their good-byes. For enslaved riders, this may have been the last time they would see the faces of loved ones, if their loved ones even had permission to see them off.

With the engine fed and the water tank full, the conductor made his final calls. William dared to peek outside. Linked to him, he knew, if only by way of rickety clasps between the cars, was Ellen, who by this time should have been seated in first class.

It would be difficult for William to see her before the train stop. Travel between railway cars was hazardous, even for experienced conductors, so much so that some railroads put up pictures of gravestones as a warning. But briefly, William could glimpse the ticket booth, where Ellen, as his master, would have purchased two tickets.

Instead of his wife, he saw another familiar figure hurrying up to the ticket window. His heart dropped. The man interrogated the ticket seller, then pushed his way through the crowd on the platform, with purpose. It was William's employer, known to him since childhood, scanning the throng as he approached the cars. The cabinetmaker was coming for him.

Beneath the tall hat, tinted spectacles, and poultices, Ellen's features were barely visible. Her eyes of variable color (brown to some, hazel to others), the heart-shaped outline of her face, the subtle cleft on her smooth chin—all were obscured. Anyone looking at her from behind a ticket counter would see a sickly young man of privilege, maybe traveling home from college.

Ellen had more than enough money for a ticket, as much as $150 by one estimate (more than $5,000 today), earned from William's extra hours at the cabinetmaker's shop, his waiting tables, and possibly her sewing work. She carried it all on her body. A through ticket for herself from Macon to Charleston (including train, steamer, omnibus fares, and meals) cost about $10, while William's fare was roughly half that. In the low voice she had rehearsed, with as confident a posture as she could muster, she requested passage for herself and her slave.

The ticket seller handed her stubs of paper, marked on one side with the names of the stations she would pass. As she could not read, she would have to track her route by listening vigilantly to the calls of the conductor. Fortunately, Savannah was the last stop on this line. If the ticket seller had asked her to sign her name, he did not actually make her do it, seeing from the look of her arm and her troubled bearing that Mr. Johnson was disabled.

There was the luggage to tend to—possibly a bandbox or carpet bag, light enough for Ellen to have carried on her "good" arm, but also, more problematically, a trunk, or even a pair of trunks, whose transport may have been arranged in advance. No one would have guessed the contents, certainly not the porter who assisted Mr. Johnson on this day. Stored deep within the folds of this baggage was a full set of a slave woman's clothes. The porter was known to Ellen: it was said that he had once asked her to marry him. This man now called her "Young Master" and thanked her for the tip she gave him—a parting gift, as he could not have known, from someone he had once loved.

Ellen boarded as swiftly as an invalid could be expected to move. She stepped up onto a platform, and as she entered the enclosed carriage, she may have eyed the exit on the opposite end—another escape, if needed. There was a double row of seats on either side of a long central aisle, with hangers and racks above, for coats and bags. A smoky anthracite stove sent out an uneven heat, barely touching the farthest passengers and threatening to scorch the nearest ones.

Ellen chose an empty seat by a window and fixed her gaze outside. East Macon lay before her. If all went well, she would soon behold the vast sculpted mounds where generations of Native people, including the Muscogee or Creek, had once lived, prayed, and buried their dead. Older Georgians still recalled the morning when the people who cherished these lands had been forced from their homes, and the cries of the men, women, and children. The rail tracks cut through the sacred grounds, now popular for picnicking. Ellen's present enslaver, Robert Collins, had overseen the construction himself. It had been his laborers, likely enslaved, who had discovered relics four feet underground, including earthenware, spoons, and human bones, among them those of a seven- or eight-year-old child. Collins's brother Charles had collected some of these relics and displayed them in town.

Robert Collins had been hailed a hero for his ability to build tracks over these final miles of ground. The Central Railroad had been plagued with problems from the start. There had been tension between Black and White laborers (largely Irish and German immigrants, and a few Italian women), employed by competing contractors, who eventually turned exclusively to enslaved labor because it was considered more reliable and cheap—and good for local enslavers, who rented out the workforce. Long, strong rains had wiped away bridges and roads; workers had sickened and died from swamp fever, which also killed the young railroad president. Then stock prices plummeted, contractors balked, and the venture seemed doomed.

That was when Collins and his friend Elam Alexander had come to the rescue, motivated by $21,000 in bonds, and pushed workers to complete the final fifty miles in record time. Cheering over barbecue in 1843, officials boasted that it was the longest railroad in the world under single ownership. Two years later, Maconites toasted to a fine new ride, said to be superior to anything in the North.

How they had feted the glorious first-class cars, where Ellen now sat, ladies and gentlemen clinking glasses of iced, spiked lemonade.

How they had marveled at the thundering of the great iron horse, the clanging of its bell, the twenty-mile-per-hour clatter over metallic T-rail tracks. There had been hitches, to be sure. Fires and black dust were common. Horses threw off their owners or bolted when the trains came near; opponents to the railroad wreaked havoc by jamming pieces of wood into the tracks. A cave-in in the home stretch buried four workers, killing two. Collins suffered financial losses, which plagued him even now. But the train's first crossing had been a triumph. As a giant banner expressed in Court-house square, the Central Railroad was "The salvation of Georgia."

Now it was Ellen's time. She had moved by her own will through Macon, unrecognized. She had convinced the ticket seller that she was a gentleman worthy of first class. She had paid for herself and her slave. She had crossed key lines by which people commonly defined themselves and judged others—race, gender, class, and ability—all before dawn. And if everything went well, she would escape on a route built and paid for by the lives and labor of enslaved men, women, and even children.

If Collins could see her now, outfitted as a younger version of himself, what would he say? And what would become of her mother? They had been forced to separate before. Still, they had known, then, that their good-bye was not for good. Ellen had not needed to fear, as she did now, that her mother might suffer retaliation, interrogation, or even torture, so often used on loved ones in the hunt for those who sought their freedom.

As she waited for the train to leave Macon, Ellen knew she could count on nothing after this ride. If she returned, she would probably be in chains. If she succeeded, she was unlikely to see her loved ones again—excepting if prayers could be answered, William. Were she to survive, Ellen would do everything in her power to emancipate her mother, but she and William would have to free themselves first.

A movement at one of the exits drew Ellen's attention: a familiar form, among the last she would hope to encounter. The cabinetmaker from William's shop peered into her car. He saw her, yet he did not register her—she was, after all, a suited White man, not the slave he sought. He turned abruptly to leave.

Beneath the double-story hat, Ellen exhaled, no doubt with a rush of feeling. She had not been detected—it was another successful passing—but her only companion, the love of her life, might soon be.

There was little she could do but wait and pray that she did not hear shouting from the cars next door.

———

In the Negro car, William drew his beaver hat low and shrank into the farthest corner. He turned his face from the exit, waiting for the man to come.

William had seen the cabinetmaker checking the cars; it was only a matter of time before the man arrived to drag him out. How he and Ellen might have revealed themselves or how this man came to know they had run, William had no clue, but he was certain that their plot had been uncovered.

William had belonged to himself for all of a morning, and now he might be convicted of carrying off Mr. Ira Hamilton Taylor's valuable property, and, with Ellen, Dr. Robert Collins's too. He listened, sound being his best available guide. Would the man go after Ellen first? There was no noise to suggest that there was any turmoil. What he heard instead was the blissful ringing of the bell, and he was startled by the sensation of movement. The journey to Savannah had begun.

———

As the train lurched forward, Ellen's attention remained at the window, her gaze turned out. Her husband had not appeared on the platform, hauled out as a runaway. No one had fired a shot. Instead, there was just the cabinetmaker, heading away from the train.

Later, Ellen would learn that the man had a funny feeling that morning that his trusted assistant was on the run, and followed his instincts to the depot. He had little time and only managed to scan the tracks and a few cars, entirely missing the Negro car before the train took off, but left satisfied, believing he had been anxious for naught.

With the train now chugging forth, her body aligned with its momentum, Ellen could finally get her bearings. It was a rough ride. The seats were hard and thinly padded, scarcely blunting the blows of the "mad dragon," as Charles Dickens had described American trains. The air was stale and rank, reeking of tobacco freely smoked, chewed, spat on the floor. Spit flew and sometimes sizzled, landing in the designated receptacles only occasionally. Above all, the train was loud, making noises that reportedly sounded like a dozen asthmatic donkeys.

Ellen turned from the window where, in the summers, travelers would lean out or even hang out their feet, eager to touch cool, fresh air. It was then, as she shifted her gaze, that she first became aware that someone was sitting right beside her, someone she knew. In fact, she had seen him the night before at a dinner he had attended as a guest at the Collins home. He had been a familiar figure since her childhood.

The old man greeted her brightly.

"It is a very fine morning, sir," he said, as pleasant as can be.

Scott Cray was no stranger to this route. A longtime resident of Darien, Georgia, he had journeyed from Macon to Savannah many times before, well before the advent of the railroad, in which he had been an investor. Cray was no stranger to Robert Collins, either—a North Carolina transplant like himself, whom he would come to rely upon as a son. He and Collins went back more than a decade, at least, helping to found the Macon Library and Lyceum Society. Cray had also known Ellen since she was a child—which is why, Ellen now suspected, he may have been tasked with her return.

There are other reasons why Cray might have been given such a charge. A onetime city alderman, canal commissioner, banker, and auctioneer, Cray was known as a man who could be depended upon to collect, manage, and return others' property, including slaves. In 1818 A. H. Powell posted a runaway notice in the *Darien Gazette* for men named Nosko and Chance, adding: "A reward of ten dollars each will be paid by delivering them to Scott Cray." In the coming summer, Cray would be entrusted with the management of three enslaved women, Kitty, Mary, and Polly. Ellen may not have been aware of these duties, but as the old man sat so close to her, she was sure that he had been summoned. After all, he had been Collins's guest just the night before. If anyone could recognize her and engineer her return, Scott Cray could.

He repeated his question, with more volume and urgency: "It is a very fine morning, sir!"

Removing herself was not an option, so should she answer him? What if he pressed on and asked her for information about herself, as a gentleman was likely to do? Could she manage the conversation without giving herself away? If he did not know her yet, would he know her by her voice?

Ellen in that moment, decided upon a course of action that might have cost her a beating or even her life as an enslaved woman—one that she hoped would save her instead. She ignored him, pretending to be deaf.

Cray was not pleased. The young man beside him, who took no notice of a fellow gentleman's sitting down, continued to stare fixedly out the window, despite two greetings.

Still no answer. Other passengers looked on with amusement, one laughed out loud. Now Cray was annoyed.

"I will make him hear," he vowed, before repeating, "It is a very fine morning, sir," his voice ringing through the car.

At last, the young gentleman turned toward him, bowed politely, and uttered a single word—not "Yes, sir," but "Yes"—before returning his gaze to the window.

From across the seat, a fellow traveler offered the old man an exit, and inadvertently, perhaps, the young one as well. It is "a very great deprivation to be deaf," he observed.

"Yes, and I shall not trouble that fellow any more," Cray agreed, his pride mollified. The men went on to chat about popular subjects among their class: slaves, cotton, abolitionists.

Abolitionists! Ellen had heard this word before, from the lips of those who would have her believe that abolitionists were people who meant her harm. As the train moved forward and the conversation continued, the meaning of the word transformed, indicating to Ellen that she was not alone in her quest for freedom or in believing in her right to be free.

The train stopped at Larksville, and, next, at Gordon. There Scott Cray disembarked for his final destination of Milledgeville, which was then Georgia's capital. Ellen could only have felt relief to see the old man go, sure now that Cray had not been there for her after all.

Eighteen miles they had traveled, a long first hour. Though it was early, the two fugitives—for this is what they had officially become—had this much to savor. Separately, they had passed their first tests, with three men who had known them well, each in a different way: an employer, an owner's trusted friend, and even a onetime suitor. They had left Macon behind.

Roughly eleven hours of travel, more than 170 miles, remained to Savannah, where they would arrive, as they had left, in darkness: time and space in which to move forward, but also look back.

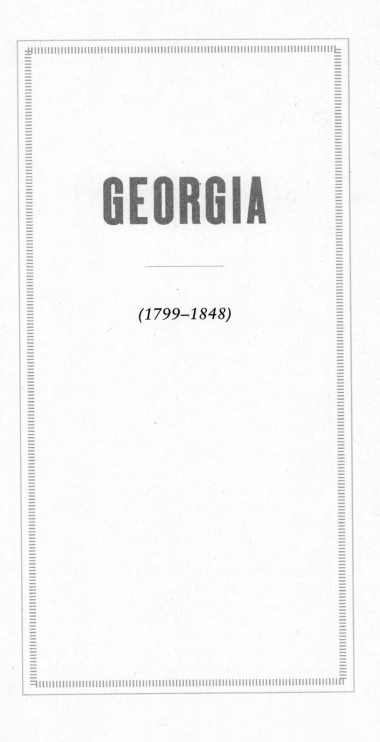

GEORGIA

(1799–1848)

THE CRAFTS

|||||||||||||||||||||||||||

Milledgeville may have been Scott Cray's destination, but for William, it was his place of birth, where he and his parents, his brothers, and his sisters had all been enslaved by one man—Hugh Craft—before that man had sold them each and all, leaving William with only his name.

Hugh Craft himself had suffered multiple family losses. Born in 1799, he hailed from an insular nook of Maryland's eastern shore known as Craft's Neck—a fierce, lonesome terrain, roughly the same geographic region where Frederick Douglass and Harriet Tubman would be born. There he had grown up encircled by other Craft families, each of whom dutifully marked their chimneys with their dates of construction. For this child, slavery was a norm, with five enslaved people in his household by the time he was a toddler.

In fact, the surname he passed on might have been Charlescraft, had it not been for his father, Benjamin, a powerfully built farmer who boldly lopped off the "Charles." Benjamin Craft would be remembered for his strong body and strong gestures. But his strength couldn't keep away death; he died when his son was seven. Hugh's mother died a few months later.

At fourteen, Hugh Craft struck out for the Georgia frontier, with plans to become a doctor, but after a brief time at the university in Athens, he quit to join an uncle in business. By twenty, the orphaned boy from Craft's Neck was a married man in Milledgeville. He was also an owner of human property. Census takers scanning the Craft home in 1820 marked seven columns for "slaves": four boys and one girl under fourteen, and a man and a woman between twenty-six and forty-five years old. It is possible that these included William's parents and older siblings.

When and how Craft acquired William's parents is uncertain, as is so much else about their lives. What is known is that William was born to them on September 22, 1823. He was one of five children, possibly more. Whereas the names and birth dates of Hugh Craft's fourteen children, born and lost, would be recorded carefully in a family Bible, those of the people he enslaved—and the losses they endured—would go unmarked. Only William's birthday (remarkably) remains.

William's early years coincided with a tumultuous time in Craft's household. When William was born, Craft was just beginning to make a name for himself. As William learned to walk and talk, the young merchant was often on the road, cutting long paths back and forth to Charleston, Savannah, and as far north as New York, where he marveled at the cliffs above the Hudson River, and splurged on tailored coats custom-cut for himself and his wife, Mary.

Three days past William's first birthday, Craft celebrated the opening of a New Cash Store, stocked with goods carried back from New York, including two giant bales of "Negro clothes" and three hundred pairs of "Negro shoes." Spun, sewn, and cut in Northern factories, these clothes were made of Southern cotton, shipped up North, and sent back home transformed.

In his absence, Mary, the wife he left to preside over the household in his absence—a devout young woman who had once gone to school in Chapel Hill, North Carolina—was becoming sick and melancholy. Winters were difficult because, as she confided to her best friend, Martha, this was the busiest season for her husband's business. Summertimes were a struggle, too, with outbreaks of fever and heat.

Then Mary lost two young children within a year. Martha offered the consolation—often given in these times—that no mother could deny her children the certainty of death, which would bring them to God's glory. But Mary withdrew deep into herself, worrying her husband in the midst of his awestruck tour of the nation's capital. Hugh Craft promised to take his wife to the springs when he returned and bring candy for their surviving son, Henry.

Mary Craft died young, leaving behind Henry and his two younger sisters. Mary's saucy best friend, Martha, married Hugh Craft shortly after, but she also died in childbirth. Elizabeth Collier became the third Mrs. Craft: she is the one whom William would have remembered as Mistress. She, too, would lose her first child but would eventually give birth to eight more.

Craft was a man who, as Henry would remember, bore his losses stoically. He was a father who never kissed his children and never cried, but who made his love known in his own way, whether through an affectionate sign off in his letters, or sweets brought from far away. Henry was as different from his father as his ornately curled penmanship was from his father's jagged scrawl. Meticulous, demanding, occasionally hurtful to his son, and doggedly optimistic in the face of repeated misfortune, Hugh Craft was, said Henry, "the strangest compound I have ever met."

Others recalled Hugh Craft differently. Fellow churchgoers remembered him as a good and generous man. He was the kind of person who offered to pay for the education of a poorer relative's children, taught Sunday school, served as an elder in his church. At his death, following years of illness and partial paralysis, he would be declared universally loved.

As a man of faith, Hugh Craft was decidedly old school. Other entrepreneurs may have embraced Methodism, a New Light religion that put salvation in a person's own hands, but Craft remained a staunch Presbyterian—the kind who believed in a masterly, authoritarian God, with an inscrutable, almighty will and judgment that could never be earned or known. (Hence the expression "Damned if you do, damned if you don't.")

In this view, you could not bribe your way to heaven with righteous deeds or kind behavior, as God had already decided your fate. Success and bounty were no sure signs of God's grace; neither did loss guarantee that God was permanently enraged. The best you could do was not so much to question as to endure. It was the view of Job, seized by an orphaned boy whom the universe had not spared suffering—a long view that would benefit Hugh Craft in business, but cost the men, women, and children he enslaved.

———

There was a brief, golden period when Hugh Craft's investments began to flourish, and he moved his family from Milledgeville to Macon. It was in this era, as he was building up a new life for his own family, that he began to tear down William's.

William, too, was part of a large family, with at least two brothers and two sisters, born to parents whose names are unknown. What he recalled most vividly about his mother and father were their loving hearts and spiritual devotion: parental gifts that would become life-sustaining models for their young son. William would also remember his parents as aged. Even as a young child, he could see in the way that they moved, or in the lines on their faces, that his parents' bodies, if not their spirits, had been weakened by too many years in bondage.

Hugh Craft noticed these changes as well. If, in fact, they were the man and woman listed as his property in 1820, William's parents may have been well into their forties by the time Craft chose to move to Macon. William's mother's best reproductive years were behind her, as was William's father's physical prime. Knowing that they were a losing business proposition, Craft decided to sell them, along with other older laborers, in exchange for younger ones.

A chart from Forsyth County, North Carolina, illustrates the businessman's line of reasoning. The price put on an enslaved person increased incrementally every year from birth to age twenty. A one-year-old was valued at $100; a two-year-old, $125. Prices rose by $25 until age seven, when they increased by $50. After a peak of $900 at twenty, however, the numbers began to drop. A fifty-five-year-old was valued at $100; a sixty-year-old at $50. Then the numbers stopped.

There was a window when older people such as William's mother and father might be forced to pass for younger than they were—traders pulled or colored gray hairs and oiled aging skin—but these tricks would work for only so long. Hugh Craft had William's parents sold separately from their children and from each other, ripping apart the boy's family and his world.

William was about ten years old when he last saw his mother and father. No records remain to tell of good-byes—whether William had a chance to exchange parting words with them, or whether they simply vanished, their sales communicated as an afterthought. William would tell only that they were "dragged off," at separate times, to different people, never to meet again.

What astounded William was that a man who made such a show of his religion (and who owned some of the best pews in the grandest church in town) would think nothing of destroying the bond between his devoted mother and father. Slave marriages may not have been recognized by law, but it was clear to William, as he believed it should have been to Hugh Craft, that his parents had been joined together by God's own hands.

Outraged as he was, William refused to let this man's irreligion shake his own faith, which would be a powerful part of his parents' legacy—that and their love, which would set a precedent for his own, lifelong union. He developed a hatred "not for true Christianity," as he would later recall, "but for slaveholding piety," maintaining his belief in an invisible, immutable, almighty justice, far more powerful than any earthly authority, and, ultimately, not only all-knowing but also avenging.

In addition to William's parents, Craft sold one of William's brothers and a sister, holding on to William, another brother, Charles, and his younger sister—at least for a time. To increase their value, Craft apprenticed the boys, William to a cabinetmaker and Charles to a blacksmith, both occupations that were in high demand. William's younger sister needed little more to enhance her value than time, for with it, her body would inevitably mature.

Severed from his family, ten-year-old William began his trade in the shop of a cabinetmaker in Macon, whom he would serve for the next fourteen years. Here, surrounded by the limbs and trunks of felled trees, William learned to cut and measure with care. He saw less and less of his actual owner, living not with Hugh Craft's family but as a boarder in town. In this line of work, William avoided the harsher physical labor of the cotton fields. Even so, he was not protected from cotton's pain.

Everyone was touched by cotton, from the enslaved people who were put to work in ever greater numbers to plant, hoe, pick, and process it; to planters and gin owners who built their capital with its profits; to mill children and factory owners in New England who turned it into cloth; to New York bankers who invested in its sales; and well beyond to all those who paid to wear the clothes spun from these fibers.

All were affected, too, when international demand for cotton fell in the spring of 1837, due to an oversupply from both the United States and India. The drop in cotton prices helped destabilize a national economy that was already on the edge. Banking practices were wild and unregulated, with individual banks issuing notes, or private currency, with abandon. Railroad companies, colleges, and municipalities, as well as individuals, accrued debt. Speculation was rampant, particularly in land.

Then, on a single day in May, the heads of the banks in New York stood up and drew a hard line, refusing to redeem paper currencies at their full value in silver and gold. Their actions spiraled outward in a terrible cascade, toppling the nation into the worst financial crisis it had ever known: the Panic of 1837.

In Macon, where armed guards patroled the warehouses in which planters paid to store their cotton (now worth less with every day), businesses crumbled. Many of the biggest, including the banks and the railroads, had their stocks tied together and threatened to bring each other down. The Monroe Railroad, which had its own bank, would soon go bankrupt. Ocmulgee Bank would fail too, and even the women's college was nearly forced to close.

Hugh Craft was tangled up in it all. He was a superintendent for the failing Monroe Railroad Company, as well as a stockholder. He also owned bank stock and speculated in Cherokee lands—all financial gambles. Before long, his lands were seized and sold by tax collectors, and he gave up his share in his business partnership. By more than one account, Hugh Craft was a ruined man.

In need of money, Craft sold William's last remaining brother, Charles, leaving just William and a younger sister: Eliza. He also took out mortgages on additional property to speculate in cotton. Unbeknownst to William, the mortgages were on him and his sister.

It was possible in these times to mortgage a person as one would mortgage a house. Buyers could pay for slaves by making an initial down payment and taking on a mortgage to pay the remainder, with interest. They could also take out a mortgage on the people they already owned, using their human property as collateral. As with real estate, they could rent out those they enslaved, adding improvements—such as apprenticeships—which increased their value. As with a house, however, human property was also subject to foreclosure, and this is precisely what happened to William and Eliza.

In January 1839 Hugh Craft signed papers detailing exactly what he would owe the Commercial Bank at Macon and its bankers should he renege on his debts. The property he named included a house; a pianoforte; five church pews; and four Negroes, including "William a Boy about 16 years old a Cabinet Maker by trade" and "Eliza a girl about 12 years old."

Within the year, Hugh Craft was gone from Macon. He moved to Holly Springs, Mississippi, where he became a land surveyor, planting his family in a wood-framed home, while planning a dream mansion across the street. An early riser, he would shame his son Henry for not sharing his industrious habits. He also profited from the labor of his remaining slaves—ten people, as counted by 1840 census takers. As for other properties Craft had left behind, they were sold off piece by piece that summer, as cotton prices plummeted to new lows, and his debts were called.

Newspapers were full of listings for debtors' sales, held before courthouses. Some people sold for debts were named or described, others were anonymous. Such was the case for those sold in Hugh Craft's name, listed alongside his furniture and reminders of his Presbyterian faith, under the heading "Bibb June Sales: 3 Negroes; household Furniture; Pews Nos. 55, 57, 58, 59, and 60 in the Presbyterian Church." Among these Negroes were William and his sister.

KNOCKED DOWN

|||||||||||||||||||||||||||

William would recall it as the day when his brain was set on fire. The June day was warm, though not as hot as it would be in a month or two, when the cotton, fully bloomed, would give the surrounding territories the appearance of snowy fields. From the courthouse steps, William had a full view of the large public square, the crowds, and, behind them, the jail. His gaze, however, was fixed on one subject: his younger sister Eliza, who waited to be sold, or "knocked down," as sales by auctions were described in these times. She would be the first to go.

A healthy girl of her age had long-term value to prospective bidders. Many first-time buyers in the surrounding counties chose, as their initial purchase, a woman in her reproductive prime. A man might be stronger in the fields, but a woman could toil while also adding to her owner's property, since, by law, any child she bore—no matter who the father was, even if the master himself—also became a slave. It was also for this reason that a girl like Eliza was at risk. And, as William had known, rape was an ever-present danger even for a child.

While he watched his sister turn, dance, or follow other commands on the auction block, William may have planned to match her efforts, to lift heavy boxes, "look lively," as traders exhorted, or even call out to his sister's purchaser, as some did, promising their best work in order to draw the same buyer. He may have prayed that a familiar person would bid, allowing them to stay in Macon, as two of their brothers had. Warren worked at the Central Hotel, a block north of the courthouse; Charles, nearby as blacksmith. But he was well aware of other possibilities, the push of westward settlement, and its unending demand for slaves.

All that disappeared, however, as the auctioneer accepted the winning bid for his sister. There was hardly time to maneuver; William was up next. Beyond the courthouse gate, he could see the man who had bought his sister hurrying her into a cart. He was not from Macon, a planter by appearance, eager to head into whatever future awaited him and his new property.

Even with the auctioneer's cries ringing in his ears, William maintained a clear presence of mind, an ability to assess a situation and improvise—skills that would prove essential to his survival in the years to come. He asked an enslaved friend to approach Eliza's new owner and plead with the man to wait until the sale was over, so that William could say good-bye. The planter sent his reply: He had a ways to travel. He would not wait.

William then got on his knees and begged. For the auctioneer, this was intolerable. William's price, which would determine how much went into his own pocket, depended not just on his strength and skills, but also on his appearing compliant. A slave collapsed on the platform, overcome, when he was supposed to stand up tall and look happy, sent the wrong signal. The man grabbed William by the neck.

"Get up!" he barked, his mouth full of curses, violence in his tone and hand.

"There's no use in your seeing her," he warned, and in this respect the auctioneer was right: his sister was vulnerable. Her behavior now, in her first moments with her new owner, could set the tone for their relationship, for her future in his house.

William never forgot what happened next. He rose, shifted his gaze forward to his sister in the cart that was moving away. Eliza did not speak, but her hands, grasped tight, told her pain. When she turned to her brother a final time, she was close enough that he could see the tears on her cheeks. She bowed to William, delivering her farewell with her body, before doubling over completely, her face buried in her lap. To her brother, the gesture was unbearable.

William was eventually sold to a local, Ira Hamilton Taylor, a twenty-six-year-old former New Yorker and aspiring man of business. At least briefly, though, William was owned by Thomas Taylor, one of Hugh Craft's creditors. It was six months after the auction that Ira Taylor went on record as paying $1,750 for William—more than twice the average price of other sixteen-year-olds. Clearly, William was a youth of extraordinary value.

He was also a young man of extraordinary resourcefulness. William worked out an arrangement where he would pay his new owner a yearly sum of $220 in exchange for being able to hire himself out. He then set his daily wages with the cabinetmaker, allowing for the possibility of working additional hours for extra pay. Technically, this arrangement was illegal, as self-employment by the enslaved was banned in Georgia. Macon had its own laws, too, meant to protect skilled White workers from competition from Black artisans such as William. But mostly everyone quietly tolerated a practice that provided such easy money for enslavers.

For young Ira Taylor, who had yet to set up a house with a bride, it was an excellent deal—akin to collecting rent on his property without any management or upkeep. Before long, he was sure to recoup his payment, especially since William's value would only go up. A field hand might peak at twenty, but as an artisan, William was not even halfway toward his prime.

William questioned the justice of it all, as he turned over his hard-earned wages to his enslaver. Yet he persevered, with a longer goal in mind. Superficially, little changed following the sale—the shape of his days remained as it had been before—but on a deeper level, every-thing had transformed. Denied his last chance to say good-bye to his sister, William had experienced a rage so powerful that, as he would recall, it stopped his tears, seemed to set his mind aflame, made him crave power for vengeance. It was on that day that he resolved one day to run.

In the aftermath of his family's rupture, William made every effort to keep track of his dispersed family members, all of whom he appears to have located, years past their removal—all excepting his last sold sister. Roughly a decade past his parents' sale, in 1844, William knew that his mother and an unnamed sister were in New Orleans, and that his father was in Savannah. Meanwhile, his two brothers, Warren and Charles, continued to reside nearby.

It was together with Charles that William would approach the chil-dren of Hugh Craft when they visited Macon, the enslaved brothers leaving traces of powerful emotions. Why William and his brother sought out their former enslavers is uncertain—the visit was crypti-cally recorded by Hugh's son Henry—but the stakes were clearly high. According to Henry, William and his brother came to Henry's sister with specific questions, and when she evaded them, the brothers began to cry.

Could their emotions have something to do with their younger sister, whose fate Henry, would not or could not recall? Though the context is lost, the brothers' expressions gave lie to the claim among enslavers that those they enslaved made and remade their family bonds with ease, and instead indicate lasting trauma.

Now, however, eight years after the devastating sale, four years after he had sought out the children of Hugh Craft, William himself was leaving Macon behind for good. And as the train chugged along toward the Georgia coast, the formerly enslaved boy from Milledgeville, now a man riding the rails, was fulfilling his deepest wish. He was up and on the run, alongside another kind of master, the woman he loved.

MANIFEST DESTINY

|||||||||||||||||||||||||

Emmett, Oconee, Tennille, Davisborough, Holcomb. The train tore ahead, with harried huffs and ear-splitting squalls, lurching to a crude halt every ten miles or so, demanding to be fed. Firemen rushed to stoke the flames and nourish the iron beast. Much of the crew, here and elsewhere, who unknowingly helped carry the Crafts to freedom were enslaved laborers, especially those who performed the most dangerous jobs.

So, too, had past laborers prepared the ground for the couple's escape. The train traversed the swamps and swells of the Oconee River, rattling over a bridge that cost many souls. Swamp fever had devastated workers. No one had wanted to touch the job, so those who had no choice were brought in: a captive labor force of the enslaved. These unsung lives succeeded in building a bridge of freedom, over which William and Ellen now rode.

By Midville, William and Ellen were midway to Savannah, their first hundred miles behind them, six more stops to go. It was something to celebrate. No wandering animal had blundered onto their tracks or impaled itself on the cowcatcher, requiring precious minutes to be pulled or hacked off. No sparks had caught on anyone's clothes. Neither did the boiler explode—something once so common that one train line put a "Negro brass band" on a car between passengers and the engine, to serve as a buffer against combustion, as well as entertainment.

Once Scott Cray, Ellen's seatmate, had gotten off at Gordon, it became possible for William, as the faithful slave, to look in on his sickly master. With eyes, if not word, or with the unseen graze of touch (the fix of a sling, brush of a sacque), Ellen and William could signal their encouragement and togetherness, as inch by inch of contested terrain receded, for now.

Set at close intervals between the swampy acres, the stations that ticked off their progress were meager. The priority was to move cotton, not people. At the better stops, passengers might devour a plate of soup or some greasy chicken, grab boiled eggs, biscuits, or other easy snacks from vendors. Or the sellers might have ventured aboard, slipping up and down the aisles with fruits and little pound cakes, before rushing away at the sound of the bell.

At a station stop, a gentleman like Mr. Johnson might have sent his valet out for refreshments or descended the train to relieve himself. For the Crafts, however, any move away from the vehicle would have been a calculated risk, since to miss the train would be to lose a day, giving any trackers that much more time to catch up. It might be well past dusk before Ellen would have access to any private facilities.

All around them, people swirled. The conductor, who had checked Ellen's ticket when they first came aboard, strode through the car with his shiny badge and money box, with an eye out for interlopers. Enslaved workers, some of them possibly children, moved through the cars too, carrying buckets of cool, free water, served with small cups or a ladle; others tended the stove. And then there were the travelers, who were notoriously chatty on this route, to the irritation of many European observers, who would much rather have been left alone.

Georgia stretched out ahead on a winding course of pine forests and swamplands. Occasionally a lonely cypress tree came into view, draped in gloomy moss. A few houses clustered near the stations. Here and there, gangs of enslaved workers might be seen traveling between plantations, carrying tools, gazing up as the train rushed by.

From behind her spectacles, Ellen watched the landscape fly past her window, the lenses tinting the barren grounds an unnatural shade of green—redolent, in a macabre way, of the fertile region where she had been raised. Men like her father had come to Georgia in pursuit of their Manifest Destiny. And now here she was, seeking to make manifest a destiny of her own.

Beyond the illness she feigned as she rode the Georgia rails, Ellen bore scars. The sleeve of her sacque and shirt covered skin damaged from a bad case of tuberculosis, which she caught when someone spoke or spat or even sang in her direction, and the disease entered her body. At a time when "consumption" was a leading killer, Ellen was lucky to have walked away with only these scars, even if they identified her. They marked her for life as a survivor.

Ellen was a survivor in other ways. Above all, the trauma of being forced apart from her mother in her girlhood was one she would return to time and again—as she considered marriage, decided to flee bondage, and traveled forward in time, every hour taking her closer to freedom, but also farther away from the mother she loved.

Her mother's name was Maria. Just three years older than James Smith's first daughter by his legal wife, Maria was said to have been bought by Smith when she was a child. Noticed for her youthful appearance, even in her later years, Maria would be recalled as a "gentle Christian woman, of light complexion" by firsthand observers. Little other testimony survives to tell of the details of her life. Maria, too, may have been fathered by a White man. She was described as mulatto and half White; Ellen, as quadroon, or a person of one-quarter African ancestry.

Chosen to work as a house slave in the Smith family home, Maria was required to spend most of her days in their private living quarters, and possibly her nights. Enslaved women tasked with caring for children were often made to sleep on the floor of their charges' rooms, ladies' maids close by their mistresses. Children training for housework, too, often slept near their enslavers.

It is said that James Smith began making nighttime visits to Maria when she was still in her teens. What happened between them remains unknown, but this much is certain, beyond the eventual birth of a baby: the enslaved child, Maria, was in no position to say no to the thirty-seven-year-old, official father of nine—soon to be more—who was her legal owner.

If he had read his Georgia law book from cover to cover, James Smith would have seen nothing regarding the rape of a slave, no protections for an enslaved person like Maria against a man such as himself, though it would have been a capital crime if a White woman were raped by a Black man. Years later, in an accounting of his estate, Maria would be tallied on the same page as his chickens and pigs, and valued at $500. Also appearing on that page was a second Maria, sixty years old, appraised at "000"—whatever value she'd once had as a worker or a mother considered depleted, gone.

Ellen was born when her mother was eighteen years old. The paternity of a mixed-race child was a matter often avoided or denied in households like the Smiths'. As a contemporary, Mary Boykin Chesnut expressed famously, "the mulattoes one sees in every family exactly resemble the White children—and every lady tells you who is the father of all the mulatto children in everybody's household, but those in her own she seems to think drop from the clouds." The paternity of Maria's child, however, was so unmistakable that it was often presumed, and the lady of the house made sure that both Maria and Ellen suffered for it.

More is known of the woman who hated Ellen than the mother who loved her. Mistress Smith, James's wife, was born into the illustrious Cleveland clan, which would one day produce an American president. Mistress Smith's own mother was an Irish immigrant who had been married, very young, once before; her father was a black sheep called "Devil John" by his kin. John Cleveland was a Revolutionary War captain and official of note, but he was also described as a "wild, reckless man." To Devil John and his wife, Catherine, seven children were born—including, second to last, a daughter named Eliza, who became Mistress Smith.

Married at eighteen, Mistress Smith fulfilled her expected wifely duties right away, bearing four sons and four daughters. In 1826 she was pregnant with her ninth child, Elliott. It was around the same time that Maria expected Ellen. Regardless of whether she was aware of it before, Mistress Smith could not escape the knowledge of Ellen's paternity once the girl was born. Time and again, others would observe Ellen's resemblance to James Smith and assume she was a legitimate child of the family.

The mistress's frustrations might have been compounded by grief. When Ellen was a toddler, Mistress Smith gave birth to a daughter—named Catherine for her grandmother—who died in infancy. (That year, Mistress Smith joined the Methodist church, carried into the waves of religious revivalism that would wash over Macon.) Soon she was pregnant with her last child, another Catherine, who died before age two. Why the two Catherines died so early is unknown: whether they, too, suffered from tuberculosis, the child-killing disease that would leave Ellen scarred for life. If so, the mistress might well have resented not only that Ellen had been born, but that she had survived.

Among friends, Mistress Smith would be remembered as a woman of few words, common sense, strength of will, and deep religion. Ellen, however, experienced a different side of the woman's character. How exactly Devil John's daughter made the girl suffer is unknown, but her authority had few limits where Ellen and Maria were concerned.

As an enslaving mistress, she could decide where mother and daughter worked and what food they ate, what work Ellen would be given, and even how often Maria got to see Ellen. Mistress Smith could punish Ellen as she pleased, striking her or having her whipped—and she could also hurt her in places that did not show.

When her youngest surviving daughter—her namesake, Eliza—was to be married in April 1837, Mistress Smith exercised one of the greatest powers available to her. She decided to give away Ellen as a wedding gift. Ellen would be Eliza's slave, and Mistress Smith would no longer have to be reminded of her husband's sexual exploitations in her own home.

Maria had limited hours to prepare her eleven-year-old daughter for a life without her. Until now, no matter how cruel Mistress Smith had been, Ellen had her mother nearby. She may have had other family in the area as well: a grandmother and possibly two sisters, as well as an uncle and aunts. In the house of her new mistress—and master—Ellen would have to fend for herself. On the brink of puberty, the girl was especially vulnerable to sexual attacks, as her mother knew well. Much would depend on Eliza's husband and how he ruled. But even if he left her alone, there was the rest of the world to consider.

What did Maria teach, tell, give her child before the forced departure? What could she provide, to help Ellen face this unknown life without her? In South Carolina, a mother named Rose would make what has been called a "survival pack" for her nine-year-old daughter, Ashley, filling a sack with a tattered dress, a handful of pecans, a braid of her own hair, and a final, life-sustaining ingredient that infused all.

"It be filled with my Love, always," Rose told her child. Rose and Ashley would never see each other again. The contents of Maria's "emergency kit" for Ellen, material or not, may not survive, but she, too, carried her mother's love as a vital sustenance.

For Ellen, the pain of separation would carry across the years and become so scarring that the very thought of becoming a mother herself struck her as a "horror." But she learned from her mother this crucial lesson: that no matter what slavers might rob or remove, the love she carried belonged to her. And she would find her own strength in this trial by fire, learning that she could make her way alone, if need be—a crucial education that would empower her to create her own future.

Ellen left her mother's world with other lessons that would help her in her new household and, one day, beyond. Among the practical skills she carried, one in particular stood out: Ellen was known as an excellent seamstress. Maria may have helped her develop this talent, which was one of the few that any woman of this time and place could depend on to earn money, and it would assist her in unexpected ways. Then there were the other, invisible forms of training. Importantly, Ellen learned the language of the White elite. She also learned to observe their manners, the smallest signs and behaviors that were typical for them, rather than one of her own, enslaved class.

Under Mistress Smith's rule, Ellen's genes had worked against her. No matter how she dressed or how deferentially she spoke, her physical features marked her as the child of the White man whom she was required to call Master. And every failure to appear otherwise—to pass muster as an enslaved Black child in the eyes of strangers—brought her fresh abuse from the mistress. Yet those failures would also give her the confidence, one day, to know that she could pass for White.

Ellen further learned to maintain her composure: to steady herself as Mistress Smith lashed out, to act quickly if necessary, or to refrain from reacting at all, depending on what the situation called for. She learned to make these calculations under great pressure—all skills that would prepare her for her performance of a lifetime.

Such was the degree of the mistress's abuse that, for all the pain she experienced at being taken from her mother, Ellen experienced a release from pain as well. Fortunately for Ellen, her new mistress, Eliza Collins, would resemble her own mother in name only. But there were other troubles to come.

MACON BOUND

Ellen's new mistress—the half sister now entitled to send slave hunters her way—was a vivacious Georgian beauty, with dark curls, flashing eyes, and a delicate, oval face, just the shape that was thought to be most beguiling in these times. If there was anything short of charming in her demeanor, at least as she was captured in her official portrait, it may have been a slight smugness in her expression—but then again, perhaps it was a mere archness in her gaze, or the mood of the itinerant painter who depicted her.

Eliza Smith Collins was eighteen when she became the bride of a widower eighteen years her senior, Dr. Robert Collins. Like Eliza's father, Collins was a pioneer, originally from Bunscombe, North Carolina. His first wife, Harriet, had died a prolonged, horrible death after years of illness. With all his skills as a doctor, Collins had been powerless to heal her. The couple lived in one of the earliest frame houses in Macon, settling soon after the Muscogees or Creeks had been forced to cede their sacred grounds.

Collins may have been old and widowed, but he was bold in ways that might have mattered to a young woman like Eliza. Some men adamantly opposed the creation of a new women's college in Macon. As one legislator huffed: "Females can never master studies long familiar to men." Said another: "All a young lady needs to know is how to weave clothes for her family and how to paint a daisy in water colors." Collins was more broad minded. He had left the South to study medicine at the University of Pennsylvania and later helped found Macon's Wesleyan College. (His new bride, however, would not be among those who enrolled.)

Collins was forward thinking in other ways. He was a man who could picture a city with running water, running trains, and electromagnetic lines that could transport messages across faraway terrains—a person who harbored a futuristic vision of what his city and life could be. He was also extraordinarily wealthy. When he proposed marriage to the teenage Eliza, Dr. Collins did not intend for her to lie in the same room where his wife had died. He hired his friend Elam Alexander to design one of the grandest mansions in town, down the road from where Alexander was building the women's college.

Clinton was ten miles from Macon, a long but manageable carriage ride along red clay roads, and Eliza may have gotten to see her future home as it went up. If she viewed it on the arm of her father, James Smith would have reason to be confident that he had given the daughter he adored everything she needed for a good start in life.

Legally, for Eliza, marriage was a kind of substitution, where she left her father's protection for her husband's—only there was loss as well. Unmarried, Eliza could inherit property, own land, claim wages, sue and be sued, and make contracts. As Mistress Collins, her legal identity merged with her husband's. What had belonged to her now belonged to him. If he were, say, to fall into debt, any property that might have been hers was up for seizure, unless she or someone around her had known enough to protect her interests.

In the coming years, Eliza Collins would prove fortunate to have just such a person in her father, even while her enslaved half sister, Ellen, did not.

Not long after the wedding, Eliza's belly began to swell—surely a welcome sight for Collins, who had no heirs. In her role as lady's maid, Ellen was likely among the first to notice, and may have been the one to let out her mistress's dresses.

Young as she was, Ellen could be called on to do just about anything for her mistress, from brushing her hair and helping her dress and bathe—intimate tasks that became increasingly difficult as the months passed—to running errands and managing her wardrobe. There were benefits to this station: Ellen avoided the cotton fields and the overseer's watch, and had access to better food and clothing. However, she was always on call, under the command of not only the mistress she knew, but also an unfamiliar master.

Few traces survive to tell of Ellen's relationship with the man who was to become her chief public adversary, Robert Collins. Records do tell, however, of how Collins and his business associates used the enslaved as collateral for their financial agreements. Other records reveal more personal views.

Collins had, in his own words, "been accustomed to slavery from his earliest days," and, from "long experience," considered himself something of an expert on the matter. In fact, his brother Charles, with whom he frequently did business, was later reputed to have been a slave trader. Robert would secure his own legacy as a slaver through authorship, penning an *Essay on the Treatment and Management of Slaves*—a kind of slave owner's manual, which details his thinking on the subject.

Its eighteen pages offer best practices on topics ranging from the practical ("Feeding of Slaves") to the more philosophic ("Discipline"), giving rationales for each suggestion. For instance, "Negro Houses" should be built two feet off the ground, sixteen by twenty feet, with one family per house, to avoid the overcrowding that would be both unhealthy and demoralizing.

Likewise, he counsels that diet and clothing be attended thoughtfully, despite the added cost. "Neatness in dress is important to the health, comfort, and pride of a negro," he observes, and should be made a priority, since "the more pride and self-respect you can instill into them, the better they will behave, and the more serviceable they will be."

Regularity is the operative word for Collins. "Proper and suitable indulgences and privileges should be granted," he advises, but only by permission, "for they are a people ever ready to practice upon the old maxim, of 'give an inch and take an ell.'"

Punishment of a slave, says Collins, "does not make him revengeful, as it would an Indian or white man, but it rather tends to win his attachment and promote his happiness and well-being." Moreover: "Slaves have no respect or affection for a master who indulges them over-much, or who, from fear, or false humanity, fails to assume that degree of authority necessary to promote industry and enforce good order." Special care, he cautions, is needed to protect the enslaved from themselves, for: "if allowed, the stronger will abuse the weaker; husbands will often abuse their wives, and mothers their children." In his view, a master class benefited all.

To Collins, it all came down to this: "Of what does the slave of the South, or his true friend to complain? There is no country, and no place upon the face of this earth, where the negro race have such security for a wholesome living, as the slaves in the United States."

Whether Eliza Collins shared her husband's views is unknown, but the Crafts would later observe that she was "decidedly more humane than the majority of her class," and credit her for "not exposing" Ellen "to many of the worst features of slavery." When Ellen displeased her, Eliza never had her sent out to be punished, or tortured—professionalized abuse that would have made Ellen further vulnerable to rape.

In time, the half sisters grew into their roles, and Ellen was so attuned to Eliza's needs and wishes that she became Eliza's favorite. Yet under one roof, these two daughters of James Smith stood worlds apart. One sister answered to the title of Mistress; the other was forced to respond to calls of "nigger." Ellen was long to remember how this word was used against her, to keep her down. For her part, she learned to have "no confidence in White people." It would take her many years to conclude that good and bad came in all colors.

––––––

As Ellen moved forward on her journey, each revolution of the wheels beneath her marking her own revolt, she traveled with a consciousness of the Collinses—who, as enlightened as they might have considered themselves, might authorize any kind of brutality if they discovered her escape. Yet, beside her enslaving sister, Ellen moved with the awareness of a second blood relative, another Georgian beauty, who pointed a different way.

Near the banks of the Ocmulgee, on a hidden clearing, lived the Healys: Mary Eliza, identified by at least one source as Ellen's mother's sister, in an illicit relationship with her enslaver, Michael Morris Healy, a White Irish immigrant. What set apart the Healys was not the fact of their sexual relations, as the example of Ellen's own father attests. The difference was that Healy considered Mary Eliza his one and only wife, and their ten children his family. Together, they lived as master and slave, husband and wife, relationships that were forbidden to coexist.

The Healys may have called each other husband and wife, but the law made it impossible for them to be anything to each other but master and slave. Private acts of manumission were prohibited in Georgia. In earlier years, it had been possible for Georgians to grant freedom in their wills, as George Washington had (albeit with conditions) in

Virginia. But in this era, Healy was powerless to liberate Mary Eliza—
or their children. It did not matter that their father was White, or if
they appeared White. What was known as the "one drop rule" prevailed: A single drop of Black blood was enough to color an entire
body. Moreover, slavery always followed the mother. Blackness and
bondage were seen as permanent conditions, not to be played with or
undone—a presumption that the Healys, and now, Ellen, turned on its
head.

Over the years, Healy had ferried, one by one, each of his children
with Mary Eliza to Massachusetts to live and study. Soon Mary Eliza
was to give birth to their tenth and last child, and then the Healys
planned to join their family up North.

Ellen was alert to the example of this family and their unconventional maneuvers—and possibly motivated by them. As she prepared
for her own arrival in Savannah, she could draw confidence from their
past successes, their reaching the North unharmed. Like her cousins,
she would use her light skin to pass. In her case, however, there was
William to bring forward as well. Savannah would be their first stop.

SAVANNAH

Day 1, Evening:
Wednesday,
December 20, 1848

HOUSE OF
STRANGERS

||||||||||||||||||||||||||

Night fell as the train rolled into the "city of shade and silence," studded with jewellike squares. Trees flourished even in winter: palmettos, pride of India, and giant live oaks, draped in Spanish moss. By day, the shade trees formed a living shield, deflecting the sun's glare. By night, they were incandescent, strung with tall hanging lamps—in some parts of town.

Where the Crafts entered the city, there were few signs of shade, light, or bloom, no view of the mansions bedecked for Christmas. Not even the Savannah River was visible in the restless dark. Instead, there was a ticket booth amid a landscape of cotton. Stacks, like towers, were moved all night along West Broad Street, up a mile to the river. In the maws of huge machines, the cotton would be pressed to a fraction of its original size and dispatched around the world. Darkened forms could be seen hauling, carrying, driving it forward, many of them enslaved. For in this era, the railroad was the biggest slaver in town.

Young Mr. Johnson stepped out into the cool of the Savannah evening, assisted by his slave. It was chaos, with travelers abounding, hack drivers calling out. Mr. Johnson, however, knew to follow the flow of travelers bound for Charleston and mounted the omnibus provided by the railroad: a long, horse-drawn car, which shuttled passengers to the wharves.

As the fugitives pulled away from the depot, they must have whispered thanks to the "mad dragon" now at rest behind them. Just six years earlier, a journey of this length in so short a time would have been inconceivable. Yet here they were, on time.

It was a miracle, really. As one traveler remarked: "If my great-grandfather had been told that his great-grandson, at this day, would dine at one in the evening and go to bed the same evening 120 miles distant, he would have called the prophet a fool." The window before departure was small, but they had sufficient time to catch the eight thirty steamer—time enough, even, for tea.

––––––

As part of its shuttle service, the omnibus was to stop at a hotel for refreshment: the Pulaski House, Savannah's original "House of Strangers," named for a Polish general of the American Revolution. Peering out from the omnibus, Mr. Johnson would have seen a handsome, four-story establishment, aglow—a place that one Dr. Collins from Macon had been known to visit, and where he would soon return.

The Pulaski was called Savannah's best house, and while some had qualms about its proprietor (a "stiff-necked, old piece of fat importance," said one visitor), few could find fault with his table. Mr. Wiltberger's wine cellar held clarets and madeiras from ports around the world. His houses were renowned for sumptuous preparations of turtle soup and fresh shad, and for fine, chilled drinks: iced champagne and an incomparable mint julep—kept frosty cool with ice dredged from New England waters. The passengers' tea would have to be fast and simple, but it would be prepared by the same expert hands.

The hotel stood at the edge of a green square, with a radiant, high-columned church and a white obelisk styled after Cleopatra's Needle. Named for a colonial governor of South Carolina, Johnson Square was Savannah's oldest and largest square, where the Declaration of Independence was read, presidents paid visit, and ethereal nighttime balls were held. Yet the trees told another story. Local legend says Spanish moss will not grow on the great live oaks here, on account of the deep suffering that took place. Whether or not there are scientific reasons for this, the lore, passed down over generations, provides a truth of its own.

The same square that harbored Georgia's first Episcopal church was a central axis in Savannah's slave economy, with the trading houses of Bay Lane above, and the courthouse auctions below. It was one of many incongruities in a city that had been intended as a free colony—free of rum and slavery—but where, in this era, there were more brothels and tippling houses than houses of worship, and the life of the city was built on bondage. Savannah's biggest slave dealer would soon run his business from Johnson Square. The largest slave sale in American history, known as "The Weeping Time," would be scheduled to take place here, too, before it would grow to such dimensions that it was moved to a racetrack.

Travelers from Macon had access to little more than snacks, at most, for the past twelve hours. Many would have eagerly disembarked for a fresh, hot tea. The invalid Mr. Johnson, however, preferred to remain on the omnibus and sent his slave for a tray. And so William entered the Pulaski House through the servant doors, which were unmistakable.

The Pulaski was known as a popular establishment for slave traders. It was rumored that there were underground pens for holding human cargo, here or at the hostelry next door, and tunnels that led directly to the river for transport. Blocked-up passages were later discovered, but their purpose became impossible to verify once they were demolished. Whether or not William glimpsed sight of such pens or passages when he entered the House of Strangers is unknown, but he is sure to have encountered the hotel's large staff of enslaved men and women. It was a space he knew how to navigate better than most, having been a hotel waiter himself.

He returned with the tea tray, and as Ellen sipped and chewed (or pushed around her food, in order to avoid having to relieve herself for a few hours more), she and William might have conferred quietly, but they were certainly on their guard. The short meal may have been the longest time the two had spent together since the start of their journey, and the most they could anticipate having for a while.

Ellen had succeeded once again by a strategy of avoidance. By remaining on the bus, she had escaped close contact with strangers, the light patter over shared meals, served by enslaved people. Importantly, she had avoided providing a signature at the hotel. She could hold off personal interactions for only so long, though, if she and William were to survive the next leg of their voyage, within the closed theater of the steamship.

Back in the omnibus, their bellies full, the Charleston-bound travelers passed the noisy, trafficked avenue of Bay Street, which stretched along the river—a heady line between slums to the east and west of the city— en route to their steamer.

The ride that awaited them, the *General Clinch*, was a small craft of 256 tons, about half the size of seaboard ships, but dependable enough to serve guard and escort duty during the Civil War. In the starlit evening, moored riverboats bobbed up and down in the waters, bumping against the docks. Around the ship, roustabouts shuttled heavy cargo, including thick bags of daily mail, while the captain greeted all aboard.

Steamships, even more than railroads, were strongly hierarchical, with position determined by class, race, and gender: the captain at the top, cabin boys and chambermaids at the bottom. Passengers were classed similarly. Small coastal steamers did not have the lavish wedding cake tiers of larger, oceanic vessels. Still, on its main deck, the *General Clinch* had separate sleeping quarters for ladies and gentlemen, as well as a gentlemen's saloon.

Below were holds for lower-class travelers, luggage, and cargo, including the enslaved. The *General Clinch* was the type of vessel preferred for coastal slave transport, and regularly trafficked enslaved people between Savannah, Georgia's main slave port, and Charleston, one of the nation's largest. During this Christmas week, at least twelve men, women, and children were transported as human cargo, including a three-year-old named Sarah, all of two feet, six inches tall, as measured by her traffickers. Two infants were also registered. All were accounted for by the ship's captain, who had to sign for every enslaved person he carried, attesting that no one had been imported after 1808, when the international slave trade was banned.

As they looked up at the *General Clinch,* Ellen's boot heels clacking down hard with every step up the gangway, the Crafts knew they faced something new. With such crammed quarters, steamers required passengers to be social. Ellen would have to eat and sleep beside unknown men, in rooms off-limits to women. William would have to find his own place and footing while aboard. The Crafts would have to work jointly to perfect their roles of master and slave. Fortunately, there was at least this advantage: Ellen had experience to guide her, having traveled this way before.

CHARLESTON BOUND

||||||||||||||||||||||

Ellen had been this way because once upon a time, early in the Collinses' marriage and in Ellen's years with them, the Collins family had moved to Charleston. Back then, there were no railroads to hasten the journey from Macon to Savannah. But steamships ran from Savannah to Charleston, such as Ellen was about to ride.

The move had come at a difficult time for the Collinses, and consequently for Ellen, to whom their fortunes were connected. From the outside, Eliza Collins's life had the appearance of a fairy tale—one that would, in fact, be painted on an immense canvas, six feet tall, four feet wide, by an itinerant painter. Her face framed by ringlets that Ellen may have shaped, Eliza stands on a palatial terrace against a flash of Romantic sky. She holds a stem of three shining grapes: two grapes touch, a third drops down, perhaps signifying her nascent family. At her knee is a golden-haired child who has removed one of her tiny shoes, and is handing it up to her mother.

Not all was well in the House of Collins, however, with tragedy striking from the start. The child in the painting was not the Collinses' first. Though Eliza became pregnant soon after her wedding, the son she bore had died at four weeks, likely of a summer fever, and was buried next to Collins's first wife. It would be four years before Eliza gave birth again, during which time Ellen had to be attuned not only to her mistress's physical needs but also to her emotional state.

Perhaps the loss compelled the Collinses to move to Charleston when they did, sometime around 1840. Professional matters may have weighed in too, as they joined households with extended family: Eliza's sister Mary and her husband, Jesse Franklin Cleveland, a former congressman, banker, and Collins's new partner in a factorage and commission business on the wharf. These were heady times for Robert Collins, who advertised his availability in the "auction and commission business." Though his speciality was cotton, he advertised his willingness to "attend to any business . . . entrusted to him."

When the Collinses relocated, they must have taken Ellen with them—a painful move for her, given that her mother, Maria, had finally moved to Macon with her enslavers, the Smiths. Although in separate households, mother and daughter had lived only blocks apart, serving mother and daughter mistresses, only to be separated again.

For the Collinses, Charleston brought new hope. Baby Juliet, the golden-haired child captured in portraiture, entered the world here on the birth date of the nation, July Fourth. With fireworks on the water and parties all around, it must have seemed an auspicious time to be born. For Ellen, Charleston summoned other memories, which she now carried on her northbound journey—ones useful to her, but also haunting.

As the Collinses' enslaved maid in Charleston, Ellen would have learned the city's layout. She knew the path toward the Collinses' old residence on Meeting Street. She recognized the Custom House as the place to purchase tickets. She had seen where, from the harbor, ships left daily to free states and free cities such as Philadelphia, Boston, and New York. From Charleston, she had learned how one could touch the world.

But she also knew the challenges that the Custom House presented: the required signature, and more. No one who went by the site in those days could pass unawares of the slave sales by its doors, where thousands of men, women, and children were auctioned—"knocked down," as William had been—and families ravaged. Then there was Charleston's infamous Sugar House, a house of torture where the enslaved were sent for punishment. Eliza had never sent her there, though she might have, easily: the Sugar House was located behind the streets where the Collinses lived, symbolic of the nearness of other fates. Memory of it, alone, served as its own brand of torment.

The Collinses' residence in Charleston was only a sojourn, for they were back in Macon within two or three years. But what Ellen had seen and experienced appears to have cast a shadow.

It was in the aftermath of the Collinses' return that Ellen would form a connection with the man whose love would prove transformative: a tall, young cabinetmaker named William Craft. In fact, they might have met before. A slip of paper kept by descendants notes that the couple first met in 1841, when William was eighteen; Ellen, fifteen. If so, they would have met soon after William lost his sister, while the Collinses were still in Charleston, perhaps when they came home to visit. Once the Collins family returned to Macon for good, the two finally had occasion to form a closer connection. Even so, Ellen kept her distance.

With all that she had experienced, the trauma she had witnessed and known, she could not bear the idea of forming that intimate connection, of creating a family that she soon might lose. She had seen too many children seized out of their parents' arms, and had been separated from her own mother time and again. This is why she made a noteworthy move.

In protest of the demands of her enslavement, which negated her will, her desire, Ellen determined that she would *not* marry William, *not* bear children—not until they escaped bondage; not until her own body—and therefore her children—belonged to her. Understanding her pain, and respecting her decision, William agreed, signifying the start of an unconventional, consensual, collaborative love.

Over months, soon to become years, they explored all methods of escape, sharply attuned to the risks. They knew that every road, every bridge was guarded. They knew of the animals in the swamps and hinterlands, and worse, the human animals and their canines, trained to hunt. They were also aware that if they failed, they would not be returned to their former lives, but exiled, at best: William, possibly to cotton fields or railroad tracks; Ellen to New Orleans, where light-skinned enslaved women were known to command high prices in the so-called fancy trade, a cruel euphemism for sex trafficking.

Separately, they might have had better luck. Alone, William stood the best chances of surviving an arduous journey at a demanding pace. Alone, Ellen might have disappeared into an all-White crowd, whereas with him, she would be seen as a White woman in the close company of a Black man—the ultimate taboo. Together, it would seem, they gave up any advantage they had singly and brought each other down.

Unable to devise a plan, yet determined to be together, they had decided, at last, to invert their goals—run later, love first. They would build the best possible life they could in the present by taking the first required step of all those enslaved: asking their enslavers for permission to marry. But even this carried risks. Robert Collins believed that the enslaved should marry others within a single estate. For, as he explained, those belonging to different owners "cannot live together as they ought, and are constantly liable to separation, in the changing of property.

"It is true," he added, "that they usually have but little ceremony in forming these connexion; and many look upon their obligation to each other very lightly; but in others, again, is found a degree of faithfulness, fidelity, and affection, which owners admire; and hence, they always dislike to separate those manifesting such traits of character."

Fortunately, in Ellen's case, Collins made an exception, perhaps because she was a favorite, or because he knew that William had financial resources, or because his wife, Ellen's half sister, wanted it this way—or even, possibly, because he recognized Ellen and William's bond as one of the extraordinary variety that he would not call by name: love.

When the Crafts were finally married, Ellen was not allowed the Christian wedding that would have sanctified her marriage as a permanent union ordained by God, rather than by earthly masters. Instead, the two were joined as husband and wife in a ceremony held sacred to them and those who loved them, where they "jumped the broomstick," a traditional wedding ritual among the enslaved. It would be another two years before the couple would seize upon the plan that now propelled them from Savannah to Charleston—a scheme whose brilliance lay in its bold suppleness, its ability to harness a prevailing wind, rather than be destroyed by it.

Their plan conjured another kind of affection. Later Georgians would wax nostalgic about a custom, among a certain class, to pair a young family scion with an older, enslaved child, one who would teach his younger charge to fish and trap, find birds' nests, and name the eggs, like some kind of Caliban and guide. It was the faith in this bond between boys that would cause enslavers to send their slaves alongside their sons to "be of service" in the Civil War.

Of all the possible connections between Black and White, this idealized bond was one that the dominant powers in William and Ellen's world loved to see. And so this is what the couple determined to enact. Nowhere would they be more closely watched, together, than aboard the Charleston-bound steamer; nowhere would their learning curve need to be so high.

UNDER WATCH

||||||||||||||||||||||||||||

Just after the second bell, the two ducked into the saloon: a claustro-phobic space in a ship of this size, furnished simply with a stove and tables. Men met here to read papers, play cards, swap stories, dine, drink, and spit. (Even in the best ships, walls and carpets were smeared with tobacco juice.)

With his master safely seated, William exited, leaving Ellen alone among the men, including the captain. She remained bundled, aloof. A gentleman in the corner, who had been yawning, checking his gold pocket watch only a moment before, was now fully alert, gazing at her intently. The whistle blew; the ship shuddered into its launch. Ellen waited for what seemed like a reasonable amount of time, then asked to be shown to her berth.

The man with the gold watch was observing, listening all the while. He had noticed the small, sick young man immediately, all covered up so that not even his eyes were clearly visible. He heard the gen-tleman introduce himself as Mr. Johnson and say that he was unwell. He watched as the young man's slave was sent for. He noted that Mr. Johnson's voice was soft, even womanly.

The berths were tiny, with bunks stuck to a wall and a mirror, at most, for adornment. A small window and perhaps another door faced the deck. The communal facilities aboard steamships were notoriously filthy, with a single towel for all passengers, a shared comb, and an unmentionable hole. Anyone using them would have wanted to move in and out fast.

William helped his master settle into his bunk. When he emerged, he sensed that something was wrong. Not just the man with the gold watch, but the captain and other passengers thought young Mr. John-son's behavior strange, and questioned William, who answered the best he could, then returned to check on his master.

Ellen directed William to take out some flannel cloth and medicine, and make a show of preparing them by the stove: this would reinforce her disguise and perhaps reassure the other passengers who may have been concerned. It was one thing to travel alongside an invalid gentleman, another to be trapped in a closed vessel with one afflicted with, say, the cholera. Outbreaks were on the rise, and the disease was known for inflicting terrible suffering, including excretions from all parts of the body. Rheumatism, in contrast, was a common complaint and safely noncommunicable.

One known remedy for this joint malady was opodeldoc, made from soap, liquor, camphor, and spirit of ammonia. Evidently, it smelled awful. As William began to warm the medicine in the saloon, two men complained about how much the liniment stank, and one threatened to throw it overboard.

William returned gratefully to his master's berth. There, he had reason to stay, while the medicine was applied. As William pressed the warm cloths to his wife's face, he and Ellen had a moment to steady themselves, with careful looks and prescribed touch, before Ellen's night alone among men. William remained as long as he could before leaving Ellen once more, freshly plastered in reeking flannel. Both had to hope that the stench was enough to ward off trouble.

Outside, the man with the gold watch paced the deck. A light from Tybee Island was still visible—the same lighthouse glare that had guided slave ships back from Africa. Survivors of the Middle Passage first landed at Tybee Island, where they were quarantined at a pesthouse, or lazaretto, before being approved for sale at a second port of entry in Savannah. Though the international slave trade was now illegal, some ships continued to slip through.

The man with the gold watch took in the last Tybee light, then turned in. William, meanwhile, stepped out on the deck. He had asked a steward where to sleep, only to be told that there was no place for colored passengers. He paced the deck awhile before finding the warmest spot he could, on top of some cotton bags by the ship's funnel. It was loud and damp on the open deck, with the engine screeching and irregular sprays of water. Within the heated confines of her berth, Ellen also heard the noise. The stars shined brightly above them both.

Through the night, the steamer wound in and out of islands, touching the waters past Bloody Point on Daufuskie, and passing Hilton Head,

Truncard's Inlet. They glided past the ruins of an old Spanish fort, plantations near Beaufort, and piers and shores crusted with oyster beds, stopping with the mail. Now they passed the island of Saint Helena, heading seaward.

With the weather so nice, most passengers were outside early, taking in the crisp breezes off the water, whetting their appetites for their morning meal. Out on the deck, the man with the watch kept an eye out for young Mr. Johnson, who soon emerged (in the same clothes as he had worn the night before, the man noticed), and sat at the boat's guard.

The man could scrutinize the young invalid more closely in the daylight, and saw that he was handsome, with dark hair and an olive complexion that suggested Spanish blood. The observer was curious to know more about Mr. Johnson, but as the young gentleman seemed to shrink from contact, he asked questions instead of his ever-present slave.

William informed the man quickly that his master, who came from Atlanta, suffered from illnesses that had baffled the best doctors in Georgia. His main trouble was rheumatism: he could hardly walk or do anything by himself. Mr. Johnson was now headed to Philadelphia to see his uncle, a renowned doctor. William spoke confidently, boldly, as his questioner recalled later, appealing to his listener's sympathy. The man felt concerned for the sick young man, but also noticed, as he watched him move, that there was something odd about the invalid's gait.

The bell rang for breakfast, and passengers returned to the saloon, where tables were laid with broiled chicken and hot coffee. The captain invited Mr. Johnson to sit at his right, and expressed concern about the young man's health, as did his other guests. Mr. Johnson was well enough to dine, but required assistance. William tended to his every need, carving up his food so that he could use his one good hand. Then came a scene that the Crafts would later narrate to dramatic effect.

When William stepped out, the captain took a moment to give Mr. Johnson some advice.

"You have a very attentive boy, sir," he observed, "but you had better watch him like a hawk when you get on to the North." However loyal William seemed, he might "act quite differently" there. The captain had personally known men who had lost their valuable property in abolitionist country. To his eye, the young Mr. Johnson was headed for trouble. Even before Mr. Johnson could reply, a fellow diner, evidently a slave trader, agreed.

"Just mention your price," he added, and he would take the burden off Mr. Johnson's hands. December being the start of the prime season for buying and selling slaves, a deal would serve them both. The slave trader had a hard face, and he locked eyes with Ellen.

"What say you, stranger?"

"I don't wish to sell, sir," was Ellen's reply. "I cannot get on without him."

"You will have to get on without him if you take him to the North," the trader shot back.

He pointed out that he was older than Mr. Johnson and more experienced at reading slaves. For a decade, he had been employed as a "breaker" of slaves by General Wade Hampton. William would best be sold in New Orleans.

"He is a keen nigger," the trader warned, "and I can see from the cut of his eye that he is certain to run away."

If William had to cover for Ellen before, now it was Ellen's turn, and she spoke strongly:

"I think not, sir. I have great confidence in his fidelity."

"Fi-*devil!*" the trader exclaimed, bringing his fist down on the table, and knocking hot coffee into another man's lap. When the scalded man sprang up, the trader warned quietly, "Don't disturb yourself, neighbor; accidents will always happen in the best of families."

The room was close: fistfights were all too common aboard steamer saloons, especially as the liquor flowed at night, but it was morning, and the journey was near its end. Mr. Johnson thanked the captain, and all dispersed for the deck. There the trader pontificated loudly, roaring above the engine's din and excited cheers as he invoked the name of John C. Calhoun—the South Carolinian firebrand who famously proclaimed slavery to be a "positive good."

As it happened, Ellen's father was an admirer of Calhoun's, believing that "State rights was the true faith of a patriot, and that Calhoun was its prophet." Of another persuasion, Mr. Johnson observed to the captain that the air was too much for him, and he returned to the saloon.

There, breakfasting late, was a young military officer whom Ellen had met en route to Savannah. The officer's type was also familiar to Ellen, as her White half brothers were cut from the same cloth. The sons of James Smith were all known to be good-looking, energetic, big-bodied young men—among them, fun-loving Bob, captain of the Macon Volunteers. The officer before her now assumed a brotherly role with Ellen.

"You will excuse me, sir," he began, "for saying I think you are very likely to spoil your boy by saying 'Thank you' to him," adding: "The only way to make a nigger toe the mark and to keep him in his place is to storm at him like thunder and keep him trembling like a leaf."

As if on cue, the man whom the officer enslaved, Ned, entered the room, and the officer demonstrated with an example. Then he sent Ned off for the luggage, observing that if every slave were drilled like this, they would all be "humble as dogs" and never dare to run.

Why not go to Arkansas, the warm springs there, the officer suggested? Then there would be no reason to worry about his slave. Mr. Johnson replied that he believed the air of Philadelphia would best suit his needs and that he could get "better advice there."

They heard the whistle, signaling their arrival in Charleston. The officer wished his young friend a safe and pleasant journey and left. Outside, the man with the gold watch looked out for Mr. Johnson, but, not seeing him, moved on. He would remember the words of a fellow traveler: that the invalid was "either a woman or a genius." Only weeks later, when he read the *New-York Herald*, would the man learn Mr. Johnson had indeed been both.

Ellen, meanwhile, paused indoors. She and William had survived their first twenty-four hours, but the biggest test was now to come: in a city that held the keys to her past but also, in 1848, her present.

THE PLAN

||||||||||||||||||||||||||

For two years, Ellen and William had endured the best they could in Macon, conscious that their situation in slavery was "not by any means the worst," which is also to say how much worse it might have been. For Ellen, Collins had done better than a sixteen-by-twenty Negro house two feet off the ground. She had access to a small, detached structure behind the Collins mansion, a space that doubled as her sewing workshop and living quarters.

On the door of this cottage was a lock. Inside, she had furniture custom-made by William, including a chest with secret, lockable drawers. Ellen spent most of her work hours as a seamstress, while William labored at a nearby hotel and workshop. Their hours together were limited, but they knew they were considered fortunate to have this much.

Another man who had been enslaved in this region, John Brown, would testify to very different experiences of "slave life in Georgia"— to the brutality of the fields and physical torture, including medical experiments he had endured at the hands of a local doctor who once had an office in Clinton, near James Smith's. To test medicines for sunstroke, this Philadelphia-trained physician had buried Brown in a smoking pit until he passed out. The doctor conducted further experiments to see how "deep" Brown's blackness went.

Among the punishments he suffered for trying to escape bondage, Brown was forced to wear around his head, for days on end, an iron contraption protruding with three-feet-long rods and strung with bells. He was also required to restrain pregnant women while they endured their punishment. Holes were dug into the ground to hold their bellies, "so as not to injure the burden they were carrying."

The Crafts had witnessed, if they had not experienced, such extreme violence. As William would attest: "I have seen slaves tortured in every conceivable manner. I have seen them hunted down and torn by bloodhounds. I have seen them shamefully beaten, and branded with hot irons. I have seen them hunted, and even burned alive at the stake, frequently for offenses that would be applauded if committed by white persons for similar purposes."

Such torments served as reminders that the fortunes of the enslaved could always change and that pain was guaranteed for those who defied order—above all, those who attempted to escape. Loved ones, too, might be made to suffer. This was a common deterrent strategy among slavers: retaliation against those left behind. Alert to all consequences, the Crafts watchfully endured, prepared to escape only if they had a worthy plan. As skilled artisans, they were ready for this, trained to measure twice before cutting, to visualize a whole from the parts.

Nevertheless, there came a time in 1848 when their limited options compressed. The Crafts would never identify a single incident that precipitated their run. It might have been, as they suggested later, a matter of timing, opportunity, and inspiration. But beyond their own forward momentum, there were pressures at their backs. For in 1848, the House of Collins was in deep trouble, and both William and Ellen knew that with their enslavers' financial difficulties, their own problems were soon to grow.

Collins was hardly new to legal and financial turmoil. Long ago, when he was still wed to his first wife, he had been accused of shady business that required him to publish a statement to clear his good name. He had squared off in court many times since and managed to bounce back each time. He was a speculator, after all, and ups and downs were part of the game. Yet the stakes also escalated with each conflict, and his backroom deals would haunt him, as would be seen by the "most trusted and most faithful" of his "house servants," Ellen.

In the fall of 1844, not long after the Collinses had returned from Charleston, when Eliza was pregnant again, Ellen had borne witness as the family mansion was sold at auction on account of Collins's debts. The family had retained the house only because James Smith, Eliza's and Ellen's father, had saved them. His winning bid was $2,000—an amazing bargain, given that the construction price alone had been ten times that amount. (Then again, the towering, hot-tempered Smith was not the kind of bidder anyone wanted to beat.)

James Smith had given the Collinses back their home, with one shrewd change. He made Eliza the owner, locking up her property in an iron-clad agreement that would protect it from her husband's creditors. The decision was wise, because two years later, saddled with new debts, the Collinses faced public auction again. This time it was human property that was up for sale.

It was a staggering list, with 106 people named in all, many of them mothers and children. There was Nicey and her infant; Nancy and her five children; Matilda and her child; Charity and hers; Harriet and her two, Lettice and Martha, with their infants; Mary, Rhoda, Francis, and Viney, all with their children too.

Unnamed herself, Ellen waited with the others for the day of reckoning that would remove from her world people she had likely come to know, work with, care for—an event that promised to replay, many times over, the agony of the separation that she had experienced in her own childhood.

The auction was scheduled to take place in 1846—the year she and William finally married. Thus, in their nuptial year, all their fears were put on display, the looming sale testament that the pain of separation was only a debt, a death, a desire away.

That Ellen's name was not on the list may have come as little surprise, since she was a favorite of Eliza Collins. What Ellen may not have known, however, was that her father's hand was also at play in what would be a curse as well as a gift. On July 1, 1845, after he had made Eliza the official owner of her home, James Smith took further steps to formalize the wedding present he had made of Ellen years earlier. Declaring his love for his daughter, he made her the legal owner of Ellen and a young man named Spencer, binding them together in a contract that would protect Eliza's property against her husband's debts.

It was a will without an end, extending not just to Ellen but also to her "increase," that is her children, and beyond. What this meant was that when Ellen fled, she escaped not Robert Collins's ownership but that of her half sister—who, thanks to their father, was now both a slave owner and a homeowner, and among the richest women in Macon. It also meant that when Ellen ran, she emancipated not only herself but also generations of her future kin.

For two years after the posted sale of slaves, Collins avoided further large-scale public humiliation. Then in the revolutionary year 1848, he

faced a suit that eclipsed all others. It began in Charleston, with a man whose name Ellen would adopt as her own.

———

William Butler Johnston was in many ways Robert Collins's doppelgänger: a savvy investor in railroads and banks, an entrepreneur with a passion for public works, and a so-called self-made man. He, too, had begun with another career, trained as a jeweler, and, with $200, had built up the biggest jewelry business between Charleston and New Orleans. It was Johnston who had required a "negro man" to sit by a tub of water on a Macon street, pretending to fish for a book in an unforgettable display of advertising.

This self-proclaimed genius, known for exacting taste in art, a passion for flowers, and a superstition about odd numbers, would one day, like Collins, take a young bride, twenty years his junior. After returning from a European honeymoon, he would build an Italianate palazzo at the top of Mulberry Street, from which he would look down on other fine houses, including the Collinses'. The Johnston palazzo would boast a magnificent art gallery with oil paintings and marble statues, one of which cost $5,000.

The year 1848 was a turning point for Johnston's extraordinary fortunes. He filed what would be an extremely lucrative lawsuit in Charleston against the South Western Rail Road Bank. Front and center, charged with fraud, was Robert Collins. Johnston accused Collins, who had been liable for a staggering $130,000 worth of debts (approaching $5 million today) to the failed Ocmulgee Bank for conspiring with that bank and the South Western Rail Road Bank to cheat Johnston of tens of thousands of dollars. Through this suit, Collins's name became linked with "trickery and chicanery," and his reputation—the basis of his livelihood—was under siege.

In the spring of 1848, Johnston was victorious. The defendants appealed, and a second court date was scheduled after the new year. Collins had much to lose in a suit that could convict him as a fraud and a scoundrel, and make him accountable, once more, for the giant debt he thought he had rid himself of long ago. The loss of public trust was serious, as Collins had seen in the example of a former bank president, L. L. Griffin, who was attacked by a mob, thrown in jail, and forced to watch his property go to auction—not just his own, but also his wife's.

Collins and Eliza no doubt worried as 1848 drew to a close. After all, the last few times the doctor's affairs had been in such turmoil, they had seen their home and property go to public sale. What more would they lose? Ellen, for one, may not have wanted to wait to find out.

As a trusted lady's maid, Ellen, if anyone, would have been in a position to know that the Collinses's fortunes were once more at risk. She might have taken note of Dr. Collins's travels to Charleston. She also knew Eliza well enough to detect her anxiety as she awaited news.

If Ellen knew that there was to be another trial with even greater stakes in the near future, she would have had good reason to run at the year's end. Christmas had practical advantages too, since it was known as a time when slavers were most likely to give days off, as well as passes. Yet others would suggest another reason why the Crafts were so urgently motivated to run. It began, they would say, with the death of a child.

The Crafts would never mention any children born in slavery. In later years, however, at least four White activists or their descendants, each of whom had a unique connection to the Crafts, contended separately that Ellen had given birth to a baby who died while she was forced to perform her duties as a slave. Published years apart, with no apparent connection among them, the accounts vary widely but suggest in common that the loss of a child compelled the Crafts to escape slavery. If indeed they were grieving parents, Ellen and William may have felt they had little more to lose—that they had already faced the worst.

Whether or not they had children while enslaved, this much is clear: the Crafts had their future children in mind when they resolved to be free. They were haunted—"above all," as they would later say—by "the fact that another man had the power to tear from our cradle the newborn babe and sell it in the shambles like a brute, then scourge us if we dared to lift a finger to save it from such a fate." It was to defy this fate, a new reiteration of the central trauma of their own childhoods, that they vowed to put their lives on the line.

A circle of silence surrounds the Crafts' most intimate experiences in slavery, especially Ellen's. Others who knew the couple would hint at further traumas: for instance, that Ellen had been a "victim of her master," and that the Collins home had been a "cradle of licentious

wickedness." Whether this suggestion was based on fact or mere speculation, intended to dramatize the horrors of slavery, cannot be known.
The only certainty is that at some point, a scale tipped, so that the need
to escape outweighed all privilege and the threat of worse to come.

Years later, Ellen's descendants would recall hearing that she did
not like to talk about the days of her enslavement. What losses she and
William suffered were theirs to mourn and own. So, too, did they own
their future, as together Ellen and William resolved to mount their
own revolution, one built on their inheritances of love and faith.

They knew this biblical verse: "God made of one blood all nations
of men." And they had absorbed cadences from the Declaration of Independence. Where the words came to them—from an Independence
Day reading on the courthouse steps; from the halls of the Methodist
church where their enslavers worshipped; from loved ones in their
own sacred convenings; or even from the mouths of their past or present enslavers—is unknown, but as Ellen would tell William at a moment when the prospect of their undertaking seemed too much, she
believed that "God is on our side." This faith in an unseen hand would
prove as essential to her performance as her visual disguise.

The plan came together fast, within four days of conception, according to the Crafts. Publicly, William would take credit for the idea.
It was safer that way, to say that Ellen had to be talked into the unwomanly act of cross-dressing. However, there is reason to believe
that Ellen had conceived the plan. First, she had the background. No
one knew better than Ellen that she appeared White, and as an expert
seamstress, she knew the power of clothes to transform. If Ellen had
accompanied the Collinses to Charleston, she also had the geographic
vision, knowing where to stay and how to travel. And she was alert to
the dangers, which would lead to a critical addition to her disguise.

According to one telling, inspiration was borne of a counterfeit
coin. The Crafts had been up at night in Ellen's cabin, and William was
counting his savings, including a fake half dollar. He wondered if he
could pass it off. He had amassed about $150—an amount that must
have seemed both so much and so little. It was not nearly enough to
buy freedom for one of them, let alone both. Yet it was too much to
keep safely. Why not use this money as a down payment, Ellen proposed, to buy the things that could help them run?

In this version of the story, it was William, not Ellen, who was skeptical. He worried that his wife was not tall enough, for example, to pass

for a man, to which Ellen replied, "Come, William, don't be a coward!" For the next few nights, the two met secretly behind the locked door of Ellen's dwelling, staying up to prepare and strategize. The plan at this time was for Ellen to be not just White and male but also wealthy. The expenses would be higher, but the added privilege would give her a social buffer from other passengers and buy her some privacy.

Over several days, William purchased the elements of the costume, each at a different shop, to avoid suspicion. He had to be careful to gauge the will and mood of the individual storekeepers, who were not legally allowed to sell anything to him without permission from his owner. Ellen sewed her pants and practiced walking, speaking, and holding herself like a man. William did his best to appear happy. She, meanwhile, was required to look sad, for in order to obtain a pass, Ellen needed to persuade her mistress that she was needed by her sick aunt. (This was a fabrication, William would admit later.)

Eliza Collins's initial answer was no. She had her own children to manage, and the holidays were busy; she could not spare Ellen. It was the night before their scheduled departure. Boots, hat, shirt—her entire costume was locked and ready. Summoning all that was at stake, Ellen burst into tears, begging to be allowed to see her aunt, who was near death. With this, Eliza finally relented.

Back inside the cottage, Ellen and William showed each other their passes and rejoiced briefly. But a memory flashed in Ellen's mind: she recalled the signatures that were required at hotels—above all, the Custom House in Charleston, where slavers were required to register their human property before clearing the port. Now, the literacy that she had craved for so long became a crucial marker between slavery and freedom.

As they sat together in the close space of the cabin, they despaired. Then Ellen, long accustomed to serving a doctor and his wife, came up with a critical addition to her disguise. "I think I can make a poultice and bind up my right hand in a sling," she proposed.

With an injured writing arm, she would have every reason to ask others to sign for her. She would make another poultice for her face, tied in place with a handkerchief, suggesting a toothache. This covering would further mask her beardless cheeks and chin, and give her added reason not to speak. She needed one more thing, a pair of glasses to hide her eyes, and the feelings they might convey. William slipped out to buy a pair that were shaded green, for eyes strained by reading or fever.

At last, Ellen was ready to transform into a young man of simultaneous privilege and disability—too important and too ill to be disturbed. This critical adjustment reinforced Ellen's mastery. Sickness, or even the appearance of sickness, could doom a slave; but an ill or disabled White master, in contrast, needed special care. Ellen's apparent illness would also require William to serve as his master's "eyes, ears, hands, and feet," playing to claims that Black people were best suited for hard physical labor and Whites meant to be served. And it would give them added reason to travel to Philadelphia, a center of medical knowledge.

Already, the guise of disability had served them well, with Cray on the train, as an excuse not to join a hotel tea, and with strangers on the steamer. Now the act would be put to its most vital test at the Charleston Custom House, where Ellen would have to convince an official to log her chosen name, William Johnson, or Johnston, as it was also spelled. Just one stop here, and they would be on their way to Philadelphia.

How ironic it would be, for Ellen to exit the South with the name of her master's archnemesis, a director of the Central Railroad. Even if the Crafts were apprehended, at least the record of this name would survive as the ultimate taunt.

CHARLESTON

Day 2, Morning:
Thursday,
December 21, 1848

TWO HOUSES

|||||||||||||||||||||||||||

Each cleared the landing: the observer on the lookout; the slave trader who had wanted to buy William; the young military officer who had urged Ellen to make like thunder when speaking to her "boy." Enslaved people stepped ashore too: Ned, bearing the military officer's luggage, and possibly others—unnamed men, women, and children who may have been traveling belowdecks. Mr. Johnson, however, would linger inside the gentleman's saloon.

More than twenty-four hours had passed since the Crafts had locked their door in Macon. William still held the key, but for all they knew, that door may have been cracked open. If they were declared missing, their owners might have dispatched bounty hunters, or used another one of Robert Collins's signature projects—the Electromagnetic Telegraph—to alert officials at the Custom House. (Words tapped out in Macon would have arrived in Charleston far faster than steamers and railroads.) Someone might recognize William, if not Ellen, from a description and seize him as soon as he stepped ashore. For this reason and more, they were afraid.

Other dangers lurked in this town memorable to Ellen. All along the harbor were tall ships and steamers, weighing the waves with their cargo: golden crops of rice, bales of cotton, chinoiserie—and chained below decks, the enslaved, a major commodity in this international port. There were slave sales near the docks, in shops closer inland, and by the Custom House, which hosted the city's largest open-air slave market on its north side, as Ellen knew. The sight was so disturbing to foreigners (and therefore bad for business) that, in a few years, the city would pass laws to hustle the trade indoors.

It was within this building, the Custom House, that Ellen would have to purchase tickets and register William as her slave. But this site was not her only cause for concern. Behind the Collinses' former residence was the Sugar House she had learned to dread—so named for its past use at a sugar factory, now where the enslaved were sent to get "a little sugar."

The Sugar House was surrounded by high walls, topped with broken bottles to cut any who dared to run away. Customers of the Sugar House could determine every aspect of the pain to be inflicted on the people they forced through its doors, from the number of lashes received, to the type of instrument used, to the duration of the torture. They could leave or they could watch.

The men, women, and children who were held captive here had no choice. As one man, James Matthews, bore witness: the "whipping room" was underground and disorienting, so dark "you can't tell the difference between day and night. . . . When you get in there," he told, "every way you look you can see paddles, and whips, and cowskins, and bluejays, and cat-o'-nine tails. The bluejay has two lashes, very heavy and full of knots. It is the worst thing to whip with of any thing they have. It makes a hole where it strikes, and when they have done it, will be all bloody."

Those sent here to be tortured would see this range of instruments before a hood was drawn over their heads and their bodies were "stretched." The most notorious instrument of punishment, however, was a giant treadmill—a "perpetual staircase"—upon which the enslaved were forced to keep up a terrible pace after being whipped, at risk of falling under and having limbs ripped off if they did not, generating profits with their pain, as the machine ground corn for consumption.

"I have heard a great deal said about hell, and wicked places," said Matthews, "but I don't think there is any worse hell than that sugar house. It's as bad a place as can be."

There were rules to follow for avoiding such a place. Here, as in Georgia, free Blacks and the enslaved alike were held to a nightly curfew, sounded by bells and drums, and prevented from congregating. Enslavers lived in deep fear of slave insurrections, such as the Stono rebellion (1739) and Denmark Vesey's revolt (1822). It was after Nat Turner's 1831 rebellion in Virginia that much of the South adopted the features of a police state. In Charleston, the rules were minute: Black people were required to walk in the roads, rather than on the sidewalks. By law, William was obliged to raise his white beaver hat to every White person he saw. City patrols kept people in line, around the clock. The Crafts had reason to dread Charleston.

William and Ellen may have journeyed some three hundred miles without detection, persuading spectators in the intimate theaters of railroad cars and steamers, but they had more to convince in this cos-mopolitan town. With a population near forty thousand, the city was many times the size of Macon, home to fewer than six thousand souls.

The pressure would be on Ellen to dodge signatures not only at the Custom House but also at all public houses. In a city known for a heightened brand of Southern charm, personality would count too. As one visitor wrote: "It would be difficult to find in the United States or elsewhere a more agreeable or hospitable people than those of Charles-ton. They have neither the pretension of the Bostonian, nor the frigid bearing which the Philadelphian at first assumes."

Charlestonians, in short, were known for a frankness and ease with strangers. A cold aloofness and unmanly delicacy might not play well here, no matter how rich or unhealthy a person might appear to be. Ellen would have to judge and adjust. William would also have to re-fine his act. His interaction with his master on the steamship had ob-viously not pleased the other men aboard, who saw in William not a dutiful servant but a keen-eyed slave bent on running away.

The Crafts waited as long as possible to hobble ashore, Ellen leaning on William. To their relief, there were no signs of alert. Still, they met bad news: the steamer to Philadelphia had stopped running for the season.

The Crafts would learn later that on the last ship out, a month be-fore, a fugitive had been found aboard. His name was Moses, and he was enslaved by a wealthy Charlestonian, Miss Mary Brown. Moses had squeezed his body into a box the size of a child's coffin—two feet deep, two feet four inches wide, three feet five inches long—addressed to "E. Mishaw," and loaded into the hatchway just before the ship was to sail. There he had lain, barely breathing, with a loaf of bread and a jug of water, awaiting delivery to Philadelphia.

Heavy seas, however, caused the ship to be delayed for two days, so that Moses was forced to break from his box. Though he managed to cut through other boxes and sustain himself with poundcake, pome-granate, and wine, he was near death when he was discovered by work-ers who had entered the hatch, preparing to unload cargo. The ship turned back to Newcastle, Delaware, and Moses went to jail. Whether he died, was returned to Miss Mary Brown, or was sold is unknown.

For the Crafts, there would have to be a change in plans—fortunate, insofar as the steamship line to Philadelphia would have been watched closely, following Moses's failed escape attempt. But the new route was also far more complicated. Now, in lieu of a single trip to Philadelphia, they would have to travel with the mails in what was known as the "Overland Mail Route." This route required a bewildering sequence of ride changes from steamers to carriages to trains, and passage through multiple cities, including the nation's capital. They might still reach Philadelphia by Christmas, but only *if* they made all their connections and left on time.

Since the steamer to Wilmington, North Carolina, would not depart until later in the afternoon, Ellen's challenge at the Custom House was delayed. The Crafts would instead have to find a place to pass the hours. They secured their luggage and hired a fly: a small, brisk vehicle that buzzed back and forth between the streets and the docks, and all over the city.

Only the best would do for a gentleman like Mr. Johnson. Ellen gave orders to head for the Planter's Hotel—considered by South Carolina statesman and slaveholding firebrand John C. Calhoun, for one, to be the finest hotel in town—in a neighborhood she had known.

———

From the steamship docks at the northern end of the harbor, the Crafts passed down Charleston's busy thoroughfare, with its City Market, and nearby, an area thick with houses of worship. Those included Baptist, Catholic, Universalist, and German Evangelical churches, as well as one of the country's oldest synagogues.

Magnolia trees and palmettos gave the city's avenues a languorous, tropical feel, but there were also, incongruously, turkey buzzards perched atop the market house and on tall poles. Visitors were often spooked, but locals were known to be at home with their unpaid street cleaners, who were protected by law. By the market, the buzzards could be seen swooping down through traffic to seize entrails dropped by butchers and narrowly averting death by wagon wheel as they soared back up, their bloody catches dangling from their maws.

They slowed down where Church Street met Queen, coming to a genteel brownstone building with a delicate, wrought iron balcony and a theatrical history. The site once housed "America's first theatre," which had served up "bawdy, raucous fare." Planter's Hotel would eventually revert to its theatrical roots, but for now, like the Crafts, it was something other than what it would become. Patrons clinked glasses of brandy, sniffed nosegays, and engaged in business of all kinds. It was said that human beings were trafficked at the street level.

To Ellen, it was undoubtedly disturbing to arrive at a site so close to the Collinses' former home, where she had a worn metal badge to identify her as Eliza's house slave. The family had lived around the corner on Meeting Street with the family of Eliza's sister (and Ellen's half sister), Mary Cleveland. Ellen may have remembered the other enslaved people who worked alongside her in the household: one young girl, three women, and one man besides herself. And she may have taken some comfort in knowing that the Clevelands no longer lived in Charleston. Jesse had died while the Collinses were in the city, perhaps precipitating their move; Mary, too, had died after returning to Macon. Still, the neighborhood was sure to have triggered memories.

As soon as the Crafts pulled up, the landlord ran out to greet them. A person of quick judgment, he could see at once that the gentleman traveler was exactly the kind of person that this hotel was named for: wealthy, refined, and important. The visitor was also clearly unwell. With great care, the landlord took the gentleman invalid by one arm and commanded a member of his staff to take the other, ordering the young man's slave aside.

Mr. Johnson lowered himself off the fly and, his weight balanced between the two strangers, the landlord and his "man," climbed the few front steps. For Ellen, this may well have been the first time that she was assisted so courteously and deferentially by White hands.

It all happened fast. Mr. Johnson wanted to go directly to his room. No refreshments were needed—or a doctor. The landlord understood. The gentleman would be shown to one of the best rooms. With assistance, Mr. Johnson mounted the wide center stairs and shut himself up to rest. The help of his own man and the comfort of his private quarters were all he required for now.

Inside, Ellen peeled the poultices off her face and handed them to her husband. William ran the bandages back down to the lobby and informed the landlord that his master wanted two hot poultices as soon as possible. Minutes later, William flew the smoking cloths up to his master's room, where—the door now closed—he promptly put them on the mantelpiece. This was the first time in two days that Ellen's skin had breathed free from the reeking wrappers, and she wasn't about to reapply them any sooner than necessary.

In all the rush and urgency, a crisis had been averted. Ellen had entered the hotel as Mr. Johnson and had not had to sign. She could only hope that those in charge at the Custom House would be just as understanding, and that she would continue to pass muster.

While Ellen rested, William went out on his own, knowing that in a hotel such as this, he was expected to work, not idle. He ordered his master's dinner, then lugged his boots outside for a polish, entering the hotel's behind-the-stairs world. There, as he would recall later, he encountered an enslaved hotel worker from Africa—living proof that the international slave trade continued from ports such as Charleston, despite the decades-old ban.

William himself was a grandson of the Middle Passage. He knew he had a grandfather who had been born in West Africa, a leader of his people, who had been deceived by White men and taken captive aboard a slave ship. He knew, too, of a grandmother who was of full African ancestry. These stories had been passed down to him, if not by his grandparents, then by his parents or others who sustained the memories. (There may have been White people in his family tree as well, but no one would speak publicly of them.)

The hotel worker, who introduced himself as Pompey, struck William as shrewd. He greeted William casually, asking in an African English pidgin where William was coming from and where he was headed with that "little don up buckra," or White man, as he described Ellen.

The hotel landlord may have perceived Mr. Johnson as entitled and high class, but Pompey saw the sick young man more clearly for what he was, fussed over and small.

Philadelphia, said William.

Pompey was jolted. Could it really be that William was headed for a place where, as he'd heard, there were no slaves?

Quietly, William affirmed that he had heard this too.

With this confirmation, Pompey dropped his work and advised William never to follow his master back, no matter how good he was. *In other words, run.*

William would not reply, except to say thanks. He picked up his boots to return to his service, but not before the other man grabbed his hands, shocking him with a tearful blessing. When you are free, Pompey added, don't forget to pray for me.

William was afraid to say much in response at the time. However, this voice of Africa—this desire for remembrance—was one he would hear and honor in years to come.

Mr. Johnson descended the great stairs into the brilliance of the Planter's dining room, fresh poultices plastered to his cheeks and wrapped around his hand. He was seated at a fine table, presided over by the mistress of the house.

William received his humbler meal on a broken plate and was sent to eat in the kitchen. He took up the rusty fork and knife, but ate little before excusing himself to look after his sick master. The hotel wait-staff tended to Mr. Johnson's every need. Still, the young gentleman, too, was unable to consume much before his travels. He paid the bill and tipped his helpers, to murmurs of praise. He is a great man—the greatest gentleman to have traveled through for the past half year, they exclaimed to William, who could not help but agree.

Now the fly was once more at the door, and it was only a quick ride around the corner and down Broad Street before the Crafts came to the Custom House. This site carried its own secrets, having once hosted a dungeon where pirates, as well as Revolutionaries, had been imprisoned. One such outlaw was the famed "Gentleman Pirate" Stede Bonnet, a former sugar planter and associate of Blackbeard's, who was rumored to have escaped capture disguised in women's clothes—before he was hanged. Now came a master (or mistress) of another disguise. The luggage came off the fly, and buried deep within it, an enslaved woman's clothes.

The Custom House, too, had illusions of an architectural kind. The jewel of a building was well balanced, according to the style of the times, with fake doors and windows to create an impression of symmetry. There were equal numbers of doors and windows on either side of the front facade, as well as at the back. In one way, however, the balance was off. Blocking off the north side of the Custom House, by a large palmetto tree, was Charleston's most prominent slave market. If they had not seen this market before, the Crafts could not miss it now—an embodiment of all they prayed to escape.

Leaning again on the strong arm of his slave, Mr. Johnson mounted the steps. The Crafts tried not to draw attention to themselves as they entered the open first-floor arcade, thronged with captains, officers, merchants, and travelers. The ceilings were high, the floor wide and bright. Light streamed in through tall glass windows that overlooked the harbor in one direction and the slave auction in another. To both sides of the entry were offices, including the one where tickets were sold for rail and steamship travel out of Charleston.

The ticket office clerk was not nearly as sympathetic in appearance as the hotel landlord had been. He was mean-looking, William decided, and cheese colored—the kind of South Carolinian who prided himself on being well bred. Swallowing whatever fears she had, Ellen, as Mr. Johnson, asked for two tickets straight through to Philadelphia—one for himself and one for his slave.

At once suspicious, the clerk turned to William.

"Boy, do you belong to that gentleman?"

"Yes, sir," was William's reply, and to his mind, it was no lie.

The clerk demanded to know where they were coming from. William answered Atlanta. If there was any danger of telegraphing, at least the officials would be put on the wrong track. Seemingly satisfied, the officer took Ellen's money—about $23 for her own ticket, roughly half that for William's—and issued the tickets.

Then he added: "I wish you to register your name, here, sir, and also the name of your nigger, and pay a dollar duty on him."

Ellen pulled another dollar from her pocket. Gesturing at her poulticed hand, she requested that the clerk sign her name instead. At this, however, the man became unhinged. He sprang up from his seat and refused. Signing for travelers was not part of his job.

Charlestonians were widely admired for their smooth gestures and velvety inflections, aimed to diffuse conflict: The sound of this man's bellowing voice caused others to turn. The Crafts were now in a place they least wanted to be—the center of attention.

What would happen if Ellen did not sign? With luck, she might simply walk away, to seek refuge in a dangerous city—and possibly await capture, if bounty hunters were on the way. But the ticket officer could also demand details about Ellen's identity and insist that she prove her slave ownership with papers or witnesses, with heavy consequences if she could not—especially if she were suspected of being an abolitionist.

Charleston had no tolerance for abolitionism. In 1835 a mob had entered the Custom House, which doubled as a post office, seized tracts sent by northern antislavery advocates and set the papers ablaze. Stark punishments awaited fugitives and their abettors, in a jail next to the Sugar House. Caught without a legitimate master, William might be sold. As for Ellen, it would be a matter of when and how officials discovered her true identity, both as a fugitive and as a woman.

And then, along came a Southern gentleman: the very same military officer who had tried to educate Ellen about schooling William just that morning. The young man had obviously enjoyed some brandy in the intervening hours, which made him both more friendly and more bold. He grabbed Ellen's good hand and shook it. In his brandied eyes, they were friends.

The young officer was apparently known in Charleston, and in this town, renowned for its hospitality, his reputation helped Ellen.

"I know his kin like a book," he exclaimed happily, and with this single gesture, the winds turned.

"I will register the gentleman's name," offered another handsome man nearby, "and take the responsibility upon myself."

This man proved to be none other than the captain of the steamship that the Crafts wished to ride. The young officer's word was good, and the sick young traveler appeared capable of affording a ticket. That sufficed for the captain to take on another paying passenger.

The captain turned to the young invalid, whose eyes were scarcely visible under his thick, green glasses. He asked the gentleman his name.

"William Johnson," Ellen replied.

It was a fine Southern moniker, and it passed.

The captain wrote the words: "William Johnson and slave."

"It's all right now, Mr. Johnson," the captain assured him.

Clearly, the young man was shaken. The military officer hoped to cheer him with a drink and a cigar, but Mr. Johnson demurred and, with his enslaved man by his side, limped off.

For Ellen, it was another major triumph. She had outwitted her challenger not just with a clever disguise, by luck or coincidence, but by the good will she had built up with a stranger. Through conversations here and there, she had persuaded the young officer she was worthy of his type and class, and in a single moment, her hard work paid off. Her success exposed both the hypocrisy of her world and the possibility: of one person's power to help another; of civilization's ability to break down what it wrongly put up—that is, when blinded to its own constructs.

Departure was scheduled for three o'clock, with arrival in Wilmington expected in the early hours of the morning. On this voyage, the Crafts could be more confident, as their place was assured by the captain himself. There would probably be one meal to endure, at most. After that, Mr. Johnson had the excuse to retire.

At one point during the ride, the good-natured captain took pains to address Mr. Johnson, sensing that the young man had been rattled. It was not out of any disrespect that he had been stopped; it was just that Charleston, as a rule, was strict. The captain had seen entire families kept at dock until more information could be had about their slaves. Matters might have been much worse.

"I suppose so," Ellen replied, and thanked the captain for his help.

OVERLAND

Day 2:
*Thursday,
December 21, 1848*

THE WRONG CHAP

||||||||||||||||||||||||

All night, fire hands stoked the furnace, and the smokestack spun out plumes and sparks, fading into the dark-blue sky. Cooks stirred great pots below decks, while passengers slept behind the curtains of their berths. High in his elevated house, the pilot kept a steady eye on the horizon and on the myriad shoals, bluffs, and inlets along the jagged shore—from the no-man's-land of Withers Big Swamp (now Myrtle Beach), up to Bald Head Island, with its perilous Frying Pan Shoals.

In the hands of sleepy navigators, even steamers might wash up on this course—or possibly explode. (The "floating palaces" were also known as "floating volcanoes," for a reason.) This steamboat connection, more than any other point along the Great Mail Route, was known for its "irregularities." Ellen and William Craft pushed through the waters, however, unassailed.

By morning, they passed around the battery of a seaside town called Smithville. Passengers could glimpse the ruins of a Revolutionary fort, ushering the way to a river that flowed to the sea: Cape Fear. Turning widely, the steamer wound its way up the tangled river lines, the currents fast, the trees thick and close. At last, the curtain of trees appeared to part, the river opened up into marshland, and, in the distance, the town of Wilmington, North Carolina, came into slow focus.

There were wharves on either side of the river, and a bracing tang in the air. The steamer bell clanged, and people seemed to pour forth from inland, ready to greet the new arrivals or the mail or start their own ride. The Crafts moved with other northbound passengers over a bridgeway, alive to the commotion—the sounds of workers' calls and shouts, the rolling of baggage cars.

It was not long into their train ride that they discovered the source of the sharp smell. For miles, there were little more than pines, reminiscent of Georgia. Only here, many of the trees were scarred with eighteen-inch wounds, as one eyewitness observed, from which the blood of the trees—turpentine—had been bled into boxes notched into the trees' own bodies. The great pines did not always die from these bloodlettings, but they did not appear healthy. Neither too, did the locals, as observed by travelers—sickened, it was guessed, by the swamps or by a poor diet consisting largely of sweet potatoes and herring.

Day plunged again into darkness, with little opportunity to rest. The passenger cars were not fitted for sleeping, and there was a bewildering number of station changes, where groggy, disoriented passengers would be prodded and shuttled into yet another car or a crosstown omnibus. At each exchange, luggage and property had to be accounted for. Among the property that was most carefully tracked were the enslaved.

The rails moved passengers and the mail, but also, more and more, people who were being bought and sold: men, women, and children who might have shared the same car as William, and could be parted on a buyer's whim. En route to Richmond, Virginia, the British novelist Charles Dickens had been shaken by the cries of children riding in the next car with their mother, after having been sold away from their father, who was left behind at the previous station.

Each time the train heaved off, the conductor rattled through with his money box, light shining off his arm from a specially fitted lantern. "Ticket!" he demanded. "Ticket!" "Negro firemen" startled passengers awake too, when they stoked the stove. Sometime they brought buckets of cool drinking water, and then men, sleeping with their feet up by the fire, their grubby socks exposed, might rouse themselves for a drink before snoring to sleep again.

If there was one comfort for passengers, it was that with each shift, the cars improved, along with the service. British travelers tended to become more comfortable in Virginia, a land settled by the descendants of "ruined cavaliers." They appreciated the Virginians' superior manners and amenities, and generally felt more confident that they were not going to die.

Mr. Johnson, too, benefited from the changes. When the train pulled into Petersburg in the early morning, he was invited to a special car for ladies, families, and invalids. It was only twenty miles from Richmond, and not a long ride, but Ellen gladly took advantage of the opportunity for some privacy and rest—though she was to learn that she would not be alone.

The car was cleaner and more spacious than most, with couches for reclining. Mr. Johnson entered the space with assistance and was soon joined by other passengers: an older gentleman and his two single daughters, who became curious about Mr. Johnson.

As William took his own place in the Negro car, the old gentleman came by to ask him about his young master. What exactly was wrong with him, where was he from, and where was he headed? William gave his now well-rehearsed answers, which seemed to satisfy the old man. He inquired further if the young man's father had any more "boys" as faithful and smart as William?

William assured the old gentleman that his master's father had many more—which, as he wryly recalled years later, was "literally true." That was all the old man needed to know. Before returning to his car, he thanked William with a tip, making him promise that he would be good to his master—a promise that William was only too happy to keep.

Back in the family car, the young people were enjoying a cozy chat. "Mr. Johnson" might not have been the picture of health or style, with a slight reek of camphor about him, but he would make up for these deficiencies with other attractions. Having served such young ladies all her life, Ellen knew exactly what type of conversation would be most pleasing to them from a gentleman like herself. Upon his return, the ladies' father inquired politely after Mr. Johnson's health and then invited him to rest on one of the couches. Ellen obliged, grateful for any excuse not to talk.

The others were eager to help. The ladies insisted on tucking their shawls under Mr. Johnson's head, and covered his body with his sacque, probably with some persuading. Ellen could only have been glad that her shirt and vest were shapeless enough to hide the swell of her chest. The old man may have done his part too, by pulling off the invalid's heavy boots. (Any misgivings he may have had about the young man's small feet, he fortunately kept to himself.) Once Mr. Johnson seemed asleep, the ladies could not help themselves, one reportedly exclaiming, "Dear me! I never felt so much for a gentleman in my life!"

Behind the cool green glasses and closed lids, Ellen's could only think: "They fell in love with the wrong chap."

Mr. Johnson soon revived himself enough to accept sweets from the ladies. As they approached Richmond, the women's elderly father extended a recipe for treating rheumatism. Ellen pocketed it fast, lest she betray her illiteracy. The old man extended a further hospitality, expressing his hope that Mr. Johnson might call on him, adding mean-ingfully, "I shall be pleased to see you, and so will my daughters." Ellen now feared that she had taken things too far, but thanked him and promised to call when she returned that way—which she privately hoped would be never again.

BOXED IN

||||||||||||||||||||||||||

They rattled over the long wooden bridge toward Richmond's shore—a tightrope, with no railings or breaks to keep the train from veering into the frothy James River, coursing hard below. It was a hush, dark hour in the city, hours before sunrise. There was the noise of the falls, of the river crashing down over the fall line, a hundred-foot drop, but little more.

Guards were awake at the Virginia state capitol, however, installed round the clock after Gabriel Prosser's 1800 slave revolt—a warning to the enslaved population downhill that an eye was on them at all times. "Give me liberty or give me death"—the summons from a famed Virginian and enslaver, Patrick Henry—was not meant for them.

The quiet cut a contrast to the tumult by day, especially where the Crafts disembarked. Richmond was a "resale center" in the slave trade, and while coffles (chained walking gangs) remained a common sight, more and more people were being trafficked by train. Many of the enslaved in Macon were known to come from Richmond, and the Crafts may have heard stories about this town, renowned as a place where tobacco was sweetened and families were broken apart.

Enslaved people riding with William would have been prodded in the dark toward one of the city's many slave jails, or pens, for keeping overnight. The most infamous was Lumpkin's Jail, called the "Devil's Half Acre." The owner, Robert Lumpkin, lived on the grounds with the mother of his children, a "nearly white" enslaved woman named Mary. One day, thanks to Mary Lumpkin, a school for Black freedmen would rise on these grounds, eventually to become part of Virginia Union University. But that future was a long way off in this darkest hour.

Mr. Johnson might have been offered the opportunity to check in his slave at Lumpkin's or elsewhere, but he would insist on keeping William close by at all times, unable as he was to function without him. The rich, young planter had his choice of a number of excellent hotels, including the palatial Exchange, with a dining room for hundreds, or the American, where the celebrated British author William Thackeray would be a guest in a few years.

At the hotel of their choosing, the Crafts performed a similar routine as they had in Charleston. William helped to rush his sick master to a room. Here Mr. Johnson might have rested, ordered fresh poultices and food, while William, once again blackening his master's boots, gleaned whatever information he could. Both of them watched, waited. They would not want to be late, not when they had less than twenty-four hours left to go on their journey, and with the red flags for slave sales to unfurl so soon.

By eight o'clock, they were out, pulling away from the Richmond-Fredericksburg-Potomac Depot, far from the docks. As the whistle shrilled, they bid farewell to this high, hilly landscape and its classical white capitol, with its stuccoed marble sheen and round-the-clock guards. With any luck, an even grander Capitol—the nation's—would soon be in their sights.

Just before the train pulled out, however, a heavyset woman seated near Mr. Johnson spotted William on the platform and started screaming that he was her runaway slave.

"No, that is my boy," Ellen objected, but the woman kept yelling. Only after William turned around, offering a full look at his face, did she finally back down.

The woman apologized, explaining that William exactly resembled a man named Ned, who had run from her eighteen months ago, after she had sold his wife, July. Whether her words were truth or fiction, the story of broken promises was all too familiar in these parts.

Just now, in fact, a Richmond man named Henry was mourning the loss of his family. Like William, Henry was a skilled worker, a self-hiring tobacconist. He and his wife, Nancy, were enslaved by different people, but they had lived together with their three children and had a fourth on the way. Then, while at work one August day, Henry got word that his family had been taken to a prison and sold to a Methodist minister who would take them to North Carolina.

Henry begged his owner, known as a kind Christian man, to help him—to no avail. The man said Henry could find another wife and start a new family easily enough. Henry pleaded with others he knew to help buy his loved ones. They informed him, sadly, that they could help in any other way, but not by trafficking in slaves.

The next morning, Henry waited on a corner where he knew the gangs of the sold passed through. He saw the wagon full of children coming toward him first. He had seen many such wagons before, but this one carried his first-born child, who cried as the wagon rumbled by. He saw his wife next, Nancy, her belly swollen, her body chained as she walked. For four miles, he walked with her, holding her hand, before they were forced to leave each other. He would not see Nancy or any of his family again.

When the Crafts passed through Richmond, Henry was near to having his own revelation. On Christmas Day, he would hear a song, receive a vision, see a box. He would carry out that vision, accomplishing what the enslaved Moses had tried and failed to do in Charleston. He would put himself in a three-foot-by-two-foot box and have himself mailed to Philadelphia. Twenty-seven hours later, he would emerge and sing his praise to God.

The world would come to know his name, and so would the Crafts. He would be called Henry "Box" Brown, and their paths would cross again.

THE CAPITAL

|||||||||||||||||||||||||||||

Sixty miles later, they were at Fredericksburg, by the Rappahannock River. Black vendors—blue black with cold, as one traveler recalled—would approach passengers here with cakes and fruit for sale, or giant triangles of gingerbread. Such fare may have provided the Crafts with needed nourishment, if Mr. Johnson and his slave had neither the time nor will to eat before. From Fredericksburg, they switched trains, rumbling over another long bridge for a fifteen-mile ride, landing at Aquia Creek, which led the way to Washington, DC.

Solomon Northup, a free Black man and violinist who was kidnapped into slavery, had been forced through here several years earlier. (In 1848, he was still in bondage, years from penning *Twelve Years A Slave*.) Northrup was one of thousands who would pass through Aquia Landing, a small but vital link connecting the nation's capital to destinations farther South. William and Ellen were among the very few enslaved at this time, to escape in the opposite direction.

The Crafts soon climbed aboard a small, fast ship—possibly the Powhattan or the *Mount Vernon*. The vessels were known to be good, far better than what Charles Dickens had complained of a few years earlier. He was especially disgusted with the washrooms, which contained "two jack-towels, three small wooden basins, a keg of water and a ladle to serve it out with, six square inches of looking-glass, two ditto of yellow soap, a comb and brush for the head, and nothing for the teeth." Everyone used the same comb and brush, he noted, and stared at him when he pulled out his own.

Travelers who were unhappy on prior legs of the journey, especially in North Carolina, generally enjoyed the ride up the Potomac. Even the toilets were said to be nice, and there was a "negro barber" on hand for a quick shave—though, of course, Mr. Johnson would decline, due to the delicacy of his rheumatic jaw.

On board, the Crafts needed to look around them carefully. The Great Southern Mail Route was well traveled by students, businessmen, and sightseers who might be known to them or their enslavers. One young man who would make this very journey a few months later (pronouncing it "delightful") was Henry Craft, the son of William's previous enslaver, Hugh Craft, the man who had sold William's family. Henry had recently finished law school at Princeton University and would travel this way with his sister.

The river ran wide and fast—more like the sea, as much as a mile across in parts, and silver: a broad, gleaming mirror, as one traveler remembered. Green fringed the shoreline, dimpled with small bays. The boat passed fancy villas and humbler farmlands, and voyagers unaccustomed to this region would startle at the closeness of the Black and White bodies they passed. Babies, light and dark, were carried in the same arms; faces of different hues appeared pressed together from within the same doorways. The river spanned two states as the boat moved north, Virginia on the left, Maryland on the right—two more the Crafts hoped to leave behind.

A bell tolled to announce the highlight of the sightseeing, which rose up on the Virginia side: Mount Vernon, George Washington's old home. Even the most reluctant of tourists usually got up on deck to take in the view. Mr. Johnson may have done so; it would have seemed odd if he did not. Some grabbed their spyglasses, while others might have sung "Washington's Grave." On a clear day, the columns of the great house were clearly visible, the red roof bold against the sky, crowning the site where the nation's first president had once lived and now was buried.

It was Washington who had authorized the act that now endangered the Crafts: the Fugitive Slave Act of 1793, which allowed enslavers to prosecute for the return of fugitives who had crossed state lines. This act was rooted in the Constitution itself, which did not name slavery, but protected the rights of enslavers to pursue those who owed them "service or labor" in Article IV, Section 2, Clause 3, also known as the Fugitive Slave Clause.

Thanks to this act, no matter where the Crafts went in the nation, their enslavers had legal right to drag them back into bondage and to sue anyone who provided assistance—that is, however, if they could be tracked. The law was notoriously difficult to enforce, especially in the North, where resistance was growing. The Washingtons themselves had troubles with an escaped slave, who had died earlier in 1848—a woman named Ona Judge, who had outlived and outrun them both. With luck, the Crafts would follow her lead.

The riverboat turned a bend toward Fort Washington, Maryland, before pausing at Alexandria, Virginia, which only a decade earlier, had been the nation's premier slave export market. From here the US Capitol was already visible, its orb above the evergreens, touching the giant sky.

As the steamer churned the waters toward the capital city, William and Ellen knew that just two more transfers remained before the end of their long journey. Of the one thousand miles to travel, they had a forty-mile train ride from Washington, DC, to Baltimore, before a final hundred miles by rail to Philadelphia. With each passing mile, possibility was becoming reality, and they could dare to believe that this would be their last afternoon in bondage.

But just as the Southern winds seemed to soften, there came a sudden chill—a reminder that their journey could reverse course at any moment. William sensed a White man observing him closely, and as they drew closer to Washington, the stranger's gaze grew hostile. He focused on William's white beaver hat, commenting to Mr. Johnson that his slave was likely to be spoiled by it. This was not the first time Mr. Johnson was taken to task for overindulging his property, but the charge now carried a new menace. The president of the United States himself could not have worn a better hat, the man accused. It made him want to go and kick it overboard.

Before he could follow his impulses, however, a friend calmed him with a touch and a few quietly spoken words: this was no way to speak to a gentleman. The other man complained nonetheless—it made him itch all over to see the likes of William dressed like himself, "dressed like a white man," and Washington was full of these kinds of slaves, free and spoiled. He wished they would all be sold down South, where the devil in them would be whipped out.

It was the first sign, however unhappy, that they were no longer in the Deep South; that "way down South" was far away. Ellen, her identity obscured by her own fine hat, decided that the less she said, the better, and simply walked away, gambling that her complainant would show the restraint required of him as a fellow gentleman.

Her instincts were correct again. A few tense minutes, and they were on shore once more, with no time to recover, only to push forward. As they steeled their nerves for the next challenge, there might have been this passing relief: that it had been William and not Ellen who had been reviled for overstepping boundaries, for daring to dress as someone he—or she—was not.

Though the Crafts may not have known it, the unpleasantness on board was symptomatic of larger tensions in the nation's capital—a year's worth of tumultuous events that had roiled the landscape now entering their view.

They docked by a great bridge at the bottom of Maryland Avenue, beneath the green expanse of the Mall. The city had an unfinished feel, especially toward the edges, like a picture half colored in. The Washington Monument was little more than a stump, while construction of the Smithsonian Institution had been stopped for the winter. Only the Executive Mansion and the Capitol appeared fixed and majestic: classical gods descended into a mortal world.

For the Crafts, the race began from the moment they docked. The steamboat landing and the depot were separated by a mile, and they needed every minute to make the connection to Baltimore. They jumped into a conveyance—a hack if not an omnibus—their sights hard on the depot and on the Capitol that led the way, guiding them like a star.

The Capitol was surely the largest building they had ever beheld, and as they inched toward its colossal form, stretched skyward with its blue-grey dome, the Crafts looked onto a space that had been consumed more and more with the fate of people like them: the enslaved, but also fugitives. Topics that had been hushed in previous years reared up in this election year of 1848, especially following an incident known as "The Pearl."

On a rainy night in April, while citizens of the city were lighting bonfires and toasting to the democratic revolutions in Europe, seventy-seven enslaved men, women, and children hid in the hull of a schooner called the *Pearl*, to be transported down the Potomac to the Chesapeake Bay and then farther North. It was an ambitious ploy, called the "the single largest known escape attempt by enslaved Americans." The plan was discovered, however, and the *Pearl* was captured, along with everyone on board.

Days of rioting followed the *Pearl*'s return to the city, and a mob threatened to destroy an abolitionist press. The event ignited both sides of the slavery divide. Slavers and sympathizers were outraged by the conspiracy to steal their human property, while antislavery advocates were horrified at the specter of so many enslaved people in flight from the nation's capital, held captive in its jails. Those who had orchestrated the escape had in mind this very outcome, not only to free a large group of people from bondage but also to stoke a national fire over slavery.

The spark lit the Capitol. For years, gag rules (lifted in the US House of Representatives but intact in the Senate) had ensured that antislavery legislation would be tabled. Emboldened by the crisis, New Hampshire's antislavery senator John Hale proposed legislation that exposed what was truly at stake in the aftermath of the *Pearl* revolt. Ostensibly, his proposal concerned compensation for property damage in the event of mob action, but his opponents knew otherwise. As Senator Calhoun warned, "I know to what this leads. . . . When this subject was first agitated, I said to my friends there is but one question that can destroy this Union and our institutions, and that is this very slave question."

Mississippi's Henry Foote then extended an invitation to his colleague from New Hampshire: "Let him visit the good State of Mississippi, in which I have the honor to reside," he said, and it would not be long "before he would grace one of the tallest trees of the forest, with a rope around his neck, with the approbation of every virtuous and patriotic citizen." Soon known as "Hangman Foote" the senator offered to help string up his fellow congressman himself.

The Crafts now crossed directly into this contested terrain, close enough to the Capitol to see the shine from its windows—panes through which the city's slave pens were also visible outdoors, as a representative from Illinois, Abraham Lincoln, would remark. The future president would long remember the appearance of these buildings, from which the enslaved were driven to Southern markets, "precisely like droves of horses." Business had reportedly been brisk over the past few weeks, with slavers in Washington concerned about moves to abolish the slave trade in the capital and selling off their human property while they could.

Meanwhile, the nation's lame-duck president, James Polk, bought and sold people from his office, though he was careful to keep his business secret. As he wrote to one agent: "There is nothing wrong [in] it, but still the public have no interest in knowing it, and in my situation it is better they should not." The president whose name would be forever linked with Manifest Destiny lived out the contradictions that his nation grappled with regarding the future of slavery. During his last days in office, Polk would write a will in which he expressed his wish to manumit his slaves. But he also made orders to buy more enslaved people, including a lone ten-year-old named Jerry.

From the Capitol, the conveyance finally rounded the corner, bringing the Crafts to the railroad station, a onetime boardinghouse turned depot, too small for the heartache it contained. This was the site where, only a few months before, fifty of the captured fugitives from the *Pearl* were forced onto trains for Baltimore, for transport farther south. Many had been house slaves and skilled, self-hiring slaves like William and Ellen, and their loved ones had come out to bid them good-bye, filling the station with the sounds of weeping. Overseeing this procession was a tall, silver-haired man about Ellen's father's age: the most infamous slave trader in Baltimore, and a man who was known to Ellen from her childhood.

Hope Hull Slatter had been a sheriff in Clinton for many years before he moved to Baltimore and put up the sign that had as its only advertisement: "From Clinton, Georgia." He was also the uncle of Jesse Bunkley, the man at the center of the identity theft case in which Ellen's father was hired as a defense attorney. "Hope Hell Slaughter," as he was sometimes called, was not known for mercy. As the *Pearl* fugitives neared departure, he had separated a husband and wife—even after the man claimed that his wife was free—and when they tried to touch hands one more time through a window, Slatter had the man clubbed down.

William and Ellen likely entered this depot as they had the others, with Mr. Johnson leaning on the arm of his slave. Although the station house was shabby, the train cars were handsome and colorful. First-class cars were adorned with painted panels, framing sites of travel and battle that competed with the views outside. There were three-by-three water closets on this line, where a gentleman might find relief, not far from the warmth of the pot-bellied stove.

William helped Ellen to her luxurious first-class seat before taking his own place in the Negro car. As the train chugged forth, and the sun slid lower in the sky, the Crafts lurched toward the last and possibly most dangerous slave port of their journey, Baltimore, for their final transfer to freedom.

BALTIMORE

|||||||||||||||||||||||||||

Daylight faded to darkness again, casting a shadow into the cars. It was the third sunset the Crafts had seen since Macon. They had hardly slept during the interim nights aboard the noisy berths and decks of the Charleston and Wilmington steamers, amid the racket of the Richmond-bound rails. They could scarcely rest now, not with the knowledge they carried. Their passes covered four days at most; today was their fourth full day in transit. With so much time having lapsed, one thing was clear: *they knew.*

By this time, back in Macon, Eliza and the cabinetmaker would certainly be inquiring among William's and Ellen's friends and family members. They might have sent word to Ellen's sick relative, and what would they learn then? That the Crafts had never come? Had someone telegraphed ahead to Baltimore?

As the Crafts drew toward the city, the weather bleak and overcast, their fear was compounded by what they knew of the place itself. Despite having the nation's largest free Black community, Baltimore was the last major slave port before the North, and thus on high alert for fugitives. Trains were watched with special care, since a number of people had escaped this way. One was a ship caulker born a Frederick Bailey, who, upon his self-emancipation, chose to be called Frederick Douglass. Disguised as a sailor, with a red shirt, tarpaulin hat, and black cravat, he carried borrowed papers showing that he was a navy man, and therefore free.

In her own disguise, rumpled from days of constant wear and travel, Ellen steeled herself for a final test. She was not required to sign a book, as she had in Charleston, or purchase tickets, since she had paid for the entire passage already and carried the ticket stubs—and money—on her body. But she would have to pass muster with the train's conductor and anyone else who chose to question her claim over her slave. William made sure during these hours to take special care of his master, showing such devotion that he drew praise from onlookers, who took his attentiveness as proof of the closeness that existed between masters and slaves.

They chugged over a massive viaduct that spanned the Patapsco River, hovering sixty feet above the water, braced by a sixty-three-thousand-ton granite structure once called "Latrobe's Folly." Then came Baltimore, visible even through the darkness, lit up with gaslights—a rare constellation of man-made stars. The iron horse was soon disconnected, and live horses hitched to the cars. In a city where the trains cut straight through, the mercurial, fire-belching engine was too much of a hazard. Real beasts would haul them through.

They pulled past the hub of Mount Clare Station, then dragged east across Pratt Avenue, past giant storehouses and factories, and, nearby, Hope Hull Slatter's old slave pen. Another man ran the operation now, silver-haired Slatter having relocated to Alabama with his young bride following his transport of the fugitives from the *Pearl*. However, the Georgia-born slave trader had left his mark on Baltimore. A foul tunnel, two blocks long, was said to traffic enslaved men, women, and children directly between Slatter's old pen and the docks of what is now called the Inner Harbor—a dark and seemingly endless space that required crawling.

The Crafts edged toward the Baltimore Basin and touched down at the depot where they were to change trains, a whiff of the wharves beyond. Ships of all sizes left the Baltimore waters for ports around the world. The depot here would be the last official station where William and Ellen would have to transfer lines before they were on their way to Philadelphia.

They jumped out into chaos: the shared station was thronged not only with passengers but also hawkers yelling out the names of hotels, jostling for hire. With minutes to spare before last call, William guided his master swiftly over the platform and through the crowd, and assisted Ellen into her car. One final transfer to one more train, one last stop.

The veteran Philadelphia, Wilmington, and Baltimore Railroad was unlike any the Crafts had encountered, fitted with sleeping berths, promising a more comfortable ride for Ellen, at least—one where she could stretch out in both mind and body. It would be a fitting way to end their journey.

If only. As William made for the rougher box of his car and was poised to step in, he felt a tap, heard a voice: "Where are you going, boy?"

"To Philadelphia, sir," William answered as calmly as he could to the petty officer who stood in his way—a man who, to his eye, appeared of lower class than his so-called master.

"Well, what are you going there for?"

William answered that he was accompanying his master, who had already taken his seat.

The officer's next words tumbled out fast. William would have to get his master at once, since the train was soon to start, and it was against the rules for anyone to take a slave past the station until he could prove his right in the office. He walked away, leaving William alone on the platform.

For a moment, William was still, his pulse so fast and hard he seemed to feel it in his throat. Later, he would recall the faith that drew him forward—his conviction that the God who had brought them so far would not fail them now. But there was this too: William had resolved that he would fight to the death rather than be taken.

He stepped back into Ellen's car. There she was at the far end, sitting by herself. She saw him, too, and smiled. He knew what she was thinking, recognized the hope in her posture, even as her eyes remained obscured—a hope that by morning, they could be free. He tried to appear cheerful too, to ease the coming shock.

How are you feeling? he asked.

"Much better," she replied, with thanks to God that they were getting on so well.

Not so well as they might have hoped, William warned, before relaying the officer's message. Ellen appeared stricken, and, for once, she spoke out of character: Were they doomed to go back? William could not answer.

All would depend on the next few minutes, they both well knew—on Ellen, and how she managed to prove her mastery by some combination of stance or word. William offered what encouragement he could, but Ellen would have to speak for them both.

They exited the carriage, crossed the platform, stepped to the office. Through the door were the breaking waves of many voices. Ellen stilled herself, her senses sharp. She addressed the officer at once: "Do you wish to see me, sir?"

"Yes," the man affirmed, and explained once more how it was against the rules for a person to take a slave out of Baltimore into Philadelphia without proving his right.

"Why is that?" Ellen demanded in a voice both low and firm, as befitting a gentleman's son. The officer seemed to have no doubts that she was a White man, but she still would have to show him that she was one of the highest class, a master.

The other man replied to her query with a chilling timber of his own.

"Because, sir," he began, if a gentleman were to take a slave to Philadelphia and prove not to be the owner, the railroad would be accountable and liable to pay. Therefore: "We cannot let any slave pass here without receiving security to show, and to satisfy us, that it is all right."

By now, the discordant tones had drawn the attention of other travelers. Some began to make noises of disapproval, stirred up at the sight of a sick young gentleman, so rudely detained. *Chit chit chit*, they murmured.

Before this chorus, the officer seemed to falter. Wasn't there someone, he asked—another gentleman in Baltimore—who might vouch for him, validate his mastery? The brotherly young military man from Charleston, with his brandied gaze, would have been helpful here, or the handsome captain who had signed the Custom House log. But Ellen didn't need them anymore.

Ellen stood tall in her double-story hat and thick-heeled boots. She and William had come too far—all but forty miles—to see an end to each other and to the love they had denied themselves so long.

"No," she said, "I bought tickets in Charleston to pass us through to Philadelphia, and therefore you have no right to detain us here."

Yes, she knew some gentlemen, but she didn't know that it was necessary to bring them along to certify that she was master of her own slave.

The man struck back: right or no right, he wouldn't let them go.

Ellen and William looked at each other, only too aware of what awaited them in the gaslit dark, those hidden worlds like the Charleston Sugar House, Lumpkins' Jail, and the courthouse square in Macon. It was as if, as they remembered it, hope had smiled, only to deceive. At the height of their performance as master and slave, they felt themselves suspended above a pit, strung by a thread that one wrong move could clip. What could they do? Run and be caught. Shoot and be killed. What could they do but pray?

Ellen chose to wait.

No one spoke. The train conductor from Washington stepped into the office. He confirmed, when asked, that Mr. Johnson and his slave had ridden with him. Then he left. The bell rang, and there was a flash of eyes, as everyone looked at Mr. Johnson and his slave. All turned next to the officer, who wavered once again.

"I really don't know what to do," he exclaimed, his fingers in his hair. Then he exhaled. "I calculate it is all right."

Run to the conductor, he told his clerk, and tell him to let the gentleman and his slave go past. The young man was clearly not well, so it would be a pity to stop him.

With a hasty thanks, Ellen moved as quickly as it was possible for a sick gentleman to do, then hobbled onto the platform, William beside her. He practically pushed her into a carriage, before running for his own car near the front of the train. The locomotive was already in motion when William jumped aboard, just in time.

Had the crowd in the ticket office known the true story, they would have done well to applaud this tremendous act—not that of the officer, but of the elegant young person who had traveled so far, in every possible way, in just four days. From her first train ride with Scott Cray, where she had uttered a quiet, simple "Yes," she'd now won a battle with a firm, emphatic "No."

But there was this too: later, William and Ellen would state their belief that "had they not been sustained by a kind and . . . special Providence," they could never have come this far. Ellen's ultimate test of mastery was also a moment of surrender, or an act of radical faith, where her trust in the moment, and an invisible grace, empowered her transcendence.

BAGGAGE

||||||||||||||||||||||||

The train rocked beneath the bodies of the fugitives, the rhythmic turning of the wheels bringing them to a state of rest. The night was wet and starless, and in the shelter of the cars, after four days of moving, running, watching hard, Ellen and William knew that they were nearly at their destination.

They chugged through a long, enclosed channel, 117 feet in a shuttered void, then burst out to the harbor. In the distance lay Fort McHenry, the site where, just offshore, "The Star Spangled Banner" was conceived. The coming of the dawn's early light, which had awoken Francis Scott Key (himself an enslaver) to thoughts of the "land of the free and the home of the brave," would hold another promise for William and Ellen.

Barring any crisis, the Crafts were near their first sunrise in Philadelphia, their first Christmas and New Year in freedom. Three stops in Maryland, then Delaware, a mere nub, until they would steam over the Mason-Dixon Line and into the free state of Pennsylvania.

William came to Ellen at every station, and, when they had their chance, they shifted the weight of their fears and hopes. In the sequestered dark, they transferred their precious remaining funds from her pockets to his—those silver coins they had counted in Macon a lifetime ago, enough to begin a new life in the North. Swindlers trolled these trains, and they would be more likely to pick the pocket of a sick, rich Southern gentleman than that of his slave. Ellen continued to keep the tickets, while, most likely, William kept the gun.

Thirty miles into their journey, past a third pile bridge, they came to Aberdeen, Maryland, and passed gently over hills. Soon the landscape smoothed out into vast fields on either side of the track, etched here and there with darkened homes. The car William rode in was far from comfortable, if it could even properly be called a car. It was more of a thin box adjoined to the luggage van, serving as a highly combustible block against the tender car in front. There was no insulation and only a few raw seats. Being so close behind the engine, it was loud and dim.

Despite the noise and discomfort, the rhythmic chuffing, William at last relaxed as he had not since the trip began. With the money and the gun hidden in his clothes, and secure in the knowledge that Ellen was tucked away safely in the next car, he allowed himself to rest his eyes.

It was eight days since either of them had really slept. For four nights in Macon, they had stayed up rehearsing, making the plans that were now all but complete. For four more nights, they had been on the road, with shock after shock, running on adrenaline. Philadelphia was just hours away, fewer than one hundred miles, and as those miles flew by, one by one, William's muscles twitched and softened, his breath grew long. It was about the worst possible time to succumb to sleep.

In the night, the Pennsylvania-bound railcar slid to a halt by a river. It was raining outside, dark and cold. They had not known they would stop here, near a pretty seaside town called Havre de Grace on Maryland's Susquehanna River—a "Harbor of Grace" that had reputedly come up one vote short of becoming the American capital.

The river's currents could be so fast and wild that no bridge had been able to tame its shores or withstand the massive ice floes, which roiled the waters with the spring thaws. Passengers would have to disembark for a short ferry ride across before transferring to new cars, as Mr. Johnson was informed. The young Southern gentleman gathered his belongings and prepared to move, confident that his slave would soon be at his side.

But for the first time, William did not come.

The minutes passed, and passengers began boarding the boat. There was hot food aboard, tables spread, and a short while to consume it. One had to be aggressive. Gentleman were known to lay civility aside and grab bread from one another's plates. It was a place where "persons of color" could also have some refreshment. William, however, was nowhere to be seen.

Mr. Johnson began to worry, and stopped the conductor to ask if he had seen his slave.

The conductor was a man with a sense of humor. He hadn't seen him for a while, now, he said, and guessed he had run away. Mr. Johnson was sure that was not the case and asked the conductor if he would please find him.

"I am no slave hunter," was the reply.

To board the boat or not? Ellen knew that William would have come to her if he could. That left three likely scenarios: he had been kidnapped, to be returned South; or left behind; or killed aboard the train. Her options were limited. She had no money. She did not know this town. She could get off the ferry, but she would not be able to afford a place to eat or stay. She was a sick, rich, young man, a stranger from the South (a prime target, if there ever was one)—even worse, an enslaved woman, not yet in a free state of the North.

Days ago in Macon, she and William had surely planned for the possibility that one or both of them would be detected, captured, or lost—Ellen, if someone saw through her disguise; William, if he were kidnapped or recognized. But here they were, so near to Philadelphia that pickpockets, more than slave catchers, were foremost in their minds. They had likely not imagined that their greatest crisis would come on the last leg of their ride, after Ellen was no longer required to prove her mastery.

Until now, she had successfully improvised. Each stage of the journey had demanded a new strategy. Avoidance worked at first, with Scott Cray outside Macon, until it became insufficient. The guise of disability had helped her in Savannah, before failing in Charleston. There the social capital she had gleaned had been her saving grace, followed by her confidence in Baltimore—her ability to conjure not debility but strength, and move by faith.

No previous strategy or preparation had readied her for the present moment, however, when her greatest challenge was not an external enemy but the prospect of being alone. Yet Ellen, a survivor, was ready for this too.

In the dark, still hour, she made her decision. She had the one-way tickets to Philadelphia. William had money and, likely, a gun. She would have to pray that she would meet him again in a free state. Alone, she would run.

The ferry ride lasted fifteen minutes. While others clustered by the stove indoors, Ellen stared out from behind fogged green glasses at the receding shore, looking for any sign of the husband she might have left behind. If she had held out any hope that William would be there to greet her as she came off, it was dashed as she boarded the cars, solitary for the first time.

Mr. Johnson took his seat unassisted by his slave, clearly badly shaken. The conductor and others aboard the train shook their heads, finding the sight amusing: a slaveless master. The luggage car and its neighboring apartment had been loaded onto the ferry and reattached to the train on this side of the river.

It was an ingenious solution that some clever soul had devised: don't bother unloading the luggage from train to ferry to train again, piece by piece. Instead, keep the luggage in its place, roll car and all onto the upper deck of the boat, and hitch it back to the engine on the opposite shore. Less trouble, less work, less time—and for the Crafts, in the end, a saving grace.

"Boy, wake up!"

William awoke with a start, feeling a hard shake to his body.

"Your master is scared half to death about you."

It was now William's turn to panic: Had Ellen been discovered? He asked the guard standing over him what was the matter.

"He thinks you have run away from him."

William relaxed, assuring the guard that his master would not think that.

What had happened, as Ellen and William learned later, was that he had slept through the entire transfer of his car onto the boat and had simply been rolled over the water with the rest of the luggage, wakened only by the prod of the guard once the train was again on the move.

William rushed to the first-class car to find Mr. Johnson, whose relief was palpable, though he was careful not to show it. He had "merely wished to know what had become of" his servant, that was all. Others knew better.

A mixed group rode in William's car: the conductor (who typically tallied his tickets at the front of the train), a guard, and one or two other travelers. When William returned, he found them having some fun at the expense of the young planter—once an object of courtesy and deference, now a laughingstock.

"Boy, what did your master want?" asked the guard.

Just to know what happened, William answered.

No, that wasn't it, the other man said—his master had thought that William had taken "French leave" and run off. "I never saw a fellow so badly scared about losing his slave in my life." The guard proceeded to give William a bit of advice about being a slave, as Ellen had been coached about being a master days earlier: "When you get to Philadelphia, run away and leave that cripple."

William, however, would play his part to the end.

"No, sir," he replied coolly. "I can't promise to do that."

The conductor himself was confounded. Didn't he want his freedom?

"Yes, sir," William answered, but he would never run away from such a good master as he had now, which was the truth. A third man told the guard to "let him alone"—he would open his eyes soon enough. But later, a Black man quietly told William of a safe boardinghouse, in case William should want to run. William thanked him, though careful not to stop his act or let down his guard.

Later in the night, they passed a large grey stone by a yellow painted house, the rock marked with an *M* for Maryland on one side and a *D* for Delaware on the other, indicating that they had crossed another state line. They paused at Wilmington, at the edges of a great river. Then came the town of Chester, which they may or may not have recognized as part of the free state of Pennsylvania, but by the time they reached Gray's Ferry, by the Schuylkill River—the last river of their journey—they knew they had arrived.

It was early in the morning of a new day, still dark. As the steam whistle blared overhead, William opened a window to feel a cold rush of air and see the city lights winking in the distance. Behind him, he heard another man call, "Wake up, old horse, we are at Philadelphia!"

Actual horses, meanwhile, pulled the train over the last few miles, hauling them across a great covered bridge and into the city. It would have been hard to see much of anything in this starlit, predawn hour, but this much was true of the landscape they passed: there were no slave pens or auction houses, with curtains and red flags; no Sugar Houses, with high, spiked walls; no whipping posts or treadmills, with pools of brined water, bottles of pepper, pockets of salt; no houses of justice, where a couple or a parent or a child might be sold.

They clattered over the rail tracks, turning into new streets, free streets, at last. William took it all in—looked and looked again, feeling as if "the straps that bound the heavy burden to my back began to pop, and the load to run off." He sent his thanks up to God. Then he ran.

The train had barely stopped moving when he leaped off for Ellen. Together they rushed to a cab: William helped Ellen inside, then threw the luggage on board and got in beside her. The door slammed shut, the cab rolled forward. They pulled out, left the station. Ellen grabbed her husband's hand.

"Thank God, William, we are safe!"

It was Christmas Eve.

They were one thousand miles from Macon.

The free city sped by.

And at the end of these days, a lifetime of running, Ellen leaned into William and cried.

CHRISTMAS EVE CODA

||||||||||||||||||||||||||||

A thousand miles away in Georgia, Eliza Collins would fret before she truly started to worry, unable yet to imagine that her favorite lady's maid had chosen to leave her. Not Ellen, whom she had seen round in Maria's belly, who had joined her in her nuptial home, and who had been by her side during her most difficult hours: from the death of her first baby and siblings, to her husband's misfortunes and the births of her children. Not Ellen, the half sister whom she never acknowledged publicly. Weeks later, when the evidence came in, the Collinses would hold open the possibility that Ellen had not made a choice but had been led away, tricked.

Down the hill from the Collinses' mansion, surrounded by raw planks of wood, waiting to take their final form, the cabinetmaker's realization likely began with frustration too, as he had taken pains to tell William to be back on time. Added to that frustration: foreboding. After all, he had felt the instinct to search for William at the railroad. If anything had happened to his trusted worker—whom he had trained since boyhood and thought he knew well—he would have to answer to Ira Taylor, William's legal owner, since he had personally written William's pass.

Then came that time, as unease or irritation grew into shock and fear, when someone checked Ellen's cabin, forcing open the door. Ellen and William had done what they could to cover their tracks, but whoever entered the cabin found a cabinet with a lock, which no one knew Ellen possessed, much less the secrets she had stored inside.

The Collinses knew what typically came next, as did Ira Taylor: Telegraph all major ports. Send catchers, offer a cash reward. Post advertisements far and wide for a tall, dark man and a short, light-skinned, nearly White woman, with scarred, scrofulous arms. But they would not—not yet.

PENNSYLVANIA

December 24, 1848–
January 1849

CITY OF
BROTHERLY LOVE

||||||||||||||||||||||||||||||

Philadelphia was then a sliver of a city, bounded by two rivers on the east and west, and wedged into a patchwork of townships to the north and south. Soon the sun would come up on this bursting grid, with Quakers headed for meeting in their dark skirts and wide-brimmed hats, but also newer arrivals: Irish families fleeing the potato famine, factory workers from England and Germany, Southerners with second homes, and, nearby, concentrated in the southern corridor where the Crafts went, the largest population of free Blacks in the North.

In and around this City of Brotherly Love, the Black community was nearly twenty thousand strong: milliners and mariners, coachmen and caterers, bleeders who leeched out bad humors, barbers who shaved cheeks smooth. There were midwives and ministers, hucksters and oyster shopkeepers, ragpickers and composers, laundresses, seamstresses, and craftsmen too. And all around town, throughout the chilled winter days, vendors could be seen and heard hawking steaming hot bowls of pepper pot soup—ox feet, intestines, all the odds and ends of things, seasoned, mixed up, and bubbled into a rich, heady brew. "Pepper pot, smoking hot!" was their cry as they ladled out their savory concoctions.

Philadelphia was a place where James Forten—a freeborn "gentleman of color" who had served the cause of revolution—had succeeded in building a fortune with his famed wind-catching sails, choosing from the best laborers, Black and White, to work in his lofts. But not all here was loving or brotherly. Forten's son had been hounded and struck by a racist mob, and Black churches, orphanages, and homes bore burn marks from similar incidents of violence. Still, it was a city that had brought generations of refugees like the Crafts into its fold, and William and Ellen could take cover there for now.

They shot toward the "colored hotel" that William had learned of on the train, zooming across Broad Street, for the heart of the African American community, which ran roughly between Shippen and

Pine, from Eleventh Street down to the Delaware docks. The carriage slowed, the horses pulling in close to the address on Pine Street that William had learned by heart but would never disclose. The Crafts lifted off their luggage and ventured forth. Ellen no longer limped but was shaky in her thick, clicking heels, alert to the sudden cold.

Whoever received them—bleary eyed or not, surprised or not by the sudden apparition of a fatigued young master with his tall slave— agreed to let them a room. This is how they would recall what happened next: they went straight to a private room, where they knelt and gave their thanks to God, ending their northern journey the same way they had begun. Then Ellen, pulling her old dress from their luggage, changed back into her familiar clothes. Together, as husband and wife, she and William came out to the sitting room, where the boarding- house landlord was "thunderstruck" to see them. (His own racial iden- tity was never specified.)

"Where is your master?" he demanded of William.

William pointed at Ellen.

"I am not joking," said the landlord. "I really wish to see your master."

Once again, William pointed at his wife, and the landlord insisted that this was not the gentleman who had come in with William before. But yes it was, the Crafts revealed, explaining their disguise. The land- lord's astonishment would later become a bit of comic relief, worked into the story the Crafts would tell many times.

The way the scene played out initially, however, may not have been so funny. Under oath, years later, William would recollect an alternate unfolding of their boardinghouse entry. In this version, Ellen alone went straight to their room, while William pulled out a gun and laid it on the parlor table. He called for the landlord, then declared that he and his wife had escaped slavery, and that he would use his weapon if he had to.

"I do not know that I would have shot him," he added, "but I told him so, anyhow."

The landlord's response was to laugh and assure the wary, sleep- deprived refugee that he could be trusted. He had clearly seen this kind of fear before. What was new to him was "Mr. Johnson's" shape- shifting form. A half hour later, Ellen would come down the stairs in her regular dress. She would not forget the shocked expression on the man's face.

Were they safe to stop in Philadelphia? the Crafts wanted to know.

The man didn't think so, but said he would bring others who would know better—and who were sure to want to hear their story.

The landlord stepped out into a city that was far more turbulent than it was presumed to be, especially for people such as William and Ellen. Superficially, Philadelphia was conceived in straight lines, forming such a tidy grid that some British travelers begged for a little spontaneity. Visitors admired the redbrick homes, shuttered green; Independence Hall, where both the Declaration and the US Constitution were debated and signed; and the magnificent marble edifices. It was a city with running water—so abundant, it was noted, that even the sidewalks were washed clean.

Meanwhile, there were alternate manuals for Philadelphia's back side. A debaucher's guide to the city, for instance, promised with a wink that the City of Brotherly Love was full of "sisterly affection" as well. A coroner's report described shanty homes that were virtual coffins, where bodies were found starved and frozen. Between the straight-edged corners of Philadelphia's planned avenues were innumerable alleys, side streets, and slums, where gangs such as the Killers, Stingers, Skinners, Blood-Tubs, and Rats roamed and fought. Mob violence soared in the nation's former capital. Running water may have washed some sidewalks, but elsewhere, human waste, decomposing carcasses, manure pens, and rotting garbage were the norm, leading to an outbreak of cholera the next year.

Earlier in the decade, the boardinghouse landlord might have had a clearer plan of action for the Crafts. Back then, a Vigilance Committee and a Female Vigilant Association, organizations for the aid and protection of fugitives, had been active. The landlord might have reached out to a secret list of committee members ready to provide food and shelter, medicine and clothing, and, above all, safety. Under the leadership of another gentleman of color, Robert Purvis, and his wife, Harriet (one of James Forten's three famously accomplished daughters), these committees had assisted as many as a fugitive a day.

Matters had since become more complicated. Philadelphia was a center for antislavery activism, with strong leadership in the Black community and long support from Quakers—who, while hardly uniform in their stance toward slavery, had banned enslavers from their religion since the last century. The country's first antislavery organization had been formed in Philadelphia, and the city now boasted multiple, inter-racial activist groups, consisting of both men and women.

Yet "Philadelphia's best customer" was said to be the South. Steps from the depot where the Crafts disembarked stood the University of Pennsylvania's Medical School. Here, the man who had so recently enslaved Ellen, Robert Collins, had once been a student, and many Southern families continued to send their sons. The townhomes of wealthy Southerners were so numerous on one Philadelphia street, between the railroad depot and the southern corridor, that it was known as "Carolina Row." The closeness of the South—and the potential for combustion, even within individual households—was dramatically on display that winter in an ugly divorce case playing out in the court-rooms of Philadelphia between Georgia plantation scion Pierce Butler and his English-born, actress-turned-abolitionist wife, Fanny Kemble.

Abolitionists, while vocal, were hardly in the majority, as evidenced spectacularly in the building and burning of Pennsylvania Hall, which had been built as a "Temple of Liberty," where antislavery meetings could convene safely. (Not even the Quakers wanted to lend their spaces for such meetings anymore, due to the threat of violence.) The Anti-Slavery Convention of American Women was among the groups that met for a grand inauguration on May 16, 1838. Then came rumors that these meetings were promoting mixed-race coupling, or amalga-mation, and an immediate end to slavery. (The abolitionists would dryly point out the irony that the *real* amalgamation was happening through the rape of enslaved women in the South.)

As women of many colors gathered together and spoke, a crowd outside threw bricks and stones and "pummel(ed) Negroes." Thou-sands thronged the hall, and the following night, insurgents torched the Temple of Liberty while authorities stood by. The blue damask couches, gold-lettered signs, and pages upon pages of protesting words were consumed by fire—"those beautiful spires of flame," as one Geor-gian journalist happily described.

Philadelphia had since turned even more deadly. In the crowded, industrializing city, where refugees flooded in not only from the South but also from abroad, nativism and anti-Catholic, anti-immigrant sen-timent bubbled hot, exploding into riots. Philadelphia's Black popula-tion was targeted for repeated, violent assault. Mobsters had set fire to Black churches and orphanages, and destroyed homes.

In 1842, after an especially brutal, prolonged race riot, the central operators of the vigilance organizations in Philadelphia, Robert and Harriet Purvis, moved outside the city, and the organization lost its vital force. By the time the Crafts arrived, the Vigilance Committee was virtually dissolved, and the work of assisting fugitives was continued mostly by individuals and families within the Black community. Fortunately for William and Ellen, and so many others to follow in their steps, there had been a promising new recruit to the cause: a young man who would one day be known as the father of the Underground Railroad.

Though he had lived in free states all his life, William Still, clerk of the Pennsylvania Anti-Slavery Society, knew the cost of escaping bondage. He knew this price from his mother Sidney, now called Charity, who had fled Maryland before he was born. Having already run and been captured with her four young children once before—and knowing she could not take them all the next time she tried to escape—she had been forced to choose. Reaching into the straw bedding where all four slept together, she woke her two girls, kissing the boys, six and eight years old, before disappearing into the night.

"Leave the boys, the oldest and strongest," she had reasoned. "Save the girls, the youngest and the weakest." She was "incurable" when it came to the pursuit of freedom, as her son was to recall. As a child, she had been made to bear witness as "her own father's brains had been blown out" by his drunken enslaver.

Still was the youngest of eighteen children, born to his mother and father after his mother's harrowing escape. His father, Levin Still, had purchased his own freedom before his wife's successful flight with their daughters, and was reunited with her in New Jersey. There they built new lives, though the memories of the lost boys lingered. Knowledge of what his parents had endured led William Still to his life's calling: the dangerous work of sheltering, feeding, aiding, and abetting refugees from slavery—and, later, writing down their stories.

Twenty-seven years old, with high cheekbones and penetrating eyes inherited from his mother, Still was newly wed to a dressmaker when the Crafts came to Philadelphia. He had started working at the offices of the Pennsylvania Anti-Slavery Society the year before, taking a second job as a janitor. He spent his days cleaning the office, organizing documents, and helping to send out the abolitionist newspaper that was printed there, on North Fifth Street, near Independence Hall. The paper was called the *Pennsylvania Freeman*.

When the boardinghouse keeper went out to find assistance for the Crafts, Still was one of the first responders, as he would be time and again. He would bear witness when Henry Box Brown rose from the box in which he'd been entombed for twenty-seven hours. Still would also be on call when a man named Peter would come looking for his kin: a mother he had lost when he was only six, called Sidney, a father called Levin. This would be Still's own lost brother, revealed to him.

All that would come later. For now, Still worked without a resolution to his own life story, to help others write theirs. And the one that came to him this Christmas Eve held the record for astonishing. When Still first saw Ellen, she was once more dressed in a gentleman's clothes. It was a vision that he would never forget—the fineness of her suit, the shape of her cloak, the boost of her high heeled boots—how Ellen looked "in every respect like a young gentleman."

A second man, Mifflin Wistar Gibbs, would also recall arriving at the boardinghouse, not knowing what to expect. A carpenter and contractor a year older than William, Gibbs would become the nation's first elected Black municipal judge. He, too, noticed the impeccable black coat worn by the young gentleman and the silky sheen to his tall hat. He also noted the "good features" and command of a second, "young colored man." "The first," Gibbs would write, "was introduced to me as Mrs. Craft and the other as her husband, two escaped slaves."

Still and Gibbs moved quickly to their first task of interviewing the fugitives—to learn and remember their story, but also as a matter of precaution. Though most seeking aid were genuine, there were those who pretended to be runaways in order to receive free food, clothing, and money. The newspaper Still helped put into print had, three days before, carried warnings of such pretenders: two men in fur caps, one a "tall black man," recognizable by a coarse blue shirt and a speech impediment; the other a "short mulatto" with a green coat and plaid vest.

Exhausted as they were, the Crafts were ready to provide all the required details. Then, as Still was to recall: "Scarcely had they arrived on free soil when the rheumatism departed—the right arm was unslung—the toothache was gone—the beardless face was unmuffled—the deaf heard and spoke—the blind saw—and the lame leaped as a hart, and in the presence of a few astonished friends of the slave, the facts of this unparalleled Underground Rail Road feat were fully established by the most unquestionable evidence." What that evidence was (or who else might have been present) is uncertain, but there were allies nearby who were in a unique position to verify the Crafts' story—among them, Charles Dexter Cleveland, a professor of classics and an organizer of the failed *Pearl* escape, who also happened to be a relation of Ellen's first mistress, Eliza Cleveland Smith.

With the interview over, Ellen could finally change out of her gentleman's clothing. Back out of view, she dropped the trousers, unbuttoned the vest and shirt, laced up her corset, stepped into full skirts. When she reemerged into company, her bobbed hair smoothed, her revised appearance made as an indelible impression on Still as her original one had an hour before. It was shocking for him to see her with no trace of the gentleman visible within this young woman's form.

There was rejoicing on both sides, no doubt, as they came together in this hour: by the Crafts, most of all, for their successful arrival, but also by the activists for the couple's extraordinary story. Powerful testimonies against slavery existed already, including from published writers such as Frederick Douglass and William Wells Brown. But the Crafts' story was unique. Both Douglass and Brown had run alone, from border states. They also had assistance, Douglass from his freeborn wife-to-be, Brown from a Quaker. Here was a couple who had traveled a vast distance in full, public view, with no one but each other, yet at the same time, together. To the wider abolitionist community, a story like this was golden. The failed escape on the *Pearl*, after all, had been engineered for humanitarian purposes, but also for publicity.

There was little time to reflect. Right away, the Philadelphia activists confirmed what the landlord had suspected. The Crafts were not safe. Legally, the couple remained vulnerable, due to the 1793 Fugitive Slave Act. It was true that this law lacked teeth (as enslavers often complained), especially in Pennsylvania, where so-called personal liberty laws had been passed to protect fugitives like the Crafts. The doors to such laws had been opened by the 1842 Supreme Court case of *Prigg v. Pennsylvania*, which had made state enforcement of the Fugitive Slave Act essentially optional. At the same time, the *Prigg* judgment had sided with the suing slavers and upheld the act's constitutionality. For this reason, the Crafts remained at risk wherever they went in the nation. Technically, American law, and the Constitution itself, sided against them.

Even beyond the law, the threat of forcible seizure in a border state such as Pennsylvania was a serious risk. No Black person, free or not, was safe from the threat of kidnapping. Children, in particular, were known to disappear. This was why, in the end, the Crafts' friends recommended Boston. The city had a strong Black community and a vocal, multiracial activist community. Indeed, among opponents, it was known as a hotbed of raging abolitionists. Only Canada would be safer, but the activists did not believe the Crafts should leave the country so soon. Besides, they warned, Canada was cold.

It was the couple's first major decision in their precarious freedom, and they agreed to make Boston, not Canada, their destination. One reason for this choice may have been a desire to remain closer to loved ones still enslaved, whom they would have an easier time tracking and possibly rescuing. Eschewing the guaranteed path to their own safety, they opted for a riskier road, setting a pattern for years to come.

Boston was three hundred miles away, a distance that could be covered quickly by train, but for the Crafts, it was thought best to go underground. They would be conducted in the very best of hands. If they were greeted at the Philadelphia station by the father of the Underground Railroad, William Still, they would travel out with its so-called president, Robert Purvis.

PURVIS

||||||||||||||||||||||||||||

If anyone could identify with Ellen's passing as a high-class passenger, it might have been the president of the Pennsylvania Anti-Slavery Society, Robert Purvis, the wealthy, thirty-eight-year-old free Black (or "quadroon") activist who had once undertaken a brazen feat of passing himself aboard a transatlantic ship—the one instance when he chose to pass.

Six feet tall, and noticed everywhere for his stunning looks, Purvis had such an impeccable Southern air about him that Irish leader Daniel O'Connell once refused to shake his hand, mistaking him for a slave owner. Assuming that he was one of them, meanwhile, slavers consulted him about "blooded horses" (racehorses) and wine.

Purvis had been twenty-four at the time of his transatlantic voyage, headed for England as an eloquent, passionate spokesperson against slavery and colonization (the resettlement or deportation of Black people to colonies abroad). Before he embarked, a Virginian planter, learning that a Black man would be on board, lodged a complaint with the Quaker shipowners. Could you make other arrangements? The Quakers inquired nervously, because Southern business was at stake. Purvis decided to travel another way, but then happened again to book passage on the same steamer as the Virginian on his return journey.

This time, he did not advertise his identity as a Black man. Once aboard, the Virginian, recognizing Purvis as a cultured, elegant gentleman, invited him to dine. Purvis soon charmed the Virginian and his circle of friends, not to mention their ladies on the dance floor. One Mr. Hayne, a brother of the late South Carolina senator Robert Hayne, expressed repeatedly on the voyage that "the negro was only a little removed from an animal" and that Black blood "in the veins of anyone could always be detected, particularly by a Southerner." This same man pulled Purvis out of his sleeping berth to dance with his daughter.

At the final dinner, Purvis was asked to give a toast, which he did happily, cheering President Andrew Jackson—who had personally intervened to make him the first Black man to receive a US passport, though Purvis did not mention this at the time. Only once New York Harbor was in sight did Purvis pass word to the "colored steward" to tell the captain's wife that he was a Black man on board. A German doctor was sent to verify this astonishing claim. Purvis's response: "Yes, go back and tell the company it is true, and I am proud of it." A distinguished judge on board was reportedly so amused that he lay flat on his belly and howled with laughter.

Purvis was the son of an English cotton broker, from whom he inherited wealth, and a half-Jewish, half-African mother. His maternal grandmother, Dido Badaracka, is believed to have been kidnapped in her girlhood from Morocco. Purvis's father had lived with Purvis's mother in Charleston as his one and only wife, before moving his family to Philadelphia. In the North, Purvis attended excellent schools, including Amherst Academy, which he was said to have left after firing a cannon as a prank with a classmate named Samuel Colt (who, as Purvis was to remark, had "an intuitive presence in firearms" and would later become famous for his legendary revolver).

Savvy in his real estate investments and other businesses, Purvis provided money to the antislavery cause. He helped fund William Lloyd Garrison's abolitionist newspaper, the *Liberator*, and was a major contributor to building Pennsylvania Hall, before it was set aflame. In fact, the sight of Purvis helping his darker-skinned wife into their carriage was one of the sparks that enraged the mob, igniting the rumors about "mixed-racial coupling." Later, as Purvis provided legal testimony about that terrible evening, he charmed everyone yet again. "It seemed so natural," he said, of offering his arm to his wife, and, for once, the court laughed.

It had surely not been an easy decision for Purvis to leave Philadelphia, where he had a long history, and he had faced down much danger before. When a fugitive from slavery, Basil Dorsey, was kidnapped, it was Purvis who raced to secure his freedom and even drove him off in a getaway carriage, dodging would-be captors. When the mob had come for Garrison at Pennsylvania Hall, it was also Purvis who had gotten him away. And he and his wife had sheltered innumerable fugitives in their town house on Lombard Street, shuttling them through a trapdoor below the children's room.

But then there had come those searing August nights in 1842, when a mob targeted his home (not for the first time) following a West Indian Emancipation Day parade, held annually in honor of the abolition

PENNSYLVANIA 129

of slavery in the British West Indies. Purvis had been on his way home from giving an antislavery lecture when he saw his children's English governess rushing toward him in terror, warning that a mob was coming for him. He would never forget the subsequent, sleepless hours he spent on his doorstep, a gun in his lap, as he stood in defense of his wife and children, house and home, ready to kill the first man who tried to knock down his door.

His own family was spared that night, but others were not. Rioters beat Black adults and children alike. Down the street, a Black church and hall burned. Purvis felt a deep despair, disturbed, beyond the violence of the mob, by "the apathy and *inhumanity* of the *whole* community," as he told a friend. "From the most painful and minute investigation. . . ." "I am convinced of our utter and complete nothingness in the public estimation." After the sheriff himself warned that he could not ensure his safety, Purvis, "miserably sick," resolved to move his family out of the city.

Purvis's new home in Byberry, twelve miles north of Philadelphia, was as fine as could be imagined, set off a generous stretch of road, across the street from a Quaker meeting house. It was not easy, to be sure, being a Black family in this country neighborhood. Even the Quakers drew lines, some reserving separate "colored" benches in their meeting places, and were not always friendly. But here Purvis knew he could continue his crusade, while maintaining some distance from the city, for the sake of his family.

Purvis was a true civil rights activist, who supported others' calls for justice, whether for Irish, Indigenous, or women's rights. He promoted inclusion in his own circles, working with White abolitionists and advocating women's equal participation. Yet the past year had put his idealism to the test, and by the time of the Crafts' arrival, Purvis had fresh reasons for frustration, if not outright despair. He was fighting multiple battles: against discrimination in the schools; for the right to vote (which Black men of property had once exercised in Pennsylvania, but were now denied); and even in his church. The year 1848 is said to have been a turning point for Purvis, when his faith in interracial collaboration began to erode, and he started to lean toward a greater affiliation with a Black activist cohort, even as he maintained a lifetime commitment to a wide spectrum of human rights.

The Crafts' case was sure to have resonated with him: how brilliantly the young couple had turned racial and gender categories inside out to their own advantage. At the same time, the couple pointed toward the need for radical action, at a time when Purvis was personally becoming impatient.

William and Ellen probably traveled to the Purvises' home by carriage. Approaching the house, they would have passed the Quaker meetinghouse and school across the street, as well as a spacious hall, which Purvis had built for antislavery meetings—a brave reincarnation of the one that had been set ablaze in Philadelphia.

High gateposts signaled their arrival at the entrance to the Purvises' estate. Gliding over the unaccustomed snow, the Crafts moved past a carriage house and two domed structures, a barn and an icehouse, before reaching the triple-story mansion, with its sweeping porch and encirclement of snow-laced fruit trees. Frozen gardens lay past where the eye could see, and farther on, stables where Purvis's prize-winning thoroughbreds (crossbred from the best local horses) were buffered inside against the winter cold.

Once within the doors of Harmony Hall, as the house was called, the Crafts would have met the rest of Purvis's family: His wife, Harriet, a founder of the Philadelphia Female Anti-Slavery Society and an antislavery activist in her own right; and their seven children, the oldest sixteen and nearly college bound, the youngest just a toddler. Attending them was their White English governess, Georgiana Bruce, originally hired to teach only the younger children but now charged with educating the Purvises' older sons, whom they pulled from public school on account of discrimination.

True to its name, Harmony Hall was warm and commodious, with a great fire roaring in the hearth of the front parlor, a floor-length hall, and a handsome central staircase. The layout was typical for such stately houses, with a spacious living room, dining room, and kitchen on the ground floor, and numerous private sleeping quarters above. Underground, however, was a secret space, custom-built for guests such as William and Ellen.

The dining room at Harmony Hall would have been the perfect place to have Christmas dinner, if the Crafts felt safe enough that they could stay aboveground. With the curtains drawn, the shutters closed, they might have taken places beside their hosts at the long dining table that shimmered with silverware and china, the candles casting a warm glow. There they could enjoy a meal grown as well as prepared by free hands. In addition to cultivating their own prize-winning produce, the Purvises were supporters of the Colored Free Produce Association, which sold food that was produced without slave labor.

From that table, the Crafts would have gazed up to see two fine paintings on the wall, both commissioned from the artist Nathaniel Jocelyn. On one side was a picture of Sengbe Pieh—also known as Joseph Cinqué—the leader of the 1839 *Amistad* slave rebellion, whom at least one observer would invoke when describing William. Kidnapped from West Africa, where William's grandparents had also been stolen, Cinqué and his companions overthrew their captors, but were intercepted near American shores. Demanding back their freedom, the Africans soon took their case all the way to the Supreme Court, where, represented by John Quincy Adams, they were victorious.

Purvis had commissioned Cinqué's painting just before the final hearing, well aware of how powerfully images could play to the American public. Following the Africans' legal victory, he had welcomed Cinqué to his home, where the rebel leader's portrait proudly hung. In fact, Purvis had wanted the painting displayed in an annual arts exhibition in Philadelphia, but it had been rejected, due to the exhibitors' fears of "injurious" repercussion.

On the walls of his own house, however, Cinqué's portrait exerted a new force. Another self-emancipated guest, named Madison Washington, would not forget the powerful image of the victorious rebel leader in a classical pose. After being recaptured into slavery, this Madison Washington, inspired by the painting, would organize a successful rebellion on the US slaver *Creole*.

A second painting by Jocelyn hung beside Cinqué's image. If the first portrait turned the Crafts' eyes to a transatlantic history of slave revolt, this one signaled their interracial activist future. Its subject was a prim and bespectacled man, with only a flush across his cheeks to suggest how he could be roused. But William Lloyd Garrison, publisher of the *Liberator*, had had those glasses knocked from his face only a few years earlier, as a proslavery mob dragged him through the streets of Boston with a rope around his body.

Unlike some who hedged their antislavery bets with plans for colonization, compensation for slavers, and gradual emancipation, Garrison embraced the call by Black activists like the Purvises for abolition now—urgently, without delay, banishment, or rewards. As he declared famously: "I am in earnest—I will not equivocate—I will not excuse—I will not retreat a single inch—AND I WILL BE HEARD."

Garrison had been a guest in the Purvises' home, as Cinqué had been. Now, Cinqué was long gone, having returned to his homeland years ago. Garrison, meanwhile, remained in Boston, and if all went well, the Crafts would meet him there soon.

The Purvises had their differences with Garrison: Robert Purvis, for one, did not share in the White abolitionist's insistence on "non-resistance," or rejection of force; neither did he agree with Garrison's refusal to participate in a tainted political system. Nevertheless, he and Harriet knew the Crafts could be ensured support from their friend and others in Boston.

Together the Purvises and the paintings that hovered above them in their dining room spoke to the Crafts of a powerful coalition: a multiracial, transnational activism born of slave revolution. The portraits told the Crafts of a journey past, present, and future, connecting them and their individual travels to an even bigger picture—a movement that stretched across the world.

TINY SHOES

||||||||||||||||||||||||||||||

After holding herself so perfectly in character, alert and awake for more than four straight days; after surviving the shock of her arrival in Philadelphia; and after feigning sickness for so long, Ellen became ill. Day and night, she dreaded the thought that kidnappers were at her back, and though it might have been safer for her and William to travel on, they remained hidden at Harmony Hall for several days, while word of their escape spread.

"Have you heard of the well-managed escape from Macon?" Abby Kimber, a teacher and abolitionist, would write to her friend Elizabeth Gay in New York. "I do not think it should be published," Kimber added, "but it is a fact to chuckle over."

Elizabeth may have received this news days earlier, when Philadelphian abolitionist James Miller McKim shared it with her husband, Sydney Howard Gay, editor of the *National Anti-Slavery Standard*. "I have just come from seeing *the* most interesting case that ever came under my notice," McKim recalled breathlessly in a letter. "When you hear the whole story, you will say that it was the best managed thing ever you heard in your life: in plan *&* execution."

Among the Crafts' many visitors was a Quaker named Barclay Ivins, who invited them to his farmhouse in nearby Bucks County, where they could rest further before moving on. His hospitality risked stiff penalties, as another Quaker, Thomas Garrett, had learned earlier that year when he faced multiple lawsuits and a fine of $5,400 (over $200,000 today) for assisting fugitives. But Robert Purvis, who introduced the Quaker to William, knew Ivins as a true Friend in all senses—ready to assume the risks of being a stationmaster on the Underground Railroad, as Purvis was himself.

With Ivins's invitation awaiting them, Ellen was soon packing her trunk again. In that trunk, no doubt, were new clothes. Warmer garments were required for this frigid weather, these unfathomable, thick falls of snow. The Purvises and others who assisted fugitives commonly provided outfits that also served to disguise. They replaced Ellen's gentleman's clothes, which, for safety reasons, she preferred to leave behind. But she carried items from her past, too—including, one person would allege, a child's shoes and toys.

Were these the belongings of a lost baby, as the Purvises' governess, Georgiana Bruce, would later contend? Bruce would maintain that Ellen spoke directly to her of having lost a child, and that she, Georgiana, had seen the child's belongings tucked into the bereaved mother's luggage.

There are reasons to be skeptical of the governess's story, which she wrote decades after the events had passed, and which included other unlikely claims. Yet her story is worth examining, for it suggests the kinds of scrutiny Ellen would endure in the aftermath of her escape from slavery. As Bruce would tell it, the child died "due partially to neglect," Ellen "having been obliged to leave it untended when delicate from teething." Even in the words of a radical abolitionist, one sympathetic to the enslaved, there is a hint that Ellen was "partially" to blame.

During the Crafts' recovery at their home, the Purvis home was full of children, with another soon on the way. (Little Georgiana Purvis, called Georgie, was to be born the following year.) Missing her own mother, if not a child, in pain, and under scrutiny, Ellen would have much to grapple with as she adjusted to living in the North, new lessons about how to tell her story, how much to reveal, and whom to trust.

FRIENDS

||||||||||||||||||||||||

Quaker Barclay Ivins, clothed plainly, met William and Ellen on the shore of the Delaware River, by Pennsbury Manor. (This was the country home of fellow Friend William Penn, the state's pacifist founding father, and also, on these grounds, an enslaver.) It was a short drive to Ivins's spacious farmhouse, shining against the night sky. There an older lady in wide, dark skirts and three younger women appeared as the Crafts disembarked.

"Go in and make yourselves at home," Ivins told his guests. "I will see to the baggage."

But Ellen stood still in the yard, unwilling to move. For, until this moment, she had assumed that Ivins, being "not of the fairest complexion," was of mixed race like she was. Seeing the women, she realized her mistake.

"William, I thought we were coming among colored people," she said to her husband.

"It is all right, they are all the same."

"No, it is not all right," Ellen insisted, "and I am not going to stop here; I have no confidence whatever in white people. They are only trying to get us back to slavery."

With that, she turned her back on the house, declaring, "I am going right off."

Then the older woman, Barclay's wife, Mary, stepped forward and reached for Ellen's hand.

"How art thou, my dear?" she inquired with a warm smile. "We are very glad to see thee and thy husband. Come in, to the fire; I dare say thou art cold and hungry after thy journey."

Pulled in by the friendly Quaker, Ellen entered the doorway, however reluctantly. The daughters of the family asked if she would like to freshen up before tea.

"No, thank you, I shall only stop a little while."

"But where art thou going this cold night?" Barclay Ivins wondered, having just returned.

"I don't know," was Ellen's honest response.

"Well, then, I think thou hadst better take off thy things and sit near the fire; tea will soon be ready."

"Yes, come, Ellen," Mary Ivins agreed, "let me assist thee." And with swift, motherly attention, she began loosening Ellen's bonnet strings.

"Don't be frightened, Ellen," she continued to reassure, as her younger guest likely recoiled. "I shall not hurt a single hair of thy head."

Mary said that she had heard all about Ellen and William's escape, and could well understand Ellen's fear, but "thou needs not fear us," she promised, as "we would as soon send one of our own daughters into slavery as thee."

This welcome was, as William and Ellen would long remember, the "first act of great and disinterested kindness" they had received from White people. For Ellen, it was a transformative moment, one where her "fears and prejudices vanished" and she came to believe "that there are good and bad persons of every shade of complexion."

The Quaker woman's hands were quite possibly the first White hands that had willingly come to her aid. And, with this mother's kindness working like a balm, Ellen burst into tears.

If the kindness of the Quakers was not enough, Ellen felt even more reassured after meeting two Black people in the Ivins home, Sally Ann and Jacob, whom the Ivinses employed. Soon all sat down for a farmhouse supper—possibly another first for the Crafts, being guests at a White family's table. It was a country feast. The farms in this area bore bright, lush harvests of beets, apples, buckwheat, and corn, which were packed, pickled, and preserved for the winter months. Barclay Ivins was particularly known for his foxite potatoes, rich and flavorful—a meal in themselves—and there was an Ivins fishery nearby, stocked with tasty shad.

When none could eat any more, the Ivinses' daughters asked William and Ellen if they could read. No, was the response, to which their hosts replied that if the Crafts wished to learn, they would be happy to teach them. Swiftly, the teacups, the plates, and the remnants of the meal came off the table. Out came an assortment of books and slates. And thus it was that within days of her self-emancipation, Ellen began her lifelong dream of learning to write and read.

Ellen had come of age in a house where education was prized, but denied to her—where she had only been able to stare at the alphabet in secret. Here was a new beginning, evidenced in the tentative series of loops and lines that she formed in her own hand—spectral, fleeting traces that she drew, erased, and drew, again, to spell out her name, *Ellen*.

For days, they practiced shaping their letters, making their words, while contributing their own skills to the household. William worked on two chairs for Barclay Ivins; Ellen no doubt impressed the women with her sewing. All the while, they forged deeper bonds with their hosts.

They might have learned, during this time, that the Ivinses had broken some barriers of their own. An Irish immigrant, Mary Ivins was not a born Quaker, and when her husband had first chosen to love her, he had been banished from his religion, which forbade marriage outside the faith. Eventually she had earned a place for herself in his community, converted, and entered the official books with the same patient perseverance with which she had entered into the affection of her guests.

Among the Ivinses, Ellen became particularly close to their second daughter, twenty-nine-year-old Elizabeth, with whom she would correspond. However, it was Elizabeth's younger brother, Robert, to whom Ellen gave the last remains of her gentleman's outfit—her "lovely, expensive boots with spurs"—fearful, yet, that these Southern relics would somehow betray her.

The Crafts would stay in many homes in the days, weeks, months, and years to come, in various states and nations. Of all, they would recall the Ivinses as the most truly like family. For the Quakers' part, they would have loved for the couple to stay on longer than a few short weeks. The Crafts, however, were not safe this close to Philadelphia. What is more, they were eager to start working and making their own way in the world.

So much might have happened next. The Crafts might have moved on to the next safe house, arriving in Boston within days. Their story might well have ended here, as they settled into their freedom, unknown to the world.

And then into their lives came William Wells Brown.

WILLIAM
WELLS BROWN

||||||||||||||||||||||||

On the page, on the stage, in song, and, above all, in person, William Wells Brown—best-selling author and "star lecturer" of the Massachusetts Anti-Slavery Society—was a virtuosic storyteller. Though the law called him a slave (even after fourteen years in the North, he was considered as much a fugitive as the Crafts), no one owned his words. He held the copyright to his life story, which had already sold out in three editions and was on its way to a fourth.

Brown's power as a storyteller came not just from how he spoke but also from how he listened. He was attuned to his audience and adjusted his music to their mood, sometimes breaking into song during his lectures. (He had also just published a book of musical selections.) And he inspired trust. "Erect and graceful," as one admirer described him, with a jaunt to his side-swept curls, Brown was attractive, charismatic, "easy." It has been observed that people, free and enslaved, had a habit of confiding their deepest secrets in this handsome, winsome, warm-eyed man.

Brown's appeal did not always work in his favor, though, even as it had helped him survive his twenty years in bondage. His mere appearance had once so pleased a "soul driver" (as slave traders were called), that the trader had tried to buy him on the spot—not for investment and resale, but to make him his own right-hand man. When Brown's enslaver rejected the offer (thereby keeping a promise to Brown's biological father—the owner's own first cousin), the trader proposed the next best thing: to rent Brown instead. It was, as Brown would recall later, the longest year of his life, and not long after, he made his move to run.

While enslaved, first in Kentucky and then Missouri, Brown worked as a house servant, field hand, and boat hand. After his escape to Ohio, he became a waiter, a wildcat banker (printing his own currency), a steamboat steward, and self-styled "Fashionable Hair-dresser from New York, Emperor of the West"—not to mention a conductor on the Underground Railroad—before becoming an antislavery agent, speaker, and author. He had a range of perspectives as few had, which he drew from in his relentless series of lectures across the North.

The life of an abolitionist lecturer was known to wear down both body and soul, with long stretches of travel among strangers on backroads and railroads, and, often, violence. Earlier that year, Brown had been hurled over the back of a speaker's platform and nearly crushed to death in an antislavery riot on Cape Cod. Frederick Douglass and William Lloyd Garrison once barely made it out alive from Harrisburg, Pennsylvania. It took a particular personality to persevere. Even the indefatigable Douglass complained, "This riding all night is killing me." For Black speakers, racial attacks and second-class accommodations increased the hardship.

By 1849, Brown had survived this way of life for more than five years, but it cost him. His wife, Betsey, whom he married soon after reaching Ohio, could not forgive him for being so long away from his family. When their baby, Henrietta, died during one of his absences, Brown may have arrived home too late for the funeral; even so, he was back on the lecture circuit in weeks. Story had it that Betsey sought company in the arms of his friend, and the couple eventually separated, with Brown retaining custody of their two surviving daughters.

Brown was in Pennsylvania longer than he had planned, having extended his tour at the request of the Pennsylvania Anti-Slavery Society. No one could move a crowd as one who had experienced slavery firsthand, and Brown lit up audiences, who then filled the antislavery coffers. (On a personal level, White abolitionists tended to like Brown better than Douglass, even if Douglass, most agreed, exuded more gravitas.) Brown had agreed to continue speaking, spending Christmas away from his girls, with two more weeks of lecturing to go before he was to return.

It was at this time, around the New Year, that he learned of the Crafts. He was immediately intrigued. Passing and disguise were not novel to Brown, who had once helped an enslaved man flee in a White woman's mourning garb, veiled and elegant. But this story was different: a fugitive love story, a romance, and he wanted to hear it from the couple themselves.

Always a resourceful gatherer of information, Brown managed to get word of the Crafts' secret location before they pushed off. As it happened, Brown was scheduled to speak in Bucks County, and although the Ivins homestead was about twenty-five miles out of the way from his lecture in Pineville, he was determined to investigate.

And so it was that William Wells Brown voyaged out to the Ivins home, tall and slim, and braced against the bad weather. The sight of the Quaker farmhouse may have reminded him of his own escape from slavery at age twenty. He was known then as Sanford or Sandy, his birth name, William, having been stolen from him on account of a White relative who was given the same name. Seven days into his journey, Brown was near death, frostbitten and starved, when he put himself in the path of a Quaker, who brought him home and, together with his wife, nursed him back to health.

Brown would honor the man in perpetuity. "To Wells Brown, of Ohio," begins the inscription to his personal narrative: "Thirteen years ago, I came to your door, a weary fugitive from chains and stripes. I was a stranger, and you took me in. I was hungry, and you fed me. Naked was I, and you clothed me. Even a name by which to be known among men, slavery had denied me. You bestowed upon me your own. . . . In the multitude that you have succored, it is very possible that you may not remember me; but until I forget God and myself, I can never forget you."

Brown made an immediate connection with William and Ellen. There was much they shared in common, as they would learn on this day and others to come. Like Ellen, Brown had the light complexion of his White father, and while he, too, had been singled out for privileged, in-house positions on account of his coloring and birth, he had also been targeted by a sadistic overseer as a "white nigger." Also, like Ellen, he had a deep bond with his mother, being her youngest child—a perennial "mama's boy," as he has been called. Like William, Brown had seen his mother and favorite sister sold, and knew the torment of a last good-bye.

Brown's time in slavery was permanently marked on his body, in a scar over his right eye, where he had been struck with a bullwhip, as well as on his back and in other places that did not show. In him, the Crafts met someone both original and familiar: original in the ways that Brown always was—eloquent, persuasive, interested, and interesting—but familiar in their shared experience of bondage. He was different, in this way, from the others who had helped and given shelter, such as Still, the Purvises, and the Ivinses. Brown knew what it was to be enslaved, and in this "first African American man of letters," the Crafts could recognize one of their own.

Brown talked to the Crafts about their next steps and learned they were headed for Boston. Brown, however, had another route in mind for them. He invited William and Ellen to join him on the abolitionist lecture circuit, to share their story as only they could, together.

Brown knew as well as anyone the enormity of what he was asking the Crafts to do. They may have been in the North now, but they were fugitive slaves by law. Any public appearance put them in danger. Even if kidnappers did not appear, there were no guarantees that audiences would be friendly. Rotten eggs and fist-sized stones were hallmarks of an "abolitionist baptism." Ellen faced added pressures as a woman. Harriet Tubman and Sojourner Truth—two women who would be among the circuit's most celebrated lecturers—were not yet known names; in 1849 Tubman was still enslaved. As a Southern female fugitive on the abolitionist the lecture circuit, Ellen would be charting a new course.

In the face of all uncertainty, however, Brown set a model of what being a public American fugitive could be. Legally, he was as vulnerable as the Crafts, but he had refused to hide, going so far as to send a copy of his narrative to the man who had once enslaved him. Brown felt strongly within himself that he "owed a duty to the cause of humanity." There were three million still in bondage, including loved ones, who shared his scars. He spoke for them and hoped that the Crafts would decide to do so as well.

There were other arguments Brown might have made to bring his young friends into this cause. As lecturers, the couple could raise money, for themselves and for others, and, if the news traveled to their enslavers, through public channels, it could reach their loved ones too. Ellen's mother might then know that her daughter had survived, no matter what others might try to tell her. The couple could also aim to purchase her freedom. This had been done before.

The Crafts had to know that Brown's invitation would prolong their travels, deferring their own settlement, and no doubt, recovery. At the same time, it offered a new way forward—one that would help them reconcile their future with the not-so-distant past. The Crafts listened to all that their new friend proposed, and in the end, Brown was persuasive. Within ten days of having arrived in a free state, they agreed to join him on a new, perilous journey.

In preparation for their public appearances, one of the first choices they had to make was what they wished to be called. Both Brown and Frederick Douglass had chosen new names. William and Ellen opted for more subtle adjustments. In Macon, William had been called Bill by some: He now chose *William Craft*, a name that would connect him to his new friend and preserve the link to his family, even while it retained a trace of his first enslaver. Ellen also decided to keep her given name, which she shared with others in her mother's household. To this she added her husband's surname—*Ellen Craft*—symbolizing the permanence of her union with William.

These choices were brave and significant. The known names would put targets on their backs, but they would also authenticate their history. With these names, they would stand their ground and, together with William Wells Brown, be wholly, defiantly exposed.

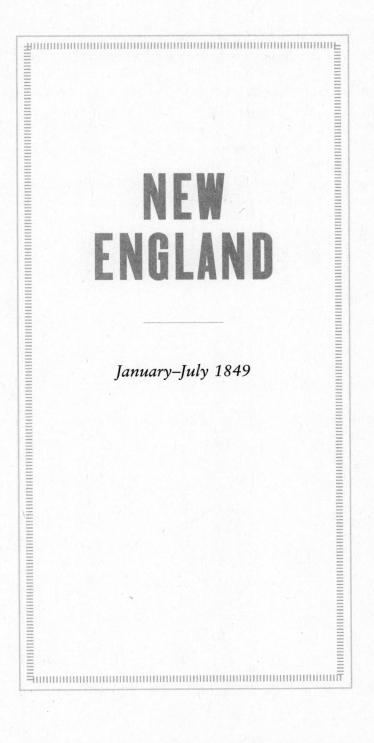

NEW
ENGLAND

January–July 1849

SINGULAR ESCAPE

||||||||||||||||||||||||||

Word was hot, just as Brown had hoped. He sent news of the Crafts and their upcoming itinerary in an exuberant letter to William Lloyd Garrison at the *Liberator*, bluffing on some details, perhaps to keep enemies off their tracks. He announced that he and the Crafts would journey straightaway to New England, where they would warm up their presentation before their grand debut in Boston. (In actuality, the Crafts probably forged ahead in secret, while Brown completed his solo tour near Philadelphia.) Meanwhile, news of the couple also moved—from pen to page, by steamer and rail, through telegraph, print, and word of mouth. By the time the trio resurfaced for their first public appearance, the word was out.

Brown's letter was reprinted, and not just by the antislavery press. Days after their news ran in the *Liberator*, ahead of their first lecture, the Crafts made the first page of the *New-York Herald* with their "Singular Escape from Slavery." (One person who was shocked to read this news item, and would take action: the man who had observed the Crafts on the steamer ride from Charleston, watch in hand.)

Front-page news of the Crafts' singular escape came at a time when the nation itself was in fast motion, now that the war with Mexico was over, and the country was a third larger than it had been. Legions of settlers were driving out west, especially to California, which was advertised loudly in all the papers. "Gold Rush!" yelled the headlines. "New ships departing!" the newsboys called. Amid all the excitement were unsettling questions, which the Crafts' flight underscored: What would be the future of slavery in these territories—and in the nation at large?

Conflicts over slavery, including the matter of fugitives, were approaching a boiling point in Congress. Southerners were so incensed over what they perceived as assaults against their rights as slave owners that they were banding together to formulate their complaints, holding meetings behind closed doors. One journalist managed to infiltrate, however, and share his report in the same issue of the paper to feature the Crafts' story. During this meeting, Senator John C. Calhoun of South Carolina threatened to dissolve the Union if slavery were forbidden in the new territories, while a Virginian compared the "grievances of the South to those of the colonies of America, which drove them to rebellion."

Meanwhile, for Brown and other antislavery activists, all signs in the recent news pointed to a new American revolution, soon to come. Witnesses to the first American Revolution smelled war in the air as well. On the day that Brown's letter ran in the *Liberator*, in weather so cold that ice floes rammed boats in Philadelphia Harbor, an elderly merchant named Thomas Cope worried in his diary: "Congress is doing but little. The slave question is the all-absorbing subject. . . . The Union is in more danger than at any former period." He closed with a plaintive cry: "May we be preserved from Civil War!"

It was in the midst of this month of frozen floes and rising heat in Congress, two days after their story had hit the front page of the *Herald*, and was ricocheting even farther out into the world, that Ellen and William touched down, gently, noiselessly, in Massachusetts.

Ringing with bells and whistles, the city of Worcester was in many ways an ideal landing spot, easy to run to—and to run from—with six railroads crisscrossing through. It was also known for being friendly to radicals: those who believed they could improve their lot by eating only certain grains or taking special baths; others who advocated women's rights. Fast on the heels of the Seneca Falls convening, the first National Woman's Rights Convention would soon meet here.

Most important for William and Ellen, the town was known to lean antislavery. The Free Soil Party, which demanded "Free Soil, Free Labor, Free Men!" in the new territories, had rallied first in Worcester, winning the county in the presidential elections. There were more hard-core abolitionists as well, who wanted not just to contain slavery but to eradicate it.

The most famous were Abby Kelley Foster and her husband, Stephen, whose Georgian farmhouse, Liberty Hall, in nearby Tattnall, was fitted with a secret underground chamber for hiding the newly self-emancipated. The Fosters had a one-year-old daughter, Alla, whom Abby had weaned early, to much criticism, in order to continue her abolitionist lecturing. She and Stephen took turns with child care and traveling, although everyone acknowledged, including Stephen himself, that Abby was the star. The Crafts would come to know the Fosters well.

Less documented in their work were members of Worcester's Black community, who, individually and communally, assisted refugees such as the Crafts. Anchored by several leading families, including the Hemenways, Browns, and Riches, the activists here were well connected to Black leaders in Boston, and together they fed, sheltered, and protected new arrivals. Much of the population—about two hundred souls all told—was young, like William and Ellen, and included barbers, an herb doctor, a basket weaver, a cake baker, and at least one "former slave."

But Worcester had other dimensions that leaned South, including a manufacturing contingent that, if it didn't actually produce cotton products, made related machinery. It was also a town rich with schools, including the College of Holy Cross, where numerous sons of slavers were known to be students—among them, the sons of Ellen's aunt Mary Eliza and her husband Michael Morris Healy, who had been sent here to board. (In fact, the older Healys themselves were making urgent preparations to move North.) As promising as Worcester was, there was no knowing whom the Crafts might encounter here in this cold, small world.

They would open with William Wells Brown at Waldo Hall, one of several grand performance spaces in a landlocked town hungry for spectacle. It was large enough to host panoramas—mammoth painted scrolls, some more than a thousand feet long—which were slowly unfurled to reveal other worlds, from Italian landscapes, to fairy grottoes, to a "dioramic spectacle of the Conflagration of Moscow!"

As the Crafts prepared to take the stage, night veiled the panoramic hall in darkness, obscuring the comings and goings of both spectators and performers alike. William and Ellen did not mount the platform from the beginning—suspense was key—and it was safer this way. But even while hidden, the young couple was surely uneasy, looking out on the unknown faces turned toward the stage, shadowy in the dimly lit hall.

If anyone could transport them from the discomfort, however, it was William Wells Brown: a seasoned, charismatic orator who could change the energies of a room within a few opening lines. A true multimedia artist, Brown used anything within reach to build a story, mixing images into texts, poetry into prose, songs into statements. He raised slave shackles high in the air, held up a letter from his so-called master and addressed it as if it were the man himself. By watching him over days and months, the Crafts would learn the techniques of storytelling from one who had mastered the art.

Brown was a convener, a conductor. Days earlier, in Attleboro, Pennsylvania, he had brought together young and old, conservative and liberal, reformers and Southern sympathizers—people who might normally fight one another but who laughed and listened instead. He spun fun into his repertoire: there was the story about how he had learned to read, for instance, by bribing White boys with barley sugar candy. For each letter of the alphabet they taught, they would get to lick the candy. He could also recount with humor how, when he had been starving and on the run, a farmer's wife had pushed aside her spouse to give Brown food. "Ever since that act," he recalled with a wink, "I have been in favor of women's rights."

Yet the expert tactician could just as easily make his audiences weep or squirm. Once, he reportedly left an audience of seven thousand with not a single dry eye. He would tell of how, as a child, he had woken to the sounds of his mother screaming as she was beaten, and, later, how he had lost her. Or he might pivot to his experiences as a slave trader's assistant, forced to pluck white hairs from the elderly captives, compel them to dance through their tears. On any given night, one never knew what kind of story Brown would share or what point of view. Perhaps even Brown himself did not know until the moment the story began to flow.

Not all approved of Brown's theatrics, including some White abolitionists, who were unnerved by his over-the-top expressions. If Frederick Douglass was told to put "a little of the plantation" in his delivery and sound less learned than he was, Brown was advised to tone down the drama. He was too "popular," too "sassy"—even, it was suggested, too self-interested—but always effective. As one eyewitness put it: "Friend Brown, perhaps, throws too much humor in his subject, and is too rhetoric for some, but to draw out an audience and to interest and enlighten the public, he is the man."

But Brown knew exactly what he was doing. Invited by the Female Anti-Slavery Society of Salem to discuss "American Slavery As It Is," Brown had this to say: "Were I about to tell you the evils of slavery, to represent to you the slave in his lowest degradation, I should wish to take you, one at a time, and whisper it to you. Slavery has never been represented; Slavery can never be represented." Now, on this frigid January evening, with the snow piled high aside the Worcester streets, the windows in Waldo Hall aglow and afog, it was up to him to represent William and Ellen's journey.

Brown had a winning plot for his lectures: start wide, tap into a core story, and open up again to stir his listeners to action. The Crafts' story provided a thrilling center, but it also required deft footwork. Brown needed to provide enough authenticating details to convince skeptics, while withholding enough information to minimize the risk of the Crafts being traced back to their enslavers. Most of all, he needed to set the right tone. The audience needed to believe in the couple, and already, there was one strike against them, for a bold lie centered their escape. Then there was Ellen, who had slipped into a man's trousers, as only the wanton or unwomanly would dare, and showed further audacity by appearing onstage. Her subversions attacked the standing social order, and not just in the South. For the audience to warm to the Crafts, Brown needed to build up his friends' reputations.

As he laid out their story, Brown dwelled on the details of how the Crafts had been able to pull off their feat, alone. Here was a man, William, a skilled artisan, who earned $220 a year for his owner, and managed to save $100 over five years for himself. By presenting firm numbers, Brown anticipated one of the questions most on the minds of audiences: How had the Crafts afforded the clothes, the travel? Brown showed that the two were honest and reliable. They had not stolen Ellen's disguise, and they did not come as beggars to the North. Far from being a liability, they would be assets to any community they joined.

With the Crafts' character secured, Brown arrived at the climax of his delivery. To this point, William and Ellen may have been hidden in plain sight among the audience, but now that he had assessed the crowd's readiness, Brown pointed out the heroic couple, sending shock waves through the hall. This was a dramatic moment, and a historic one. Though Ellen may not have been the first woman of African heritage to lecture in the state, she was almost certainly the first self-emancipated female public speaker from the South. What is more, though she was identified as a former slave, and therefore Black, she appeared White to the crowd.

Audiences invariably gasped when they saw her: this stunning young woman who looked, as many observed, no less White than their own wives or sisters, and gazed quietly back at them. Ellen Craft was not an "unfortunate slave," who required their help. After all, she had saved herself and her husband. Together she and William demanded that others not look down at them, but eye to eye.

Brown now gave the audience the chance to ask questions of William and Ellen—any ones they wished, the curious and skeptical alike. (Brown was well aware that people wanted to be sure that while they were being entertained, they were not being duped.) It was a risky move, since the conversation could go anywhere, and the Crafts were novice lecturers. Yet they were already masters of improvisation. Indeed, they had been required to perform since they were children: Ellen made to smile through days without her mother, William forced to remain calm as his sister was sold. Ellen had faced the performance of her life when she stood down White officials. No test could be as demanding as those they had already passed.

The challenges came fierce and fast. Somewhere along the way, the Crafts had revealed (at added risk to themselves) that their journey had begun in Macon, Georgia. From all around the room, spectators aimed a volley of questions at William about Macon and its people, several referring to locals who had relocated to that city. William parried back answers without hesitation. Not only could he identify most of those named, but he added details about where they lived and worked, and discussed their businesses with a specificity that only an insider could have known.

With Ellen, meanwhile, audiences were eager to know her personal story—namely, how a woman with skin as light as hers could be a slave. (Hovering unspoken were the twin taboos of sex and rape.) Ellen let it be known that she was the daughter of her first owner, who had died leaving directions that she and her mother be freed. His male heir, however, had ignored his wishes, and kept them enslaved. All the while, of course, James Smith was very much alive and well in Macon, still legally the master of her mother, while his daughter Eliza held title to Ellen.

One can only guess what motivated Ellen to modify her story. Perhaps she intended this as a decoy, to keep the focus off the relatives who still enslaved her mother. Perhaps she did not want to talk about her half sister and mistress, about whom she would never publicly say a negative word. Whatever the reasons, one thing is apparent: in this fiction, where she killed off her father while changing the gender of her sister-enslaver, Ellen assumed narrative mastery.

The audience was enthralled. With his "shrewdness, intelligence, and talent," as well as his "ready wit," William was deemed "no ordinary man." Ellen was declared "equally intelligent." By the end, all were convinced that the Crafts were "worthy" of the stolen birthright—freedom—for which they had run. This was exactly the reaction that Brown and other activists were hoping for: a first step in empathy, which would break through the malaise of apathy toward the nation's "peculiar institution," pushing the moral matter of slavery back center.

From the distance of Worcester and like towns, it was easy to be lulled—to suppose that, however terrible slavery might be, it was not the North's problem. Common was the claim that Blacks were happier in Southern slavery, where they were taken care of, and even better off than the Northern poor. If they were freed, so the argument went, they would be unable to support themselves—or they would flood the North with their poverty and cheap labor. This, after all, was part of the Free Soil argument: while there were those who genuinely opposed slavery, there were others whose commitment to Free Soil hinged on a desire to keep new lands free of Black workers and Black bodies.

Other foes of abolition commonly argued that ending slavery would be bad for business. Like many manufacturing towns, Worcester depended on trade with the South. Do we want to lose our business, and is it worth the price of sending our sons to battle, so soon after the war with Mexico?—a cautious New Englander might ask, hearing news of Calhoun's thunder.

Still others shrugged and said slavery was on its deathbed. The markets would correct the system; slavery did not pay. Why force the issue? There was too much to settle, as the nation grappled with its immense new territories and big questions about how to manage them. Leave the South alone, for now.

Seeing the Crafts, however, forced audiences to confront what they might have dismissed previously as abstract horrors, or even denied. As one reporter noted, the Crafts remained outlaws, even up North. Slave catchers might come at any time and drag them out, backed by the government. No one in the audience could help them—indeed, if they did, they, too, would be penalized, criminalized for acting with conscience, robbed of their own liberties.

The Crafts finished to great applause—an inaugural triumph. Brown was no doubt pleased that the handsome young pair had held their own onstage, boding well for Boston, and beyond. But the performance was not over yet. Once the talk was complete, collections taken, it was tradition for audiences to greet speakers and shake their hands. Within weeks, the crowds who came to see the Crafts would surge, engulfing the young couple. Eventually the Crafts would choose to exit early. On this night, the numbers were likely smaller, but it was surely unsettling for William and Ellen, as strangers strained forward and reached out to touch them—this laying on of hands another initiation into the many ways of telling and receiving their story.

The next three days were a whirlwind of word and motion. From Worcester, the Crafts and Brown headed southward, most likely by train, for another lecture in Pawtucket, Rhode Island. Traveling past snow heaves and frozen waters, a foreign winter landscape, they experienced a different kind of travel from what they had known in the South, though it carried its own history of prejudice.

It was not long ago that "Jim Crow" segregation was violently enforced in Massachusetts. (Ironically, this term—which was taken from the name of a White minstrel performer, and became synonymous with segregated travel—began among White Northern railroaders.) Earlier in the decade, Frederick Douglass had been physically assaulted and thrown off a train for trying to ride first class in Lynn. But he and other activists had ultimately prevailed with boycotts, sit-ins, petitioning, and other protests. Their past actions empowered the Crafts and Brown to choose their own seats.

After leaving Pawtucket, they headed north again. At last, they crossed a wide, marshy water, strangely colored from the pollutants it carried: the Back Bay tidal basin. To one side, plumes of smoke puffed up from scattered factories, while on the other, church spires stretched skyward. As in Richmond, Virginia, and so many other cities the Crafts had seen, one mighty edifice rose high above the crowded skyline. The Massachusetts Statehouse, with its glistening dome, signaled the Crafts' arrival in Boston, their final destination. Little did they know that their reputations had already preceded them.

CRADLE OF LIBERTY

||||||||||||||||||||||||||

They traveled on back ways, behind the Boston Common—past the mansions and brick townhomes, luminously gas lit—steep down to the other side of Beacon Hill, dubbed "Nigger Hill" by neighbors. They were lucky to have William Wells Brown leading them through this mazelike city, shaped, it has been said, like a fist, so unlike Macon's wide-open grid.

If the ground was cold and sodden here, the winds harsh at the bottom of the slope, they were spared the stench of factory waste, entrails, and other pollution that came off the Charles River on warmer days. The cadences of many tongues echoed through these streets, from the lyrical songs of Irish immigrants, to the rolling lilts of other refugees from the South, to the flattened vowels common to Boston. Within this working-class neighborhood, rife with alleys and folds, William and Ellen briefly slowed down.

Brown himself had a place on West Cedar Street—near the river, and the construction site for an elaborate new prison—but he hustled the Crafts to another home where he knew they would be safe. Soon they arrived at an unassuming brick structure on Southac Street, where they were welcomed by Lewis and Harriet Hayden, a husband-and-wife team of revolutionaries who met them, as they had received so many others, with open arms.

The couple had escaped bondage in Kentucky only six years earlier, aided by two White abolitionists, a preacher, and a teacher. Like the Crafts, the Haydens had worn disguises, their faces powdered with flour, to make them appear fair from afar. The couple made it to Canada, along with their son, but, concerned about those left behind, they returned to the United States, settling first in Michigan and, finally, in Boston. Now the family made its house on Southac Street an activist headquarters, along with Lewis Hayden's secondhand clothing store.

The Hayden house was fronted with a short step and narrow door, but that was not the only way in or out. A second door led out from the basement, while a secret tunnel, a dark crawl-through space accessible only from the subbasement, allowed other visitors to enter and exit the house unseen, and traverse to an unknown location, possibly across the street. As many as thirteen people could hide at once on the top floor, and other Southern refugees ate, slept, and boarded in this building when William and Ellen first walked inside.

There were few places where they would have been better protected than in this house, this neighborhood. Through intricate alleys, fugitives could be ferreted away from enemies, while strangers easily lost their bearings. A spirit of resistance was alive and well. This was, after all, the adopted hometown of David Walker, a militant Black activist born of an enslaved father and free mother, who had claimed equal citizenship for Black Americans and whose words had sent chills of terror throughout the South—tremors still palpable two decades later.

In his *Appeal . . . to the Colored Citizens of the World*, a pamphlet he had secreted South, Walker had exhorted Black Americans to rise up with arms, if necessary, to overthrow those who enslaved them and claim their rightful place as equal citizens of the nation they had helped build. "Look upon your mother, wife, and children," he famously commanded, "and answer God Almighty; and believe this, that it is no more harm for you to kill a man, who is trying to kill you, than it is for you to take a drink of water when thirsty." Walker called out the hypocrisy of the clergy and White Americans, cannily quoting the Declaration of Independence and asking, "Do you understand your own language?"

Walker's words and prophesies galvanized his fellow colored citizens while terrifying slavers, intensifying their paranoia of being poisoned, burned, murdered. (These words from Walker were not enough to assuage their fears: "Treat us like men, and there is no danger. . . . Treat us like men, and we will be your friends.") Those in power cracked down further, passing severe laws against free Blacks and the enslaved. The state of Georgia put a $10,000 bounty on Walker's head. One year after he was declared a wanted man, Walker died suddenly in Boston, reportedly of tuberculosis, but the terror he fueled—as well as the spirit of resistance—lived on.

Only a few blocks uphill from the Haydens, meanwhile, were the luxurious homes of financiers—among them, cotton mill owners and other locals who profited, directly or indirectly, from the labor of the enslaved. These streets were "choked with cotton dust," as described by

Wendell Phillips, a White abolitionist who had grown up here. However, such Bostonians were not likely to set foot downhill, where their cooks, caregivers, and coach drivers resided.

The community at the bottom of the hill was on its guard, with business people and entrepreneurs, Masons and other club members, preachers and churchgoers, ready to mobilize in case of trouble. Two years earlier, when a slave hunter dared to invade the neighborhood, Nancy Prince—polyglot activist missionary, businesswoman, world traveler, and soon-to-be author—led a group of women and children to chase him off with rocks.

Others grabbed fugitives from courthouses, putting their own bodies between the law and re-enslavement. The Haydens, among others, were known to keep firearms. Certain White abolitionists may have insisted on nonresistance, but those who knew slavery and were at risk of being carried back could be more practical about their need to defend themselves and those they harbored.

The Crafts soon saw that there was good reason why William Still, the Purvises, and others had urged them to head for Boston—into the "honeycomb," as this neighborhood was often described. Though it was far smaller than Philadelphia in numbers, this was a world in which they could easily disappear and be powerfully defended. Ellen and William, however, would not hide.

Scarcely had the Crafts caught their breath, when it was time to debut at Boston's celebrated Faneuil Hall. Atop the classical brick hall, with its three floors of arched windows ablaze on a January night, perched a glittering, glass-eyed grasshopper, slowly spinning with the winds: a whimsical weathervane, with a time capsule planted in its belly.

This shiny bug had seen and heard much in the century since a coppersmith named Shem Downe had made it for Peter Faneuil, the Boston businessman and philanthropist who gave the hall to the city as a gift. The so-called Cradle of Liberty had rung with cries of "Freedom!" and "Revolution!" from within its depths. But other cries had been heard here too. For besides molasses and fish, wine and wood, Peter Faneuil traded in enslaved human beings, who were sold off Dock Square, in front of the very building the Crafts now entered. This was the kind of irony that William Wells Brown noted well. If America were a cradle of liberty, he once quipped, it had rocked its baby to death.

The hall that had been funded by a civic-minded slaver was now packed with a different kind of crowd. The vast and brilliantly lit space, often crammed with standing spectators, was laid out in orderly fashion with rows of settees, or low-backed benches, that would allow for ladies to spread their skirts. It was to be a "promiscuous" crowd—meaning mixed gender—as well as mixed race. Above, balconies allowed for even more spectators. Slipping into the throng on the main floor, likely incognito until the time was right, William and Ellen were surrounded on all sides, across the floor and up to the balconies, by antislavery advocates of many colors.

This was the seventeenth annual convention of the Massachusetts Anti-Slavery Society, the home terrain of America's most infamous White abolitionist, William Lloyd Garrison, and one of the biggest "Garrisonian" events of the year. The founders of the group had first met on a stormy night in the basement of the African Meeting House (also used as a schoolhouse) in 1832: twelve White men in all, with leaders of the veteran Massachusetts General Colored Association bearing witness. As the ceremonies closed, Garrison declared, "Friends, we have met tonight in this obscure schoolhouse, but, before many years, we will rock Faneuil Hall."

Since then, the Garrisonian antislavery organization had grown dramatically, deployed agents, spread out across the country. And now, honoring Garrison's prophecy, they were indeed rocking Faneuil Hall—an interracial coalition of women and men, thousands strong.

Looking out at this convening, the Crafts would have gazed upon a sea of faces—a few of them, such as the Haydens', whom they already recognized, others strangers whom they would soon know well. Among them was that skinny, nearsighted man whose gentle, bookish demeanor belied the fire beneath. People were always shocked when they met William Lloyd Garrison: This was the man who *would be heard?* He looked more like the kind of man who liked cats, who would get down on his knees and play with children, who enjoyed fussing over policy matters—all of which he was as well.

True to his calm demeanor, there was a fundamental peacefulness to his approach. Garrison opposed the use of force, even in the face of violence, sure that "moral suasion" was the way to end slavery. On this matter, he disagreed with David Walker. To anyone threatened, spat upon, assaulted—as he himself had been at the hands of a "gentleman's mob" in Boston—Garrison would counsel passive resistance.

At the same time, Garrison was militant and uncompromising in his approach and goals. *"No Union With Slaveholders!"* was his rallying cry. This meant breaking from church and state, if need be, sacrificing whatever was required to purge the nation of the sin of bondage, immediately, without compromise. As Garrison saw it, the Constitution itself was a proslavery document, tainting the nation from its roots. The only way to create a more perfect Union was to break from the old and start afresh. All were welcome in the fight against the Slave Power, as far as Garrison was concerned, regardless of race, religion, or gender, the goal being not merely abolition but also equality as citizens. These were the radical core tenets of Garrisonianism.

When the Crafts were poised to make their debut, the Garrisonians were organizationally at loose ends—spent, after a long day full of quibbling over terms, and an even longer year. In some ways, the activists could not have hoped for better. Slavery was all that anyone talked about in the press and at the US Capitol. The future of the slave trade in Washington was under bitter debate, as was the territorial extension of slavery. Senator Calhoun was riled enough to openly declare his most rabid views, providing a clear target for attack. The nation's two major parties seemed to be cracking under the pressure. Antislavery, it seemed, was now mainstream.

For Garrison and his cohorts, however, a time of relative peace created other problems. At least in crisis there was bonding. Their biggest headache now was a softer enemy, the Free Soil Party, which, as one unfriendly journalist snickered, had "stolen Garrison & Co's thunder"—and their funds. Much to the horror of all those who championed an immediate end to slavery, it appeared that the antislavery message they had been signaling so fervently had been co-opted, sung to a modified tune. The issue over slavery was no longer about uprooting a moral wrong so much as it was about redrawing lines and keeping slavery contained, or so Free Soilers advocated.

Even some antislavery advocates believed that this was the more reasonable path: that it would be better to quarantine slavery and manage the problem incrementally. Wouldn't it be wiser to keep slavery where it was, rather than explode the Union? Disunion might lead to the creation of an even more powerful slaving empire, one where the fate of the enslaved human being, as well as free Blacks, would only worsen. To some antislavery activists, it was the Garrisonian radicals who were towing a dangerous line with their unrealistic, all-or-nothing demands.

All day long, there had been fractiousness in the convention, with tedious arguments over procedure. What the group needed on this night, more than ever, was a sense of shared purpose and urgency. As Garrison expressed, a person did not walk slowly and reasonably when his house was in flames and his family trapped within. The problem was how to make others aware that there was a fire in the first place. How to conjure that heat? It was now that the Crafts arrived to bear witness, with no one better able to raise the temperature in the room than William Wells Brown.

EVERLASTING YEA

||||||||||||||||||||||||

For William Wells Brown, it was a triumphant return. One year earlier, when he had been the Massachusetts Anti-Slavery Society's featured fugitive, he was in a far different position, having just received a letter written by his enslaver. No matter that it had been Brown himself who had initiated contact. The letter, which left no doubt about the slaver's power to sell Brown, left him shaken. Then there had been the problems with his estranged wife, who went knocking on doors in Boston telling such stories about him that the leaders of the Massachusetts Anti-Slavery Society, Brown's employers, began to worry.

But Brown had buoyed himself on the abolitionist stage. In a dramatic reversal of power, he had held up his master's letter, spoken to it, talked it down. He had used that letter in lectures all that year. He had kept up a furious pace on the circuit and was widely recognized as an abolitionist superstar. And now, with this heroic, handsome young couple, Ellen and William, beside him, he was once again taking the stage at Boston's revolutionary hall.

Once more, he waved a valuable page from the South, this time an article newly minted from the *Newark Daily Mercury*, written by a man who called himself only "A": the very man who had studied the Crafts on the Charleston steamer while checking his watch, and read later of their "Singular Escape." Brown could not have made the article more evocative and interesting himself. "A" not only wrote down the facts, but also set the scene of his starlit sighting, closing his remembrance with the remark from a fellow traveler that Mr. Johnson was either "a woman or a genius." The article was an ideal opening, not only because it provided drama but also because it established proof.

As he had in Worcester, Brown conveyed the outlines of the young couple's journey. Then, the moment his instincts told him it was right, he summoned the Crafts to the stage.

In his own lecture years ago, William Lloyd Garrison had exhorted a skeptical crowd: "Suppose that, by a miracle, the slaves should suddenly become white. Would you shut your eyes upon their sufferings and calmly talk of constitutional limitations? No, your voice would peal in the ears of the taskmasters like deep thunder."

Now it was as if the miracle had been made manifest in Ellen. As the pastor-turned-activist Samuel May Jr. would marvel: "Ellen Craft . . . is a woman who may be called beautiful; she has no trace of African blood discernible in her features, eyes, cheeks, nose, or hair, but the whole is that of a Southern-born white woman. To think of such a woman being held as a piece of property, subject to be traded off to the highest bidder, while it is in reality no worse or wickeder than when done to the blackest woman that ever was, does yet stir a community brought up in prejudice against color a thousand times more deeply than could be effected in different circumstances."

Seeing Ellen, the audience reacted once more as if an electric current ran through the hall. Eyes widened, bodies turned, and the space rang with thunderous applause. Feeling the tempo, the crowd's pulse, Brown prepared to raise it all even higher. He would put forth three questions, "that they might be answered in hearing of these fugitives."

First, he called: "All present who will help return a slave to his bondage, will please to say *yes*."

For the Crafts, this was their worst nightmare, especially when a voice, lone but distinct, called "Aye!" from a settee at the back of the hall. Ignoring it, Brown pushed on.

Second: "All who would stand still, and do nothing, for or against him, will please to say yes."

Now there was not a word.

Third, Brown cried, "All who would aid in protecting, rescuing, and saving him from slavery, will say *yes*." And the hall exploded, resounding with a chorus of voices, rising together in waves of affirmation—an "immense and prolonged assent" that washed over the stage, over William and Ellen, again and again, an "everlasting yea." It was a sustained sound, surely unlike any the couple had heard before.

Then it came down to a single voice in song. Rather than draw the Crafts forward for a question and answer session, as he had in Worcester, Brown would close their appearance with an antislavery melody, likely from his songbook *The Anti-Slavery Harp*. These were not spirituals or work songs, the kinds of songs that Brown himself would have heard or sung on the docks. Instead, they were radical lyrics set to popular tunes such as "Oh! Susannah" and "Auld Lang Syne." Crowd-pleasers.

One song that might have fit the mood was "Lament of the Fugitive Slave," about an enslaved mother left behind, or, on a related theme, "O, Pity the Slave Mother," which evoked stories left unspoken. Or, if a livelier tune was called for, Brown might have called up the abolitionist hit "Get Off the Track," which kicked off with a mighty "Ho!" and touted "Freedom's car, Emancipation!" (What better way to fire up support for an Underground Railroad, than with fugitives who had ridden to freedom in an authentic ironclad train?)

For William and Ellen, it must have been uncanny to hear their story told and sung, in tones somber and exultant, by their newfound friend before this passionate gathering. Brown sustained his final note, and the hall erupted in applause again, closing their sensational Boston debut.

The conveners wanted more: of William, "a very intelligent-looking black man," and Ellen, a "pretty nice-looking girl . . . with strait black hair," whose behavior was "pretty and natural," as Anne Warren Weston, one of three activist sisters known as part of the elite "Boston Clique," would describe them to her sister Deborah. The next evening, the Crafts were invited back to Boston's Great Hall, and yet again the night after that. By now, the Crafts were such a sensation that even critics joined the crowds to see them, including a reporter from the *Boston Post* who surveyed the scene, askance, as dusk fell.

The abolitionists were lit up. William Lloyd Garrison called for the *immediate dissolution of the American Union*—a "Union," he cried, "based on the prostate bodies of three millions of the people, and cemented with their blood—a Union which gives absolute power and perfect security to the wholesale traffickers in human flesh . . . —a Union in which freedom of speech and of the press, the right of petition, and safe and equal locomotion, are cloven down."

So enraged was Garrison over faithless Northerners who claimed to hate slavery and yet were so willing to compromise with the slaveholding South, that he resolved to commend the voice of Slave Power, South Carolina senator John C. Calhoun. At least Calhoun, Garrison declared, truthfully proclaimed his belief in slavery as a positive good. Next, collections were taken for a "Catholic slave girl" who would be sold south if funds could not be raised. Then it was time for William Wells Brown to introduce the celebrated fugitives.

Standing at the center of the platform, opposite the hanging lights, the crowd, the giant clock where the heartbeat of the hour ticked forward, Brown began by lightening the mood. He joked that though his father was one of Kentucky's aristocracy, he, Brown, was "not too proud to speak to common white people in Faneuil Hall." His comment drew laughs, but it contained a lesson: that the lines that made one person "higher" than another, or "master" over another, were arbitrary and wrong.

Before his listeners could enjoy too prolonged a chuckle, Brown changed the mood again. He threw his weight behind Garrison's resolutions, then illustrated all that was at stake by sharing stories about his own family—stories that shook William and Ellen.

His precise remarks are lost to history, but the stories Brown recounted most often were about his separation from his favorite sister and his mother, losses that both William and Ellen had known. He had lost them both within days. Fresh off his dreaded service as a slave trader's right-hand man, the teenage Brown had learned that his sister, Elizabeth, was sold and bound for Natchez, Mississippi. Having just spent the worst days of his life journeying to Natchez and New Orleans, he knew exactly where she was headed, to a slave-trading hub, famed for sex trafficking. He snuck into the jail where she was being held captive. There, he remembered, his sister put her arms around him and broke down in tears, then told him to take their mother and run.

Brown convinced his mother to escape with him, though she was reluctant to leave behind her other children—a pain alive to all who ran. They left St. Louis at night, stealing a skiff for the Illinois shore, and hid in the woods, surviving rainstorms. Just when Brown began to dream aloud about finding work in Canada, buying his siblings, and reuniting his family, slave hunters came on horseback. Mother and son were separated, and Brown's mother was sold downriver to New Orleans. Brown last saw her chained aboard a crowded boat. Unlike his sister, she could not move, speak, or cry, but when her son begged her for forgiveness, she assured him this was not his fault. Like his sister, she told him to run.

Only a month earlier, Ellen and William had been living in the world that Brown conjured, and his words touched wounds. It was the curmudgeonly reporter from the *Boston Post* who noticed that as they heard Brown speak of his family, both William and Ellen cried.

Their tears were still visible when their friend pulled them onto the abolitionist platform.

Perhaps this is why Brown swiftly changed his tune again, launching into an animated tale of the couple's journey that once more held the audience spellbound. The famed orator Wendell Phillips, son of old Boston, was so moved by the Crafts as to prophesy, in ringing tones, "Future historians and poets would tell this story as one of the most thrilling in the nation's annals, and millions would read it with admiration for the hero and heroine of the story."

With the current of the night's energy jolting them, a once lumbering organization became fleet-footed. When the leaders of the convening called for a final vote on the resolutions they had been arguing over for three days, the measures unanimously passed.

According to the *Liberator*'s report, the Crafts "electrified" Fanueil Hall. Boston had not been so overcome since George Latimer—a man whose case stood as both an example and warning to the newly anointed fugitives. Light-skinned Latimer had "passed" out of slavery with his pregnant wife posing as his slave—a kind of mirror image of the Crafts' escape. When Latimer was recognized and jailed in Boston, activists of all colors were galvanized, showing how robustly Bostonians could stand up. They took to the streets and courts, flooded the legislature with petitions. They purchased his freedom and finally pushed for the passage of a "Latimer Law," or personal liberty law, which interfered with slavers' ability to pursue their human property.

For White abolitionists, the shock of seeing an enslaved young man as white as themselves was especially motivating—as was the case in their excitement about Ellen. Yet Latimer's case was not entirely happy. He was promoted and then put aside on the abolitionist lecture circuit, proving not to be as charismatic a speaker as organizers had hoped. The romance of his escape was further undercut by personal troubles: eventually George Latimer would desert his wife and children. His example showed that life in the North offered no guarantees.

As they packed their things for the next phase of their journey, launching from the home of Lewis Hayden—who had also experienced troubles on the lecture circuit, and may have shared his own stories of being promoted and abandoned, midtour—the Crafts knew they needed to steel themselves against multiple dangers ahead, on the stage and off.

From an activist's point of view, the attention this bright young couple received could not have been better for the cause. And yet, to the fugitives themselves, the spotlight was no doubt concerning. For the words that Brown had spoken in Boston radiated out through the press to travel the country far and wide, reaching back down South.

MACON AGAIN

IIIIIIIIIIIIIIIIIIIIIIIIIIII

Word flew again, or rather, it rode, carried by telegraph and rail, along some of the very routes that William and Ellen had traveled on their revolutionary journey. And on a mid-February morning, the Collinses woke to the story in their local paper. There they were: "A good-looking mulatto man, and a still better looking almost white girl, with straight hair, lately escaped from their master in Georgia" were now in Boston "as man and wife." Lest there be any doubt, the paper noted that the slaves would be recognized at once as those belonging to Robert Collins and Ira Taylor.

A few blocks above the offices of the *Macon Weekly Telegraph*, high on Mulberry Street, in the mansion that fronted the abandoned sewing studio and slave cottage, the Collinses were forced to reckon with these words on the page—and with Ellen, who had not only run away but also had done so in the most scandalous way.

Ellen, riding aboard a train in a White man's clothes; Ellen, having her boot removed by a traveling stranger; Ellen, drawing palpitations from a "marriageable" White girl—all of it was shocking titillation. Moreover, the story made it clear that Ellen had played an active role in her own escape, that she had not been carried off, though the paper left open the possibility that she had been "decoyed," and Collins himself would continue to blame William.

The challenge was what to do next. Being a man of action, Robert Collins may have been tempted to pursue the fugitives. He knew they were around Boston, where he had friends, and he had connections to people who could handle this sort of business. He also knew that inaction could have disastrous consequences. Collins, a stickler for order, believed that "regularity and a strict adherence to the rules" were essential for slave management. He knew, as he would express later, that Ellen's successful escape was sure to inspire others.

The threat to order extended far beyond his household, and for this reason, he was also aware, he would have support from other slavers. In fact, his very position was being spelled out in the press. On the same day that the Crafts appeared in the *Telegraph*, the paper also published a version of an *Address of Southern Delegates in Congress to Their Constituents*, penned by the sickly, wild-haired senator John C. Calhoun, who argued that the problem of fugitives was not just an individual or local matter, but a looming national crisis.

The nearly sixty-eight-year-old former vice president, secretary of war, and secretary of state was wracked with a terrible cough and living alone in a Washington boardinghouse, his wife, Floride, having abandoned the city decades earlier to manage their South Carolina cotton plantation. There, at night, he plugged away on a book called *A Disquisition on Government*; worried about his children, including his favorite, Anna, who was headed overseas; and hoped that Floride had not added yet another room to their sprawling estate. None of his personal stress was visible, however, in the steady, firm-fisted *Address* he produced on behalf of his Southern congressmen.

Over the past several months, Calhoun and other Southerners, still riled up about the failed *Pearl* escape, had become increasingly anxious as their colleagues served up bold, new antislavery proposals. The Southerners were especially incensed over attempts to limit slavery in the new territories and in the capital, where it was even suggested that free Blacks and slaves be invited to vote on the matter. The problem of fugitives was another point of fury. Southern congressmen had convened in protest; Calhoun's *Address* was the result.

As Calhoun first articulated, the rights of Southern slaveholders were protected by no less than the Constitution itself: Article IV, Section 2, Clause 3, which promised that those "held to service or labor in one state," who escaped to another, would be "delivered up." Without this promise, the South's forefathers would never have signed the compact that drew them into the Union. Without the guaranteed rights to slave ownership, in other words, the United States of America would not exist. And yet, these promised rights were under siege daily, as fugitives disappeared into the North. This was the first grievance stated in the *Address*, and it spoke loudly for Southerners like Collins.

As Calhoun saw it, the escape of fugitive slaves and the failure of their return was no minor transgression but a step toward the end of Southern slavery, which would ultimately end their way of life. Emancipation, he warned, would quickly come, and that would not even be the worst. Former slaves, empowered with the vote, would soon join hands with the North, to "hold the white race at the South in complete subjection."

"We would, in a word, change conditions with them," said Calhoun, "a degradation greater than has ever yet fallen to the lot of a free and enlightened people, and one from which we could not escape . . . but by fleeing the homes of ourselves and ancestors and by abandoning our country to our former slaves, to become the permanent abode of disorder, anarchy, poverty, misery, and wretchedness." It would be a world turned upside down.

Not all Southerners shared Calhoun's anxieties to the same degree. To some, the three-time presidential hopeful and former vice president went too far, and they dismissed him as a radical disunionist—a charge he shared, oddly, with his arch nemesis, William Lloyd Garrison. The final *Address*, as signed by the Southern congressmen, was toned down, few being ready at this time—in slave states or free states—to push the conflict to its ultimate conclusion: war.

For his part, Robert Collins was strongly pro-Union. Beyond ideology or politics, he had practical issues to consider. As Calhoun had vividly conveyed in his *Address*, the task of pursuing a fugitive in the North could be costly and messy—even deadly. Collins had witnessed others' struggles, the trials of his friend Colonel S. T. Bailey serving a case in point.

Bailey's "servant" (as he called the woman he enslaved) had escaped bondage in Vermont, where Bailey and his family had been traveling. The Colonel succeeded in tracking and capturing her, only to be chased across three states, as he claimed, by "Abolitionists, with the energy of blood hounds." Back in Vermont, Bailey was arrested for kidnapping and stood to face ten years in jail. Though acquitted, he remained shaken. As he told Collins and other friends, "Demons from Hell could not have manifested more ferocious malice than the gang who arrested us."

If Colonel Bailey had faced an uphill battle, Robert Collins's prospects were far worse. Bailey's case had taken place only five years ago, but legally it seemed a different era, due to new personal liberty laws, which made it much more difficult for Southerners to recapture the enslaved out of state, denying assistance from state judges and police, as well as the use of local jails. What is more, Boston was notorious for its abolitionists. Were Collins to pursue Ellen, he would have to wager all for a single escaped slave, at what could not have been a worse time for him personally.

Collins was still in the throes of a legal battle with his entrepreneurial doppelgänger, William B. Johnston—the battle that may well have precipitated Ellen's run. Having lost the first round, Collins was preparing for an appeal in the spring, with hundreds of thousands of dollars on the line, the equivalent of millions today. Given these stakes, one runaway slave—however dear she might be to the family, however shaming the situation—was not worth the effort.

Then there was Eliza, Ellen's legal owner, who might have played a role in the decision or possibly made the call herself. Collins would describe later how "Ellen has been, from her youth, the most trusted and most faithful of my house servants; and in consequence, my family were much attached to her." In the past weeks and months, Eliza had been confronted with the fact that this "house servant" who had so expertly tended to her needs was someone whom she herself had little known. When Ellen had cried at her refusal to grant a pass, Eliza had gone against her instinct to refuse, but instead had trusted her and that trust was betrayed.

Yet, whatever her feelings or her rights, in the end, Eliza Collins did not insist on the action that was legally hers to take—and which her father, if not her husband, might have pursued on her behalf. She would not force the return of the half sister she enslaved. William's enslaver, Ira Taylor, seems to have assumed the same stance, perhaps having consulted with Collins. A younger man—scarcely older than William—with none of the doctor's connections or capital, Taylor had less to wager and more to lose. And he was about to marry. Preparations for his future bride would take precedence.

The news must have reached Ellen's mother, Maria, as well. Since William and Ellen's escape, she and others may have paid a price, as the Crafts were well aware. If those known to them had not been threatened with direct punishment or torture, at the very least, watchful eyes would follow their every move, passes be reconsidered, privileges revoked.

One thousand miles away, Ellen and William pressed on. Unable to communicate with those left behind or divine what the enslavers intended, the couple continued their travels on the lecture circuit, fighting to destroy the system that had once enslaved them, laying their lives on the line.

THE CIRCUIT

Lecture time was showtime in 1849, with a star-studded roster of performers on the road, including Ralph Waldo Emerson speaking on "Great Men," Henry David Thoreau on "Civil Disobedience," and Senator Daniel Webster of Massachusetts on constitutional history. All three topics would find expression in the story of the "Georgia Fugitives" who rode all over New England on their own circuit tour that season, in the care and company of William Wells Brown.

The Crafts were fortunate; their grouping was not the norm. Garrisonian organizers liked to send out Black and White lecturers in teams (often with higher salaries for the White speakers)—Frederick Douglass with William Lloyd Garrison, for example. The couple was lucky to have linked up with Brown in other ways. Their friend was not only a great speaker but also an expert publicist, fund-raiser, and navigator who was personally acquainted with both the sweet spots and danger zones on this abolitionist road.

Just six months earlier, on a smoldering day in August, Brown and two other speakers had been mobbed and beaten in Harwich, Massachusetts. Young and lovely Lucy Stone had been there too, but she emerged unscathed, having demanded gentlemanly protection from one of her attackers. She was savvy at other times in her self-defense. When someone once hissed her at a lecture, Stone spat back: "Hiss it again, my fat friend, for it is a shameful fact and deserves to be hissed," sending the audience into gales of laughter—and the man out of the hall. Nonetheless, crowds had seethed when they saw her, a White woman, sharing a stage with a man like Brown. Brown would not take his friends anywhere near Harwich, skirting Cape Cod altogether.

Instead, he led the Crafts to another salty spot on the shore: New Bedford, Massachusetts, famed as a whaling town, as well as a haven for self-emancipated people. Refugees arrived in all manner of ways: nailed in boxes, dressed as Quakers, riding trains, tucked into a barrel marked "Sweet Potatoes," or so it was told of a child named Isabelle White, four or five years old, who arrived alone that very year. It was a place where loved ones torn apart in slavery were known to find one another and where many chose to settle. New Bedford was home to a sizable community of color, including Indigenous and multiracial people (such as entrepreneur and activist Paul Cuffe) and a greater Southern-born Black population, percentagewise, than New York or Boston.

Brown had a personal attachment to this town, since for the past two years, his ten- and thirteen-year-old daughters, Josephine and Clarissa, had boarded here with the same activist couple who had once welcomed Frederick Douglass: Polly Johnson, a celebrated confectioner, whose creations were said to "sweeten" abolitionist business, and her husband, Nathan, a caterer. In this sweet-smelling home, where buoyant sponge cakes, tender macaroons, calves' feet jelly, candied pears, and lemonade were made, the girls lived and attended public schools. (Brown would not have them in Boston, where only a lone schoolhouse was available to Black children in the city.)

The girls had been shielded here, too, from the drama between their parents, whose bad marriage was spiraling out of control, despite their physical distance. In fact, Brown had not shared the girls' location with their mother, Betsey, until the summer before, when the girls and their mother had an uneasy reunion—along with a new little girl, whom Betsey had brought, but Brown never recognized as his own. For Brown to meet his daughters again in New Bedford was another kind of homecoming, and so, for many reasons, the right place to launch.

The crowd was great that night, thanks to Brown, who had sent ahead word, along with handbills, promising the appearance of a *"white slave."* It was a line and an idea he had used before, one calculated to rouse both empathy and fear in White spectators, in particular. The handbills did their job, assisted by the weather. In the dead of winter, when the harbor was frozen, and there were endless days stuck inside, the event promised excitement. Liberty Hall was thronged well before the Crafts were due to appear—not just with the usual coalition of Black activists and people of color, Quakers and other allies, but with strangers to the cause, who wanted to see the "white slave" for themselves.

There were gasps and pointed fingers when Ellen stepped forward, William by her side.

"Could it be possible she was held as a slave?" went the murmurs of wonder. Then: Did they call you a "nigger" in the South? A lady asked Ellen.

"Oh yes," she said, "they didn't call me anything else. They said it would make me proud."

Questions came fast for William, too—for example, about what he would have done if someone tried to capture him during his flight. William spoke with a fire in his eye that reminded some of Cinqué, hero of the *Amistad*.

"I knew the consequences," he replied in his deep, steady voice. "I had made up my mind to kill or be killed, before I would be taken."

If the audience had not been united before, it was by the time the Crafts were through. The assembly resolved to support an end to slavery and, even further, to extend to those escaping to Massachusetts—men and women like William and Ellen—"the same protection of life, liberty, and the means of pursuing happiness that we claim for ourselves."

These were mighty promises: not merely of rescue but also of equal opportunity. With ayes from the crowd, wide awake on this winter night, the resolutions passed unanimously. As would be true in many towns to follow, New Bedford was newly lit and ready to resist.

From New Bedford, they shot out all across the state. In Kingston, they shook hands with a sea captain with a branded palm—marked "slave stealer" after a failed attempt to sail seven enslaved people out of bondage. Then they rode up to the shoe and leather town of Abington, as far west as Springfield, and back to the friendly village of Upton. Their pace was unrelenting. Audiences filled halls to overflowing, while zealous abolitionists exhorted them to keep moving. A week into their journey, Brown signaled that William would soon start working at his trade; moments later, abolitionists unanimously passed a resolution to have the Crafts lecture on.

Ride, arrive, greet, perform, sleep, wake, repeat. On any given night, the Crafts never knew where they would rest or eat, and they never had more than a few days between lectures and locales. If one were to have plotted their positions on a map, the dots would have seemed to dance all over, without reason. But there was a logic to their travels. All the places they spoke fell along or near station stops on the railroad, which once more defined their journey.

Travel could be uneasy. While the "jimmy cars" and "paddy cars," restricted to Irish passengers, were no longer official, the dominant population of New Englanders who ran and rode the trains tended to be watchful, if not hostile, toward "colored travelers." As Douglass observed once, "Prejudice against color is stronger North than South," adding, "it hangs around my neck like a heavy weight."

Sometimes the heaviness entered their meetings. In a packed town hall in Northboro, a farming and manufacturing community nestled in the heart of Massachusetts, William—now with only a brief introduction from Brown—gave a "thrilling account" of his and Ellen's escape, which kept his audience in "breathless" suspense. Then a proslavery man came forth, demanding that William name the governor of Georgia from seven years ago.

William might have been used to this kind of grilling, but he was unprepared to answer. Fortunately, he had won over the crowd, and someone threw the same question back at his interrogator: "Who was the governor of Massachusetts seven years ago?"

The man was stumped, and the hall rang with applause.

Whispers then blew through the space like trapped winds: *I want to hear his wife speak*. Ellen came forward to meet them, and afterward there was a near hysteria as people rushed the stage, reaching out for her and William.

It was a scene played out again and again, in other packed halls that crackled with applause, where everyone wanted not only to be near these celebrities but also to touch them. For a couple who had escaped slavery only two months earlier—who had already traveled one thousand miles, and were now required to replay the story of their lives night after night—it was surely exhausting as well as unsettling. Still, they moved without pause.

So too did their news, which spun out to Maine, Ohio, New York, Maryland, Wisconsin, Louisiana, and Georgia, where the Augusta *Daily Constitutionalist* slyly tipped its hat to Ellen with a header borrowed from the *Baltimore Sun*: "Shrewdly Done." All this took place as Southerners in power were becoming frenzied in their opposition to fugitives and abolitionists, whose most vocal ranks the Crafts had officially joined. In Congress, Southern men registered complaints about abolitionist propaganda and the lax enforcement of the Fugitive Slave Act, while in Macon, an anti-abolitionist rally met on the courthouse steps. Among the attendants: Robert Collins, who maintained his public silence on William and Ellen.

So well known had the Crafts become in this turbulent season that some worried for their safety. For their part, the Crafts continued flexing the fullest muscles of American citizenship, speaking and moving in defiance of their legal status as fugitives. And in their spoken word and their unfettered travel, denied to them in bondage, there was, for William and Ellen, freedom and power.

With experience came confidence. The Crafts now entered halls side by side with Brown, their dazzling entrance timed a little later to add to the thrill. In February they shared the stage with Abby Kelley Foster and her husband, Stephen, making a handsome quartet: two women celebrated for their guts and beauty, alongside their supportive men. As the days lengthened, they voyaged out to harbor towns such as Hingham and to mill towns like Lowell, where young girls wrangled giant power looms to transform Southern cotton into cloth.

Many of their destinations were working-class enclaves where those who rallied were not privileged, grey-haired intellectuals or Quakers, as abolitionists are often represented, but younger men and women who worked with their hands, such as farm workers and artisans. As Thomas Wentworth Higginson recalled, abolition was a "people's movement," stronger in factories and shoe shops than in pulpits or colleges, strong among those with their own demands for justice. "Radicalism," as he expressed, "went with the smell of shoe leather." At the core of the movement were Black activists and activists of color such as the renowned Remonds of Salem. Though "colored citizens" were fewer in numbers in the places the Crafts visited, and less visible in the surviving records, they, too, would have cheered the couple on their unrelenting journey.

While Thoreau may have found the time to pause in solitude at Walden Pond, the Crafts and Brown did not tarry in Concord, one of their many stops. Instead, from there they continued to move back and forth across eastern and central Massachusetts, well into April, when they appeared with Garrison and Wendell Phillips at Boston's Tremont Temple. By now, the trio were enough in demand that they charged admission—unusual for an abolitionist meeting.

Here, as elsewhere, William narrated his and Ellen's adventures, enthralling audiences. Still, it was Ellen that everyone wanted to see. And several stops later, when they pulled into the shipbuilding, maritime town of Newburyport, it would be her turn to tell the story.

As many as nine hundred eager spectators overwhelmed the Court Street meeting house, known as Elder Pike's Place, tucked blocks away from the boats and rails. Even more were turned away at the doors, such was the hunger to hear and see the famed Georgia Fugitives.

For William Lloyd Garrison, who had grown up in poverty here, Newburyport was a place of ghosts. He had once been refused a chance to speak by a local church, and to this day, he would not return to lecture. William Wells Brown, however, was popular in town. As usual, he warmed up the audience, followed by William, but on this spring night, Ellen would tell their tale.

She stepped forward with a style all her own. In her speech, there would be no shrill bells or whistles, no epic Underground Railroad heroics, no sobbing or sensation, as conjured by some White male abolitionists. Neither would she excite her audience to breathlessness with her "thrilling" adventure, like her husband or Brown. Instead, Ellen spoke "in simple and artless a manner," as reported by a local blacksmith. Yet in the very ordinariness of her speech and appearance, she struck at the prevailing norms.

Anyone who saw Ellen as White, as many did, had to accept that this visibly White woman had chosen to love a Black man—no small challenge in a state where interracial marriage had been banned until a few years earlier. Ellen required audiences to question the meaning of all those categories that seemed to pin the social order in place, whether it be North, South, Black, White, master, slave, or husband, wife. Together Ellen and William turned popular racist arguments upside down: claims that Black people were menaces to society, or charity cases at best; that they needed salvation; that they wanted to be White.

What Ellen herself said at this meeting is unrecorded, except for the blacksmith's brief report. He noted that audiences were satisfied, adding that he hoped for an even bigger hall next time Brown came around. For Ellen, however, this event was a turning point. Afterward, the Crafts paused their tour, and from then on, she seems to have ceased her public speaking.

Why she did so is an open question. It has been suggested that she was "silenced"—possibly by the two Williams—or by general expectations that she fit a certain quiet, womanly, middle-class mold. Untold threats may have been at play as well. Had bad news come from the South? Ellen was only too aware of the ways in which the fury of the slavers could be revisited on her loved ones, and her mother was never far from her mind.

But silence might well have been something Ellen chose, her refusal to speak of the pain she owned. Strangers did not hold back from asking terrible questions, probing trauma. She might have decided that she had simply had enough. It may also have been strategic. Ellen was a person who had repeatedly asserted herself, in her life and on her northbound journey. She had engineered and navigated her own emancipation, outsmarted everyone she met on the road. Her silence can be seen not as that of someone unprepared or forbidden to speak, but as a variation on a theme—an act of resistance no more passive than her travel on a first-class train.

Just as she had on the train ride from Macon, so too, Ellen let others talk and explain on the abolitionist stage, while drawing power from the weight of spectators' assumptions and using that power to propel her further along in her goal: formerly, to reach her destination in the North, now to fuel antislavery flames. With silence, in other words, she harnessed the power of a prevailing wind, just as she had on her travels from Georgia. Audiences might clamor for more—gasp at her appearance, ogle her skin and hair, grasp for her hands—but she would communicate in her own style, answering to none.

Twelve days after Ellen told her story in Newburyport, the Crafts resumed their journey in the full green of spring, packing halls from Quincy to Cambridge, Taunton to Roxbury, before arriving, once more, at the Johnsons' sweet-filled home in New Bedford. Three months and a week had passed since they had launched from there. During this time, they had logged more than one thousand miles—the equivalent of their journey from Georgia.

They finally had a reprieve when Brown left for the annual gathering of the American Anti-Slavery Society in New York. Until now, they had experienced no sustained rest, no time on their own. These two weeks gave them the longest break of their lives.

The New York convention was a big opportunity—a national stage, with all the top activists in attendance—but was probably considered too risky for the Crafts, after recent rioting, as well as the kidnapping of another refugee from slavery. By skipping the convention, the Crafts missed the chance to meet the abolitionist greats. Yet the biggest Garrisonian event of the season was still to come: a blockbuster convening at which the Crafts would be two of six self-emancipated stars.

THE SIX

||||||||||||||||||||||||||

A new man strode onto the abolitionist stage: a Virginian who had burst from a box about three feet long, two feet wide, and two and a half feet high. In that box, with all five feet eight inches, two hundred pounds of him folded in, knees to chest, with just a cow's bladder full of water to keep him cool, Henry Brown had taken the same Overland Mail Route that William and Ellen had traveled, boxed for twenty-seven hours straight.

Like them, he had traveled up to Washington, on Aquia Creek, passed through Baltimore, and had been thrown over with luggage at Havre de Grace. And he suffered. Though the box was labeled, "This side up with care," Brown had been turned upside down, once for nearly two hours. The veins on his face swelled as thick as his fingers. He thought he would die.

In Philadelphia, James Miller McKim, the agent who received the box with William Still, had feared he had a coffin on his hands, but Brown emerged triumphant, as wet as if baptized, and soon sang a psalm. "You are the greatest man in America!" McKim hailed, overcome.

This "greatest man" would now join the Crafts at the first night's meeting of the New England Anti-Slavery Society at Boston's Melodeon. Named for a hybrid American instrument (part reed, part keyboard), the Melodeon had a past life as a theater, with pageants featuring the Biblical Queen Esther and a live menagerie, including elephants. For the crowds (drawn through torrential rains), the Crafts and Henry Brown were major attractions. But for these newcomers to the abolitionist arena, there was a formidable veteran to behold: thirty-one-year-old "prophet" and revolutionary, Frederick Douglass.

Six self-emancipated people took the stage on opening night—"six fugitives," as the papers would proclaim (or in Douglass's case, former fugitive, since his freedom had been bought while he was abroad, a fact disapproved by some Garrisonians as giving in to "ransom"). Together they proudly stood: the two Crafts, Henry Brown and William Wells

Brown, a man named Watson, and Frederick Douglass. Henry Brown would be newly named that night, anointed as "Boxer" by the ever clever man of letters, William Wells Brown, and soon go by "Henry Box Brown."

The following night, the new stars of the convention, the Crafts and Brown, told their stories. Introduced by William Wells Brown, Henry Box Brown "excited a thrill of sympathy," and closed to "deafening shouts." Then Douglass presented William and Ellen.

After more than sixty lectures on the road, William was now an experienced performer, and he delivered a rollicking account of their adventures. He remembered his late-night preparations with Ellen, his nervousness over the too-wide coat, Ellen's assurances that sacques in this style "never fit!" He absorbed Ellen's point of view, describing how a porter, her former suitor, called her "Young Master." He recounted how he had so perfected his performance as a "servant" that Southerners pointed him out to their Northern friends as an example of how wonderful the bond between master and slave could be. And he recalled how throughout, Ellen never lost her nerve, though she came close when she landed at Havre de Grace, alone.

That the Crafts chose to detail their method may not have sat well with Douglass, who had personally refused to reveal the means of his own escape so that others might use it too. He and others were all too aware of the tragedy of two men, Alfred and Swanky, who had recently failed to escape by box, no doubt compromised by the recent publicity surrounding Henry Brown. (They were taken in transit, their boxes opened by the mayor of Richmond himself.) But none of that displeasure was visible when William closed to resounding applause.

"What an exhibition!" Douglass cried to a crowd that was high with feeling. "What an appearance is here presented!"

"Are the slaves contented and happy?" He gestured to the others on the stage, as well as himself, as proof to the contrary—their escapes proof, too, that they were "worthy to be freemen."

At the crowd's urging, Henry Box Brown then returned to perform the hymn he had sung when he first burst out of the box. The words from Psalm 40 spun to the rafters, free falling in the silence: "I waited patiently for the Lord." And when the notes soared to a finale—"The Lord be praised"—the very air seemed to shatter with applause.

The mood among the abolitionists was ebullient, never mind the down-pour. Wendell Phillips would later credit the self-emancipated speakers for the rise in energy, saying, "It is the slave, the fugitive slave from the plantation, whose tongue, inspired by oppression, speaks most forci-bly to the American people." In his excitement, he made an error, for none of the star fugitives at this gathering were plantation laborers but skilled, urban workers. It was the kind of elision that showed the need for education, even among the abolitionists.

Frederick Douglass, meanwhile, was in no celebratory mood, as he would soon reveal in an incendiary speech that would give the Crafts a new way of framing their experience in America, nationally and inter-nationally. "Give us the facts," a White abolitionist had once insisted— that is, just stick to your personal story—adding: "We will take care of the philosophy." Douglass was ready as ever to give them both.

Handsome and leonine, as he was often described, with his dark, wavy hair parted smartly on the left, his wide-set eyes meeting any gaze (including the camera's, which he would invite, but never smile for), Douglass had covered more mileage than most people he would meet. He was born in Talbot County, Maryland, to an enslaved mother whom he longed to remember, and a White father, who may have been his first enslaver. At nineteen, he fled bondage via the same railroad that the Crafts and Henry Box Brown would later ride. Since then, he had lectured across the world, speaking to thousands in England, Scot-land, and Ireland, as well as in the United States.

Unbeknownst to those who met him in these days, in wet and light-less Boston, Douglass, too, was under a cloud, his lungs ravaged, his muscles sore, suffering ailments similar to those Ellen had feigned: in-flammatory rheumatism. It was not just his body that was low. Doug-lass was troubled personally and financially. He was also on the verge of a "breakup" with his onetime friend and mentor, William Lloyd Garrison.

Garrison had been thunderstruck when he first saw the twenty-three-year-old Douglass rousing a crowd on Nantucket Island, mix-ing biblical lines with classical oratory and revolutionary notes, into a preaching all his own. The admiration was mutual. Of Garrison's *Liberator* and its publisher—a tireless man who had been abandoned by his father, scavenged for food as a boy in Newburyport, trained as a shoemaker, and grown up to be a printer and a fearless advocate for the enslaved—Douglass once said: "I not only liked—I loved this paper, and its editor."

But the two stubborn giants of abolition had since grown apart, especially after Douglass's return from England, where he had opened his eyes to another world, one in which he was seen and accepted as a man. Once back in the States, Douglass had grown increasingly angry, disillusioned, and impatient with American abolitionists, who moved so slowly and too often betrayed their own prejudices, subtle or not. Even some in Garrison's closest circle were known to utter racial expletives on occasion.

Soon after his return, Douglass and Garrison had gone on the road together again, taking blows side by side in an epic western speaking tour. But rather than come together, they only pulled further apart—even more so after Douglass started his own newspaper, the *North Star*, a long-held dream for himself and his people, which Garrison opposed. Douglass also began exploring politics and meeting other kinds of activists, including a White man named John Brown, who would one day stage an uprising at Harpers Ferry. Garrison and his friends might counsel turning the other cheek, but Douglass—who at sixteen had physically defeated a hired "slave breaker"—knew firsthand the value of force.

It had been a difficult spring for both men. They were both sickly, and Garrison had recently lost a child: six-year-old Charlie, only a year after the death of a baby girl. Douglass, in the meantime, welcomed a second daughter and now had five children to support in an unhappy marriage. Financially, he was barely able to make ends meet, struggling to get his paper off the ground—and, it has been suggested, headed for a nervous breakdown. Help had come with the arrival of an English friend, Julia Griffiths, who would assist in press and household, but rumors about their relationship would cause further damage.

Both men had thrown themselves into their work, lecturing heavily. Yet even as they fought a shared cause and appeared together, they were headed toward an ideological collision, as would be evident when Douglass gave a speech unlike any the Crafts had ever heard.

The weather was lousy for the third evening in a row, but the abolitionists had an incandescent new venue: Faneuil Hall, where they met once more under the glass-eyed gaze of the man-made grasshopper, which spun on its windy perch. The hall was testy, with a motley crowd of lawyers and physicians, merchants and mechanics, farmers and divines. There were veteran Black activists and grim Garrisonians, but also hostile young men, stampers and hissers, not to mention a few insistent "crackpots," whom organizers disdained.

Douglass smoothly greeted all. "Mr. Chairman, Ladies and Gentlemen," he spoke, warming up his resonant bass voice, "I never rise to speak in Faneuil Hall without a deep sense of my want of ability to do justice to the subject upon which I undertake to speak."

So much for the humble introduction; Douglass began by taking on one of the most popular statesmen in the country, "the Honorable Henry Clay," a senator whose renowned feats of diplomatic compromise would one day alter the lives of many present, including the Crafts. The very name drew applause. Douglass's intention was not to cheer, however, but to take aim.

In his sights: Clay's plans for ending slavery. The Kentucky senator was a longtime owner of human property, but he spoke of slavery in different terms from his colleague Calhoun, calling it an "great evil to both races." And yet, like so many others, Clay was unable to picture an America shared by Black and White. His solution: gradual emancipation, with mandatory colonization, which would rid the nation of slavery slowly, systematically—and rid the country of the enslaved.

By Clay's plan, all children born after 1860 would be freed at age twenty-five, whereupon they would be required to work for three years in order to earn fees for their deportation to Africa. For people like the Crafts, this plan would not only put freedom out of reach, but exile any children they had after 1860. All the while, enslavers might sell or mortgage their human property as they pleased.

"And this is the plan of the good Henry Clay," said Douglass, "whom you esteem and admire so much," eliciting both hisses and cries of "Shame!"

From Kentucky, Douglass turned to New York. He recounted how, days earlier, he had escorted two White English ladies (likely Julia Griffiths and her sister) to dinner aboard a steamer, "forgetting all about my complexion, the curl of my hair, or the flatness of my nose, only remembering I had two elbows and a stomach, and was exceedingly hungry."

Laughter filled the hall again, but the mood soon changed as Douglass described the turmoil that followed. He was denied service and ordered to leave, which he finally did, after the captain appeared, flanked by four or five other men. As Douglass explained, he "had but one coat," which he did not care to have torn. What he did not say, but others knew, was that he and his lady friends had recently been attacked, struck on the head, by White men who were enraged at the sight of them walking arm in arm along the Battery in New York.

Douglass would never forget how other diners cheered when he left. Not a single person showed even a troubled look, much less a word of support. One lady, a slaver, betrayed a typical prejudice when she claimed she was afraid even to be near Douglass, a Black man—all while other Black men remained in close proximity, serving their dinner.

"This," said Douglass, "tells the whole story."

He called out his fellow Americans for their fundamental hypocrisy. Black Americans like himself had helped build the country, fought for the country from the beginning, yet without receiving any of the benefits reaped by their White counterparts.

"Our connection with this country," he observed, "is contemporaneous with your own," pointing out that, "in the same year that the Pilgrims were landing in this State, slaves were landing on the James River, in Virginia."

"We are lovers of this country," he further declared, "and we only ask to be treated as well as the haters of it." It was an outrage that even recent immigrants—"who know nothing of our institutions, nor of the history of our country"—would "have the audacity to propose our removal from this, the land of our birth."

For his part, Douglass declared his intention to stay in the United States and fight for justice. He might have lived comfortably abroad but had chosen to return, believing that the nation could transform. Only recently, interracial marriage was illegal and railroads were segregated, with people of color confined to "Jim Crow cars." Douglass remembered when he himself, newly arrived in Boston, and working at the shipyards, was hesitant to eat with White people, some of whom refused to eat with him. But Wendell Phillips had shown another way, telling guests at his home that "if they did not like to sit at a table with me," as Douglass recalled, "they could have a separate one for themselves. . . .

"It is all false," he insisted, "this talk about the invincibility of color. If any of you have it, and no doubt some of you have, I will tell you how to get rid of it. Commence to do something to elevate and improve and enlighten the colored man, and your prejudice will begin to vanish. The more you try to make a man of the black man, the more you will begin to think him a man."

Then he headed for an explosive turn, with "A word more."

There were now three million people in slavery, Douglass observed, held in bondage with the support of the American government—and Boston's own citizens, who were bound to bear arms in the event of slave insurrection, in defiance of the spirit of the nation's own revolution. Douglass's ensuing battle cry shook the hall.

"When I consider . . . the history of the American people . . ." he thundered over the heads of the restive New Englanders, sons and daughters of revolutionaries, "I say . . . I should welcome the intelligence tomorrow, should it come, that the slaves had risen in the South, and that the sable arms which had been engaged in beautifying and adorning the South, were engaged in spreading death and devastation there."

Cries and hisses now erupted—a "sensation," as one eyewitness recalled.

"There is a state of war at the South, at this moment" Douglass declared, his voice angled high above the stamps and shouts. "The slaveholder is waging a war of aggression on the oppressed. The slaves," he said, "are now under his feet."

Douglass would not say it any more directly, but the message was there. The time for rising up had come. His audience sensed it too: there had been revolutions around the world in 1848, revolutions cheered by Americans North and South. They had celebrated the barricade against the king in France, crying, "Long live the republic!" and "Liberty, Equality, Fraternity," an homage to an even earlier revolution.

"And should you not hail with equal pleasure," Douglass demanded, "the tidings from the South, that the slaves had risen, and achieved . . . against the iron-hearted slaveholder, what the republicans of France achieved against the royalists of France?"

The great hall was awash in dissonance, the freeborn, the freed, the legally enslaved, all engulfed in the uproar, as Douglass made it loud and clear: it was not, as Garrison and Calhoun claimed in their opposing ways, that the Union needed to be broken, but that America needed to be remade—that in the spirit of democracy, in truth to its founding principles, the nation's unfinished revolution needed finally to be won.

After Boston, William Wells Brown traveled alone. He had more great plans: nearly two weeks of lectures in Maine and Massachusetts, including Nantucket. The Crafts did not accompany him, however, possibly alerted to a new danger to their safety.

Brown returned from his travels bursting with news. He had been invited to be a delegate at the International Peace Congress in Paris come August, and he wanted the Crafts to join him on a tour of Europe. It was a momentous decision, as the move would guarantee their safety. The Crafts, however, declined once more. For them, a life of itinerant activism, as meaningful as it was, was not the goal. They had dedicated themselves to community justice for months, and now they were ready to settle down. They would commit themselves to building their lives in a country that held their past, but also, as Douglass had drawn for them, their future.

Ellen would take one public step, however. Before Brown's departure, she had her picture made. The portrait could not have been more different from the giant oil of her half sister and enslaver Eliza, who appeared resplendent in silks, with a fanciful background, smiling baby, and plump grapes in her delicate grip. Ellen's likeness, in contrast, was male and modern, conceived by machine in Luther Holman Hale's daguerreotype office on busy Washington Street.

She may have entered this space in a dress, but she carried a gentleman's change of clothes, which she layered on, piece by piece, replaying the ritual of a distant morning in Macon. Ellen's hair had not fully grown out since then: she pulled out a few curls, arranging them above her ears. She also hung a sling around her neck and draped her cloak over her shoulders, letting the tassel dangle. She would leave out the poultices—"because the likeness could not have been taken well," as explained later.

With her left hand, she fingered the lining of her cloak and kept her right hand free, leaving the sling empty. It was manliness, not illness, that would be on display. Ellen wore her glasses, though, as she gazed out, sitting perfectly still as she awaited the camera's shutter to close. For a few breathless moments, she held her pose and composure, just as she had on her journey, and as she had for hours, for months, on the abolitionist road.

It was a position she had mastered, and once again it gave her power. Reduced in size so that it could be pocketed, her image would be slipped from hand to hand, to travel the world.

There was a party on July 16, to send off William Wells Brown and honor William Lloyd Garrison. On behalf of the "Colored Citizens" who hosted the event, Brown's good friend William Cooper Nell—a writer, historian, and until recently, an editor of Frederick Douglass's newspaper—presented Garrison with a silver pitcher inscribed with the motto of his paper: "My Country Is the World—My Countrymen Are All Mankind."

Two days later, Ellen, William, and Nell stood with Brown at Boston Harbor, awaiting his passage on the steamship *Canada*, for travel to Liverpool. Among the things Brown carried: copies of his book, letters of introduction to British society, and sketches for an epic panorama of slavery. He also carried Charlotte Brontë's *Jane Eyre* and Thomas Macaulay's *The History of England*, parting gifts from his friends, as well as slave shackles and an iron collar given to him by those who had broken their bonds. Finally, he carried the pictures of Ellen.

Brown said good-bye to his friends, and as he looked out over the ship's edge at the Back Bay, through the hot glare of the noonday sun, past the dots of parasols held aloft by well-wishers on shore, he glimpsed William's fluttering white handkerchief, high above the others. With odd prescience, he wondered when he would see his friends again. It would be longer than he ever imagined, and Brown would prove lucky to have left the country when he did.

THE
UNITED
STATES

1849–1850

CITY UPON
A HILL

|||||||||||||||||||||||||

William and Ellen entered New England at the height of its so-called flowering, as Elizabeth Peabody was gathering up transcendentalist philosophers in her cluttered downtown bookstore, and Utopian experiments were all the rage—from the bookish Brook Farmers, to even more radical groups such as the free-love Oneidas and the celibate Shakers.

It was a season of big literary fruits. In the year of the Crafts' arrival, Nathaniel Hawthorne drafted *The Scarlet Letter*, while eighteen-year-old Emily Dickinson played precociously with verse. Henry David Thoreau published "Civil Disobedience," and Herman Melville was soon to begin *Moby-Dick*. Three new self-emancipated authors published books this year as well, including Henry Box Brown.

The Crafts, however, would wait to write their story, focused as they were on crafting the narrative of their lives. After months of perpetual movement, this was their chance to live the life they imagined, in Boston, a place that Puritan John Winthrop had envisioned as "A Model of Christian Charity"—or a "city upon a hill"—as he anticipated his own arrival on Massachusetts shores. (He would become a Colonial governor here, as well as an enslaver.)

Far from the lush nature that made cool-eyed Emerson swoon, and closer to where young Louisa May Alcott experienced the most impoverished years of her life, the Crafts landed in a densely packed city—a dangerous proposition in the summer, when the stench of tainted waters came off the wharves, even more as a global epidemic raged. The cholera outbreak was centered in the tenements on the eastern side of the city, where Irish immigrants, already weakened by famine, lived too many to a house, a privy, a room, than was considered safe or sanitary. Writers of the cholera reports that year were shocked by the living conditions mere blocks from their homes.

Where William and Ellen lived was crowded, too, but in ways that could be reassuring. They lived at the heart of Boston's Black community, in the safe house of the Haydens, where they were surrounded by other Southern refugees. There was Peter Custom, a nineteen-year-old tailor born in South Carolina; Harrison Crawford, a Virginian cook; William Griffen, a Carolinian trader who, in his forties, was an elder; and twenty-three-year-old Frank Wise, another South Carolinian, profession unnamed. The only children reported were the Haydens' two youngsters, a boy and a girl. But Ellen had Harriet Hayden for female company, as well as a young White English immigrant, Bridget, who made a living cleaning other people's homes.

Beyond this safe house, roughly one-quarter of Boston's Black population was Southern born. A few houses down from the Haydens, a Baptist church was going up, attended by so many Southern refugees that it would become known as the "Fugitive Slave Church." The Crafts journeyed farther on Sundays to the Melodeon to hear the radical Reverend Theodore Parker preach rousing sermons to a multiracial congregation of thousands. To venture past the hill was to take a risk; even in Boston, no one who had escaped slavery could ever be entirely at ease. Yet in their worship and other choices, the Crafts refused to allow fear to define how they lived.

No sooner had William Wells Brown set sail for England when William ran his first advertisement in the *Liberator* (to be followed with a listing in the Boston City Directory):

WILLIAM CRAFT,
DEALER in New and Second Hand FURNITURE,
No. 62 Federal Street, Boston.
N.B. All kinds of Furniture cleaned and repaired
with despatch, in the most satisfactory manner.
The patronage of his friends and the
public is respectfully solicited.

William chose to open his store not on Cambridge Street, by Lewis Hayden's clothing store and other Black-owned businesses, but on Federal Street, on the other side of the Common, not far from the fine house where Louisa May Alcott was able to find refuge from the summer's heat and disease as a guest of her wealthy uncle.

William spent much of his time at sales and repair, as opposed to cabinetmaking—possibly on account of local prejudice—but the business was entirely his own and gave him standing in a community where opportunities for skilled Black laborers were all too rare. (Ironically, most craftsmen like himself hailed from the South.) He put in orders for loads of pine and would soon have such demand that he would need to hire another worker.

Ellen, meanwhile, adapted her stitches to heavier folds of fabric than she was accustomed to in Georgia—the cloths thicker, still, as she began to learn the art of upholstery from a local woman named Miss Dean. Her work took her in and out of homes not far from where she lived, but a world away, with their chandeliers, oil paintings, and generous hearths—stoked not with the cheap wood that smoked, but well-dried cuts that burst into flame.

Her clients included one elegantly outfitted woman, whose rich husband—an India merchant and railroad man—was known for his exacting tastes in how the women of his household were dressed. He was also reputed to be a proslavery sympathizer. Though his daughter, Caroline Healey Dall, was an abolitionist, friends worried for Ellen's safety in his house. But Ellen, like William, had the confidence to move without limits, and her judgment on the Healey family would prove to be correct.

The weather cooled, and with it, thankfully, the cholera receded. Trees did not grace the dark alleys by where the Crafts lived, but as they passed the Common, they could see some thousand elm trees on the Common burnishing gold. Then came time for wool stockings and thick-soled boots, and the Crafts were lucky that their work was not seasonal, like that of the draymen by the wharves.

Two stories became the talk of the town as fall turned to winter in 1849: the first, a grisly murder in which the severed, charred bones and thorax of one Harvard professor were discovered in the chemistry lab of another, not far from the neighborhood where William and Ellen lived. Say what people might about the vice in the slums—the night-walking and rat-fighting in the North End, or even about the north side of Beacon Hill (called "Mount Whoredom"), where men of all colors were known to ogle gyrating dancers while slurping stiff drinks—none of the local crime reports compared with the scene left behind by these Harvard faculty.

Even closer to home—and soon also to be judged by Lemuel Shaw, father-in-law of Herman Melville—was the case of Sarah Roberts, a five-year-old who had to walk beyond five other schools before arriving at the lone school designated for Black children. The girl's father, a printer and activist, sued to have his daughter attend a closer school, launching a fight for desegregation that would divide Boston, and within it, the Black community.

Both cases were to make history. The Harvard homicide established the catchphrase "reasonable doubt" as a threshold for crime. Sarah Roberts's failed bid for school integration set a precedent for *Plessy v. Ferguson* (1896), which would legalize segregation, while also anticipating arguments made *Brown v. Board of Education* (1954), which declared forced separation inherently unequal. Both sensational cases, of the schoolgirl and of the murderer, showed that for all the Utopianism that flourished in this region and in these times, New England in its fullest flowering was hardly an ideal world.

With Christmas at hand, there were festivities to look forward to, such as the Anti-Slavery Bazaar, and now it was the Crafts' turn to take seats in lively halls, not as performers but as spectators. Ellen was one among many to experience the thrill of minister LaRoy Sunderland's mesmeric "Wonders of Mental Science," reportedly "fascinated." Newer refugees, meanwhile, took center stage at abolitionist gatherings, including a teenage mother named Betsy Blakely, who had stowed away aboard a steamer from North Carolina but had been forced to leave her baby behind.

Still, the Crafts had a unique star power. When the celebrated Swedish novelist Fredrika Bremer visited Boston, it was the Crafts whom Garrison arranged for her to meet. To Bremer, the couple "appeared to be sincerely happy," but her own interactions with them indicated further complications.

Bremer asked Ellen why she had fled her enslavers, wondering if they treated her badly.

"No," Ellen replied, "they always treated me well, but I fled from them because they would not give me my rights as a human being," adding: "I could never learn anything, neither to read nor to write."

She might have added, too, that she had made solid progress on both counts. When census takers would pause at the Hayden home the following year and ask who in the house could not read, one lone man was counted, not William and Ellen. The letters of their names, which they learned to form with chalk and slate at the home of the Quakers less than a year earlier, were now more sure, and the Crafts had plans to attend school in the evenings.

Others asked William how it could be claimed that slaves were commonly flogged and beaten, when other visitors to the South insisted they had "never seen any thing of the kind"?

Smiling, with a "keen expression," William answered: "Nor are children whipped in the presence of strangers; this is done when they do not see."

Bremer would meet the Crafts again with poet Henry Wadsworth Longfellow, who would recall how Ellen "hung her head" after Bremer spoke of her escape in men's clothes. Ellen said she "did not like it mentioned," that "some people thought it shocking."

The poet recalled that Bremer "laughed at this prudery," and the two writers urged Ellen to be proud of what she had done. But the reality was that Ellen was not welcome to exhibit such pride. No matter what the literati might say, she knew that her future depended on her appearing the lady and her husband being the one who proudly wore the pants.

There was sure to have been some surge of feeling, however, as the Crafts looked back on the year that had passed. They had rung in 1849 while hiding with the Purvises in Byberry, gazing up at paintings of Cinqué and Garrison. Now they were living in the world those paintings evoked. In their newly written lives, the Crafts were becoming models for self-reliance, as defined by Ralph Waldo Emerson in his famous essay by that name. Yet the time for "Civil Disobedience" was soon at hand.

COMPROMISE

IIIIIIIIIIIIIIIIIIIIIIIIIII

Even before the clock struck midnight to 1850, there had been tremors on Capitol Hill. When Congress opened in December, members of the House and Senate were name-calling and close to brawling over what Senator Henry Clay would call "this vexed problem of slavery."

It happened every time the nation grew bigger or redrew its borders: this explosiveness over slavery's future and whether it, too, should be allowed to grow. Three decades earlier, late in the wake of the Louisiana Purchase, Congress passed the Missouri Compromise, engineered by Clay, "the Great Compromiser." It decreed that slavery would not extend north of that magical line the Crafts had crossed between Maryland and Delaware: the Mason-Dixon.

But now came California, long and lean, daring to sit astride that boundary, far, far west. It leaned antislavery, and New Mexico, too, when the nation hung in balance, fifteen slave states to fifteen free—a congressional equilibrium, which the West threatened to undo. Slavery's stakeholders knew what that would mean, and a growing number pledged to fight it, no matter the cost.

Everything was a cause for conflict—not just slavery in the territories but also slave trading in the capital (the sight of which Clay himself considered an "abomination"); the lines around the slave state of Texas (which had its eye on New Mexico); and, increasingly, clashes over fugitive slaves. This was a tinderbox that recent high-profile escapes, such as the Crafts', helped to light. Slavers considered it a "constitutional right" to recapture their human property, and were enraged by the fugitives and their accomplices, who made a mockery of this right. Inspired by the stories of people like the Crafts, opponents considered their recapture a crime.

Soon after the New Year, two Southern senators proposed measures to update the Fugitive Slave Act, so as to make the capturing of fugitives a national duty as never before. In the months that followed, these measures weighed on many minds, including that of the man whom everyone hoped to negotiate another great compromise.

Henry Clay was one of the "Great Triumvirate," a sick and dying breed of men who had politicked the nation through turmoil in the past. There was Western-facing Clay from Kentucky, the South's John C. Calhoun, and New England's son, Daniel Webster. The three men didn't like one another, yet a bond ran deep. As Calhoun expressed, "I don't like Clay. He is a bad man, an imposter, a creator of wicked schemes . . . but, by God, I love him!" Whatever their differences, they had learned to work together, at least before this time.

They knew what might happen if they did not. Clay and Webster, in particular, were alive to the personal costs of battle. Clay's favorite son and namesake had died fighting in the recent Mexican-American War; Webster too, had lost a son, and buried a beloved daughter the very same day his boy's body came home. All three had opposed that war, predicting that to expand the boundaries of the nation yet again would be to bloat it beyond what it could peaceably hold. And now here was America, talking of Civil War.

It was Clay who made the proposal on a historic winter day, rising to speak in a claustrophobic chamber that was stuffed with far more senators than the space had been built for. Over six feet tall, famously long bodied, with a winning grin, Clay has been described as possessing the kind of robust charisma that made ladies line up to kiss or dance with him. But the Kentucky charmer, now seventy-three years old, and newly returned to the Senate after an absence of eight years, had been sleepless, coughing, torn.

Clay was one of his state's major enslavers, having inherited human property at the age of four. In contrast to Calhoun, however, he believed not that slavery was a "positive good" but that it should end. His own preference was gradual emancipation, a solution that Frederick Douglass had mocked and fellow slavers condemned. Thus the measures put forth on this day signified not just a compromise for the nation but also for the man himself.

The hall went hush as he named them, one by one: California would be admitted with no restrictions on slavery and, likewise, the other territories from the Mexican Cession. Texas would give up its border dispute with New Mexico in exchange for debt relief. Congress would not abolish slavery in the District of Columbia, but slave trading in the capital would be banned.

Then came the quietest resolution—the shortest, but the key upon which the new compromise would hang. Clay moved for a "more effectual provision" for the "restitution and delivery of persons bound to service or labor": a new fugitive slave law. As a final compromise, Congress would have no power to interfere in the interstate slave trade.

Clay hoped he had achieved equilibrium, with something for each side, but in his closing, he warned that it was the South that had more at stake, and he drew a dramatic picture to bring home this lesson. He conjured the South's darkest nightmare: an apocalypse of slave uprising and rebellion. This, he warned, could come to pass, if the reins of slavery were released too much, too soon—if lawmakers failed to act. It was fine and well to contemplate slavery as a moral issue when one was in the North, but for Southerners, Clay warned, its future was a matter of life and death. Men like Henry Clay were well aware that they were outnumbered.

He conjured a house on fire, where women and children screamed among the leaping flames, the falling rafters.

"Whose house is that?" he demanded. "Whose wives and children are they? Yours in the free States? No. You are looking on in safety and security, while the conflagration which I have described is raging in the slave States, and produced, not intentionally by you, but produced from the inevitable tendency of the measures which you have adopted, and which others have carried far beyond what you have wished."

It was a house not divided, but burning that he foresaw—the very image Garrison had evoked, only here it was Blacks who had the power, Whites who stood to burn, a world turned upside down.

Clay's words raced by telegraph all across America, down past Macon and up to Boston, where they met resistance in the Hayden household. Lewis Hayden had fled bondage in Kentucky, and he remembered Clay as the man who had bought his first wife, Esther Harvey, and their son, and under whose ownership this wife and child had been sold into the Deep South. The thought of his child sold, to "nobody knows where," was unbearable to him.

Now Hayden—joined by Ellen and William, and a multiracial coalition of more than one hundred—would sign a petition of protest. Declaring a list of grievances, including the imprisonment and sale of free Blacks into slavery, but above all, the constitutional compromise that allowed Southern slavers to "hunt and seize their fugitive slaves" on Massachusetts soil, they called for a "peaceful SECESSION FROM THE AMERICAN UNION."

They were not the only ones advocating for extreme measures. Fanning the flames on the other side was the so-called "cast-iron man who looks as if he had never been born and could never be extinguished": the man dear to Ellen's father, John C. Calhoun.

They said that when he limped into the Senate for the last speech of his life, he already looked like death, his body enshrouded in black, his hair like live grey wires, his face shrunken, his eyes too bright. He would not use his voice that day, relying on a younger Southern congressional colleague to read his words instead.

Calhoun's call was explicit: inaction would lead to the end of the Union and possibly to war. Words were not enough. "The cry of 'Union, Union, the Glorious Union,'" he proclaimed, "can no more prevent disunion than the cry of 'Health, health, glorious health!' on the part of the physician can save a patient lying dangerously ill."

To love the Union, truly, was to love the Constitution that created it, and to love the Constitution was to protect it and perform the "high duties" it called for. And had these duties been performed? Not judging by the treatment of fugitive slaves, a matter whose "violation" Calhoun called "notorious." (Though he would not tell it here, this was a matter Calhoun knew personally, through the escape of a man named Hector and a trusted house slave called Alec, who had fled "for no other reason but to avoid a correction for misconduct." Calhoun had Hector hunted down, and Alec captured, imprisoned, and whipped.)

To Calhoun, compromise was no solution. The South had already given up so much that there was no more to surrender. Instead, the salvation of the Union lay entirely with the North. Calhoun was vague on the details but specific on the consequences, his final words ringing low.

"If you . . . cannot agree, say so," he declared, and the states could separate peaceably. "If you are unwilling we should part in peace, tell us so, and we shall know what to do, when you reduce the question to submission or resistance." Remain silent, he warned, and "you will compel us to infer by your acts what you intend." The unspoken word that everyone heard, was *war.*

Calhoun's words were fuel to the fires already raging up and down the Eastern seaboard and beyond. The *New-York Herald* reported that "civil war and massacre may commence" without "a moment's warning." Even congressmen arrived on the high steps of the Capitol armed with bowie knives and guns. Now, more than ever, a unifying voice was needed, and the president—General Zachary Taylor, whom all three Triumvirs considered inept—was of no help.

Enter Daniel Webster. Before Calhoun's last words had landed, the Massachusetts statesman rose to volunteer his voice, which many Americans heard as *the* voice of the Union. "Liberty *and* Union, now and forever, one and inseparable!" he had famously cried, in his debates against South Carolina's Senator Robert Hayne—words that schoolchildren learned by heart.

Webster's positioning on slavery was cagey. He would not join the "Conscience Whigs," as antislavery members of his party were called. Yet he was remembered deeply for his spellbinding 1820 oration at Plymouth Rock—when, swaying, roused, he had decried the American slave trade. "I hear the sound of the hammer," he thundered, "I see the smoke of all the furnaces where manacles and fetters are still forged for human limbs. . . . Let that spot be purified," he called, again and again. It was this speech that first earned him the epithet "God-like Daniel."

Webster was known, too, for having purchased the freedom of several enslaved people, including a celebrated chef named Monica Mc-Carty, whose fried oysters and soft-shelled crabs had people recalling her name for years, and who was now employed by Webster, a noted gourmand. Webster also paid $500 for Henry Pleasants—"the best spent money I ever laid out in my life," said Webster, tears streaming, as Pleasants, who had gone to fight in Mexico alongside Webster's son, brought the dead son's body home.

But "God-like Daniel" was a complicated man. From childhood, he had been called "Dark Dan" and "Black Dan" because of his coloring. (It was said he was darker than Ellen Craft.) These names would be invoked for his personal habits as well.

The sixty-eight-year-old senator was an arresting person, with his gigantic head, operatic lung power, and eyes that smote. It has been suggested that when it came to their private lives, he and Calhoun played against type, swapping roles: teetotaling Calhoun, a grim-faced farmer's son and Yale man, was the natural "Puritan," Daniel Webster, the "Cavalier" of wild appetites.

Webster was the only Senator who had his own drinking room inside the Capitol, and he carried among his possessions an exquisitely
painted miniature of a woman's glowing breasts—a self-portrait by the
painter Sarah Goodridge, who presented the gift when Webster was
newly widowed, and between his first and second wives.

Webster would be dogged by rumors of excessive drinking, woman-
izing, and reckless spending, especially that spring. Many such stories
would be dismissed or waved away, including reporting by a pioneering female journalist who would lose her place in the Capitol after
charging that Webster had fathered mulatto children. But at least one
young enslaved man, Robert Yancey—later called Robert Webster—
would claim that Daniel Webster was not only the purchaser of his
mother's freedom and her employer, but also his biological father.

This was the complex figure who came forward on the seventh of
March. In many ways, his dilemma was symbolic of a crisis of conscience facing the North. Personally, Webster was against slavery and
believed it should end. But at the price of the Union? At the expense
of another child? (His son Fletcher would die in the Second Battle of
Bull Run.)

There were political and practical calculations as well. Would Webster wager his last bid for the presidency that he desperately wanted?
And, as a debtor, his financial lifeline? These were the kinds of choices
that every American would face in the years to come, a question that
might boil down to this: How much are you willing to give up, sacrifice personally, for what you believe in, for events in another part of
the country, for souls on the other side of the world?

No one really knew what Webster would say this day, when he
took center stage in the Senate hall. The space was overflowing with
senators, their families, and spectators, such as the Congress had never
seen, including a vast number of ladies, who surrounded the vice president's chair, some even occupying senatorial seats (yielded graciously
by statesmen).

Advocates of abolition hoped and prayed, and wrote to Webster,
thinking he could turn the history of the country on his word. Yet
"Cotton Whigs"—men of his own party, with ties to the South, men to
whom Webster personally owed debts—also considered him a friend.

Webster had benefited from some foreknowledge of his fellow Triumvirs' remarks. Clay, though no friend, had shown up at his door on
a rainy, cold night to drink and talk. Meanwhile, Webster had visited

Calhoun in his quarters two days before the South Carolinian's decla-
mation. Now these men—and the nation—waited to hear his position
in a speech that, as Benjamin Silliman wrote to Webster, "may be the
turning point in the life of this nation." Webster was sick with anxiety,
as he confided to his son Fletcher.

To the packed house, Webster intoned his first line: "I wish to speak
today, not as a Massachusetts man, nor as a northern man but as an
American, and a member of the Senate of the United States . . . I speak
today for the preservation of the Union."

For nearly four hours, he would rally across the divide, suggesting
that there were good people on both sides and advocating for balance.
He dismissed extremists who saw everything as "absolute—absolutely
wrong or absolutely right. . . . These persons," he said, "are disposed
to mount upon some duty as a warhorse, and to drive furiously on, and
upon, and over all other duties that may stand in the way. . . .

"Thus," he concluded, "wars are waged, and unjust wars."

This renowned constitutional defender proceeded to take both the
South and the North to task for failing to respect the aims of that sacred document that brought them together in union. He began with the
South. Once upon a time, he suggested, everyone could agree, North
and South, that slavery was wrong. The most eminent men all considered it "an evil, a blight, a blast, a mildew, a scourge, and a curse"
upon the country. As Webster saw it, early Americans questioned not
whether slavery was evil, but "how to deal with it as an evil?"

The solution at that time was to set deadlines and limits on slavery, with the assumption that it would die naturally. Webster pointed
out that the word *slavery* was *not* included in the Constitution: James
Madison, later the fourth president of the United States, and himself
an enslaver, had made sure of that. The Constitution did not say that
"fugitive slaves" had to be returned but rather "persons bound to service."

But cotton changed everything. The South became greedy for territory and for slavery's spread. It pushed for new lands, including the
Louisiana Purchase, Texas, and now the territory ceded by Mexico.
This South, Webster argued, was far stronger than others had made it
out to be, and it was ravenous.

Yet the South, Webster believed, had rightful grievances too. And
now, speaking at a strange and halting pace, just loud enough to be

heard, the Massachusetts senator turned to the wrongs of the North. As he did, he made his values absolutely clear: the defense of the Union, and the Constitution, came first. If the South had violated the spirit of the Constitution, the North was not true to it either. There were wrongs, as well as rights, on both sides.

One wrong, above all, stood out. And here Webster steadied himself for the lines that would change American history, touching the lives of William and Ellen and so many more. Among Northerners, he said, there was "a disinclination to perform, fully, their constitutional duties in regard to the return of persons bound to service, who have escaped into the free States."

No one could miss his point, since he made it explicit: "In that respect, it is my judgment that the South is right, and the North is wrong."

Every citizen, said Webster, was required by the Constitution to fulfill this duty. He called out his fellow Northerners, demanding what right they had to "get around" the Constitution? His answer: "None at all." In the words of one historian, this "might have been the moment that saved the nation from secession, or at least for a decade, staved it off."

His massive forehead wet with sweat, his eyes like "balls of fire," Webster turned his hot gaze to a single, dying face—that of his colleague John Calhoun—and invoked a hated word.

"Secession!" he cried, "Peaceable secession! Sir, your eyes and mine are never destined to see that miracle. The dismemberment of this vast country without convulsion! . . .

"There can be no such thing as a peaceable secession. . . ." he stressed. "No, sir! No, sir! I will not state what might produce the disruption of the states; but, sir, I see it as I see the sun in heaven—I see that disruption must produce such a war as I will not describe. . . .

"Why, sir, our ancestors—our fathers, and our grandfathers . . . would rebuke and reproach us; and our children, and our grandchildren, would cry out, Shame upon us!"

Webster kindled hope one last time. "Instead of dwelling in these caverns of darkness," he pleaded, "instead of groping with those ideas so full of all that is horrid and horrible, let us come out into the light of day; let us enjoy the fresh air of liberty and union." He willed the nation to come together again in mutual support of this Union, which was unlike any other.

"In all its history," he said, "it has been beneficent; it has trodden down no man's liberty; it has crushed no State. Its daily respiration is liberty and patriotism." Larger than ever before, he observed, "This Republic now extends, with a vast breadth, across the whole continent. The two great seas of the world wash the one and the other shore."

Webster ended this empiric vision with an evocation of Achilles's shield, as described by Homer in the *Iliad*, bordered around with ocean, a "living silver" that "bound the whole." What he neglected to observe was that this great work of art, with the expanse of the ocean all around, failed to protect the anguished Greek warrior who carried it, who sacrificed his immortality and knew already that he was doomed, even as he marched toward war.

When all was done, senators and spectators rushed to extol the exhausted senator, whom many saw as the hero of the day for having sung a song of unity to the tune of compromise, giving wings to the proposals of Henry Clay. "God-like Daniel" was hailed a savior in many quarters, the markets responded and prices shot up, and even John Calhoun took "great pleasure" on some of Webster's points—most of all, his position on fugitive slaves.

In his home state, eight hundred leading citizens signed a letter singing their senator's praise, saying he had saved the Union. In April five thousand admirers cheered him at Boston's Revere House. Webster personally ordered up a thousand copies of his revised speech to share with neighbors and countrymen. There were other signs, however, that the senator was not at peace. One contemporary reported that following his pronouncement on fugitive slaves, Dark Dan would never sleep more than four hours a night, that he was ravaged in his dreams.

Others condemned him too. Cotton Whigs may have been pleased, but many more in his home state and beyond denounced the senator's treachery. As Wendell Phillips challenged him, "If, in the lowest deep, there be a lower deep for profligate statesmen, let all former apostates stand aside and leave it vacant. Hell, from beneath, is moved for thee at thy coming."

An "anti-Webster" meeting was held at Faneuil Hall. Among those who rallied were the Crafts. Ellen's name was invoked repeatedly. Theodore Parker, the White rebel preacher whose house William and Ellen had visited the night before, asked his audience to imagine a scene of "hot pursuit" of Ellen Craft down Merchant's Row.

"Suppose the weary fugitive takes refuge in Faneuil Hall, and here, in the old Cradle of Liberty . . . the bloodhounds seize their prey! Imagine Mr. Webster . . . looking on, cheering the slave hunter, intercepting the fugitive fleeing for her life."

But it was a dynamic younger preacher, Reverend Samuel Ringgold Ward of New York—known as the "black Daniel Webster"—who brought down the house. This self-emancipated preacher had already been considered for the vice presidency of the United States by the Liberty Party and would soon make history as the first Black person to be nominated for that office. Ward excoriated the "Northern doughfaces"—pliable collaborators—who would "lick up the spittle of the slaveocrats and swear it is delicious."

He, too, spoke of Ellen, whom he had accompanied that night, noting: "She is far whiter than many who come here slave catching." When he called for rebellion, declaring "the right of revolution," the applause was "rapturous."

Two days later, at the African Meeting House, Ward would urge his fellow "colored citizens" to "be ready in the trial hour"—to "live *freemen* in Boston and die *freemen* in Boston"—noting that "slave hunters were already infesting Boston."

Ward was right: Webster's words alone had emboldened slavers and kidnappers to spring North. Ellen was the first to feel their force. At an abolitionist assembly in Plymouth, it was reported that six slave hunters had come for her. (Nothing more is known, only that they did not succeed.) Other reports described another Macon slave hunter on the prowl. However, the Crafts might have faced their closest call yet not from professional kidnappers but from two moneyed gentlemen who greeted William inside his own store.

———

William recognized his brother's enslaver—Isaac Scott, tall and gaunt, and dark for a White man, with a striking physical resemblance to Abraham Lincoln, as a friend recalled. Scott considered himself a "self-made man," or "one who without means or education has done well so far in this world." Like Hugh Craft, William's former enslaver, Scott, was an orphan who left school to become a businessman. But unlike Craft, he won most of his bets as a cotton broker, banker, and railroad magnate, and more and more, his business took him North. One day in the future, Scott would leave the South with his family, steaming his way to New York at the end of the Civil War. But for now, he styled himself as a proud Unionist of the South.

Next to Scott stood a second businessman, Joseph Story Fay, whom Scott affectionately called Story. Born across the river in Cambridge, Massachusetts, Fay lived in Savannah, where he made his money in cotton and was also an enslaver. Standing together, they showed that the lines between Northern and Southern business interests—"Lords of the Loom" and "Lords of the Lash"—could be fine.

For his part, Scott had the practiced eye of a businessman. He could surely see that the man known in Macon as "Bill" was prospering in his store. Scott was known as a man of few words, strong likes and dislikes, and powerful grudges. He got to his point: Wouldn't William— or Bill—like to buy his brother's freedom?

No doubt William would have longed to be reunited with Charles, a blacksmith, the last sibling whom their enslaver had sold before William and his sister, but the risk was too high. He could be sure of nothing but the threat to his safety and to Ellen's. He did what he could to appease the men, and once they left, he moved his business.

The new site was near the rancid waters and the planned county jail, but it was also close to the Haydens and others who would stand by him. The men's visitation had sounded a warning, for if Scott had found William, so too could Robert Collins. And if the Crafts guessed that the men had ties to their enslavers, they would have been right. Not only Scott, but Fay considered himself a friend to Collins, and he was in a good position to keep an eye on the Crafts—especially now that he could identify William by sight.

Henry Box Brown would have his own close call. "Attempt to Kidnap!" the papers read. Brown was in Providence, Rhode Island, exhibiting a moving panorama, *Mirror of Slavery*, which told a story containing graphic images of Black bodies being seized, sold, tortured, and included a picture of Ellen in flight. He was walking in broad daylight when a group of men encircled and savagely beat him, and tried to put him in a carriage. But even outnumbered, Brown "proved too strong" for his attackers, and then fought back in court.

Nowhere in New England was safe, and William and Ellen must have considered their options: settlements in Canada, for instance, their original destination. But once again the Crafts surveyed the possibilities with what some might have called optimism, others recklessness. They refused to leave the lives they had built and stood their ground, praying all the while that the compromise proposed by Clay and endorsed by Webster would not become the law of the land. On this wager, they lost.

OCTOPUS POWERS

|||||||||||||||||||||||||

Cannons boomed on Boston Common, one hundred shots in controlled succession, signaling the passage of the Compromise of 1850—and with it, a new Fugitive Slave Act. The sound carried over Boston and for miles beyond, touching draymen at the wharves; laundresses with soiled, wet clothes; Harvard professors; merchants with fine-tipped pens; mothers nursing babies. Any and all may have paused to listen and wonder. What, if anything, would the sound mean for them?

The Compromise had passed over extreme divisions, bearing a presidential signature not from a slaver—for Zachary Taylor had died of a fever after enjoying too much iced fruit on a hot July Fourth, or possibly, it was suspected, the cholera—but by his replacement, a man from New York. Despite being a Northerner, Millard Fillmore did not favor abolitionism, as Southerners had feared, and was more supportive of the Compromise measures than his predecessor, finally signing them into law on September 18, 1850. The president was not alone. As Samuel Ringgold Ward would point out, Northerners outnumbered Southerners in Congress: "This law of barbarism was passed, therefore, by Northern men."

None of the Great Triumvirate was there to see it through. Within a month after Webster's speech, Calhoun's body was laid out in the Capitol, with both Clay and Webster as Senate pallbearers. Clay had since left the Capitol, along with Webster, who became Fillmore's secretary of state, and in that role, the new Fugitive Slave Act's chief executor.

The first shot from the cannons, enraged and dissonant, held everyone in its sound—then gave way to vastly different reactions. For "Union men," free White citizens such as Fillmore and Webster, the sound bursts were the drumbeat of celebration, of a nation saved. There would be joyful Union parties in Boston, as there would be across the land, the cannon's call echoed in glasses clinking to cheers. At one dinner party, a well-heeled Bostonian was heard expressing his hopes that "the first fugitive slave who should come to Boston would be seized and sent back!" For others, though, the firing of the weapon could not be separated from its original purpose: war.

The new law granted enslavers what Ibram X. Kendi has called "octopus powers," enabling them to "stretch their tentacles out to the North." Now, miles away in Macon, people such as Collins could reach long into other states, on their own or with proxies, and, by-passing state officials, appeal to federally appointed commissioners who had outsized powers, too. On Collins's word, and those of two identifying witnesses—with no testimony allowed from the alleged fugitives—these United States Commissioners could send people like the Crafts (or those who might be mistaken for them) back to slavery. They would earn $10 for every positive judgment, $5 for dismissals.

Should there be resistance, "reasonable force and restraint" might be deployed, armed posses raised to hunt down the fugitives. "Every good citizen" was required to answer the call to serve as nothing less than slave patrol. This is how the octopus squeezed. Those who assisted fugitives—hid them, fed them, got in the way—faced the prospect of up to six months in jail and a $1,000 fine, plus $1,000 more for each person who escaped.

The octopus law had outrageous reach, affecting everyone from judges, to ordinary citizens, to Southern refugees, to anyone who might be pointed out as a slave, as property—and, as Ellen's case reminded all, whether visibly Black or not. There was no due process, no jury for the "accused," no rights of habeas corpus, simply the enslavers' word and eyewitness affirmations.

Now, more than ever, every Black person in the United States of America—formerly enslaved or freeborn—was in danger, since, with no means of self-defense, any Black person might be kidnapped into slavery. To each, it came down to a terrible calculus: stay (to hide, wait, or fight) or leave the country.

As quietly as they came, with hard-earned belongings, with loved ones or alone, with history and urgency, Black people slipped out of this city upon a hill, by train, foot, carriage. Some were mothers and fathers with babies in their arms, determined that their children would never see the world they had left. Some were seasoned elders, others young and Northern born. They left in haste but with the best defense they could, with many of them "well armed."

Most did not leave their names, their stories, but they left holes. Within twenty-four hours of the law's passage, the Reverend Theodore Parker reported, more than thirty Black Bostonians were gone from the city. Church pews soon sat empty, none more dramatically than in Reverend Leonard Grimes's Twelfth Baptist Church—the Fugitive Slave Church—where a full third of the faithful, some sixty parishioners, disappeared. Construction was paused indefinitely, and whereas the church-in-progress once shone as a sign of what the community could build up, the unfinished house of worship now stood as a ghostly reminder of the work still left to be done, in the city and the nation. In the coming years, twenty-thousand refugees would escape to Canada in an unprecedented mass "exodus."

The choice came to the Hayden house—not just to those who sought refuge there but also to their hosts. Lewis Hayden was legally emancipated: only recently, he had negotiated and paid for the release of the minister who had helped him escape bondage and who had been in prison all this time. Hayden's own freedom was included in the deal. But Hayden's wife, Harriet, and therefore their children, remained enslaved by law.

Hayden knew too well where this might lead. He was haunted by his remembrances of loved ones lost, his beautiful, "part-Indian" mother, who suffered such abuse at the hands of the rapist who bought her, that she had "crazy turns." As her son remembered, her long, black hair turned all white. She tried to kill herself, by knife, by hanging. Once, when Hayden was seven or eight years old, his mother was let out from jail to see her children, in the hopes that their presence would help her "get quiet." He recalled how she had sprung at him, saying, "I'll fix you so they'll never get you!" She was soon tied up and carried away.

"Sometimes," he added, "when she was in her right mind, she used to tell me what things they had done." He remembered these stories too, though he would not reveal them publicly.

Like William, Hayden could recall the sale of his siblings one by one; he himself was traded for a pair of carriage horses. But Hayden remembered another transformative event, one that continued to sustain him and prepare him for a new role in the present moment.

In his boyhood, the Marquis de Lafayette had come to town, inspiring celebrations in Kentucky, where Hayden was enslaved. All the people lined the streets to see "America's favorite fighting French man" as he drove by on a fine barouche. As he passed the child Hayden sitting on a fence, the general quietly bowed, offering a greeting of respect and an acknowledgment of his humanity that Hayden would never forget.

"That act burnt his image upon my heart," as he expressed, "so that I never shall need a permit to recall it." This act, owned as a memory, inspired Hayden's self-emancipation and ignited a revolutionary zeal. Now, with a general's spirit, he determined to make a stand in Boston, mobilizing his people for battle.

The choice came to William and Ellen. They, too, knew what would be wagered in this war and the cruelties that might await them if recaptured into the South, including beating, branding, immolation. For the couple, this was a bittersweet time. After months of hard work, William reported a yearly gross income of $700, and Ellen's business was evidently thriving too. From their earnings, each would contribute a quarter of a dollar to the antislavery cause. Combined, their earnings may have allowed them to move into their own small home by William's store, and they were about to start night school.

There may have been flutters of another dream. A Scottish abolitionist who came to know the Crafts, Eliza Wigham, would report later that just as the law passed, the Crafts were expecting a baby. As with claims made by other White activists regarding a child born in slavery, this statement goes uncorroborated. If Ellen was pregnant, neither she nor William would ever speak of it. But at the very least, the dream so long deferred was a dream once more imperiled.

Together William and Ellen had risked their lives in flight to this American "cradle of liberty," where the hand of Robert Collins could not extend—until this moment. With the granting of "octopus powers," neither they nor any life they created, now or in the future, could be at rest. Even so, the Crafts resolved to stay, exercising the full right of mobility: to move *and* stop at will. Joining hands with the Haydens and other community activists, they would help lead a new revolution.

REVOLUTIONARIES

|||||||||||||||||||||||||||||||

The African Meeting House was lit against the dark October night. A school, a church, a sanctuary, the building known as Black Boston's Fanueil Hall held a "vast concourse," as the *Liberator* reported, with "fugitives and their friends."

Lewis Hayden was president of the meeting, with his right-hand man, William Craft, standing by him as one of three vice presidents. Beside them were other leaders in the movement to come, including two whose work demanded they leave no footprints, but whose just steps walk a line to the present.

Together with Hayden, William Cooper Nell and Robert Morris were their own Great Triumvirate. Nell, a journalist and historian, would act as a conduit between the Crafts—and others like them—and the outside world in the coming days. He could fill volumes with what he had seen, as he would write in exhausted haste to an activist friend. But he would not leave further evidence of his part in their story, a sad irony, since he personally ensured that others' heroism would be remembered and recorded.

Then there was Robert Morris, who lived out the legacy of a powerful gift, a trust he would transfer. Now a stylishly suited man of twenty-seven, Morris had been just thirteen years old, waiting tables, when a White lawyer, Ellis Gray Loring, recognizing exceptional qualities in him, negotiated with Morris's mother to have him work in Loring's home. Eventually, with Loring as his mentor, Morris trained in the law to became one of the nation's first Black attorneys.

Morris would pass on the gift he received. Just now, an impoverished boy was fresh off the boat from Ireland. He had lost his father, was spat upon and reviled as an outsider (as the Irish often were), and faced beatings at school. Like Loring before him, Morris would see something exceptional in this child, hire him in his office, and mentor him. The boy's name was Patrick Collins, and he would rise to become mayor of Boston.

In the church where Morris, Nell, and others stood as leaders were the foot soldiers in the mobilization to come. Filling every pew and gallery, and streaming in through multiple doors, they came: draymen and domestics, seamen and seamstresses, and "men of over-alls," or "men of the wharf"—people of labor and action. It was these "Colored Citizens," as they called themselves, uncredited in many histories, who would perform the riskiest, most essential work of helping and protecting fugitives, putting their lives on the line in the days to come.

Morris called for a reading of the report that the elected leaders had written, William among them. Then Nell rose to deliver the soaring words: the "Declaration of Sentiments of the Colored Citizens of Boston."

Remember, these Colored Citizens declared valiantly, that "God made all men free," and that America's Revolution was their history, too—that the first martyr to the cause was colonist Crispus Attucks, a "colored man," shot and killed in the 1770 Boston Massacre.

Remember, they exhorted, that "colored men" had fought in the American Revolution and in the War of 1812, believing that all who fought would be "invited to the banquet" in the aftermath.

"But lo!" went the cry: "The white man's banquet has been held, and loud peals to liberty have reached the sky above; but the colored American's share has been to stand outside and wait for the crumbs that fell from Liberty's festive board."

As earlier revolutionaries had cried, "GIVE ME LIBERTY OR GIVE ME DEATH!" so the Colored Citizens proclaimed that they, too, would "*die* freemen rather than *live* as slaves." They proposed a League of Freedom to lead the resistance and called upon the citizens of Boston to join them at Fanueil Hall, to show truly on which side of freedom they stood.

Then spoke the soloists, one by one. Joshua Bowen Smith, a genius "Prince of Caterers," who would refuse his culinary services to Daniel Webster, advised all to arm themselves with a Colt revolver, selling their coats if need be. But it was Robert Johnson, doctor to the people, who struck the most poignant chord.

Johnson had been stolen as a child from his home by the Gambia River and endured the horrors of the Middle Passage. The doctor would recall his hometown in West Africa as a place of community, where his last free act was to pick fresh figs with his aunt, whom he never saw again. He reached out then to the women in the hall—washer women, domestics, all those who labored in hotels and boardinghouses—asking them to be on "the constant look-out for the Southern slave-catcher or the Northern accessory" and to "be prepared for any emergency."

The women heard him with pleasure and proudly affirmed, reminding all that it was women like them who had helped rescue two enslaved women from Boston's Supreme Court, singing, "Go—go!" "Don't stop!" This spirit, they promised, was alive and well in them.

William Lloyd Garrison also stood to speak, one of several White activists present. Though he declared his own preference for nonresistance, he voiced his support for those convened and the choices they might make. The passage of this Fugitive Slave Act had inaugurated a new era of militancy, in line with the nation's own War of Independence, which pacifists and philosophers, try as they might, could not deny. Garrison promised to submit a letter to clergy, causing cheers to reach the rafters as he read the call for these men to "lift (their) voices like a trumpet."

Would they rise? Would others lend their voices and their power, to stand beside their fellow colored citizens at Boston's boasted Cradle of Liberty? Such were the questions that flew forth from the warmth of the Meeting House and into the surrounding darkness.

Ten nights later, they answered the call by the thousands—from three thousand to six thousand, depending on the count, engulfing Faneuil Hall. They were young and old, of all colors, women and men, many in serviceable clothes that marked them as members of the working class. The galleries, reserved for ladies, were filled, while outside, hundreds more were turned away. It was the "bone and the muscle" of society, brought together like one mind—"like kindred drops into one," as a reporter marveled, feeling the pulse. "There was a considerable number of our colored population present," as it was observed, "listening as for their lives."

Less represented, this night, were middle-aged "men of prominence," or White men in their prime, as noted by one who fit the bill: Richard Henry Dana, author of Two Years Before the Mast. But it was one such man, Charles Francis Adams, son of one United States president and grandson of another, who would serve as this meeting's president. Likening the Fugitive Slave Law to a thunderbolt, he declared it time to act, to repeal, to empathize.

Now the hall began to shake with loud chants from every corner, demanding the great man who had been summoned by telegraph for his clarion call: *"Douglass! Douglass!"*

Frederick Douglass had ridden a long way from Rochester. He was visibly tired. But he soon cleared a path toward the stage, as palm struck palm.

Douglass conjured the law and its consequences: the outrage that "any villain" who made an oath could cause any person he chose to be "seized anywhere, ironed, and carried back into bondage." The thousands yelled back, *"Shame! shame!"*

Douglass spoke to the fear he saw even in Boston, among those who knew that recapture meant revenge. As he explained, the slavers themselves were well aware that "one who has tasted the sweets of liberty can never again make a profitable slave."

Cheers interrupted him, but Douglass pressed on: "They therefore pursue the slaves in order to make examples of them; and the slave knows that, if returned, he will have to submit to excruciating torture." (*"Sensation,"* noted one journalist.) "Hence these tears, hence this dark train going out from the land, as if fleeing from death."

Douglass told of a woman in New Bedford who had hidden herself in the hold of a ship, unmoving, despite efforts to "smoke" her out. She had run before and knew the consequences. Once, her enslaver had stripped and whipped her, then "washed her back in brine, and nailed her by the right ear to a fence rail and in her agony, she tore off the outer rim of her ear."

Douglass demanded whether they would let the slave hunters carry the woman back. A universal *"No!"* was the reply, with more roars of *"No!"* as he called the questions again.

One affirmative was heard, however, from a journalist who yelled, "Yes, the laws until repealed, must be obeyed!"

Immediately, an impeccably dressed Black man, small in frame but large in stature, stood in his way, staring hard, prompting the reporter to ask: "I believe, young man, you are the errand boy of Mr. Ellis Gray Loring?"

"No, sir," was the response. "I am Robert Morris—a lawyer, and a Justice of the Peace."

No further affirmatives were reported again.

The cheering only grew more frenzied as Douglass declared his people's resolve "rather to die than to go back."

"That's the talk!" they shouted, *"Repeat it again!"*

Support this bill, Douglass warned, and be "prepared to see the streets of Boston flowing with innocent blood"—"to see suffering such as perhaps no other country has witnessed," to see the slave hunter "bear the chained slave back, or . . . be murdered in your streets."

It was a long way from last May at the Melodeon, when Douglass's evocation of bloodshed had played to boos and shouts. Now this new revolutionary hero was hailed with rounds of torrential applause. As Douglass made clear, the time for action had come.

What kind of action was required? This would be the burning question, for each and all. A Committee of Safety and Vigilance (or Vigilance Committee) was called for, but it would be loose and general in its positions, holding together, as it did, so many disparate minds. There were already signs of tension. Some, such as Charles Lenox Remond, a Black activist of Salem, demanded a harder line.

Remond's stance gained traction at the end of the night through Reverend Nathaniel Colver, the White abolitionist Baptist pastor of Boston's Tremont Street Church, who shouted to deafening applause: "CONSTITUTION OR NO CONSTITUTION, LAW OR NO LAW, WE WILL NOT ALLOW A FUGITIVE SLAVE TO BE TAKEN FROM MASSACHUSETTS."

Colver closed with a story of a "strong and athletic Rhode Islander," who, while traveling, heard "cries of distress" from a log cabin. There he found "a man unmercifully beating his wife." Grabbing the man, the Rhode Islander "enfolded him in his strong embrace, hugging him up until the bones cracked, crying out, 'How I love you!'" until the man cried for mercy.

"Now," the preacher said, "if the slave hunter comes, and nobody else love him in this manner, I will." As Colver ended his speech, his hearers called for his declaration to be made resolution, passing it with a "tremendous 'Ay!'" at eleven o'clock.

The unity came none too soon. For at this late hour, the octopus had already begun to extend his tentacles. Slave catchers from Macon were en route to Boston, with Ellen and William in their sights.

MASTER SLAVE

||||||||||||||||||||||||||||

One thousand miles away in Macon, Robert Collins was ready. It had been a strange summer, fearsomely hot, even for Georgia, the temperature rising to a record 104 degrees in Jones County. Fresh food was fast to spoil, as was the temper of any person caught up in the debates over the Compromise—or submission, as it was sometimes called.

There had been strange deaths, too, that summer, beyond President Taylor's. Ellen's aunt Mary Eliza Healy had died suddenly, just as she was planning to be reunited with her children up north. Within months, Michael Morris Healy (her legal enslaver, who called her his wife) also passed. As he was otherwise healthy, it was suggested that he died of a broken heart.

Healy's personal property went to auction—the shotguns, the picture frames, a racehorse called Dunganon, all sold at bargain prices—while forty-nine-people he enslaved were hired out. Not included in the tally were the nine Healy children. Six were already in the North, passing at exclusive academies, while the youngest were trapped in Georgia. Only later did it become known that one of the older sons, perhaps disguised with whiskers, wig, and glasses, had secretly traveled South to rescue the younger siblings he had never seen—very possibly riding the same railroad lines north that their cousin Ellen Craft had ridden before.

The Healys would go on to remarkable lives. Among their achievements, one would become an Arctic explorer, another president of Georgetown University. Meanwhile, they were willed into a terrible paradox where, even as they were considered slaves by law, they became beneficiaries of the labor and sale of others. By their father's will, all other Healy slaves were sold when the Healys' youngest child came of age. One woman, Margaret, sued for freedom. When she lost, she and her children, William, Julia, Violet, and Martha Ann, were sold apart.

Upon hearing of Michael Morris Healy's death, Robert Collins may have eyed the property for sale—that quiet riverside land, the enslaved available for hire. But he kept his eye trained even more sharply on his family's legal property, or, technically, his wife's: Ellen, whom the Great Compromise, with its new Fugitive Slave Law, had finally put within reach.

Collins was no raging fire-eater gunning for war, not like the secessionists who roared into Macon by the thousands for a mass meeting—men like Robert Rhett of South Carolina invoking the late John C. Calhoun. Though long a Democrat, Collins was above all a Unionist who praised his country and its Constitution, and was known as a man of peace. When on a hot Georgia night, extremists had threatened to lynch a local newspaper editor, whom they suspected of abolitionist sympathies, it was Dr. Collins who talked everyone down, kept the man from hanging, and was celebrated for his justice.

Collins had kept busy since Ellen's disappearance nearly two years ago. His legal and financial battles had not stopped after the court appeal—indeed, he would continue to fight William B. Johnston for years. But somehow, as always, Collins had managed to come out on top. Among other ventures, he had been exploring a national railroad to California. Throughout this time, he had endured the scandalous news about Ellen and refrained from action, even when her location in Boston became known. The new law, however, gave him power and purpose.

Collins would claim that he had "no personal desire" to re-enslave Ellen—"the most trusted and faithful of my house servants"—that he was, in fact, "no more opposed to her freedom than those who would buy her liberty," as he would recount in a letter. Nor were her labor and monetary value his priorities. Instead, Collins believed he needed to pursue Ellen for reasons beyond himself: first, as an example to other slaves who might be tempted to follow in her and William's footsteps, but also as a test to prove that the rights of the South could be secure, and that the North would be true to the spirit of the Compromise, the Constitution, and the Union, or, in short, its word.

Here was his higher calling. Recapturing Ellen was no longer about restoring balance within Collins's own household or mastering his own fears, but about bringing order to the nation itself. Collins was convinced that the Fugitive Slave Law could and would be "faithfully executed," even in abolitionist Boston. In this, he stood opposed to many of his fellow slavers, who were sure the new act was as useless as the old, and would rather see him fail—and thereby motivate the South to secession—than broach a Compromise (or, they would say, submit). By bringing back Ellen, Collins hoped to prove the fire-eaters wrong, and keep his country whole.

Collins's ultimate goal was to preserve not only the Union but also an institution in which he fervently believed. Slavery, he maintained, was *not* the "moral, social, and political evil" that the North made it out to be, for there was "no system of servitude, on the globe, attended with less evil to master and servant, and to society, than that of slavery in the southern states."

He went so far as to say: "the free negroes of the south are in a far more desirable condition than the free negroes—and fugitive slaves, at the North." But it was the slaver's "privilege and right to determine when and how—and who of our slaves ought to be made freemen." And by his privilege and right, he willed that Ellen, for one, would not be one of them.

Collins was ready to take the lead, not just as the master of his house, but beyond, with larger political goals. Despite the recent attacks on his reputation, Collins was renowned for his financial investment in public works, the telegraph, and the railroads. That fall, he headed the Unionist ticket for election to an upcoming state convention that would decide Georgia's position on the Compromise, and he knew that capturing Ellen would boost his prospects. Next year, he would aim even higher, for the governorship. As he prepared for these elections, Collins aimed to make himself "the first public claimant of a fugitive slave before the people of Massachusetts," to prove that the Union should, and could, stand.

On a Friday in October, when the high heat of Georgia had finally calmed, he summoned two young local men to execute his word. He prepared the necessary documents, including a description of Ellen: "very light complexion, low and rather heavy in stature, about 22 years of age, straight hair, brown eyes," with "a scrofular effection," or scarring, "on one of her arms." Ira Taylor also presented a description of William: "cabinetmaker by trade, tall and well made, about 27 years of age, black (or rather brown), with black, woolly hair, and dark eyes."

Their main agent would be Willis Hughes, the blunt-mannered Macon jailer who Collins knew could be counted on to carry out difficult jobs, including physical punishments. Indeed, he was called a "public Negro whipper," and had once reputedly beaten Ellen's uncle nearly to death. As the city jailer, Hughes had dealt with fugitives and knew how to maintain order among the volatile mix of men, women, and children who were housed together in a single building. With him was tall, dark-haired John Knight, who, along with Hughes, hoped to launch his own business, making buckets. Knight was a few years younger than Hughes, still in his twenties, and more naive than his partner, but he had worked in the cabinetmaker's shop alongside William, and could identify both William and Ellen.

Collins and Taylor bid good-bye to their agents, with the hope that their proxies would soon return with their captives in bondage. Others, meanwhile, prayed for failure. There were Collins's enemies, for one, who dubbed him a "Sub," for submissionist, and would be charged in later days of publishing news of the agents' departure in a deliberate act of sabotage. Then there was the community known and beloved to William and Ellen.

At the secessionist meeting in Macon, a journalist observed a "large crowd of blacks" who listened as the "talk became *very peculiar* about the Northern people being about to make war upon the South, for the purpose of liberating the slave population." Fearing such language "in the hearing of the blacks," the majority spectators drove away the Black listeners.

Too late. No matter the burn of the fire-eaters, the enslaved in Macon who heard these words had been touched by the heat of other houses, like the African Meeting House in Boston—a different kind of fire, aimed to warm them.

From Macon, Hughes and Knight boarded the train to Savannah and, days later, arrived in Manhattan, where they were greeted by Joseph Story Fay—the man whose visit with Isaac Scott prompted William to move his store. Fay gave them letters of introduction to "gentlemen" of wealth and power in Boston, men who would stand by the law. They left for Boston at five o'clock on Friday, October 18, arriving near sunrise the next morning at a depot a few blocks east of Boston Common and opposite the largest hotel in New England.

The United States Hotel was a luxurious establishment, with hundreds of rooms, warm baths and showers, and three different dining rooms, all furnished in the modern style. Eschewing all comfort, Hughes signed the hotel book with a fake name. Within ten minutes, he went straight to work—now just a twenty-minute walk from where William and Ellen lived.

MEN FROM MACON

|||||||||||||||||||||||||||||||

The Crafts' would-be kidnapper, Willis H. Hughes (or William Hamilton of New York, as he was registered at the hotel) was a "short, rowdyish-looking fellow, five feet two, thirty or forty years of age," with "sandy hair, red whiskers, black short teeth" and a tendency to "chew and smoke," as would be recalled by unfriendly Bostonians in the coming days. Upon arriving in Boston, he probably worked his way through more tobacco than usual.

Finding the Crafts was no problem. In the public directory, William was listed under "cabinet makers" at 51 Cambridge Street, a quick stroll across the Common and over Beacon Hill. But getting him—with Ellen—was another story, and for that, Hughes required legal support, beginning with a warrant. This should have been easy enough to obtain, with all of Fay's contacts, including a lawyer. But that lawyer, one Mr. Sohier, was out of town, and so Hughes was left to venture forth alone to the courthouse square to meet an incompetent succession of men, who passed him from one to the next, as if in some absurd children's game.

Judge Levi Woodbury of the United States Circuit Court, a balding man with a sad, worried brow, claimed that he was not the "proper person" to issue the warrant. George Lunt, US district attorney, then refused the job, calling it "unpleasant business." Next there was Benjamin Hallett, who, as a federally appointed commissioner, had special powers under the new Fugitive Slave Law—powers that remained inaccessible to Hughes. But Hallett was unreachable all day, so that finally, an hour before midnight, Hughes went directly to the man's house at Louisburg Square, atop Beacon Hill.

Hughes made it known he wanted a warrant—now—so that he could "have the Negroes arrested." (In fact, the Crafts lived over the hill from the commissioner, five minutes away.) But to Hughes's astonishment, the commissioner said he should make the arrest without a warrant, *then* come back to him. Go to the heart of the Black community and remove the fugitives, without a posse, without the law? Give Hallett a pair of false ears, Hughes would later rage, and he would make a great addition for P. T. Barnum as a "fair specimen of a Boston ass."

Hughes handed the man a copy of the Fugitive Slave Law, to show him what he must do. After a brief study, Hallett said he would consider it overnight and respond in the morning.

Hughes trudged back to his hotel and resolved to hedge his bets. He would meet the commissioner in pursuit of the warrant, but he would also dispatch his partner, John Knight, to William's store—with a lure. At the very least, Knight would be in a position to provide positive identification of William, maybe more.

"Bill," or "Billy" was how they knew him—not *William* or *William Craft*, as he chose to be called. And so "Bill" was likely how he was greeted, inside his own store.

The shop stood around the corner from the Haydens' home, in a bustling building. Next door, Mr. F. C. Shephard managed his lace goods, Mrs. Eliza Stewart bred her foreign leeches, and Messrs. Brown and Garland painted their fancy signs. Horatio Jennings lived here, too, in the back of the house. There were many to bear witness should William shout.

William was also prepared. He had followed Joshua Bowen Smith's advice and kept a pistol beside him on his workbench. Still, the sight of the lank, lean, dark-haired man he had last seen last in Macon must have been jolting, even if life had prepared him to appear centered in the midst of the worst possible turmoil.

John Knight was about five foot ten, shorter than William not only in height but also in artisanal mastery. In the cabinetry shop where both had worked, it was William to whom clients handed their most treasured items for repair, not Knight, whose job was simply to take orders.

Knight expressed his joy at seeing his long-lost associate. William asked the man from Macon (pistol in hand, visible or not), Had he come alone? Knight said he did, explaining that he happened to be in town on business, and that he hoped that Bill would be willing to show him around.

When William said he was too busy, Knight suggested that perhaps William could come by the hotel later, with Ellen. They could talk about Ellen's mother—he knew that Ellen and Maria were close—and he could even deliver a note.

Knight soon left, but it would not be his last contact. Late that night, a messenger from the United States Hotel delivered a letter to William, signed with Knight's name. It read:

> *Boston, Tuesday, Oct 22, 1850, 11 o'clock, P.M.*
>
> *Wm Craft—Sir: I have to leave so Eirley in the moring that I cold not call according to promis, so if you want me to carry a letter home with me, you must bring it to the united States Hotel to morrow and leave it in Box 44 or come your self to morro Eavening after tea and bring it. let me no if you come your self by sending a note to Box 44 U.S. Hotel so that I may no whether to wate after tea or not by the Bearer. If your wif wants to se me you cold bring her with you if you come your self*
>
> *JOHN KNIGHT.*
>
> *PS I shall leave for home eirley a Thursday morning. JK.*

Knight would call the letter a forgery, and, in fact, it was—penned and signed by Hughes, who unwittingly gave himself away. Hughes's plan, as he would explain later, was "to get Craft into his (hotel) room & secure him." If they captured William, or so Hughes believed, "there would be no trouble about Ellen."

Instead, William learned from the hotel messenger that Knight had been lying. Not only had Knight *not* come alone, but he was traveling with the man the Crafts knew as the vicious Macon jailer.

The Crafts realized that they were now in far greater danger than when Isaac Scott had appeared in William's shop with Fay. But this time, they would not relocate. Having declared his resolution at the African Meeting House, William returned to his place of work the next day—taking care, however, to lock his door and keep his pistol fully loaded.

Over the hill, Willis Hughes also prepared. The morning after he had visited Hallett at Louisburg Square, the commissioner—not surprisingly—had put him off again, saying he needed to "make out his charges in a legal form." For this, Hughes knew he needed a good lawyer. It was fortunate for him that, with his employer's connections, he would have counsel arranged for him by the highest-ranking lawyer in the land: none other than Daniel Webster.

WEBSTER'S MEN

||||||||||||||||||||||||||||||

Since leaving Washington earlier in the month, Daniel Webster had been "a good deal sick," as he complained to President Millard Fillmore. He had been on the road continually, shuttling between homes in Marshfield, Massachusetts, and Franklin, New Hampshire, and then to Boston, where he was no longer senator from Massachusetts, but secretary of state of the United States.

The role was awkward. As Webster was quick to remind others, he had not been in power to vote for the Fugitive Slave Law, which had all the abolitionists up in arms. (He considered their conduct "wicked and abominable in the extreme.") Personally, he would have preferred amendments, including a jury trial, for example. Such modifications would do nothing for people like the Crafts, who had advertised their own fugitive identities, but it would provide a line of defense against kidnappings, which were becoming all too common. Still, Webster believed the act was constitutional, and that, as the law, it needed to be upheld.

President Fillmore shared his views. The very day after Knight visited William in his shop, Fillmore wrote to Webster that he intended to uphold the law, no matter the cost—even, if necessary, using military force. The matter was a delicate one that required further exploration. But, he wrote: "I mean at every sacrifice and at every hazard to perform my duty."

As he explained: "God knows I detest slavery, but it is an existing evil, for which we are not responsible, and we must endure it, and give it such protection, as is guaranteed by the Constitution, till we can get rid of it without destroying the last hope of free government in the world." Fillmore's letter to Webster was likely in transit when Hughes was seeking counsel, but it mattered little, for his secretary of state already shared his mind-set, and Webster knew just the man to pursue the Crafts.

Forty-three-year-old Colonel Seth J. Thomas was not a Boston Latin man, a Harvard man, or a Dartmouth man, as Webster was. Nor was he any relation to "those" Thomases, ancient Tories of wealth and privilege, who occupied the loveliest parts of Marshfield, on Boston's south shore. Pedigree and upbringing alone set Thomas apart from all the other counselors Hughes had consulted.

Thomas and Webster may have shared geographical ground in Marshfield, but Thomas had come up on the "other side of the Neck," by the South River, while "Squire Webster," as he was known, cultivated a thousand-acre estate on the Green Harbor. There Webster lovingly fertilized the sandy ground with seaweed, and trained geese and duck to roost at his pond. Thomas was in his late teens when Webster moved to Marshfield at the height of his fame, and was mesmerized by the great man's charms.

By the time Robert Collins—and, by proxy, Willis Hughes—was looking for a lawyer, Thomas had risen up in the world. Despite his "lack of educational opportunities in early life," he had trained his mind and body in business and the military, through politics, and law. Originally a Hanover Street hatter, he had left the trade to study under Daniel Webster's partner in Boston.

Thomas became especially known for swaying juries. He was a good speaker, "genial" (as would be recalled), methodical in his presentation, and, with his life experience behind him, unafraid to take a difficult stand. He also shared a hallway and a toilet with Webster, occupying a small office across from Webster's large one, on the corner of Court and Tremont Streets in Boston. When the secretary of state was in town, the two men crossed paths nearly every morning.

Webster had just arrived in Boston when the Georgians needed an attorney. Called upon to connect them to counsel, he had only to look across the hall. While others would make the actual introduction, Webster took time to write his request—and expectations—on his fine stationery (which Thomas, for one, appreciated). Though the letter is lost, others would recall his points. He said he sought in Thomas a lawyer "who could not be intimidated," and he made clear that the "existing law should be executed, no matter how unpopular."

"Unpopular" would be an understatement. In time, as he came to represent more Southerners, Thomas would be called the "legal pimp of the slave catchers," and worse. Others sympathetic to Thomas would say it was a "repugnant duty," and that he took on such cases with "great personal reluctance," but he understood the national stakes. As Thomas reflected later: "They were not pleasant cases, but I conducted them the best I could."

Thomas and Hughes were both trained for combat, Hughes in the Second Seminole War and as a member of the Macon Volunteers; Thomas in the Massachusetts militia. Together the two men marched into Court Square, ready for battle.

Unfortunately, they hit a wall with Judge Peleg Sprague. Even with a lawyer by his side, Hughes encountered the same infuriating delays. As it so happened, Sprague had been approached by other men that day. The Georgians had their allies, but so did William and Ellen.

The evening after Knight had visited William, the Vigilance Committee had convened at 46 Washington Street, in the legal heart of the city. The coalition born at Fanueil Hall was now eighty members strong and growing exponentially, with many subgroups, including a legal committee formed to watch for warrants, construct legal obstacles, and "alarm the town." Such vigilance was urgently needed, since beyond the Georgians, other kidnappers were on the prowl.

Attorneys Ellis Gray Loring and Samuel E. Sewell visited Judge Sprague in his chambers, demanding whether he had issued any warrants. Sprague declined to answer, but also on that day, he refused Hughes's warrant request, "equivocat(ing) and shuffl(ing)," as Hughes would recall in writing, just like all the others before.

A breakthrough finally came with George Ticknor Curtis, one of Daniel Webster's close friends. Curtis had stood by Webster in the setting sun as a crowd cheered the then-senator on his return to Boston earlier that year soon after the seventh of March. Curtis and his brother, Benjamin Robbins Curtis, were commonly called Cotton Whigs—Northern Whigs who were close with the cotton planter class.

The "Curtii," as members of the prominent Curtis clan were called, were famously conservative. It was another Curtis relation, Charles P. Curtis, who had been heard declaring his hope that the first fugitive slave who came to Boston would be "seized and sent back!" Yet the Curtii would prove unpredictable. That very year, 1850, a man named Dred Scott won an interstate suit against his enslaver, but his case would eventually be appealed before the Supreme Court. George T. Curtis would be his counsel, and Benjamin R. Curtis would be one of two justices to dissent when the Supreme Court finally rejected Scott's claim to freedom.

Commissioner George Curtis, too, would take his time, earning Hughes's wrath, but he would ultimately be supportive. As he would explain to Hughes and later to Daniel Webster, he was perfectly willing to execute the law, but because the stakes were so high—this being the first test case in Boston, and with so much talk of resistance—he believed that the warrant should not be issued by a mere commissioner, as permitted by the Fugitive Slave Law, but by the Circuit Court of the United States.

The Georgians' lawyer agreed that a court warrant was preferable, but pointed out a challenge. A big patent case was under way, and it would tie up the court for days. This is where Curtis proposed a novel solution. He offered to broker a special meeting with the judges, promising that if some agreement could not be reached there, he would issue the warrant himself. Either way, the Georgians would have their warrant by nine o'clock the next morning.

So, the secret meeting began. At five thirty, the court was cleared, the heavy doors pulled closed. Present were four commissioners, two judges, and a deputy marshal—most of whom Hughes had already met. In fact, all but one of the officials whom Hughes had previously approached were in the room, and together they proved willing to take action.

The patent case that was tying up the court was also being judged and lawyered by the men present, who agreed to suspend the case in the morning, so that warrants could be issued for the Crafts. They agreed further to pause the patent case again once the Crafts were arrested, so that the fugitives could be swiftly processed and released to their agents. Despite all of their delays, Boston's legal minds were collectively resolved to uphold the Fugitive Slave Law, and to have the Crafts sent out of Boston as soon as possible and back in bondage.

When the doors reopened, Hughes and his lawyer had to be relieved by the outcome, if not exactly elated. The warrants would be issued in open court, which guaranteed that the events would play out in full public view. But if Hughes and Thomas worried the public issuance of the warrant would give the fugitives advance warning of their imminent arrest, they were mistaken. The word was already out.

THE COMMISSIONER'S WIFE

|||||||||||||||||||||||||||||||||

Ellen was working when she heard the news. While she was at a preacher's house on Mount Vernon Street, learning upholstering, the wife of a United States commissioner—fortunately, a friend—came by. This was Susan Tracy Howe Hillard, who lived over the gemlike green of Louisburg Square, a stone's throw from the house of another Commissioner, whom the Macon jailer had visited two nights before.

Hillard did not want to alarm Ellen, so she tried to be subtle, saying only that she needed Ellen to help her with some work. Ellen, however, read the untold story on her face and burst into tears. After a short, fierce cry, she grew quiet, as Hillard would remember, and was fully composed by the time they reached the street. She remained outwardly serene in the hours to come, as the two women moved quietly to the commissioner's house at 62 Pinckney Street.

Susan Hillard and her husband were of two minds when it came to politics, as they were on other subjects, their marriage suffering early on from the death of their only son at two years old. Though George Hillard's legal partner was Charles Sumner, a noted abolitionist, Hillard was an "ardent Webster Whig." His wife, in contrast, hid fugitives in their attic. However distant he might have been, he must have known. Nevertheless, he did not breathe a word.

In the ell of the house was a closet, and in the ceiling of that closet, a trapdoor that led to a space beneath the slanted roof: a single shaft, which opened beneath a skylight, brought in air. It was here that Susan Hillard delivered Ellen.

The Crafts would be apart that night, with Ellen at the Hillards' and William hidden in the South End. Both were now in the heart of the proverbial lion's den, as they waited to learn if justice would be served come morning.

"TO THE RESCUE!"

||||||||||||||||||||||||||||

The judges delivered. In an open court ablaze with excitement, the warrants for William and Ellen Craft were made out fast, then signed by a curious hand. Though credit would go to Judge Woodbury, the signature came from Roger B. Taney, chief justice of the US Supreme Court, who was riding the circuit at that time, and would later be remembered for his ruling in the Dred Scott case.

There was no containing the news as the Georgians, warrants in hand, marched to the offices of the US Marshal, one floor down. Hughes was rearing to "go and point out the negroes," sure that William was at his shop, less than fifteen minutes on foot, even closer by horseback.

The young marshal might not have been so keen, however. Thirty-year-old Charles Devens was a lifelong Massachusetts man, and relatively new to his position. Personally, he was against slavery, he had a legal background, and he had been warned. Lawyers from the Vigilance Committee had paid him a visit, advising him that since this was a civil matter, not a criminal case, it would be illegal to force or knock down any doors. Anyone who did so would be sued. There to remind the marshal of the limits to his power, if need be, was one of the most important behind-the-scenes players on the Vigilance Committee: Robert Morris, officially on its finance team, but friend and counsel to the Crafts.

What happened next would be disputed; Hughes would blame Devens for dawdling, while Devens would point to other delays. But on this much, all would agree: the hunt for the Crafts did not begin right away. Instead, as the warrants were examined and corrected (words blackened and crossed out), the marshal went to the navy yard to arrange for a special jail. For, no matter his private beliefs, Devens was ready to execute the law and prepared for the eventuality that William and Ellen would be caught.

If the Southerners nurtured any hope of keeping their mission a secret, it must have vanished the moment they emerged from the courthouse—unrecognized, thankfully. As far as they could see were men and women, Black and White, mixed together in a spectacle of protest.

Most shocking to Hughes was the presence of a well-dressed White man on a street corner, lifted high atop a dry-goods box, who urged the "Negroes and their friends" to arm themselves with Bowie knives, daggers, and pistols. Resist unto death! he exhorted. "Shoot down all slave catchers from the South"—disturbing signs of troubles to come.

By noon, signs flew all over Boston's streets:

TO THE RESCUE!
Three fugitives about to be Arrested!!
WILLIAM CRAFTS SUPPOSED TO BE ONE!
BE ON THE ALERT!
NO TIME TO BE LOST!

The third fugitive, one William Jones, soon left for Canada, while the man hired to capture him remained in town for the "general hunt." Some of the Crafts' friends urged them to flee as well. They were too much in the light—a temptation for bounty hunters, as well as a trophy for slavers if they were caught. This, however, was exactly why the couple resolved to stay, for if even they could be chased out or captured, what hope was there for anyone else?

One thousand miles were enough; William did not intend to run any farther. He had seen enough carnage for a lifetime. He had seen people he had known and cared for chased down and tortured by men like Willis Hughes. But this was not the South. Here he was named in census records as a business owner, possessed a gun and other property. He vowed to face down any and all who tried to rob him, for his own sake and for his people—to die, if need be, in freedom's war.

Making his shop his fort, his clothes and bed moved alongside his workbench, doors barred, he set himself calmly to work, a pair of pistols and a Bible by his side—full protection, body and soul. Reporters would describe him as a "Spartacus of his race" or "champion of his people," ready "to sell his freedom with his life," a hero for his times.

Outside his store on Cambridge Street, friends stood guard. The "negro population," as it was reported, "were in a state of intense excitement, armed and determined upon resistance. No man could approach within a hundred yards of Craft's shop without being seen by a hundred eyes, and a signal would call a powerful body at a moment's warning."

Meanwhile, the spy hired by the marshal's office would somehow miss it all. The thirty-four-year-old moonlighting night watchman might not have been the ideal person for the job: when first approached, he made it clear that anonymity and avoiding personal injury were his priorities. If not actually a double agent, he unwittingly served the other side. Citing his repeated reports that the Crafts were nowhere to be found, the marshal's office would insist that it was doing all it could. The office would further claim that the Georgians had opposed a direct charge into the neighborhood, as the marshal and his men were sure to be recognized, Hughes railing: "You might as well go with a drum."

But newspapers told different story. According to one source, constables and police officers had voiced their protest to the marshal's office, "flatly refus(ing)" to capture the alleged fugitives. Scouts, moreover, were said to have reported that the only way the Crafts could be seized was if an outer door was broken, and in that case, "the process could only be served by bloodshed." One day Charles Devens would distinguish himself as a general in the Union army, and be wounded in battle three times, but in 1850 it seems he was not prepared for a war.

By Friday afternoon, the door that protected William belonged to Louis and Harriet Hayden, who had convinced their friend to move back into their home. It was reported that Lewis had prepared two kegs of gunpowder, resolving to blow up his home rather than surrender his guest. Those who witnessed the moment never forgot the "heroic frenzy of the resolute black face" as Hayden stood ready, match in hand.

Ellen, too, wanted to stand beside William in the resistance but was finally persuaded to remain in hiding "for his sake"—and perhaps for the cause. All along the lecture circuit, as well as on their journey from the South, the Crafts had assumed complementary roles, William performing to applause, Ellen playing to expectation. Here, too, it would be no different. Ellen knew well that while her husband might be celebrated as a warrior and revolutionary—or a martyr—she could provide better publicity by her absence, not presence, on the front lines. Her personal desires would be on hold for now.

At some point, the Crafts were reunited briefly, and made a last good-bye, as they had at the door of a cottage in Macon not so long ago. William was fully aware as he beheld his wife that it might be for the last time. For just as he had then vowed to kill or be killed, so he resolved to make good on his promise to "live free or die," while Ellen—in defiance of all expectation that she would be "no trouble" without her husband—determined to take her own road and live on.

Ellen climbed into a horse-drawn chaise, where a middle-aged White doctor, Henry Ingersoll Bowditch, held the reins. Beyond the Common, over the long Mill Dam into Brookline she rode, the rank water high on either side of view, as she passed the tracks of the Boston and Worcester Railroad. By dusk, Bowditch's faithful steed, Fannie, pulled to a stop at an elegant mansion. There, a stylish young woman walked the piazza.

Mary Courzon would recall their arrival with excitement. In a smoky mist, a chaise pulled up fast, and Dr. Bowditch bounded up to the door. He asked for the family of Ellis Gray Loring, who were tenants. She told him they were away, but she might deliver a message. The doctor said he would be frank: he had Ellen Craft in the chaise, because a warrant was out for her arrest, and Loring's wife had offered her protection any time. Courzon did not hesitate, and moments later, Ellen emerged, to take shelter indoors.

She walked alone, but behind her stood an army. For the Colored Citizens convened again at the African Meeting House, William among them, even as slave hunters were known to be near. Together the community resolved again to "resist unto death," their voices rising in chorus with others who made like promises across the land, in towns small and large, in churches, halls, and kitchens. That night, two hundred souls would pledge their lives to defend Ellen and William. Meanwhile, others prepared to mount another kind of offensive.

"SLAVE HUNTERS
IN BOSTON!!!"

|||||||||||||||||||||||||||

The next day, Hughes returned to the marshal's office, ready to lead a posse, serve out the warrant, and take the Crafts. But as Hughes would tell it, Charles Devens claimed that William had left town—his lookout had said so. When Hughes countered with his scout's report, the conversation devolved. Hughes recalled: "He said his man reported that Bill was not there. I then stated my man reported Bill was there. He said my man was mistaken, for his man was reliable and could not be mistaken." In fact, Hughes's man was right, but the Georgian would have no time to prove it, since, just as he hoped to be bringing in his fugitives, he himself was placed under arrest.

This was the work of the Crafts' legal team—not the official legal arm of the Vigilance Committee, which included Charles Sumner, Samuel Sewell, and Richard Henry Dana, who went by the book, but an alternate, rogue tier of lawyers who worked with the glee of pranksters.

Hughes and Knight were charged with slander for having called William Craft a slave and thus "causing damage to his business and character," and for carrying dangerous weapons with the intent to assault William. Bail was set at the extraordinary sum of $10,000 each—an amount that few could meet, and was expected to keep the slave hunters off the streets. Sheriff Erastus Rugg escorted the men back to Court Street, joined by a crowd that included a member of the Vigilance Committee, who demanded to know if Hughes was pursuing anyone else besides the Crafts.

"No!" roared the Southerner. "I've come for nobody else, and, damn 'em, I'll have *them* if I stay here to all eternity! It isn't the niggers I care about, *but it's the principle of the thing!*"

At the sheriff's office, Knight, too, nearly exploded after being slighted by the striking, if standoffish, soon-to-be senator, Charles Sumner, all of six feet four inches tall. As Knight extended his hand, the massive man pulled back his own, saying he would not be contaminated by the touch of a slave catcher. Knight then rose to a "towering

passion," and "began to talk in the Southern style of having satisfac-
tion." In fact, Sumner would one day suffer brutal retribution in this
Southern style, when a proslavery representative from South Carolina,
Preston Brooks, bludgeoned him with a cane on the floor of the United
States Senate. On this day, however, luck was on Sumner's side.

Luck was with the Georgians too, for their bail was quickly and
secretly met. And, while everyone was preoccupied with unmasking
the moneymen, the Georgians were able to slip out separately through
back doors, past the protesters who were eager to demonstrate their
fury but could not yet recognize their enemy.

That was soon to change. The purpose of the arrest was not only
to occupy the Southerners, but also to confirm their identities, Hughes
having sowed confusion with his hotel pseudonym. Now that they had
been seen by others who could describe them, new posters were made
up to alert all of Boston.

"SLAVE HUNTERS IN BOSTON!!!" the handbills screamed. They
included unflattering physical descriptions of the Georgians, with the
kinds of information about size and color usually found on public notices for escaped slaves.

Back at the hotel, while his world was still quiet, Knight saw "Negroes in large number." With a quick disguise, and his best impersonation of a New Englander's voice and manners, he moved cheerfully
among the assembly to glean news of the "kidnappers from the South,"
little imagining how fiercely he and Hughes would be pursued in the
coming days. The hunters would soon become prey.

THE COOLEST MAN

||||||||||||||||||||||||||

Over the Common on Beacon Hill, the battle cries rose. Hughes and Knight were not the only slave hunters in Boston. As Joshua Bowen Smith—the "Prince of Caterers" who advised his compatriots to invest in Colt revolvers—reported to fellow members of the Vigilance Committee, a posse of five or six had been seen stalking two restaurant workers in Court Square.

On Saturday, when Hughes and Knight were busy with their arrests, William had his own scare. He had been on Southac Street, talking with Frederick Douglass (lately returned to town), when a coach drove up dangerously close, with three or four menacing figures looming so near to William that it appeared they might grab him.

But William remained still, observing with "utmost coolness": "They can't have me alive." When the coach moved on, Douglass asked William if he "hadn't better leave the state."

"No," was the younger man's reply. "Our people have been pursued long enough." He would "live here and be free," or die.

Douglass took his friend's hand and, saying his name, offered these words in parting: "If you die, our people will live." In martyrdom, that is, William would give the cause new life.

He was called "the coolest man" in the city, who "armed himself with pistols" and "walked in the streets in the face of the sun." Reverend Theodore Parker saw him at the Haydens' house, at a table laid with weaponry. For William, the rebel preacher was a welcome anomaly. Too few clergymen dared to use their pulpits to fight the Fugitive Slave Law; some even preached its support. One minister, Orville Dewey, said he opposed slavery but called on fugitives to submit, declaring that he would "send his own brother or child into slavery, if needed to preserve the Union between the free and slaveholding States." William's feeling was that since he had done his turn in slavery, and the Reverend was ready to sacrifice, Dewey should take his place.

Theodore Parker was of another mind. He had never borne arms, but he was proudly descended of revolutionary ancestry, and his appetite for combat was palpable as he surveyed William's arsenal. "His powder had a good kernel," the minister reported, "and he kept it dry; his pistols were of excellent proof, the barrels true and clean; the trigger went easy. . . . I tested his poniard; the blade had a good temper, stiff enough, yet springy withal; the point was sharp.

"There was no law for him but the law of nature," was Parker's conclusion. He was armed and ready, as the Unitarian minister himself would be in time.

That very day, an offer came to the Crafts, one that might end their troubles, and restore order to Boston, or so some hoped. J. T. Stevenson, a friend of Daniel Webster, sent word that if William would "submit peaceably," he and Ellen would be purchased from their owners, "cost what it might." But William spoke on behalf of an entire community when he declared that he and Ellen represented *all* fugitives, and that if he gave up, "they would all be at the mercy of the slave catchers." Therefore, even if his freedom could be bought "for two cents," he would "not consent to compromise."

Back in Brookline, Ellen rejected the offer, too, though she did not speak as forcefully against the possibility of moving again. When asked about going to Canada, Ellen responded simply: "William does not want to go further."

Seared in her listener's memory was the look in Ellen's eye, "as if she had counted the whole cost and scorned to fear what man could do to her." There were rumors about what this might mean. According to Theodore Parker, Collins's plan was to sell Ellen "as a harlot in New Orleans." Whether or not the report was true, it was within his rights as an enslaver.

All that Saturday night, Ellen could barely sleep, startling at every sound. The day had been quiet, if tense, filled with fitting and stitching a dress for Mary Courzon, the young woman who had welcomed her. Mary could detect no outward signs of distress, for Ellen showed "perfect sweetness of temper and grace of manner" for hours on end, prompting Courzon to announce, "I liked her ever so much."

An afternoon messenger had brought a note in William's hand—a brief relief—but then the evening paper had come, dramatizing the dangers William had faced. Ellen took refuge in her room, and her hosts grew worried as they heard her weeping, and later, crying out in her sleep.

Ellen had a nightmare that she and her husband were running. Hughes, the jailer, was right behind them, followed closely by Daniel

Webster, who pointed a loaded pistol, ready to shoot. The dream may have played upon a feeling, for Daniel Webster was indeed close by—likely still in New Hampshire, but planning to head for Boston, with his eye trained on them.

On the Sabbath, the streets were thankfully still. William was exhausted, however, and in need of greater quiet, as was clear to the forty-two-year-old physician and vice president of the Massachusetts Anti-Slavery Society: Ellen's driver, Henry Ingersoll Bowditch.

William's militancy was making some around him nervous. As the Unitarian minister James Freeman Clarke was to recall: "He said he would kill the United States marshal if he attempted to arrest him. But some of his friends told him that this would be a very bad thing for his race and would only make their condition worse."

Figuring that it was unlikely that the slave catchers would have their writ served on Sunday, Dr. Bowditch offered to drive William to Ellen in Brookline, so that the couple might spend time together, and so William could rest. Inwardly, the doctor thought it "probable," despite everyone's best efforts, that William would be captured, and therefore that this might be "the last meeting the two of them would have in this world."

William accepted the buggy ride on one condition. He put a small weapon in Bowditch's hand as he said, "Doctor, I will go with you provided you will use this pistol."

William himself carried another pistol, along with a Colt revolver that Bowditch's own brother had given him. William was ready to use his weapons, and he needed to be sure that, if it came to an attempted arrest, the doctor would as well, no matter the Garrisonian's stance on nonresistance.

The doctor was shocked, being ordinarily in the business of stitching bodies together, not shooting them. But it would not be the first time he stepped outside his comfort zone. Eight years earlier, without thinking through the consequences, he had invited Frederick Douglass—whom he had just met—to his house for dinner. Even to walk beside a Black man in Boston had been a radical step, much less share his table at his home, especially where the doctor lived.

He had walked in fear then, as he did now, the stakes even higher—especially because, seated next to the doctor, between him and William, was his ten-year-old son, Nat, for whom this expedition was meant to serve as an antislavery lesson he would not forget.

But the words that came to the physician were these—"to do for others what you would wish done for yourself"—and thinking that he would "glory in slaying anyone who attempted to make me or my wife a slave," Bowditch answered, "Yes."

Giddy, willing, and no doubt more than a little scared, the doctor drove his horse over the Mill Dam bridge, past the toll—pistol in his right hand, reins in the left, his child to his side, the coolest man beside the boy, armed with a revolver and a blunderbuss (an ancestor of the shotgun).

"Together we might have shown a pretty smart fight," the doctor thought to himself, and it might well have been bloody, for his pistol, as he would discover, was loaded with three buckshots. Later still, Bowditch would store the gun in a memorial cabinet for his beloved son Nat, who would die after leading a charge during the Civil War.

The doctor was deeply relieved when they reached Brookline, passing no one but the toll man. They were greeted at the door by Mary Courzon, who was pleased by her beautiful new dress. (She loved to talk, and it would be very difficult in the days to come for her to keep silent when others asked her who had made her exquisite gown.) The Crafts were sequestered in the upstairs room at once, with strict orders from the doctor to keep that door closed, undisturbed.

Within ten minutes, they were back out. William declared that it was not right to stay, since, as he had learned from Ellen, Ellis Gray Loring was not in the house. This was not the first time William had taken such a stand. He had insisted that Ellen leave Commissioner Hillard's house because Hillard would risk not only high fines and jail time but also, potentially, his job.

Courzon and her aunt tried to persuade William to stay, with Ellen weighing in as well. Since it was late, and the weather was bad, might they stay until morning? William, however, was adamant and went to the door, while Ellen strapped on her bonnet, reportedly in tears.

With a guide leading them into the night, they moved to the home of Eliza and Samuel Philbrick, a few streets over, where they hid in the hired man's quarters, armed. The lady of the house was terrified that they would hurt themselves with their gun, but they would keep it loaded beside them, ready to discharge.

A WORLD TURNED
UPSIDE DOWN

||||||||||||||||||||||||||||

Across the river in Boston, the Georgians faced their own terrors, now that they were known. They could hardly step from their hotel before street boys pelted them with refuse, screaming obscenities. Others stalked them, throwing stones, alongside the boys. The cries went up everywhere: "Slave-hunters!" "Thieves!" "Bloodhounds!" Worse was still to come.

They had scarcely recovered from the weekend when, once again on Monday, the two men were greeted by a new Boston sheriff, Daniel J. Coburn, who informed them that they were under arrest, this time for conspiring to kidnap William Craft. Bail was set at another $10,000.

They were lucky that the money came fast, thanks to two locals: Patrick Riley—the deputy marshal, who had bailed them out previously, and had the marshal's blessing—alongside broker Hamilton Willis, Louisa May Alcott's cousin. Willis stood on Webster's side this day but would later lend his support to others like the Crafts. The bailing, however, was just the beginning of what would be, for the Georgians, an indelible day.

They emerged to see Court Square holding a vast army of men, women, and children—about two thousand people, by Knight's estimate—with "negroes" outnumbering White protesters three to one. Journalists reported far more White faces than Black, but whatever the composition, the protesters were united, shouting the refrain that Knight had come to loathe: "Slave-hunters! Slave-hunters! There go the slave-hunters!" Some called for feathers and tar.

A hackney coach soon drove up with a pair of white horses, wild with excitement. With the sheriff pushing through the crush, Hughes managed to jump inside, but "not without losing his hat and getting somewhat hustled about." Knight, meanwhile, was caught behind and forced to retreat, as protesters hissed and jeered, and tried to break the carriage doors. To his amazement, his partner was actually laughing from inside the coach, "making sport," though not for long.

The crowd became like one body, single-minded, with long, strong arms, as it covered the coach and rocked it from side to side, intent on taking the passenger. A Black man, it was reported, smashed open a window, aimed his weapon, and, for a quivering moment, had Hughes within his sights. But an unnamed member of the Vigilance Committee pulled him down.

The driver raised his whip and cracked it high, and with that, the coach convulsed forward, doors akimbo, people hanging off all sides. They held on, gripping the carriage spokes and dragging the wheels to stop the turning as some tumbled down, with one protester falling motionless before Parker's restaurant, where slave hunters had recently trolled.

The coach barreled up Court Street, the crowd chasing after it, screaming threats, and the city rang with their cries, the rage of the oppressed. Too late, others remembered Knight, who had managed to duck down and slip away, his hat pulled low. Though he would complain of hissing and coat tugging, and was made uneasy by the sight of a single Black man trailing him, he managed to hail a cab and return to the United States Hotel in safety.

All the while, a "mob of negroes" kept up with Hughes's carriage on foot. In blind flight, the coach careened up Cambridge Street, past a decrepit jail, and by Raymond's Wharf, where the cool blue of the Charles River awaited.

The carriage clattered over the Craigie Bridge, speeding through the toll, driver and rider hoping that the fare would deter the protesters, who clung hard. But a generous soul paid for all who persevered, and the protesters kept up, gaining fresh legs as they called out that a slave hunter was inside. Above all the others, one "colored man" straddled the roof, riding "in triumph through the street of Cambridge." It was protest in motion.

Only many miles later, in a landscape of cattle markets, slaughterhouses, and racetracks, where the animal stench was high, did the carriage at last outrun the protesters, rolling to a stop at Porter's Tavern in North Cambridge. But the driver, spooked by the ordeal, refused to continue service, leaving Hughes to find his own way back to Boston.

As he crossed the river, Hughes could little have imagined that the

Crafts, too, had passed over the Charles that very day, on their way to the home of Theodore Parker, at Exeter Place—just two blocks away, or a "good rifle shot," from the United States Hotel on Beach Street, where Hughes and Knight soon sat down for tea.

It must have been with shaking hands that the Georgians took up their cups late in the day. Then, before they were properly recovered, came Sheriff Coburn, again joined by a lawyer for the Crafts, Charles List, to say that the Georgians were under arrest for the third time, for conspiring to kidnap Ellen. They would have to return to Court Street to make their bail, set at $20,000 each (double the previous bailings), bringing the total dollars pledged in their defense to $80,000, or over $3 million today.

It was too much for the Georgians to bear. They had left Macon as heroes and expected to return triumphant, captives in hand. Instead, they had been the ones chased, ridiculed, spat upon, hunted down by law, man, woman, and child. Not only would street boys take aim at them with spoiled eggs and other garbage, but Boston's higher society mocked them for being uneducated, low class, trash, as if it were they, and not the ones they were there to capture, who dwelled at the bottom of the world.

The men refused to leave the hotel for Court Street, unappeased by the sheriff's assurances that no one was aware of their arrest. The Georgians knew better. Just outside stood a small army of Black protesters, while hostile White men lurked in the halls. The sheriff saw little to fear but offered to take them back to his own house to await bail. Fortunately, the Georgians' lawyer came to say that the bailers were on their way, so there would be no need to move. They would wait where no one would expect to find two hard-edged men from the South: in a room for ladies.

The bailers finally appeared, and according to one of them, Deputy Marshal Patrick Riley, Knight was particularly anxious to finish the business, as he was "engaged to go to the theater that evening with a lady." (He would manage to slip off.) Hughes, in contrast, did not feel well that night, and was sure to have felt worse when he learned that his instincts had been right about avoiding Court Square. An armed mob had gathered at the sheriff's office (mostly Black protesters, it was widely reported) who waited to greet him and Knight—among them, a Black man on horseback, who swore that he would be the "first man to shoot Hughes."

For the Georgians, who came from a world where there were laws against Black people owning horses, where even a free Black person carrying firearms stood to "receive upon his bare back thirty-nine lashes," when to harm the body of a White person was a capital crime, it was truly a world turned upside down. Unfortunately for them, the tilting of the axis had only just begun.

THE UNITED
STATES HOTEL

||||||||||||||||||||||||||

The Georgians were distracted with calls from visitors all the next day. First came one hundred White men, by Knight's count, who tried to intimidate them into leaving town; next a committee of sixteen, who warned that a mob would strike. The visitors were sent away by the hotel proprietors, who remained committed to their unpopular guests, and the law. When confronted by Francis Jackson, treasurer of the Vigilance Committee, the hotel treasurer insisted he would stand behind the law, even "if it was to apply to his own daughter."

Last came the ladies—the only visitors the Southerners regretted missing. Boston women were mobilizing for their own rights as citizens at this time, including the right to vote. The first National Woman's Rights Convention had met in Worcester the previous week, drawing activists such as Sojourner Truth, Abby Kelley Foster, and Frederick Douglass. The Georgians were out when the ladies of Boston made their call, however—and thus, as Knight would gallantly express, he and Hughes were "deprived of the inexpressible pleasure of seeing them."

Determined to be hunter, not prey, yet having lost sight of his targets, Hughes went to the marshal's office, where he could learn nothing. Then the Georgians were bombarded.

It was as if the would-be slave hunters carried placards on their backs, announcing, "Arrest Us." No sooner would they soothe their spirits with a little tobacco, when they were slapped for "smoking in the streets" (which, where they came from, was a punishable offense for Blacks). Exclamations of distress led to charges of "profane swearing and cursing." Monday's traumatic chase into Cambridge resulted in more accusations of toll jumping and "fast driving." The Georgians, who appeared frightened to those who saw them, faced further reprimands for carrying concealed weapons—even as their Black adversaries, as the papers described, were "armed to the teeth." The worst was the fun that locals seemed to be having at their expense. As one paper expressed, tongue in cheek: "Truly the Bostonians are a law-abiding people!"

Indeed, the Crafts' rogue lawyers were enjoying themselves as they worked down an elaborate schedule of harassment, but there were also more serious legal maneuvers in the works. Should the marshal attempt to arrest the Crafts, he would be served an obscure writ to contest their detention. William was also prepared to be charged with a criminal offense, so as to be arrested and removed from the path of the Georgians. Debt, violent assault, and even fornication were all possibilities. Because the Crafts were not legally wed (that is, by the laws of any state), they could be arrested for living in sin. William, if not Ellen, reportedly consented to this plan as a last resort.

The couple's allies hoped it would not come to that. Their intention was to keep Hughes and Knight so thoroughly occupied with being chased that they had no time for chasing—and they seemed on their way to success. The Georgians' own lawyer suggested quietly that they retreat to New York for a few days, then perhaps try again once the furor subsided. Hughes, who was still not feeling well, turned over the idea but was not yet ready to leave. He was still there in the early morning, when a rebel preacher came knocking at his door.

———

Theodore Parker wanted the job badly. The Vigilance Committee had recently held yet another urgent meeting behind locked doors, blinds pulled tight, with Lewis Hayden, Frederick Douglass, and Samuel Gridley Howe reportedly among the attendants. (Celebrated as a doctor for the blind, Howe had his eyes open in other ways.) There, as they had discussed how to scare off the slave catchers, Parker's compatriots had expressed skepticism about his abilities as an emissary. This was no business for a man of God.

Just weeks earlier, at Faneuil Hall, they had heard him counsel peaceful action, urging, "Let not dangerous weapons be resorted to, but use those which nature has provided to impede the progress of the slave holder." But now this renegade preacher promised he would do whatever it took, declaring: "Gentlemen, this committee can appoint me to no duty I will not perform." Parker might have been an abolitionist before, but the passage of the Fugitive Slave Law—and his commitment to the Crafts—carried him even further out of proper bounds.

The minister was not fully radical in his thinking. Like many on both sides of the slavery debate—abolitionists as well as enslavers—he held to some conventional racist views, which Black activists such as William Cooper Nell took pains to challenge. Parker was comfortable, for example, ranking the races, with White Anglo-Saxons at the top, Jews lower down, and Blacks on the bottom. Even so, he preached a common humanity, reaching far and wide. Two phrases used to inspire Americans for years to come originated with Parker: Abraham Lincoln's "government of the people, by the people, for the people," in the Gettysburg Address, and Martin Luther King Jr.'s "The arc of the moral universe is long, but it bends toward justice."

Parker would cast such pearls to the hundreds, even thousands, in sermons, lecture stages, and on the page, but on this early November morning, he had an audience of only two—really one, since it was clear to all that the smaller man, the jailer Willis Hughes, was in charge.

Parker traveled from his house, just two blocks from his destination, at an hour when the city streets and railroads were still dark. Hotel staff informed him at once that the men he was seeking were out. Undeterred, he had a card sent up to their room, which was promptly returned with a misspelled message: "Mr. Hughes is inguage."

Whether the slave hunter was engaged or not, the minister was soon joined by more vigilantes, some sixty men in all, who spread out through the warren of parlors and dining rooms. Finally, seeing that Parker and his cohort were determined not to leave, the hotel proprietors consented to make an introduction. With a knock, the door to room 44 opened, and the preacher and the slave hunter were eye to eye.

Parker was appalled by what he saw in the face of the other: "total depravity incarnate." Hughes did not like what he saw, either in the bald-headed preacher with the sharp blue eyes. He said he knew that Parker was supposed to be a moral man, "but this don't look much like it."

"What doesn't look like it?" Parker asked.

"Mobs and violence."

"But I came to prevent that," insisted the minister.

"But we came here to execute the law."

"Yes," Parker agreed, but they had to know that they would not be able to arrest the Crafts, much less take them from the city. And then the Georgians began to complain. Bitterly. They were being treated so badly—no sooner did they go outside when they heard the awful chanting, "Slave-hunters! Slave-hunters! There go the Slave-hunters!" Knight thought it especially unfair that even though he was not a slave hunter, he was being treated as badly as Hughes, who was.

Parker informed the men that they would not be safe another night, but that he and others would give them "safe conduct."

"We don't want safe conduct," was Hughes's rebuff. "We can take care of ourselves."

Parker said that he had already saved them from violence once and could not promise to do it again. But Hughes would make no promises either.

The two men, the minister and the jailer, gazed at each other once more, neither liking the other. Then they bid each other a good morning. Though Hughes did not blink, Parker may have gained an edge, for as they parted, the minister detected not just depravity but fear in the eyes of the other.

The doors of the hotel were under surveillance all that day. It was reported that the slave hunters never came out. Only later was it announced that they had left by the two o'clock train. The news was baffling to those on patrol, since no men fitting Hughes's and Knight's descriptions had passed through. This led to speculation that they must have escaped using the same strategy that Ellen had: by using the mantle of gender to become invisible, and waltzing by as two ladies, past watchful eyes on the lookout for only two men.

Before leaving, Hughes had a message sent by telegraph to his employer in Macon. Transmitted in cool, raspy taps: The "negroes were secreted." Hughes would head for New York City to await further instruction.

THE LION'S DEN

News reached the Crafts at their latest refuge, the home of Simeon and Betsey Dodge in the seaside town of Marblehead, on the Massachusetts North Shore. Far from being secluded, the house was situated conspicuously on a street corner, near the heart of town. So thick were the spies that Simeon, a carpenter like William, had built a trap door through which fugitives were to escape in the event of a raid. Beneath the floorboards they had hidden, William's six-foot frame enfolded beside Ellen's smaller one, young voices above, for the Dodges had many children, with another one on the way.

Where to go next was the overwhelming question. Was it safe to return or best to move on? They were already twenty miles north of Boston and might have kept going, to resurface in Canada. Some members of the Vigilance Committee had been urging this course from the beginning, and there was further support for going abroad, now that the British abolitionist George Thompson was in town. Thompson knew how easily Americans could get out of hand. On his last visit to Boston, sixteen years ago, he too, had been sent to the Dodges in Marblehead, after a "gentleman's mob" had threatened to tar and feather him. (This is when Garrison had been attacked instead.)

But Lewis Hayden, for one, argued against sending the Crafts out of the country. He made his case to a room that included Wendell Phillips, Theodore Parker, Charles Sumner, and even, reportedly, Ralph Waldo Emerson, who was never a member of the Vigilance Committee but for whom, like many, the Fugitive Slave Law—and now, the Crafts—were catalysts that turned the realm of philosophy into action. It was a sign of the Crafts' power that such diverse congregations of people cohered on their behalf, and that individuals who might ordinarily take aim at one another were willing to put aside their differences and act as one for them.

William and Ellen would agree with Hayden. They knew that in their choices, their actions, they had the power to move the world. And so they would not run to safety but in the opposite direction, straight back into the lion's den: to Daniel Webster's Boston, to the house of Lewis and Harriet Hayden.

George Thompson visited there on the first Sabbath of November, led through the maze of Boston's backstreets by William Lloyd Garrison. The house was heavily guarded, the windows barricaded, the doors double locked and barred, and was every inch the arsenal, now that rumors abounded that bigger guns were taking aim at the celebrity fugitives within. The *Liberator* reported "telegraphic intelligence" that President Fillmore was determined "to sustain the Fugitive Slave Bill, at all hazards," adding, "Let him try!"

Inside, Thompson and Garrison saw Lewis Hayden with "his young son and a band of brave colored men, armed to the teeth and ready for impending death struggle" with the marshal and his posse. Years later, William would recall a night when he and Hayden stood ready to ignite a keg of gunpowder—together, this time—"should any attempt be made to capture" him and Ellen.

The Crafts were prepared to meet all consequences, even at the expense of being together. While William remained with the Haydens, Ellen soon returned to Theodore Parker's. Climbing four flights of stairs to the top of Exeter Place, she entered a spare chamber across the hall from the minister's study. There she would wait the days and nights, keeping busy with needle and thread, or possibly books she was learning to read. Every floor of the house was crammed with tomes, some seventeen thousand volumes in all, which the minister was always happy to lend.

For company, she had Parker and his wife, Lydia; their adopted son George (Lydia Parker's dead brother's teenage love child); and Hannah Stevenson—a close friend to the minister and his wife, who had cherished dreams of having biological children during the unhappy early years of their marriage but had since found other ways to expand their family and domestic circle. Hannah Stevenson was an astute, discreet, and unconventional woman, who would one day mentor Louisa May Alcott as a Civil War nurse. She also happened to be rebel kin to the Curtii, and sister to J. T. Stevenson, Daniel Webster's friend, who had tried to convince the Crafts to submit to the law, in exchange for the purchase of their freedom.

Parker instructed "the girls," as he likely referred to his domestics, to go nowhere near the doors. Should anyone break through and charge up the stairs, the enemy would meet his fire first. He prepared his sermons with weapons at the ready: a sword in the open drawer under his inkstand, a pistol within easy reach—"loaded, ready, with a cap on the nipple." From time to time, he glanced at his grandfather's Revolutionary War musket, which hung on the wall and provided silent counsel.

Across the dying green of the Common, Douglass sensed a bloodbath. As he wrote a fellow activist, Amy Post: "The excitement in Boston about the contemplated recapture of W. & Ellen Craft is beyond description, and every moment is liable to bring with it bloodshed and carnage." "Boston boiled like a pot," another eyewitness observed.

It was not just Boston, however, for as word tapped and flashed across the wires by telegraph to the South, Macon's pot bubbled hot as well.

Robert Collins was just celebrating a successful election as a delegate to the upcoming Georgia convention when he received the telegraph from Willis Hughes, news that he would keep close. He was even less forthcoming with his curious neighbors about a second telegraphed item regarding an offer to buy the Crafts. (Such deals, proffered by men like J. T. Stevenson, were presented to both sides.)

It might have ended here, the Crafts' years of movement, if Collins had named his price, and the Crafts agreed to be bought. For Collins, however, as for the Crafts, the value of their bondage—or freedom—was beyond measure. As he wrote to a friend in Boston one day after the telegraph arrived: "We had rather have the money than to have them; we don't want them again among our slaves, we want no personal injury done to them." But this case, as he saw it, was "more important than any twenty others," due to the "romantic manner" of the Crafts' escape and their public lecturing—all of which had made them "notorious," North and South.

"There can be no plainer case made," he stated, "and none better calculated to test the law; and none to which the public's mind is much attracted at this time; and certainly, none, where the truth will do so much good, as harm, to the country." At stake was the "very salvation of the Union. . . .

"If," he proclaimed, "it is seen that the Fugitive Slave Law will be executed in good faith by the Northern people, the South will be satisfied, and quiet restored among our people; but if that law is resisted and cannot be executed," he warned, "the Union will be in imminent danger."

"Your policy," as he explained later, "would free those who are unfit to be free; it would render discontented the slaves they left behind; it would organize companies of freed slaves to conspire for the freedom of others; it would encourage abolition societies, free soil parties and associations for the protection and defense of fugitives." (In fact, all of this had already come to pass.) Collins explained to his friend that he would be happy to sell Ellen "*at fair rates*," but only after she had been returned to him.

Passive waiting, however, would not do. On November 2, 1850, Collins would seek to sway the one man in the best position to force the North to the South's will. With the power of his pen, he sought the aid of none other than President Millard Fillmore.

DISAGREEABLE DUTY

||||||||||||||||||||||||||

In Washington, Millard Fillmore faced trials he could little have imagined only six months earlier as a vice president on the sidelines. During his first summer in the White House following the death of President Zachary Taylor, he had found himself not only at the center of a sectarian crisis but also a global pandemic: the cholera. Legions of Washingtonians suffered from diarrhea and were terrified of eating cucumbers or berries, which were believed to have killed Taylor and were associated with the sickness. Since then, the air had cooled and so, too, the epidemic. But political fevers raged unabated, South and North, and the new president struggled to contain them.

A New Yorker who had been put on the Whig ticket as a ballast against slaver Taylor, Fillmore had been scorned by Southerners even as a vice presidential nominee. Now, four months into his presidency, the thirteenth chief executive of the United States drew fire on all sides on account of the Compromise he had signed into law. Charles Sumner said of Fillmore: "Better far for him had he never been born; better far for his memory, and for the good name of his children, had he never been president!" Others wanted him dead. Threats came through the mail, from North and South alike, some etched with bones and skulls.

A "dough face," he was called in the North, soft and plush. The new Fugitive Slave Act aroused protests across the North—in Philadelphia, where a recaptured fugitive had been stolen from a jail, and in Boston, where it seemed fugitives could not be captured at all. Southern extremists, meanwhile, rallied for secession. A new Southern convention was to be held in Nashville, with firebrands running the show, while in Charleston, there was talk of overtaking a federal fort—an eerie premonition of the move that would ignite the Civil War.

But there was more firmness to Fillmore than his gentle jowls suggested. As one who knew him recalled: "Behind that smiling face and courteous bearing there slumbered a world of latent passion and of power like the fires in the furnace of a great ship at rest, banked and watched, ready at call." The new president was determined, above all, to stand by the Compromise and the Fugitive Slave Law, and to use military power, if necessary, to take on what his old mentor and new secretary of state, Daniel Webster, called a "disagreeable duty" of the highest class.

Rallying a sea of supporters in Boston that spring, Webster had exclaimed, "Any man can perform an agreeable duty. . . . It is not every man who can perform a disagreeable duty." The question was whether Massachusetts—and America—would stand by "her sworn obligations."

Others now asked the same question of Fillmore and Webster, and in early November it seemed there was an answer. The very day after Robert Collins penned his letter, newspapers began to report stunning news that troops had been ordered to the port of Boston.

"THE PRESIDENT AND THE FUGITIVE SLAVE EXCITE-MENT," ran one headline from Washington. "It is stated, on good authority, that President Fillmore gave orders, on Saturday, for the immediate concentration of all the disposable force of the United States Artillery, and Infantry, at Boston Harbor." The *Baltimore Sun* disclosed more specifics, reporting that troops from as far away as Maine, Maryland, and Virginia were ordered to Boston, with a majority to be stationed at Fort Independence, less than four miles from Theodore Parker's, home where William and Ellen continued to hide.

Was it true or just a rumor, as other newspapers claimed later? In the days following, a paper close to the president, the *Washington Republic*, vehemently denied the allegations (a beat too late, other papers observed), but Daniel Webster's own letter to Fillmore suggest that an order was in place. On November 5, Webster wrote: "I see the ordering of troops into this quarter, which is very well," adding, "but I have no apprehension they will [be] needed."

By this time, Webster himself was back in Boston, having missed the most heated action that had driven out the Georgians, and the mood in the city had calmed, as he was happy to inform the president. Webster did not think there would be any resistance should a fugitive be arrested—and if so, hundreds of young men had volunteered to serve the marshal and could move at "a moment's warning."

If further action *were* required, however, the secretary of state implied it should come quiet and fast. "As our people are naturally jealous of the exercise of military power," he warned, "I incline to think it wise to say very little about it beforehand."

Together Fillmore and Webster had already begun to consider more practical matters. Should a receiving ship be used to hold the fugitives? Fillmore thought no: the marshal was already empowered to provide temporary jails. Just the same, he was thinking ahead, as everyone was, to the future of imprisoning the Crafts and returning them to the South.

For William and Ellen, it came to another excruciating decision. "Live Free or Die" may have been their motto, but with troops rumored to be heading their way, many more lives would be on the line than just their own, including those of the two hundred friends who had pledged to defend them to the death. Meanwhile, their new English friend, George Thompson, who had visited the Haydens' house with Garrison, gave fresh support for a third alternative: not living free or dying in America, but living freely and boldly abroad.

England was famed for freedom ever since James Somerset (who had been enslaved by both a Virginian and a Bostonian) claimed liberty on British shores in a landmark 1772 ruling. In the Queen's dominion, as the Crafts were assured, they would find true friends—among them William Wells Brown, who had been abroad for well over a year, and was moving and charming audiences by the thousands. With him, the Crafts could continue the antislavery resistance.

Even before others pressed them, William had already begun thinking it would be best to leave the country on "his wife's account," as Samuel May would recall. If Ellen had deferred to William's wishes previously, it seems he may now have been attentive to hers. But the future of their children may have been the strongest motivation of all.

Whether or not they were expecting a child, as a friend later suggested they were, they wished to live in a country where "we and our dear little ones can be truly free," with "no one daring to molest us or make us afraid." The determination to have a family on their own terms had launched them on their original journey of mutual self-emancipation out of Macon, Georgia, but it was now evident that this travel was still not over—that it was not from the South, but from the United States of America that they needed to run.

With this revised reality, a continuing spirit of adventure and improvisation, and their love for each other as a guide, the Crafts pivoted with full force. They would leave the "land of the free" for an alternate promised land, passing through Canada en route to England.

Ellen bid good-bye to the Parker household at a dusky hour, half past six on Wednesday, November 6. Together she and William would spend their last night at the Haydens' on Southac Street, with the friends who had supported them throughout their trials, lifting their spirits through the tedium as well as the terror. They would leave Boston—and the nation—the next day.

But before they went, they wanted to execute one last, critical, dangerous move, requiring an accomplice. William Cooper Nell hurried back to Parker's house to ask the minister this favor: Would the minister marry them tomorrow?

HUSBAND AND WIFE

‖‖‖‖‖‖‖‖‖‖‖‖‖‖‖‖‖‖‖‖‖

The rebel preacher agreed to officiate a ceremony for the Crafts, but the new marriage laws required a dangerous first step. William and Ellen would have to obtain a marriage certificate from the City Registrar's Office at 21 Court Square, around the corner from Daniel Webster's office.

On the morning of their legal wedding day, November 7, they passed like a whisper, right under the noses of all the lawyers who had worked against them, and boldly registered their names: William Crafts (as it was sometimes spelled), cabinetmaker, 25; Ellen Crafts, 23; both born in Macon, Georgia, with just one space ("names of parents") left wide and empty.

By noon they were back at the Haydens' house, where their minister met them for the ceremony. As he came through the door, Theodore Parker spied a Bible and a blade on the front table, lying side by side, as they had on William's workbench weeks before. He made a note to use them both.

It was an intimate gathering, likely including William Cooper Nell, the Haydens, and possibly other tenants, as well as Calvin Fairbank, who had helped the Haydens escape slavery years ago. Parker began with his standard remarks for grooms and brides, then spoke of William's "peculiar duties." He said that as an outlaw, unprotected by the laws of the land, William had a "natural right" to resist to the death any man who tried to recapture him into slavery and, further, to protect Ellen's life and liberty at all cost—even if it should mean digging his own grave "and the grave of a thousand men."

As he pronounced William and Ellen husband and wife, Parker took up the two objects he had spotted by the door. First, he placed the book in William's right hand, instructing him to use it "to help save his own soul, and his wife's." Then he took the weapon, a fearsome "Californian knife," and, pointing the hilt toward William, directed him to use it "to save his wife's liberty, or her life, if he could effect it in no other way."

Parker added that he "hated violence," but if there was any case where such instruments should be used, it was this. He gave William one final charge: "to bear no harsh and revengeful feelings" against those who once enslaved—or sought to enslave—him and Ellen, for if he could not strike his sword without hate, his actions would "not be without sin."

Parker's ceremony would go down in fame, or infamy. The rebel preacher would personally boast of it to Daniel Webster. For the Crafts, of course, it was a confirmation, not a creation, of their lifelong commitment to each other and to a resolution they had made when they fled Macon together, a prayer on their breaths, pistol in hand.

Yet the marriage ceremony also gave them this: "What therefore God hath joined together," the Bible said, "let not man put asunder." For anyone to claim and separate them now would be to challenge the laws of God as well as of man. This was no mere romantic gesture, but an empowering legal move to legitimize their children, as well as their bond. Two were joined as one, their singular legal identity now represented by William, the husband.

For Ellen, this move presumed to take away rights she never had as an enslaved woman in the South: her legal identity "covered over" by her husband's in a process called coverture. Married women could not form their own contracts, sue or be sued, and the children they bore belonged legally to their husbands. And yet for the Crafts, there was in this legal subtraction, a simultaneous adding on, the creation of a new equation—as, by sanction of church and state, William and Ellen were defined not by the terms master and slave, but husband and wife.

NORTH

|||||||||||||||||||||||||||||||

With Bible and blade to protect them, Ellen and William slipped out of Boston, an avuncular minister by their side. Samuel May Jr., kin to Louisa May Alcott, provided excellent cover. His entire bearing spoke to his respectability and privilege, betraying no sign of the rabid Garrisonian abolitionist he was, willing to risk fines and jail for a couple who were ready to die.

May had kept a watchful eye on the Crafts since their first arrival in Boston, noting Ellen's impact on audiences. For weeks, he had been pushing for them to leave for England, where he had traveled on antislavery missions and knew the couple would be welcomed. Now, finally, he was satisfied to see them on their way.

As the general agent of the Massachusetts Anti-Slavery Society, May had plotted countless speakers' journeys, but he had agonized over which path to take with the Crafts, since all routes were watched closely. The Portland train from Haymarket Square proved just right.

The new trio rode northeast, blurs of fading foliage flying past their window frames, and during that ride, May exhaled, knowing they had passed out of the US marshal's jurisdiction and were on course for the Crafts to be out of the country that night. Their plan had five final moves:

the train ride to Portland, Maine, with Minister May;
a night boat to Saint John, New Brunswick—Canada—alone;
a second steamer on to Windsor, Nova Scotia;
a short stage ride to Halifax; and, finally,
a British Royal Mail Ship, the *Canada*, to Liverpool, England.

Those five moves might have collapsed into one—William Wells Brown had taken the *Canada* straight out of Boston Harbor—but this was impossible now, with all the spies. The Crafts would meet the ship a week later, as it stopped to refuel in Halifax.

A soundless exit out of Boston and a silent arrival in Portland might have felt auspicious, but the luck did not last. In contrast to their first virtuoso travel experience out of the South, William and Ellen would find themselves repeatedly out of sync on this journey. Upon landing, they learned that their ship out of Maine—out of America—had collided with a schooner and was too damaged for travel.

They raced to the home of Oliver and Lydia Dennett, at 133 Spring Street, near the center of town. The Dennetts, fearless Garrisonian abolitionists, had a routine for hiding fugitives and a span of horses at the ready. May needed to return to Boston, with urgent business awaiting him. But the Crafts made a rare plea for help, entreating him to stay, and so together they waited for the ship to be repaired, praying that it would sail in time for the Crafts to make their connection in Halifax.

Across the miles in Macon, Robert Collins waited too. John Knight was on the road at the same time as the Crafts, and he soon returned home to recount the terrors of Boston: the thousands hissing and hounding him, all those "negroes" near insurrection. Knight told his story and got to see it in print, on his own terms. Ellen, he said, longed to go back south; William had told him so himself. (It was the first of many such claims, which Ellen would deny and despise.)

Though shaken, the young man expressed optimism, feeling that many Bostonians supported the Southern position, and that Hughes, still in New York awaiting orders, would be successful in the end. Not, of course, if the Crafts' friends had their way.

"Watch the Slave Hunter!" read an urgent message from Dr. Bowditch to New York editor and Underground Railroad operative Sydney Howard Gay. He warned that Hughes was in the city, and the New York Vigilance Committee should quietly try to get him south if they could. (How, exactly, the doctor did not advise.) At the very least, they should telegraph if Hughes was returning to Boston, so that insiders might do what they could to get him off track. Anything to delay until November 14, when the Crafts *should* be aboard the steamer for England.

In Portland, the Crafts anxiously followed their ship's repairs. Finally, two full days behind schedule, they learned that the SS *Commodore* was ready to sail. May checked out the ship a few hours early. After seeing it bobbing on the water, he decided it would be safe to depart and leave the Crafts to board alone. Still, he was anxious as he said his good-bye.

Ellen had become very sick. Her head was hurting badly, due to her "protracted alarm and anxiety," May supposed. Though Ellen assured him she would make it, her suffering was palpable, and May had his doubts.

"Is America the 'land of the free and the home of the brave?'" he had written an English friend, in a letter that the Crafts would carry with them aboard the ship. "God knows it is not; and we know it too."

At the appointed hour, a crowd approached the boat, hoping for a glimpse of the celebrity fugitives whose arrival had not gone unnoticed. William and Ellen managed to smuggle themselves aboard unobserved, however. The Crafts left American shores on November 9—a date that would have meaning for them in other ways, for it was also on this day that the president of the United States responded to Robert Collins.

It was not what Collins wanted to hear. In words penned by his secretary, President Fillmore acknowledged the contents of Collins's letter (which included newspaper accounts of the drama in Boston), but concluded that there was no evidence of wrongdoing or evasion of the law on the part of the authorities—or any need to take action at this time. If any person had failed in his duties, he would be removed from office. And if Collins's men had been persecuted, the courts could redress those violations too.

The letter ended on a strong statement of unity. Between North and South, he insisted, "Every effort should be made to cultivate a fraternal feeling. We should be a people of one interest and one sentiment, knowing no local decision and tolerating no sectional injustice. Our Union, so dear to the heart of every true American, can only be preserved by a strict observance of the Constitution and impartial administration of the laws."

The president's letter was printed widely, much to the delight of Collins's enemies, who considered it proof of the failure of the Fugitive Slave Law—indeed, of the United States—to protect Southern interests. But Collins and his allies chose to read the letter another way. The president clearly stated that he would stand by the Fugitive Slave Law and that he was prepared to use force. There was still hope, especially now that Daniel Webster was back in Boston.

After staying clear of the Craft case and the city altogether, Webster was settled back in at Court Square and ready to take more aggressive action. Weeks earlier, when a fugitive crisis had flared in Pennsylvania, he had stood in agreement with the president that the "law must be executed," adding this advice: "There must be no flinching, nor doubt, nor hesitation. The thing should be done as mildly & quietly as possible; but it must be done."

Webster demanded that Marshal Devens execute the warrant for the Crafts or publish his reasons for not doing so. The marshal's lack of execution had made every Northerner look bad, up to Webster and the president. Then came a tip that the Crafts had been aboard the SS *Admiral* and sailed back into Boston Harbor. Willis Hughes, who had been standing by in New York, now stormed up to Boston. All this time, the marshal's office had maintained its inept spy on its payroll, and tapped out its own secret telegraphic messages ("Mr. Jones is not in the city," meaning that William had not been found). A beat behind, it sent a scout to the *Admiral*—only to learn that no Black passengers, much less the Crafts, had been on board.

Hughes turned around immediately, to head back south, riding the SS *Florida* from New York to Charleston, then traveling on to Macon, where he was finally relieved of his duties. Moving in the opposite direction, meanwhile, his would-be captives sped for that invisible line between the United States and Canada, and points even farther away.

———

"SUCCESSFUL RESISTANCE," announced the headline from Portland, affirming the Crafts' departure from that city—news that soon went out across the country.

"You have whipped Daniel Webster and turned Massachusetts right side up. You are a glorious set of fellows," exulted one celebrant to Charles Sumner. Meanwhile, a Georgian journalist lamented: "So much for the Fugitive Slave Bill—the great lullaby of the South."

Always one to know when to cut his losses, Robert Collins soon called off his hunt. Though he initially pursued litigation (pressing Samuel May, among others, for knowledge about when, if ever, the Crafts planned to return from England), these efforts went nowhere, and Collins would have his writ for the Crafts revoked within the month.

Despite these failures, and his past warnings that the nation was in peril, Collins's support for the Union remained unwavering. In fact, at a convention called by the governor, where the fate of the Compromise was decided, it was Collins's efforts as a peaceful broker that helped build the so-called Georgia Platform, which played a key role in averting secession and thus civil war.

The nation's crisis was hardly over, however. While many Northerners cheered the Crafts' successful flight from Boston as a victory, the case deepened ruptures within, as well as between, North and South. In Boston, a celebration for George Thompson at Faneuil Hall descended into chaos, as speakers were shouted down, the lights blown out, and enemies rushed the stage. Days later, when a "Union Meeting" was held in the same hall, Webster's name brought cheers, while his friend Benjamin Robbins Curtis (soon to become a Supreme Court justice) called fugitives a "class of foreigners"—who, like the impoverished Irish, however oppressed, had no right to "invade" the "peace and safety" of Massachusetts, no claim to the United States.

Meanwhile, in Macon, there were new fears of excitement among the enslaved—inspired by the Crafts—after it was learned that a "Negro" was caught reading the news from Boston "to a number of his own color!" All were surely punished, as it was illegal for Black people to read or gather in groups larger than seven. But it was too late, for as the journalist who reported the story knew too well, words—while they might be exchanged or borrowed—could not be returned.

What exactly these articles contained the reporter did not say, but he singled out the *Boston Chronotype*, which included one widely circulated article, "Noble Determination in Crafts." The central point of this article was William's declaration to Frederick Douglass: "Our people have been pursued long enough."

It was an extraordinary moment, this reading of the news in Macon, which told that from more than a thousand miles away from where the Crafts now stood, their people heard them.

By Thanksgiving, the Crafts' friends in Boston were cautiously exultant, believing that they were safely en route to Liverpool. Theodore Parker was so assured that he wrote to Millard Fillmore directly, flaunting his own role in marrying the Crafts and sending them overseas.

Certainly it was a victory for the couple to have thwarted the Fugitive Slave Law—without injury or loss of life, and even with some humor, at the slave catchers' expense. To hear some speak of it, it was as if all of Boston were in on the joke: from the judiciary who dragged their feet, to the street boys who hurled spoiled eggs and stones. The genre of this story had changed from imminent tragedy to comedy gone wild. But the celebration came too soon.

Although William and Ellen had indeed sailed out of Portland and crossed the border into Canada, their travels had not gone as planned. Their battle against the Macon slave catchers may have come to a close, but a new battle had since begun, this one against both nature and time.

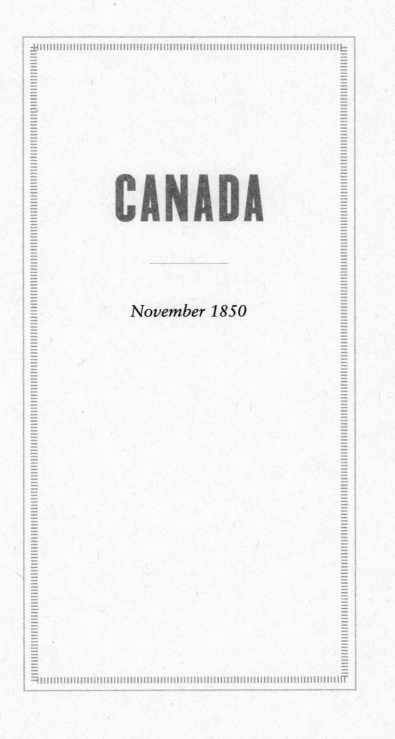

CANADA

November 1850

STRANGERS

||||||||||||||||||||||||||||

When they touched Canada, Ellen and William achieved the original goal they had set for themselves in Macon. While still in bondage, they had heard of this distant land, as had generations of refugees who fled here in waves—during the Revolution, the War of 1812, and, most recently, with the passage of the Fugitive Slave Law. The journey may have taken on more miles and years than they had intended, but with their arrival, the Crafts had finally reached a land where slavery was outlawed and where their children would be freeborn.

Yet this land, too, had known slavery—including the enslavement of Indigenous people—and traces of the history lived on. Maritime locales such as Saint John and Halifax had been a haven for Black Loyalists, who had been promised the very liberty Americans demanded during the Revolutionary War; at the same time, these same sites had seen their own slave auctions and advertisements for runaway slaves (albeit in far fewer numbers than in the United States). Indeed, some who were enslaved in Canada fled to the United States to escape bondage.

And just as New Englanders did not all welcome fugitives from the South, just as Northerners profited from their connections to the South, so Canadians also had mixed responses to refugees from the United States. Efforts to restrict Black settlement or to expatriate new emigrants were ongoing. Many recent arrivals struggled to get a footing in Canada, having fled with little in the way of food, clothing, and supplies, and there were numerous reports of starvation and poverty.

For the Crafts, there could be no true safety here. Legally, extradition was unlikely, but there were no guarantees—not when their recapture had such high stakes for the country they left behind; not when seafaring vessels steamed up directly from Savannah, Charleston, and New Orleans; not when they were strangers in a strange land.

They arrived in blustery Saint John, New Brunswick, among the crash of giant falls, with two days to pass before a steamer would carry them to Windsor, Nova Scotia, their last stop before Halifax, their departure point for England. In this town of fourteen thousand, they sought to find shelter as man and wife.

At the town hotel, William was first to approach the staff.

"We wish to stop here tonight," he announced.

The butler looked uncomfortable, noting that they had "plenty of room for the lady," but that they never took in "colored folks."

"Oh, don't trouble about me," William replied smoothly. "If you have a room for the lady, that will do." He then went out for a stroll, while the luggage was sent up to a room.

On his return, he asked to see the "lady," causing twitters when he boldly entered her room without knocking. Ellen caused even more excitement when she requested dinner for two.

"Dinner for two, mum!" was the astonished waiter's response as he glanced from Ellen's face to William's, then hurried out the door.

The butler knocked next, and he, too, uncomprehending, asked Ellen to verify her order.

"Yes, for two," she confirmed.

A maid followed, saying that the lady of the house wished to know "whether you will have dinner up now or wait till your friend arrives?"

"I will have it up at once, if you please."

The house was in a minor uproar when the landlord appeared. He had heard about Ellen and William from the steward of the *Commodore*, and, learning that they were destined for England, his own native land, and possibly of their celebrity, he cordially welcomed both Crafts as his guests—all of which boded well for English hospitality, if not Canada's.

One weekly steamer left from Saint John to Windsor, and, mercifully, William and Ellen made it on board and onto the daily stagecoach to Halifax. It was raining, however, and William was forced to sit on top of the careening vehicle with the luggage, as there was no space for "colored" inside.

For nearly forty miles, he traveled this way, blinking against the wind and rain. Then the entire stagecoach tipped over, throwing everyone out, with William landing on top of the driver, whose head was entirely submerged in the mud. As this man had said he "always objected to niggers riding inside with white folks," William was "not particularly sorry" to see the driver deeper in the muck than himself.

Inside or out, lady or man, passenger or driver, White or "colored" did not matter in the end; all were dirtied, jolted, and bruised, and required to tromp through the heavy slickness of earth and rain, with browned pants and sodden skirts, for the last seven miles to Halifax.

At last, they entered the town, crunching over oyster shells and debris. The storefronts were dark, the docks quiet, too, for, as the Crafts were dismayed to learn, the Royal Mail Ship *Canada* had come and gone two hours earlier, taking its mail and passengers, and leaving them behind. The next steamer for Liverpool would not arrive for two weeks. There was nowhere else to go but a single run-down inn across the street from the shuttered market—a "miserable, dirty hole," as William judged from the outside.

They would take no chances. Ellen went in to request a room, while William waited in the rain for the mended coach, which brought the luggage. Suspicious of William's presence near the bags, the innkeeper hurried to Ellen to ask: "Do you know the dark man downstairs?"

Ellen confirmed that indeed she did: he was her husband.

"I mean the black man—the *nigger*?"

"I quite understand you; he is my husband."

"My God!" the innkeeper exclaimed, then ran out.

The reactions to the Crafts, here and elsewhere, go a long way to show how the success of the couple's earlier journey relied not just on Ellen's passing as White, but also on her passing particularly as a wealthy, disabled, White man. The Crafts could travel together as they did because they betrayed no sign of their intimacy or relations as husband and wife—their "sexual kinship," to quote one scholar. Now that this relationship was revealed, they would face far more judgment than they had on the journey from Georgia. Even outside the South, outside the United States, the Crafts' roles of master and servant, if not master and slave, were accepted in ways that husband and wife were not.

In the morning, the innkeeper informed the Crafts that they would have to find a new place. It was not that she was prejudiced, she insisted, noting: "I think a good deal of the colored people" and "have always been their friend." It was just that there would be trouble for her business.

The Crafts replied that they would be happy to leave, if only she could find them other accommodations. But after a morning of making inquiries, she had no success and finally referred them to "some respectable colored families" who might take them in.

Though larger than Boston, Halifax had a Black community approaching the same size: roughly 1,700 in the city and vicinity, including rural Black settlements such as Hammonds Plains and Preston. Diverse peoples of African descent had long lived in this region, among them Black Loyalists, Jamaican Maroons, and former inhabitants of the United States, as well as those native born. Within Halifax were Black churches, an African school, and an Abolition Society, together comprising a community that knew how to absorb and take care of newcomers. But Halifax was also, as the Crafts had experienced, already wired with racial tension. Only three years earlier a race riot had raged between Black and White Haligonians.

A Reverend Cannady and his wife extended Christian charity, despite the Crafts' obvious illness, for by this time, the rain, chills, and close to seven-mile trek to Halifax had made them both extremely sick, Ellen especially. The Cannadys might have known about the Crafts, whose news had been published in a local paper, but even if so, they kept their own news close.

For nearly two weeks, as they waited for their ship, both William and Ellen were bedridden. After all that they had endured both physically and emotionally over the past weeks, months, and years, their bodies had been pushed beyond limits. That a doctor was called indicates the severity of the situation. Ellen would remain weakened for many months.

The couple might have been pressed to postpone their journey, but time was at a premium. They were still a mere boat ride from the South, and with every day they stayed, they consumed the funds they had received from the Vigilance Committee: $250 in total. The fare to Saint John alone had cost $14, while tickets to Liverpool were $150, leaving little to spare.

The next available ship was a sister to the one they had missed: a little older, a little slower, and perhaps a little less lucky. It was called the *Cambria*, and among abolitionists, it was infamous.

Frederick Douglass had taken the *Cambria*, a Royal Mail Ship of the Cunard Line, back and forth to England just a few years earlier, with trouble on both rides. On his way out, he had paid for a first-class ticket but had been forced to ride in steerage, in the dank and noisy front part of the ship, most prone to explosion. While he slept in these unquiet quarters, he went above decks by invitation to join his friends by day, and was even asked to deliver an antislavery speech. But a wide world of travelers rode aboard this vessel, including slavers, and a riot broke out, with men threatening to throw Douglass overboard. They backed down only after the captain threatened to put any troublemakers in chains.

On his return, Douglass was allowed a cabin, but on the condition that he take his meals in his room and stay clear of other passengers. Hearing of this, Samuel Cunard, the self-made man from Halifax with the eponymous shipping line, promised that no such prejudice would mar his steamers again, but his promises had yet to be kept, as the Crafts soon learned.

Twice William set out to buy tickets; twice the ticket sellers told him lies. Passage could be booked only once the steamer arrived, they said. William knew this was not true. Too late, the ship was full, they told him next: "Better try to get to Liverpool by other means."

Finally, William used a letter from Francis Jackson, treasurer of the Vigilance Committee, to contact a powerful local man, who chastised the office. Only then was William able to make his purchase, just in time.

Launching from Boston, where the majority of passengers were to embark, the *Cambria* finally rode into the waters of Halifax, firing its salute, on November 29, 1850. William and Ellen, sick but determined, now braced themselves for a final transatlantic journey, while mariners gazed gloomily at the dark and turgid waters.

THE *CAMBRIA*

||||||||||||||||||||||||||

They mounted the narrow gangway to board the black, wood-hulled steamship, flags flared. With two mighty sails flanking a gold-painted paddle box and a fiery-red smokestack, the *Cambria* was a strong, seasoned vehicle. While not as plush as, say, the hot new American Collins Line, with its mirrored saloons, nor as affordable as a sailing packet, with its cheap steerage fares, it could be depended on to weather the winter storms and reach its destination in about ten days, as opposed to weeks or even months.

There were some complaints about the tight berths: traveling on a sister ship a few years earlier, Charles Dickens called his room an "utterly impracticable, thoroughly hopeless, and profoundly preposterous box," grumbling that his mattress was as thin as if it had been plastered on. But the economic design promised that no decorative elements would crash onto one's head when the ship hurtled into a wave. A small window could be opened to let in light and air. Cabin passengers could also count on having their beds made, their slops thrown out, and their shoes shined by morning. And a ladies' lounge offered plump, velvet sofas, while the saloon promised a full bar from six AM.

There, if one had the stomach for it, one might sup on hot roast pork or crimped cod, cold tongue or warm rolls, boiled potatoes, puddings, or bright-green pickles, served on long, white-topped tables by skilled waitstaff. Overhead were glimmers of gold gilding, and on the walls, paintings of the places one had been or hoped to go: Boston, New York, London, Liverpool, Glasgow.

All this was on offer for a first-class ticket. The Crafts, however, traveled in steerage, as Douglass had, set apart by race and class. Despite Cunard's promise, segregation was the norm, ship magnates being mindful of Southern business, some of their best-paying customers.

Steerage was on the far side of the ship from the ladies' and gentlemen's cabins, wedged next to the engineers', firemen's, and crewmen's quarters, not far from the livestock carried aboard for meat and milk. It was the darkest, noisiest, wettest front end of the ship, which shouldered every bump and wave, and here William and Ellen made their voyage.

Though steerage spaces were limited on the Cunard ships, and went unadvertised, the Crafts might have had company. Josiah Henson—who would soon go down in fame as the inspiration for the title character in Harriet Beecher Stowe's *Uncle Tom's Cabin*—was reportedly on board with his son. Neither the Crafts nor the Hensons, however, would mention meeting.

Transatlantic travel was invariably brutal for first-time passengers, with seasickness a rite of passage. For the first few days of every voyage, the public areas would be vacated, while nauseated passengers could be heard emptying their stomachs in the privacy of their cabins. For William and Ellen, these discomforts were magnified by their position on the ship, by Ellen's worsening health, and, in a final stroke of bad luck, a series of gale storms.

Winter journeys were always a risk, which was why so few chose to ride at this time through what has been called the "graveyard of the North Atlantic." The fogs off Newfoundland were infamous. Icebergs might appear suddenly, seemingly from nowhere, and dangerous mixes of warm and cold currents could combust into hurricanes. The Crafts' journey went from bad to worse, as severe gales blew into the *Cambria* from the wrong direction, pushing it away by force, knocking into its bow at full blast. Waves could rise to the height of buildings, up to sixty feet, crashing over the masts and decks, shaking the passengers within.

In storms of this scale, passengers were thrown from their bunks. Hot meats, soups, slops, wine all flew. Glasses shattered, despite all attempts to rig them to holds in the ceiling. Anything untethered might go upside down or sideways, as the ship rolled from one side to the other, from one wave to another, wild waters overwhelming the ship's scuppers.

Fear ran high aboard a ship in a gale, with passengers often comparing the experience to war. All the while, Ellen waged a battle for her life. With her head pounding, her stomach no doubt heaving, she endured the delirium of days and nights in an airless, lightless quarantine, where time collapsed, with sun and stars invisible. Only the distant bell punctuated the hour, and the cries of the working men—and sometimes the passengers. The engine pounded, sending vibrations through the body of the ship and through her own body, as the firemen, close below, labored day and night to feed the fire, desperate to fuel the ship against the rages of the opposing sea.

The terror of a gale storm, as Charles Dickens recalled, defied representation: "Its howling voice—is nothing. To say that all is grand, and appalling and horrible in the last degree, is nothing. Words cannot express it. Thoughts cannot convey it. Only a dream can call it up again, in all its fury, rage, and passion."

It was a nightmare from which William feared Ellen might not wake.

For thirteen days, the *Cambria* coursed through the wretched waters—an unusually long course, given that William Wells Brown had made his transatlantic journey from Boston in nine days and twenty-two hours. There was this shipboard tradition: each day, passengers would place bets on how far they had traveled overnight, and at noon, the captain would come down to the cabin to post the results. It was a game that *Cambria* riders might have given up.

If there was a saving grace, it was that the ship was in the hands of Captain John Leitch. The thirty-four-year-old Leitch would become known for his heroism a few years later, when he commandeered a sinking vessel and delivered six hundred souls to safety, holding to the promise that he would be the last man to leave. At his death in 1883, he would be celebrated for his luck at sea.

The voice of this handsome captain rang above decks, crying out orders over the rush of the torrential winds and waters, the boatswain's whistle carrying them through, the team of mariners moving expertly in response. Finally came the day when the noontime bets were joyous. On December 11, days after it was due, the *Cambria* swung past the green coast of Ireland, broached Saint George's Channel, into the Irish Sea, circled over Holyhead, and turned onto the River Mersey, where a local pilot came on board to guide the ship home to Liverpool.

There was a rush, then, as passengers freshened up the best they could before shuttling, with all their baggage, into a smaller boat that pulled them ashore. Here, at last, the Crafts could emerge safely, Ellen possibly for the first time, to take in the sharp, fresh air, and squint at the mastheads, piers, steeples, and smoke rising from Liverpool's grey, noonday shore.

For many, it was hardly a sight for sore eyes. Once the slaving capital of England, Liverpool was a port of extremes, transacting in untold riches while also a site of terrible poverty, from which many sought to flee. Record numbers of refugees waited here to fill the steerage of packet ships bound for America, in an epic wave of immigration that was fast transforming the country. Long before Lady Liberty's famed proclamation, the United States was already receiving the tired, the poor, the "huddled masses yearning to breathe free."

But today, the breath blew the other way.

Generations earlier, Ellen and William's ancestors—including William's grandmother and grandfather—had been kidnapped into a brutal transatlantic journey aboard a slaving ship, which may well have launched from Liverpool. For William and Ellen, their arrival meant that they were finally beyond the reach, legally and physically, of the generations of enslavers who had since claimed to own them and their kin, and who were empowered to do so by American law.

They had survived slavery in the South, outwitted kidnappers in the North, outrun the laws of the nation they once called home. They had overcome illness and, finally, the throes of nature itself, to find freedom, at last, on a new shore.

They had run so many miles: one thousand from South to North, a thousand more across New England, and these last three thousand miles over troubled waters. They had run for each other, with each other, and now had each other in this place and time, where, strong enough together, they would have room to explore their own identities apart. Whomever, whatever they may have lost, they could fulfill their dreams of building a family that no one could break down.

How they could have kissed the ground, as they would recall, when they stepped off that last boat, knowing, for the first time, that they were truly free, that an open terrain stretched far ahead of them in time and space. Exactly how they would use that ground, that freedom, remained to be seen.

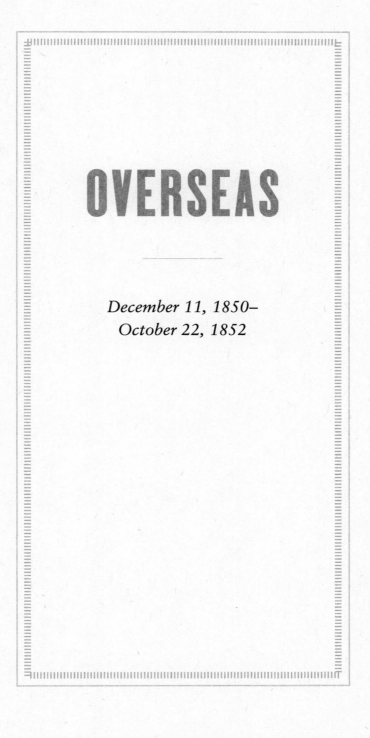

OVERSEAS

December 11, 1850–
October 22, 1852

MAN OF
THE WORLD

||||||||||||||||||||||||||

With the ground finally still beneath their feet, the Crafts hustled past the salty stench of the docks and through the megalithic new customhouse, stone faced and domed. Their baggage duly checked and stamped, they rode a coach a short ways to Brown's Temperance Hotel on Clayton Square, known to be friendly to abolitionists as well as to teetotalers. Lying low, they could finally begin to recover, as they pondered new questions and how next to move.

They had letters connecting them to a few individuals, but were otherwise strangers. Their journey had set them back physically and financially. They had skills to make a living, but they had no people, no home, and no road map for how to begin. They had been told Britons would be welcoming, yet experience gave them reason to doubt.

Then there was the past and the question of how to help those they had left behind: the anonymous millions, as well as their loved ones; those trapped in bondage, but also held hostage by American law. Would they be able to redeem their enslaved family members and support their compatriots, as well as fulfill their dream of starting a family of their own?

It was fortunate for them that, as quiet as they kept it, word of their arrival reached the one man who was perhaps best equipped to help them navigate such questions, a friend who had embraced them as refugees before: William Wells Brown.

In the eighteen months since his send-off from Boston Harbor—the white flash of William's handkerchief no doubt imprinted on his memory of the American shore—William Wells Brown, man of letters, had become a man of the world. He had traveled through England, France, and Ireland, thrilling to a newfound identity as a tourist. He especially loved Paris, where he perused paintings at the Louvre, strolled the boulevards, and enjoyed sipping coffee at sidewalk cafes. He had stood, blood chilled, at the Place de la Revolution, in the very spot where Louis XVI and Marie Antoinette had been guillotined, their bloody heads held up to the sky; he had even (by accident) driven up to the presidential palace, where a liveried servant opened his coach door and, bowing, asked if he had an appointment with the president. (In his "best French," he said, *"Non."*)

If Brown could not get enough of the world he toured, the world could not seem to get enough of him. He had republished his life story, which sold out repeatedly, and spoken to crowds of thousands, telling his own story and the stories of other American refugees, while denouncing the unjust laws of the United States, the so-called land of the free.

He had scaled up his rhetoric for international conferences, churches, and concert halls, brought it down low for exclusive, intimate gatherings, private dinners, clubs, and soirees, where he mingled with political and literary giants such as Alexis de Tocqueville and Victor Hugo. So high was his status, and so changed, that a fellow traveler aboard the *Canada*, who had sneered at him on account of his race, now sidled up to Brown, holding his hat as he requested an introduction to Hugo and his friends. Brown was only too happy *not* to give it.

As easily as he carried himself, however, Brown had faced his share of difficulties since the Crafts had seen him last. To be sure, he was applauded in wealthy, high-powered circles, and occasionally received massive gifts. A year ago, the mayor of Newcastle, England, presented him with a handmade purse on behalf of the ladies of the city, filled with twenty gold sovereigns worth thousands of dollars today. Working-class Britons also supported Brown: in Sheffield, employees at a silver-electroplating factory filled a purse for him as a "token of their esteem."

Even so, the income was erratic, and it remained a struggle for Brown to make a living for himself and his daughters, who were still in America and whom he had never expected to leave for so long. He would have been back months ago but for the Fugitive Slave Law. Brown was doing everything in his power to arrange for their travel overseas. In the meantime, he sent them anything he could, at risk to himself.

On one particularly "dark day" in London, after sending nearly all his earnings to his girls, he had been unable to pay for fare to his next lecture site, which was not nearby, as he had believed, but more than a hundred miles away. Brown had a single shilling left when he encountered a formerly enslaved man from Maryland, standing by a lamppost. The man had no work, no money, and no food that day. After hearing his story, Brown split his money with the man, who burst into tears as he received it, saying, "You are the first friend I have met in London."

Brown would not soon forget this stranger, one of many impoverished fugitives he met on his journey. He would encounter so many, in fact, that within a year, he would warn others not to come to England advising them, as he urged the man from Maryland, to try the West Indies instead.

Brown was also encumbered by attacks from America by his estranged wife, Betsey, who was desperate for support as well as for news about her daughters. (Brown had left without telling her where they were.) An article entitled "A Stray Husband" soon ran on the front page of the *New-York Daily Tribune*, quoting her charge that Brown "had become so popular among the Abolition ladies that he did not wish his sable wife any longer," and had left her and her child "penniless" and "destitute." (This was the child whom Brown never recognized as his own.) Brown had finally published a response, and friends stood by him, yet even so, Betsey's claims ignited new political controversies overseas, for the man who had famously charmed so many in America had acquired surprising enemies on British soil.

As the Crafts would soon discover, the world of abolition here was both small and divided—ironically, along fault lines set by the American antislavery movement, which had split over similar issues, namely, women and politics. Ten years ago, when Garrisonians had proposed to seat women at the World's Anti-Slavery Convention in London, the dominant British abolitionist group, the British and Foreign Anti-Slavery Society (BFASS), had stood opposed. There had been bad blood between the abolitionist groups ever since—more a matter of personal acrimony than political difference, much of it around the polarizing figure of William Lloyd Garrison. However, these divisions were soon to devolve into what Brown would call "open war."

While they had been in Massachusetts, firmly Garrisonian country, the Crafts, as well as Brown, had steered clear of these politics, and Brown had purposely gone overseas without any affiliation. However, as he had since discovered, a mere association with Garrison could be damning in places where the BFASS was strong. He soon became embroiled in a nasty feud with a founder and secretary of the BFASS,

John Scoble, a man once described as "smooth as an iceberg." Scoble had assisted numerous American refugees before, paving the way for successful lecture tours, but in Brown's case, he took Betsey Brown's words to heart and seemed as intent as she to bring Brown down.

For all these reasons and more, the Crafts could not have come at a better moment for Brown. He had been pained to hear of their ordeals. As he had told Douglass, he had held out hope for Northern resistance, until he read their news. But he would be glad to see his old friends, whose fresh testimony from Boston was sure to cause a sensation—just at the start of the prime lecture season in England, which ran from November to May.

In contrast to his own personal troubles, here was a couple whose love story was guaranteed to enthrall Victorian audiences. Brown had seen people leap to their feet for the Crafts in America, and he foresaw that here, too, the applause would be torrential. Brown wrote to the Crafts at once and asked them to join him, while writing ahead to his Scottish contacts about scheduling a tour for these new American refugees, whom they would not want to miss.

Back at Brown's Temperance Hotel, William Craft received his friend's letter with excitement. "I need not inform you that I was pleased on getting your letter," he wrote back, "but I should have been much more so, to have seen you." They would go to him, William promised, though not right away, as Ellen was not well. They would aim for the following Thursday.

As the day came, however, Ellen remained too ill to move, and so the couple improvised a new plan. William would go first to meet Brown, no doubt soon to join him at lectures, knowing their friend. This was no permanent solution—the Crafts knew what it meant to be on the road in Brown's incomparably tireless company, and they were already physically exhausted. To travel with Brown would also be to defer their domestic dreams. Brown's itinerant lifestyle might be suitable for a "single" man, but it was not conducive to building a happy marriage or family. Still, joining forces with their old friend was an opportunity for international activism that would also give them a lay of the land, and their best way forward for now.

Ellen would stay behind with a dissenting minister, Francis Bishop and his wife, Lavinia, who lived in nearby Toxteth with two young children and a servant girl named Mary. (Bishop would be so moved by the Crafts that he would plan a trip to Macon to speak with their enslavers, a trip later cut short.) Far from the chaos of the docks, Ellen would aim to heal, rejoining the Williams as soon as she could.

It would be the Crafts' longest separation since leaving Georgia, a move necessary, novel, and perhaps symbolic. The new world they had entered would give them the space to be together, but also to be apart, empowering them to transcend the paired roles that defined them in America—master, slave, husband, wife—and forge their own ways forward. They parted nearly two years to the day since they had left Macon, William moving ahead of Ellen for a very different kind of partnership.

TWO WILLIAMS

||||||||||||||||||||||||||

On England's well-laid rails, William moved swiftly across the terrain—from Liverpool on the western shore, to Newcastle upon Tyne, on the eastern coast, with colossal, new, gaslit railway stations on either end—to greet the older brother figure who was also the only man he knew in this part of the world. With William ready to join William Wells Brown on the abolitionist lecture circuit, the two Williams soon took another train, bound for Edinburgh in Scotland. Together, they would ring in the new year, and their Scottish adventures would begin.

If the trains themselves were impressive—speedier, shinier, cleaner than their American counterparts, which were bespattered with tobacco juice, as the British commonly complained—the spectacle of Edinburgh was even more unreal. They rose up from the station to a fairy-tale city complete with castles and dungeons, darkly winding wynds, and underground communities, belying picturesque avenues laid with rows upon rows of sandstone homes.

Frederick Douglass loved Edinburgh, pronouncing it one of the most beautiful cities in the world. It comprised an "Old Town" and a "New," both terms relative. Construction on the New Town predated the birth of the United States. The station came up at a low point between the halves, near where noxious waters used to be. Gleaming architecture rose all around, the Palace of the Holyrood to the east, Edinburgh Castle to the west, neither yet visible but soon to be seen.

Almost as soon as they exited the station, the two Williams were treated to a vision beloved by Brown: that of a new, sky-high monument to Sir Walter Scott (from whose novel Douglass had taken his name) sitting inside what appeared to be his own private Gothic cathedral, beside his faithful dog. It was a quick jaunt, two blocks up, past Princes Street, to Cannon's Hotel, where they would spend the coming days.

The hotel stood at the edge of St. Andrew's Square, in the neat and classy, newer part of town, edged with banks and fine houses. A towering fluted column, honoring a British leader who had stood against abolition, cast its shadow here, but not on the plans of the Williams, as they caught up and prepared for their new abolitionist journey.

Brown was no doubt eager to hear directly from William about the crisis in Boston, and the Crafts' escape from slave catchers—all of which would be incorporated into their upcoming presentations. Meanwhile, William was sure to have had questions about a vastly different cultural and political scene.

The British were proud of their emancipation history, and there were now antislavery activists in the very highest ranks. Queen Victoria's own husband, Albert, had given an antislavery speech. Whereas in the United States, angry mobs might have greeted abolitionists, here the speakers were cheered, and none more so than emancipated Americans like Brown and the Crafts. There was a national passion, as one journalist put it satirically, for "the genuine black."

Yet support for American abolition was hardly universal. The United Kingdom also benefited deeply from trade with the United States and alliances with the cotton slavers in the South. Glasgow, Bristol, and Liverpool, among other commercial centers, had all been enriched by their ties to American slavery. Moreover, the United Kingdom was undergoing its own share of social upheaval, with tremendous poverty, conflicts over labor, and fear among the well-to-do of political unrest—all of which, as newcomers, the Crafts would have to navigate with care.

If they perceived less racial prejudice here than in America, and more acceptance by the elite, the Crafts were soon to be introduced to extreme touchiness about money and class. They needed a way to raise funds, but they could not seem overly interested in "money speculation for their own benefit." They would also need to be strategic in their messaging, as they played across class lines.

Then the sad surprise: infighting among the abolitionists. The Crafts would strive to maintain their independence, but they were already identified as friends of Garrison's by virtue of the letters they carried, and formerly enslaved speakers like themselves were pressured to choose sides. In fact, such speakers were becoming so numerous—Henry Box Brown and Josiah Henson among them—that some organizers were growing concerned. As William Wells Brown himself would later report to Frederick Douglass, "too many of our fugitive brethren are of opinion that because they can tell, by the fireside, the wrongs they have suffered in the prison house of slavery, that they are prepared to take the field as lecturers." Many became "little less than beggars."

The Crafts, however, held a distinct advantage. Their story had already been well publicized. Even more, Ellen would be a pioneer on the British lecture circuit. As in America, she was one of the first self-emancipated women from the South to take this road.

Her appeal would have to wait, however. As the date of the Crafts' first lecture approached, just before the new year, Ellen was still not well enough to travel. And so William, with Brown beside him, headed to the Nicolson Street Church to tell their story on his own.

The meeting was organized by the Edinburgh Ladies' Emancipation Society, and the "respectable audience," as a newspaper described it, was large, drawn by the promise of the Crafts. Joining the two Williams on the platform were several distinguished clergymen, as well as abolitionist organizers. There was disappointment as it became clear that Ellen would not be present. But William would captivate his listeners from his opening line, which he closed with the exclamation "Thank God, I am free!"

As William Wells Brown had predicted, the crowd exploded in applause. William went on to introduce the Fugitive Slave Law and his trials in Boston, before coyly offering to tell the story of his and his wife's escape.

If people came in expecting to hear a story full of violence and trauma, they experienced instead one punctuated with deadpan humor. William first drew laughter when he told of how he requested permission to travel by informing the man who hired his time that he wished to accompany his wife to visit her sick aunt. "At last, I was permitted to go," said William, "but my wife, instead of going to see her aunt, went to see her uncle in Philadelphia!"

He regaled audiences again when he set the scene at the grand hotel in Charleston, and as he described how he had to hold up his "lame" master, to keep him from falling over. But the loudest reaction of all came when he recounted how, on the train ride to Richmond, he heard a besotted young lady sighing about Ellen, "I never felt so much for a young man in my life." Laughter now rang up to the rafters.

Long before the dramatic climax in Baltimore, the finale in Philadelphia, it was clear that William, alone, had done his job in moving his audience into action. Here, as elsewhere, an organization that had formerly lacked energy was newly fired up. Immediately after he spoke, two reverends sprang up to voice their support, and the group unanimously resolved to do everything in its power to promote the overthrow of slavery in the United States of America.

Even without Ellen, William, as Brown declared, promised to become "a favourite with the Scotch." The two Williams could not have asked for a better way to end a fraught year and a more auspicious way to enter 1851.

They continued to captivate Edinburgh. After ringing in the new year together, they attended a soiree held by the Edinburgh Temperance Society at the Music Hall, earning honorary lifetime memberships and proud praise from the society's president.

"What a humbling thought it will be . . . ," the president exclaimed, for Americans to hear that the very men they deemed so unworthy were now "in the midst of educated Edinburgh, thought fit to hold even the first rank upon our aristocratic platform."

"Down with the iniquitous Slave Bill!" He cried. "Down with the aristocracy of the skin! Perish forever the deepest-dyed, the hardest-hearted system of abomination under heaven. . . . Perish American slavery."

By night, the Williams lectured; by day, they saw the sights. Brown was an insatiable explorer, with a vast curiosity about everything, from history, to politics, to the visual arts, and led the way, a four-hundred-page guidebook heavy in hand. They traveled the "Royal Mile," going from Edinburgh Castle, now occupied as army barracks, to the Palace of the Holyrood, where an elderly woman with a ruddy complexion, "secondhand curls," and an astonishingly wide cap gave the two men a tour of the very room in which Mary, Queen of Scots's reputed Italian lover had been murdered.

They visited the former home of the famed, fiery preacher and writer John Knox, where Brown was moved to see the words inscribed above the door: "Lufe God abufe al and yi nychtbour as yi self." And they admired epic canvases at Edinburgh's Royal Institution, including lush oils by Rubens and Titian, though a seventeenth-century portrait of the Lomellini family—dour faced, somber toned, by Sir Anthony Van Dyck—drew the biggest crowds.

Yet for William, the most astonishing sights might have been the most ordinary. On the morning after his debut, as he and Brown strolled back from a fine breakfast, they crossed paths with a White man walking arm in arm with two Black women.

William remarked drily: "If they were in Georgia, the slaveholders would make them walk in a more hurried gait than they do," meaning that racists would surely drive them out of town. Brown quipped back that they need not go any farther than Philadelphia or New York for that kind of prejudice. But Brown knew what William meant, for he had experienced a similar phenomenon, as had Frederick Douglass and others before them: the feeling of being both seen and unseen in unaccustomed ways—of being visible as a person, as a man.

Brown took pleasure in observing William become initiated into his new reality. "When walking through the streets," he wrote to a friend, "I amused myself by watching Craft's countenance; and in doing so, imagined I saw the changes experienced by every fugitive slave in his first months' residence in this country." Even after all this time, sixteen months since his own arrival, Brown, too, retained his wonder.

There was also this, for William: as he watched the interracial trio walk by, undisturbed, he was invited to imagine a new life for him and Ellen—one where the two of them might exist, both seen and unseen, together.

1   The Collins family home, 830 Mulberry Street, Macon, Georgia, 1916. The grounds from which the Crafts would launch their epic journey from slavery to freedom in 1848.

2

Ellen Craft in disguise. A "most respectable-looking gentleman," to quote her husband.

3

Ellen Craft circa 1870. "Oh, how I should like my old mistress could see me now," she was heard to say.

4

William Craft circa 1870–1875. Called "the coolest man," his calm under pressure (along with Ellen's) would be critical to their successful escape.

5

Robert Purvis, president of the Underground Railroad. A native South Carolinian who was frequently assumed to be a White man and who, with his wife, Harriet, would come to the Crafts' aid.

6

William Wells Brown, the showman. An author, performer, and activist extraordinaire who dazzled audiences across the globe and taught the Crafts how to tell their story.

7

Frederick Douglass, the prophet. An ally to the Crafts who, in a moment of national reckoning, would urge William Craft, "If you die, our people will live."

8

Robert Morris, the lawyer. One of the nation's first Black attorneys, who would be one of the unsung heroes of the Crafts' revolution.

9

Lewis Hayden, the general.
A leader in Boston who was
prepared to blow up his own
home in defense of the Crafts.

10

Harriet Bell Hayden, keeper of
safe harbor. A self-emancipated
activist who, with husband
Lewis, fed, clothed, and
sheltered countless refugees from
slavery, including the Crafts.

11

Theodore Parker, the rebel preacher. A clergyman who would square off with slave catchers and prepare his sermons with a sword and pistol within easy reach.

12

Daniel Webster, the US secretary of state. Massachusetts's shining son, whose job it would be to supervise the recapture of the Crafts and send them back to slavery.

13

Harriet Martineau, the author. A British celebrity who wielded her mighty pen as an antislavery sword, despite death threats, and who would use her influence to assist the Crafts.

The Crystal Palace. A transparent global stage upon which the Crafts would walk the world.

14

15

Charles Estlin Phillips Craft,
Ellen and William Craft's
"first freeborn child."

16

Ellen Craft Crum,
a daughter of Ellen
and William Craft.

PANORAMAS

||||||||||||||||||||||||||||

On the third day of the new year, Ellen was well enough to travel to Edinburgh and finally joined the Williams. William Wells Brown gave the couple a night to spend alone in the fairy-tale city, while he departed for a gloomier landscape in Glasgow, where the trio would soon take the stage.

Ellen would make her international debut at Glasgow's city hall, located deep in Merchant City, mere blocks away from a region that Friedrich Engels decried as one of the worst slums in Europe. During the revolutions of 1848, hungry bread rioters had stormed around the building, clashing with Glasgow's pioneering police force—the first in the country, founded by a man known as the Father of Glasgow, who had made his fortunes in Virginia tobacco, grown by the enslaved.

Different crowds now encircled city hall, thronging its Grand Hall, Glasgow's biggest public arena, which stood above an indoor fruit market, from which ripe smells rose. Here Douglass had once inspired audiences to scream down American slavery with cries of "Shame!" This night, every seat in the house—three thousand in all—was filled for Ellen and William, with hundreds more turned away. The event was billed as the "GREAT ANTI-SLAVERY MEETING," with the two Williams featured as speakers, and Ellen advertised as the "WHITE SLAVE"—an expression she did not like but tolerated for now.

For more than three hours, Ellen held a place of honor beside her husband, Brown, and Glasgow's leading citizens, including a member of Parliament. She gazed out on the thousands as they roared their assent to the promise and the prophecy that "American slavery shall one day fall to not rise again." And, if the advertisements were correct, she sang, lifting her voice to meet Brown's smooth, dulcet tones, and her husband's deeper range. Which songs they chose they did not say, but one of Brown's originals, "Fling Out the Anti-Slavery Flag," set anti-slavery lyrics to the Scots' beloved anthem, "Auld Lang Syne." When, late that night, William presented his wife to the Scots, the applause for Ellen was "rapturous."

At the end of the evening, Ellen was probably escorted, along with her husband, to a mansion a few miles away, where Brown had been staying. Owned by a businessman whom Brown had met in London, it was one of the most magnificent homes for miles, located high on Laurel Bank, Kilpatrick Hills, far from the slums that Engels had deplored. Even Brown was impressed, describing it to Douglass as "one of the loveliest spots which I have yet seen." Such was the new landscape in which Ellen and William were received.

The Crafts and Brown continued to take Glasgow by storm—even more powerfully, as they were joined onstage by an oracular picture, map, and history, all in one, an epic panorama reaching hundreds of feet long, centuries deep.

Once upon a time, two years before he met the Crafts in 1847, William Wells Brown had himself been entranced by such a mesmeric map, as he had joined hordes of tourists in Boston for a virtual river cruise in John Banvard's celebrated Grand Panorama of the Mississippi River— claimed to be the largest picture in the world. In a darkened room, to lights, music, sound, and story, he watched the "Three Mile Painting" slowly unfold with lifelike views of the cities he had once traveled as a steamboat steward, as well as a slave trader's assistant, including Saint Louis, Natchez, and New Orleans.

Audiences worldwide loved this *Grand Panorama*, including Charles Dickens, Queen Victoria, and Senator John Calhoun, who praised its "truthfulness to nature." Brown was also amazed, but for different reasons. To be "sold down the river" was to be trafficked on this route. For all the care lavished on chalk bluffs and Spanish moss, on the subtle lights of night and day, no word or stroke evoked the world he knew. The people he loved, their labor, lives, and heartbreak, were invisible. From that moment forth, Brown vowed to make his own panorama and to put himself and his people back into America's picture, where they rightfully belonged.

Brown worked up artists' sketches in Boston, but it was overseas that he finally raised the funds to hire painters and execute his vision: a continuous painting of twenty-four scenes, advertised as "2,000 feet of canvas," but likely smaller, about thirty feet long, ten feet high. Brown curated his scenes with care, refraining "from representing those disgusting pictures of vice and cruelty which are inseparable from Slavery," so that slavers could not claim exaggeration. Henry Box Brown, whose own panorama included graphic scenes of torture, as well as an illustration of Ellen escaping, had faced complaints not just from slavers but also from the British press.

Brown's panorama had debuted successfully that fall, despite what it lacked in movement, size, and flash. Unlike Box Brown, who engaged a trio of "minstrel fairies" (the youngest only six) to play the cello, harp, and violin beside his moving picture, William Wells Brown spoke and sang alone before a still, painted scrim. Nonetheless, Brown's panorama was judged superior and was soon to have the ultimate accompaniment in the Crafts—above all, Ellen.

The *Illustrated Lecture on American Slavery* would be shown at Glasgow's Trades' Hall at half past seven, a quiet hour, when smoke from chimneys became one with the sky. Having paid six pence admission (or a half shilling for front-row seats), spectators climbed the double stairs to enter an elegantly gaslit space, where the panorama waited. Ellen, too, awaited the twenty-four scenes, before the room was darkened, and William Wells Brown cued a light, illuminating, part by part, a world both like and unlike anything she had seen.

As a divine he flew, hurtling through space and time, requiring all to bear witness to the everyday suffering on fields from which the daily comforts of soft cotton clothing, sweet tea, and savory snuff all first sprung. He showed handsome buildings that served as houses of torture, slave pens, and sites for human sales, while shining a light upon the people: light-skinned sisters, auctioned high ("for what purpose," the audience might guess), a mother in a chain gang who was being whipped for refusing to go on without her child.

Such scenes were known to Ellen. Yet a new narration also emerged, one that memorialized Black resistance. There was no Underground Railroad dramatized here, no saving Quaker charity. Instead, the heroes were men, women, and children who freed themselves and others. Ellen listened as Brown spoke of a man who, disguised as a woman in mourning, marched straight past his enslaver and city officials to board a Buffalo-bound steamer—as artfully as Ellen had—and later went back for his wife. He told of a mother who jumped from ice floe to ice floe with her baby in her arms. He orchestrated a climactic battle in which freedom fighters rose up as one. For Ellen, it was an invitation to imagine herself in this community of heroes.

For all, it was a mandate. Once the lights came up, Brown welcomed spectators to see an actual slave collar he had described, gifted by a woman who had worn it—proof that this was no mere picture show. Brown also indicated how Britons could effect change. They could exercise their purchasing power, buying free-labor goods. They could fund abolitionism and buy Brown's books. They could also purchase a palm-sized image of Ellen, not as she appeared that night but as she had escaped, in a high hat and jaunty tie, still, yet moving ever forward in time.

SOIREE

So many invitations. For the next several weeks, the trio hovered near Glasgow, where hundreds were turned away from their final, crowded lecture. They took on smaller towns, too, such as Paisley and Campsie, Gouroch and Greenock, the names of these places as unfamiliar on their tongues as the tang of the Scots' famed haggis might have been on their American palates.

As they finally galloped north on their latest iron horse, Brown was personally relieved to see the city's tall chimneys and smoke fall back, giving way to cottages and farmlands, sculpted terraces and picturesque trees. He was filled with longing at the approach of Stirling's magnificent hilltop castle, the site of murders and coronations, and would have dragged the Crafts out to sightsee but for their engagement in Dundee, on the River Tay.

There, sixteen hundred people paid handsomely to see their panoramic production. Among the spectators was the city's most celebrated citizen, who called on them within hours of their arrival. The three were nursing cups of strong, hot tea. Brown, for one, was near dozing and in no mood to receive guests, but he jumped to his feet, wide awake, upon hearing the name of the small, sprightly, seventy-six-year-old gentleman who had come to see them.

In his many years, Dr. Thomas Dick had been a schoolmaster, defrocked minister, Christian philosopher, and, against his parents' early wishes, an astronomer. At age eight, after witnessing a meteor that seemed to set the sky on fire, young "Tam" began fashioning old spectacles into astronomical instruments. His father, Mungo Dick of Dundee, a weaver, threw up his hands in disappointment, raging: "I ken nae what t' dae wi' that laddie Tam, for he seems t' care for naething but books and glasses."

Since then, Dr. Dick had become the renowned author of *The Solar System*, as well as an abolitionist. He greeted Ellen memorably. As the old astronomer pressed her hand, a tear ran down his thin cheek. Observing him, Brown mused: "How I wished that the many slaveholders and proslavery professed Christians of America, who have read and pondered the philosophy of this man, could have been present."

On their last day in Dundee, the trio rode out to the scientist's hilltop cottage at Broughty Ferry. Moving from the formal parlor, through the observatory, deep into the old man's home, they were invited, one by one, to peer into his instruments—the microscope and telescope—to gaze first at the world in miniature, and then out at the stars.

The group's celebrity continued in Aberdeen, city of granite, between Rivers Dee and Don. Lines of Scots and clusters of schoolchildren waited their turns to ogle Brown's twenty-four American scenes and hear the American fugitives speak. Throughout, the two Williams dominated the spoken word, while Ellen sat by her husband, gazing out, and rising at the end to curtsy. Still, her presence was key, with audiences disappointed when Ellen was not there.

Why her public silence? It may have been a strategic choice, in a land where there was an even greater stigma than at home against a woman speaking onstage—no matter that Britain's monarch was Queen Victoria. Ellen was also keenly aware that any publicity in her name would "only ensure more cruelty" to her mother, as she would warn friends in the coming months. Artistic differences may have been another factor, especially over the term white slave, which the Williams "rather liked," in contrast to Ellen, who would always identify with the Black community, and whose complex ethnicity the term erased. It is even possible that Ellen did not want to be on the road at all.

What is known is that Ellen spoke forcefully offstage when she wished. One journalist would remember a dinner party, soon after the Crafts' arrival overseas, where Ellen was asked "if the slaves generally were intelligent enough to take care of themselves if they were emancipated."

Her reply: "At present, they take care of themselves and their master, too; if they were free, I think they would be able to take care of themselves." This impromptu wit would prove essential, as the petty politics that they had thus avoided soon threatened to engulf them all.

From Aberdeen down to Edinburgh, the trio moved by steamer rather than the train, simply for the pleasure of it—to experience the coastal line in the unusually warm weather, which felt less like February than April. They had just lectured before the Total Abstinence Society, and it was near midnight when they boarded, but as Brown, ever energetic, would rhapsodize, "The night was a glorious one. The sky was without a speck; and the clear, piercing air had a brilliancy I have seldom seen. The moon was in its zenith—the steamer and surrounding objects were beautiful in the extreme."

The trio was welcomed to the ship's drawing room, where the staff was entirely at their service. Brown was happy to spy a copy of Frederick Douglass's newspaper, the *North Star*. Moved, he put his own copy of the *Liberator* beside it, "to keep it company." Then they were shown to the best berths on the steamer—another courtesy that was so much at odds with all they had known in America that the Crafts "seemed almost bewildered," as Brown recalled. Though two months had passed since the couple's arrival, the ordinary retained the power to shock.

Back in Edinburgh, they resumed their lecturing and sightseeing. They climbed to the top of Calton Hill, where the half-formed shape of a classical Greek temple framed the blue winter sky, and the entire city seemed to unfold down below: a live panorama at the top of the world. At a tour of the infirmary, Brown—a doctor's assistant while in slavery—was especially stirred to see Black faces among the medical students. Crossing the street after a lecture, he was stunned to see Black and White university students walking arm in arm.

Brown and the Crafts were also invited to breakfast with one of Edinburgh's biggest celebrities, George Combe, and his wife, Cecelia. Combe was an expert in phrenology, a popular science in which head shape was used to understand human behavior (and used by some to promote racist stereotypes and justify slavery). Combe had felt more than a few eminent skulls in his decades of practice, including those of Queen Victoria's sons. Cecelia Combe was well known, too, as a member of England's first family of theater. Her late mother was the Shakespearean tragedienne Sarah Siddons, famed for her incomparable hand-wringing as Lady Macbeth.

Through Cecelia Combe's relatives, the couple had a personal connection to America's "peculiar institution." Combe's first cousin was the famed British actress Fanny Kemble, whose charisma caused the halls of Harvard to empty during her American tour. Some young men reportedly slicked their bodies with molasses so that they could slide through the throngs. Among the besotted was a young Wendell Phillips, who had paid to see her nineteen times. (Whether he was one of the molasses rubbers is unknown.)

Fanny had married Pierce Butler, heir to a vast slaveholding fortune, amassed by one of the signers of the Constitution, and the creator of the original Fugitive Slave Law. Her visit to his family's Georgia plantation ignited her abolitionism, and the couple's spectacular divorce. In 1859 Butler's mounting debts would lead to the biggest slave sale in American history, originally set to take place in Savannah's Johnson Square, where the Crafts had passed through: the square of heartache with the great live oaks, where Spanish moss refused to grow. The sale was eventually held at a racetrack. The rain did not stop for days, as 436 men, women, and children were sold in an event remembered as "The Weeping Time."

Whether or not she read Fanny's Georgia journals, which circulated privately, Cecelia Combe had no doubt heard of American slavery from her favorite cousin, to whom she would eventually bequeath a prize possession: a glove alleged to have belonged to William Shakespeare. Combe had also traveled through slave states herself, greeting President Martin Van Buren and drinking tea with the wife of a Mississippi senator. In Boston, her husband dined with Daniel Webster, with his "majestic overhanging brow."

Cecelia Combe took pride in her table, keeping meticulous record and recipe books, documenting more than seventeen types of pudding alone. Over such morning delicacies as ham omelettes, served hot and quick, or pancakes, rolled like logs and piled high, the Combes and the trio had the opportunity to discuss people known in common, as well as the institution they deplored. Brown noted that as she listened to Ellen's story, Cecelia Combe repeatedly cried.

The trio's return to Edinburgh was not entirely triumphant, however. Indeed, what might have been seen as a crowning moment—a highly touted soiree—would prove to be the opposite, making waves overseas.

Enter Dr. James W. C. Pennington, a self-emancipated Black preacher, teacher, and PhD (newly minted, with an honorary degree)—also a best-selling author, classics scholar, veteran lecturer, and, at forty-four, the trio's elder. Diminutive and debonair, with friendly eyes, Pennington had a large following in Scotland, but friends of William Lloyd Garrison considered him an enemy, suspecting him of financial mismanagement, bad alliances, and, most of all, bad-mouthing Garrison overseas.

When an invite came for the trio to take the stage alongside this man, the Crafts and Brown knew there would be trouble. To rebuff the joint appearance was to snub Pennington and his Scottish supporters, while to accept was to insult the Bostonian patrons who had helped launch this journey. In the end, the middle road they tried to choose proved to be a disaster. Two Scottish organizers gave the trio conflicting instructions on what to say that evening. Inevitably, one was disappointed, becoming so upset that he "scolded them in no measured terms," infuriating Brown. Worst of all, though, was their own experience with Dr. Pennington.

Ellen's patience ran thin as she heard the older man declare piously he would personally never resist recapture but consider it the "Lord's will" and submit—all the while expressing anguish about the Fugitive Slave Law. He had never faced down this law as she and William had; nor would he do so in the future, since friends would soon purchase his freedom.

One of Pennington's fans turned to Ellen and asked if his sentiments weren't "beautiful." Custom expected that a lady would agree or demur: Ellen, however, chose to laugh.

For Ellen, it was more than the low point of a dispiriting night, for she was coming to realize that, for all the people who lined up to see them, the world of abolition was smaller and less functional than she had been led to believe. Meanwhile, other British activists would soon warn that the field of lecturing was already crowded, and the Crafts needed to find another way to make a living. For Ellen and William, securing their future meant not only supporting themselves but also possibly raising funds to free loved ones, such as their enslaved mothers.

Their best chances of finding another path lay, as they would discover, with a singular woman: an author and traveler with a quick eye and a bad ear, an audience of one.

HARRIET MARTINEAU

|||||||||||||||||||||||||

They swept from Scotland back to England, William Wells Brown leading them at his usual manic beat, though the Crafts learned to draw a line. While returning to their inn after a late-night lecture, they neared the ruins of Melrose Abbey, much to the delight of Brown. He began quoting Sir Walter Scott, who had immortalized the site in verse. No, they would not stop, and neither would the Crafts agree to rise early to see it. Brown would make that moonlit jaunt alone.

They joined Brown after daybreak, however, to tour Scott's stone mansion, striding through the great hall, with flashes of silver armor, and Scott's personal library, lined with twenty thousand books, the warm leather spines turned out. Brown tested Scott's chair, and together the trio beheld the wide blue coat and plaid pants that Scott had lived and died in, now enshrined in glass. They even glimpsed Scott's real-life granddaughter, who looked like she did not want to be there.

At Dryburgh Abbey, they paused by Scott's ivy-covered gravesite before speeding down by the afternoon train to lecture in Hawick, then Langholm. From there to Carlisle, Brown—possibly joined by William—was forced to ride on the outside of the coach, the vehicle strapped high with luggage, not because of any prejudice but simply because the vehicle was full.

Their last stop in Scotland was Gretna Green, famous for fast weddings. Then came the River Eden and a bucolic valley, sprinkled with farmhouses and grazing sheep. Thick columns of smoke rose in the distance, and by the time they arrived at the English city of Carlisle, even Brown was fatigued. Just one night stood between them and their destination, however, in one of the most legendary landscapes in England, immortalized by Wordsworth and Coleridge, and women of letters too: the home of Harriet Martineau, a celebrated writer, thinker, adventurer, and economist who had barely made it out of America alive.

Harriet Martineau was thirty-two and already famous when she sailed for New York in the hot summer of 1834. Best known for using stories to explain subjects such as political economy to general audiences, Martineau had burst onto the literary scene with *Illustrations of Political Economy*—a nine-volume work that also put her on the map for being antislavery.

Despite her antislavery reputation, Martineau was determined to approach the United States with an open mind. The nation was not ready to respond in kind. A proslavery heat raged, and not just in the South. Racist violence erupted in New York while she was en route, and as the ship circled the shore, the captain worried for her safety, due to her reputation.

But Harriet Martineau had already reached that place in her life where she did not much care what others thought or did. She had survived a miserable childhood and fought to be educated. She had lived with disability, having lost most of her hearing by age twenty. (She would carry an ear trumpet to the end of her days; anyone wanting to be heard clearly would need to speak straight into it.) She had written through chronic illness and the stigma of spinsterhood, defying all expectations of what a woman like herself could do or be. And she was determined to see the nation—and slavery—"as it was."

Ironically, it was not Southerners but Northerners who would challenge her most. Her troubles began when a Philadelphian asked whether Martineau would object if someone she knew were engaged to marry a Black person. The Englishwoman brushed off the questions, replying that she did not consider it her business to interfere in anyone's engagement, never mind their color. The lady flew away with a flutter of kisses and good-byes, then proceeded to spread the word that Harriet Martineau favored "amalgamation," or interracial love. Martineau thought it all absurd, but her American friends panicked, and warned her not to go South.

In Washington, DC, Americans continued to play against type. Southern senators greeted her warmly, telling her that they wished for her to see their "peculiar institution" for herself, with the expectation that she would publish exactly what she saw, both bad and good. In Kentucky, she stayed with Henry Clay's daughter, next door to the senator's plantation, while in Charleston, she was escorted by none other than John C. Calhoun.

Initially, Martineau was charmed. She was a guest at the Planter's Hotel, where Ellen had stayed in disguise. There she awoke to find little gifts on her window seat—nosegays wrought with hyacinth, pretty dishes filled with marmalade, and a "piece of Indian work"—all slipped into her room by unseen hands. Six carriages arrived daily, with chauffeurs at her service, competing to take her where she pleased. Martineau loved climbing to the top of a church steeple, from which she glimpsed the headscarves of "mulatto" women carrying water and fruit atop their heads; the shiny points of yucca trees; the blue of the distant rivers and the islands.

Friends insisted she see the Saturday evening market, run by slaves, and pointed out their apparent cheer as they sold handicrafts and fruit—a sign, they believed, that the enslaved were happy. But Martineau was determined to see another type of market, and her visit there changed everything.

Martineau would recount the scene with precision. Two auctioneers stood on a table. One held a hammer, the other called the bids. Behind them and below stood the people to be sold. A mixed-race woman came up. She wore a yellow head kerchief and an apron, and she stood with her two children. Her baby was in her arms. Another child held on to her skirt. The mother's eyes, as Martineau would never forget, darted from side to side.

Martineau thought that the woman's obvious agony would have shut up the crowd, but instead, everyone was energized—the auctioneer most of all, joking and zealous. It was, she remembered, the most hellish sight she had ever seen.

Meanwhile, her hostess, a Northern-born writer, offered this commentary: "You know my theory, that one race must be subservient to the other. I do not care which; and if the blacks should ever have the upper hand, I should not mind standing on that table and being sold with two of my children."

The author had no words in response that she considered fit for print.

Next, a small boy of eight or nine stood up alone.

"There was no bearing the child's look," recalled Martineau, and her group left quickly.

It was then as if the lights went out of the city and all became awash in a macabre glow. They went to a "young heiress's first ball," and as bouquets were presented, and the girls waltzed in their breezy dresses, and a child was brought to kiss her cheek, and men railed against tariffs and tyranny, Martineau looked upon the Black faces in the room in a new way.

Later, she asked questions, and though she would report far more on the slavers' perspective, she was moved to say: "Whatever I learned that lies deepest down in my heart, of the moral evils, the unspeakable vices, and woes of slavery was from the lips of those who are suffering under them."

Martineau did not withhold her horror from her hosts, and to their credit, as Martineau told, they remained as gracious as ever. She never had concerns for her safety while she was in the South. Instead, where she began to feel true fear was once she went back North.

Here she saw her first proslavery riots. In Boston, she drove past the crowds hoping to destroy Garrison—the "gentleman's mob" that first had its sights on her fellow countryman, George Thompson, but dragged Garrison through the streets instead. She was nearly mobbed herself at a ladies' abolitionist gathering. Rioters could be heard screaming outside, hurling dung and rocks against the walls of the house, when she was asked to speak. Harriet Martineau then faced an excruciating decision—one of the most painful moments of her life. Would she go public with her own views, as she was implored?

She did, and her life was never the same. In Boston, the press carried the story, and the city turned on her. Meanwhile, as word traveled South, she received chilling invitations to "come and see how they would treat foreign incendiaries. They would hang me: they would cut my tongue out," throw it on a pile of excrement.

Late one night, Ellis Gray Loring showed up to warn her against traveling west and south. There was already a lookout for an English lady, recognizable by her ear horn. He spoke clearly through that instrument: "You will be lynched."

Martineau headed to Michigan and the Northern Lakes instead, where, for several months, her first thought in the morning was whether she would live to the end of the day. Once finally back in England, her relief was keen, but even at home, she continued to receive threats, most postmarked from Boston.

Not one to be silenced, the writer fought back with her pen, providing a systematic condemnation of American racism. If she had once been inclined to be wary of wild-eyed abolitionists, she became fully converted to abolitionism herself and ready to use her platform to rail against the "oppression of the negroes," the nation's "grossest vice."

Martineau was not without her prejudices. She once observed: "The voice of a white, even of a lady, if it were authoritative, would make a whole regiment of rebellious slaves throw down their arms and flee. . . . They will never take the field, unless led on by free blacks." She once recalled as "disgusting" the sight of an enslaved woman in the field. At the same time, seventeen years after her American journey, she was more committed to the cause than ever and among the first to reach out to the Crafts.

Truthfully, Martineau did not have high expectations for the coming days. As she would later tell Ellis Gray Loring, she approached the weekend as a duty. But she awaited her guests as others had welcomed her, with an open door.

"Mrs. Martineau" was her preferred title—"Miss" being an unworthy "juvenile prefix," as she believed, serving only to advertise her availability for marriage, which she never wanted. Now, at forty-eight, she lived surrounded by strong country women—"Amazons," she called them—in a house she had designed, on farmland she cultivated, in a community she chose. In the British town of Ambleside, she lived out her ideals, supporting local housing projects and free lectures for the poor. She both wrote and entertained as she pleased. Charlotte Brontë, George Eliot, and, later, Florence Nightingale were among her fellow Amazons. Soon to join that roster was Ellen Craft.

Martineau's home was in the heart of the Lake District of England, a short walk from that of her late friend William Wordsworth. The poet had helped make the region a destination, as did the rails, which now shuttled tourists from all over England up to Lake Windermere, shining like a mirror on a spring afternoon.

Arriving lakeside, the Crafts and Brown took a coach to Ambleside's Salutation Hotel, where it was only a short ride past an ancient bridge house and a winding brook to Martineau's celebrated hilltop home, the Knoll. It was dark by the time they approached. The trio mounted the steps and were shown to the library, from which warm lights glowed.

The spacious room was decorated tastefully, with engravings and busts of deceased literary figures, including Shakespeare, and a Continental map. From there, they entered a cozier space with watercolors scattered on a circular table, terra-cotta sculptures, a small table covered with half-opened letters and just-published books—and at the center of it all, with her ear trumpet in her left hand, her right hand out to them, Mrs. Harriet Martineau.

She had deep-set eyes, expressive and wise, and she was just as William Wells Brown had pictured: tall and stately, only more youthful-looking than he imagined. Martineau was eager to hear Ellen and William's story and soon invited them to sit close beside her.

She held up her trumpet, the narrow end to her ear, the bell to William's lips, and through the body of that instrument moved the sound of their travels and travails. William Wells Brown had once said to a ladies' abolitionist society that were he truly to represent slavery and its evils, he would need to whisper to them, one by one. Here, through the trumpet, a story now flowed.

Brown noticed the tears running down Martineau's cheeks, and he would not forget the words she spoke once William leaned away from the trumpet: "I would that every woman in the British Empire could hear that tale as I have, so that they might know how their own sex was treated in that boasted land of liberty." As they sat together surrounded by books, she was especially moved by Ellen and William's dreams of an education and vowed to take action.

Martineau would later tell friends and family how her guests far exceeded her expectations. She wrote her cousin Lucy: "I found them sensible, full of information in their own way, simple & upright, & as true a lady & gentleman as I have seen for many a day." She was not shy about picking favorites: of her three guests, she found Ellen most charming, then William. As for Brown, "she did not find him so agreeable as the Crafts."

Brown himself, however, might never have known it. That night, he went to bed wound up with joy. As he would recall: "The idea that I was under the roof of the authoress of *The Hour and the Man*"—a novel about Haitian Revolutionary leader Toussaint Louverture—"and that I was on the banks of the sweetest lake in Great Britain . . . drove sleep from my pillow." He lay wide awake, in full anticipation of more lakeside adventures in store.

———

Lakeside would not disappoint. Early the next morning, the trio walked to the "finest spots in the valley," led by a host who, only a few years earlier, had been bound to home and bed, seemingly destined to be an invalid. Through mesmerism, Martineau had made a stunning recovery, and, since then, had gazed upon the Pyramids, raced desert bandits on horseback, and wrote about it all. Around the Lakes, she had become such an ardent walker—and an unconventional one, reportedly preferring gentleman's boots and smoking cigars—that William Wordsworth had taken her to task, saying too much walking was "mischief" in a woman.

Now she summoned her new friends into an enchanted landscape: serene country villages, where the green hills loomed so close as to appear touchable; forests where deer and rabbit bounded through the green; and the occasional, astonished pheasant. There were man-made streams, lakes and brooks, and here and there, exquisite statues darkened with moss.

The quartet was sure to have worked up an appetite for lunch, though Martineau, to Brown's astonishment, had absolutely no sense of taste or smell. For the afternoon, a neighbor, Sir J. K. Shuttleworth, sent his luxurious barouche, and, tucked, into that smooth vehicle, the group rode off to the village of Grasmere. By six, they were back at Ambleside, where they took their tea before their evening lecture.

The Americans raised an impressive sum of money. As Martineau told friends, "The negroes carried away" six pounds, seventeen shillings, and four pence—the pence coming from a small child. Martineau would have liked to know more about the Crafts' finances, especially whether they might have saved up funds that might go toward their education. William, however, was typically American in his silence, as she observed, and would not give her a clear answer.

The next day, a Sunday, the author's guests would briefly separate—perhaps a first for the group. Ellen went to Hawkshead with new Quaker friends, William worked on a letter (the Crafts could "just read & write," Martineau observed), and William Wells Brown nearly killed himself going up Loughrigg Fell on a donkey.

The group reconvened in the afternoon for more bucolic driving. Just as the sky was turning rose and gold, they came upon a medieval stone church. Martineau led them through a quiet yard to a grave beneath a young yew tree. There they paid their respects to William Wordsworth, then returned to the Knoll, where they packed for the next leg of their journey.

As the trio left Ambleside the next day, they were far better refreshed than when they had arrived, chilled and exhausted after nonstop traveling. Harriet Martineau had fortified them with her British hospitality, giving them a store of energy that they would need as they journeyed on, no longer among the custom-made homes of the intellectual elite or the thatched cottages of Cumbria County laborers, but nearer the smokestacks and factories of Leeds and York. Meanwhile, their new friend would wield her pen on their behalf, clearing another way forward.

"FUGITIVE'S TRIUMPH"

||||||||||||||||||||||||||

Within two weeks, Harriet Martineau had an answer—and a question. *"The thing can be done,"* she exulted in a letter to William Wells Brown. Everything was arranged. The Crafts could have their education, as they wished, in the most idyllic of settings, thanks to a baroness.

Lady Byron, widow of the famed Romantic poet, had agreed to take them on as students in one of her charitable industrial schools: William and Ellen could teach their crafts, cabinetmaking and sewing, in exchange for their schooling, room, and board. Additional funds would be required, but Martineau was sure they could be raised, with Lady Byron herself willing to contribute.

The school was in the village of Ockham, of "Ockham's razor" fame. Centuries ago, philosopher William of Ockham had put the site on the map when he popularized the idea that in problem solving, it made sense to take the simplest route. However, if the Crafts had pored over a traveler's map, they would have had to squint to find the village, with no visible railway lines, a pinprick in Surrey County. This may have been one reason why the Crafts were reluctant to commit, opting for a different plan.

It was still high lecture season, with invites pouring in, and the Great Exhibition was soon to open: the first World's Fair, organized by Prince Albert, consort of Queen Victoria, to be held in London in the coming months. Piece by piece, a giant Crystal Palace was going up on the grounds of Hyde Park. It would be the event of the year, which no one would want to miss, least of all the trio. The Great Exhibition promised an unprecedented opportunity to educate the world about slavery, in a transparent global arena. Until then, they would not slow down.

Harriet Martineau was personally eager for the Crafts to take action. She had written her friends the happiest of endings, an abolitionist fairy tale come true. A heroic couple, very much in love, had escaped bondage in the cruel American South, fleeing the so-called land of freedom for sanctuary in England, where they fulfilled their educational dreams under the noblest British patronage and lived happily ever after. All that was needed to end a lifetime of drama was a word. As Martineau wrote Brown: "Now, you must please just let me know whether the Crafts accept this offer: & how soon they wish to settle in Ockham." The Crafts, however, deferred.

By the time Harriet Martineau mailed her letter, the Crafts and Brown were far to the east in England, where they celebrated an unexpectedly happy ending to another fugitive story in Boston. Shadrack Minkins, a self-emancipated man who had been captured, jailed, and bound to return South, had escaped from prison with help from the Crafts' old friends, including Lewis Hayden.

They told this story in Newcastle, then spoke to more rapt audiences in Sunderland, York, Bradford, and Leeds, now playing to working-class crowds. Their story of exploitation and invention, of survival by wits, of families broken by an all-consuming system of moneymaking and greed, struck a chord among those who toiled in sweatshops and factories. (Calling Ellen a "white slave" only reinforced this connection.)

There was a difference, though, as the Williams pointed out, countering arguments by proslavers that American slaves were better off than so-called wage slaves. William drew cheers as he exclaimed that while he knew the poor here suffered, "the poorest man would not exchange positions with the best slave; or if he would, he was not fit to be called an Englishman."

William lectured heavily, having come into his own as a speaker. No longer did he go straight to the escape, the chase. Now he might now open big, with a critique of slavery worldwide, reminding audiences that slavery had come to America from England, that Britons were duty bound to help end what they had started. He spoke more personally of his own bondage and the pain of his separation from his family members, whose freedom he worked to purchase. And he played a bigger part in the drama.

Whereas in America, the origins of the plans remained vague, William now claimed the idea. *He* had seen that his wife could pass for a rich White gentleman. *He* earned the money, made the plans, procured the disguise. The Ellen he spoke of, meanwhile, was reluctant, as passive in the planning as she appeared in the lecture hall. Only with her husband's persuasion and her faith in God did she agree to put on a man's clothes.

William might well have recalibrated his story for the British, who were more worried about propriety than American audiences. His precise motives—and Ellen's part, if any, in changing the story—cannot be known. What has been reported, however, is her discomfort with the language used to describe her in advertisements and handbills, produced by the more vocal Williams, who outnumbered her. The term "white slave" persisted, and Ellen herself was often described as a "white woman" in the press.

Some of these tactics would soon change, though, as the trio traveled west to meet a father-daughter team of activists, friends of Harriet Martineau: John Bishop Estlin, a renowned eye surgeon, and his only child, Mary. Brown considered Estlin one of his closest friends in England, and the Crafts would too, as the aged doctor and his beloved daughter welcomed them into their home, where they would be warmly received, but also closely watched.

Sixty-five-year-old Dr. Estlin and thirty-year-old Mary were both in terrible health, the doctor suffering painfully from rheumatism, Mary from an unnamed disease. Even so, Estlin had been one of the first to reach out to the Crafts upon their arrival overseas, writing to Brown: "If the Crafts do not find ready friends where they are, send them to Bristol, and I will keep them at my expense."

The elderly eye doctor was not rich, but he was known to be generous. He gave free medical treatment to those in need; had lent Brown money for his panorama; and contributed whatever he could to the abolitionist cause. He and his daughter, his lone companion since his wife's early death, had woken to this purpose after traveling to the Caribbean, where they were jolted by what they saw firsthand of slavery.

The Estlins greeted their guests with such open arms that the Crafts were reminded of their Quaker friends in Pennsylvania. Both father and daughter especially loved Ellen, moved by her gentle manners and quiet confidences. Over shared cups of tea, she spoke to them of the oppression she had known in Georgia, of her beloved mother, who endured on the other side of the world and remained ever present in Ellen's mind. And in these moments, her hosts received an unprecedented education.

Like Harriet Martineau, they ranked their guests, with Ellen on top—only William was now at the bottom. "Craft has none of Brown's energy," Estlin observed, adding: "my impression is that he is a little indolent." As for Brown, Estlin saw that the Crafts "could do nothing" without him, yet he, too, lacked "that knowledge of English custom and society, which it is important he should have, to maintain Ellen Craft in that position which she ought, and might easily hold." Estlin thought both men too "showman-like" in their sensibilities, too crass, which might have been another way of saying too low class in tone, especially next to ladylike Ellen.

For her part, Ellen found renewed female companionship in the Estlins' home. Besides Mary, there was Emma Michell, Mary's aunt, who came to run the household when Mary became too ill. For months on end, Ellen had been living out of her luggage while on tour. In Bristol, she finally had the beginnings of a community and perhaps something more. "They are quite like the family in this house," said Mary's aunt, and she and the Estlins were quietly thrilled whenever Ellen referred to their shared residence as "home."

With the Estlins strongly backing Ellen, the trio's program subtly transformed. In Bristol, they drew throngs to their lectures and displays of their "painting," as the panorama was artfully renamed. Among the spectators: one thousand curious schoolchildren. To Ellen's "great delight" (as Dr. Estlin would report), the Williams were persuaded to remove the term *white slave* from advertisements. She also enjoyed a "higher position" in public gatherings. At a large meeting in Broadmead, Ellen had a place of honor on the doctor's arm and swept onto the stage in a circle of antislavery ladies. Newspapers highlighted her entry into a hall filled with "a most respectable audience," noting that Ellen "seemed somewhat embarrassed" by the attention.

As an activist, Ellen swung into high gear. She mobilized committee meetings, taking on Mary Estlin's share of duties when her host became ill. Far from the days of the disastrous soiree with Pennington, Ellen became an expert navigator of messy political situations, strategically jettisoning some invitations, while graciously accepting others. Together she and William answered "wrenching" questions and defenses of slavery with a steadiness that humbled their hosts. And, no matter that some friends of Garrison were *still* complaining about the Pennington affair, they helped raise the profile of the editor and his allies.

So effective and popular did Ellen become—and so confidently did she carry herself—that there were some who became "a little alarmed," as Emma Michell wrote to a friend, that she would be "made vain, or above her condition in life." In response, Ellen demanded, "How can they think that one who is only so lately allowed to feel herself a woman, to know that she is no longer considered merely as a thing, can be set up by being treated as a fellow creature?"

The nearness of that time would strike all, when a letter arrived with news from Boston and from Georgia, illustrating just what was at stake if and when they ever went back.

———

It was a cold day in May when the Crafts, Emma Michell, and Dr. Estlin gathered around the hearth for the tidings from Samuel May Jr. Everyone listened intently as the doctor read aloud the tragic news about Thomas Sims, a young bricklayer from Savannah who had escaped slavery aboard a Boston-bound steamer. No one had come after him until Sims, in deep financial need, wrote to his wife, a free woman in the South. His enslaver then sent a proxy to hunt him down, just as Robert Collins had done with Ellen.

The same allies who had helped the Crafts jumped in to help Sims flee. They prepared mattresses outside his jailhouse window, so that he could dive down three stories into a getaway carriage. But the way out was barred, and this time, Daniel Webster, as secretary of state, and Seth J. Thomas, the enemy lawyer, were more successful in their pursuit of the law. On an early April morning, when most of the city still slept, Sims was marched to the wharves in the escort of hundreds of armed men and the city police, with local volunteers on high alert.

"Sims, preach Liberty to the Slaves!" Someone cried as he boarded the ship.

"And is this Massachusetts liberty?" Sims called back.

The Crafts knew what he would face in the South. William shocked Dr. Estlin by observing that Sims should have killed a guard in Boston: better to hang in Boston than to be sent back to Georgia alive.

As the ordeal played out in the press, a Savannah paper, griping about the expense of pursuing fugitives, suggested tongue in cheek that his owner recoup costs by sending him to the showman Barnum, to be exhibited as a "great curiosity," the *first fugitive slave* ever brought back from Massachusetts." In the end, Sims was lashed in public thirty-nine times.

The news about Thomas Sims articulated to William and Ellen more clearly than ever not just what they might have suffered had they not succeeded in their escape, but what they could still suffer should they hazard a return to America. Meanwhile, another exchange of letters between Georgia and Boston, soon to be published widely, would rule out that option entirely.

The exchange had begun earlier that spring, when a Boston businessman, J. S. Hastings, personally reached out to Robert Collins, asking him to name his price for Ellen. This was hardly the first such offer Collins had received, but he had reason to take it seriously. From a businessman's perspective, it was free money. Collins knew that his chances of recapturing Ellen were next to none. In essence, the deal would serve as insurance for the Crafts, making it possible for them to return to America without the fear of being hunted.

Equally important, Hastings was no raging abolitionist. He approached Collins sympathetically, saying that he could tell from Collins's own words that he was a man of humanity. And he made it clear that he and other Bostonians could and would support the Fugitive Slave Law, writing: "The enforcement of the law with us is not longer a matter of doubt. We have the power and the will to do it." Though he did not mention it by name, the fate of Thomas Sims stood as a case in point. The Crafts, however, had become fugitives *before* the law's passage. On this basis, Hastings wanted to know if an exception might be made?

Collins returned a respectful but resounding no. Money was not the issue; neither was his purpose to re-enslave Ellen, about whom he had only positive things to say. (William was another story: Collins held him accountable for "abducting the slave Ellen.") It was precedent and principle that mattered—and power. Collins insisted on a slaver's rights to bestow freedom as a gift. "A good slave," he said, "can acquire his freedom without being a fugitive." In fact, this was not true, for emancipation was not possible in Georgia, where a person like Ellen, however "good," could never be freed, only sold.

Practically speaking, Collins's letter was hardly transformative, since the Crafts remained opposed to having their freedom purchased.

And yet Collins's statement closed a door. Other slavers had been known to strike deals—Douglass's, for example, and, in a few years, William Wells Brown's. Collins, meanwhile, wrote for all the world to see that he would not relinquish his mastery. William and Ellen could never return to America, not as long as he remained alive. To be free, Collins—or slavery itself—would have to die.

As much as they were haunted by the past, the Crafts now needed to look into building a future in England, not as guests but as settlers. What would they do, how would they live, not from day to day, but in the long term? These questions long deferred became increasingly urgent, especially as their abolitionist friends pressed them for an answer.

For weeks, they traveled from Bristol to other towns in western England—Taunton, Bridgewater, Gloucester, Cheltenham, Exeter, Bath, and then to Wales—with the Estlins watching them and dispatching reports. As spring turned to summer, the Estlins became increasingly frustrated and critical: not of Ellen, but of William, whom they considered guarded and intractable, even unreasonable. As they saw it, he was the holdout on Ockham, while Ellen was willing—though there might also have been some wishful thinking on their parts. Whatever their artistic differences, the Crafts and Brown were always a team. Dr. Estlin admired how they spoke only positively of one another, although he also thought that if it were not for Brown's "unusual good temper," they might not have gotten along so smoothly.

Yet, above the din, from Collins's dark aria, to even darker tunes from Georgia, over the abolitionists' chorus of complaints, Ellen's voice rose. As she addressed gatherings, slipped from drawing rooms to great halls, conversed with ladies one-on-one, shook hands, and made herself at home, she spoke this wish, time and again:

"Oh, how I should like my old Mistress could see me now."

Whether she referred to Mistress Smith, the woman who gave her away as a wedding gift, or Mistress Collins, her half sister, is unknown. Quite possibly, she meant both.

Still another song was heard in Bristol during these late-spring months. Days after the news of Sims reached them—on the very day J. S. Hastings wrote Robert Collins—Mrs. Michell paused at the stairs, moved by the sound of Ellen singing: "I am a slave no more."

The song Ellen sang to herself was "Fugitive's Triumph," and it closed with these powerful words:

Tyrant! thou hast bereft me
Home, friends, pleasures so sweet;
Now, forever I've left thee.
Thou and I never shall meet;
. . . .
Joys, joys, bright as the morning,
Now, now, on me will pour,
Hope, hope, on me is dawning,
I'm not a slave any more!

THE GREAT
EXHIBITION

||||||||||||||||||||||||

If Ellen's old mistresses could see her now indeed, as she prepared for an event beyond all imagining: the Great Exhibition of the Works of Industry of All Nations. On opening day, the first of May, in London's Hyde Park, Queen Victoria herself swept in, with its chief architect, her husband, tall beside her, surrounded by a fleet of red-clad guards and dignitaries from around the world. (There, too, was the captain of a Chinese junk ship, who in his exotic silken clothes, was taken for a high-ranking official and managed to slip into the official painted picture.)

The purpose of this great exhibit was to convene the wonders of the world's industries and technologies—not to sell or barter, but to display the possibilities of human ingenuity and to share the dream of what humanity could achieve for all. Ticketing reflected this purpose. Early admission was priced high, but then came the weekly "shilling days," which made it possible for any and all to see the world for as little as a shilling apiece.

The exhibit was celebrated as the eighth wonder of the world. Here were pulsating mechanisms of every variety: threshing, sewing, washing, and cotton-spinning machines—even a shoe-cleaning machine, to ease and possibly replace the burden of human toil. There was a machine that turned out crisp envelopes, all gummed; a hybrid piano-violin that could be played by a single performer; beds that woke slumberers by tipping them out. One of the most awe-inspiring exhibits was a printing press from the *Illustrated London News*, which could spew out five thousand copies per hour—and had, in fact, fired off so many pictures of Ellen, in disguise.

Then there were the vehicles: a gleaming, shell-shaped phaeton, muscular locomotives, and even a submarine. And there were natural treasures from all over the world, including a 191-carat diamond called the Koh-i-Noor, and other gemstones kept in cages like wild beasts.

The site itself was a Crystal Palace, built of thousands of rectangles of sparkling glass, which thousands of laborers had stacked on metal trusses in a matter of months—a marvel of coordination and problem solving, of orchestrated labor, which no machine could replace. It was exactly the kind of organizational, technological, and cultural feat that the Collinses would have loved. Macon would hold its own agricultural fair the next year, where Eliza would use her discriminating eye to judge a competitive needlework exhibit—and her husband would present his manual for managing slaves.

Southerners of rank and wealth were expected at the London Exhibition, one of the reasons why the Crafts and Brown were determined to attend: to challenge them on slavery, with the world as their witness. Unbeknownst to the trio, Brown's enslaver, Enoch Price, would be among the Southern tourists, and he would try to reach Brown, leaving a card with a friend. The move would shake Brown, despite his easy manner. Thankfully, Price would do no more to pursue him.

The plan was for the two Williams to settle first in London; Ellen would join them a few days later. The Estlins grumbled, worried about Ellen's health and nervous that there was still no fixed, long-term plan. But they were delighted to have Ellen all to themselves. As Mary Estlin would express: "I am never so happy as when she is under our immediate protection."

The trio stepped into the London immortalized by Charles Dickens: a landscape of spectacular royal palaces but also one of smokestacks and squalor, ruffian gangs of Oliver Twists. (In fact, William Craft may have expected for Dickens himself to call on him: the Estlins would say this was one of the reasons why he got more expensive accommodations than they approved of, over the advice of Brown.) Nearly two and a half million people lived in London, many crammed into ramshackle housing. These numbers swelled with the tens of thousands of visitors who came to see the exhibition every day—six million souls in under six months.

At the center of it all, at the edge of Hyde Park, below the Serpentine Lake, was the crystalline palace, stretching precisely 1,851 feet to mark the year. From a distance, it rose from the velvet green, a shining, spectral transparency of glass and iron, at once fragile and strong.

Some sixty-five thousand daily visitors descended on the exhibition during the week of the trio's arrival, the clear summer weather an added draw. As they approached the site on a shilling day, the grounds teemed with people of all classes and kinds, chugged in from around the country and steamed in from around the world. Nearby streets were jammed with packed omnibuses and bright carriages, manned with drivers dressed in red and gold.

They passed through a high iron gate, where visitors jostled to pay their way, then into the vast glass palace. They entered the transept, a sheer atrium, three stories high, to behold a dazzling, pink-glass fountain, twenty-seven feet tall. It threw light skyward, as water coursed down in magical spirals, the light beams flecking the leaves of full-sized elm trees that towered above, entirely contained within the building. Glass galleries stretched out on either side of the atrium as far as the eye could see: to the west, those of "Great Britain and Her Dependencies," or colonized countries, with foreigners on the east. It was enough to make Brown speechless. Later, he called it "the greatest building the world ever saw."

Brown marveled, too, at the spectacle of the world convening: Europeans and Asians, Americans and Africans, in communication. Interpreters offered translations in twenty-one languages, including Russian, Arabic, Turkish, Mandarin, Bengali, and Hebrew. Brown would note the "exclusive Chinese, with his hair braided, and hanging down his back," striding through the palace "in his wood-bottomed shoes," and he was especially proud and pleased to see "coloured men and women," stylishly dressed: "a good sprinkling of my countrymen."

"There is a great deal of freedom in the exhibition," Brown would observe further, in this extraordinary space, where "the Queen and the day labourer, the prince and the merchant, the peer and the pauper," and people of all colors and walks of life might collide, meeting on equal ground. Here was an "amalgamation of rank," a "kindly blending of interests," a "forgetfulness of the cold formalities of rank and grades," which dazzled Brown as much as the exhibits.

It would have been impossible to see it all in one day—100,000 items in 13,937 exhibits, over ten miles of space—one of the reasons why the trio made repeat visits. (Brown would visit a total of fifteen times.) But there was another reason why the trio went again and again. They intended not merely to observe but to stage. Together they aimed to present a key missing piece from this beautiful jigsaw puzzle of the world.

Karl Marx was among those who criticized the Great Exhibition as an "emblem of the capitalist fetishism of commodities." Conspicuously absent in this extravagant display of all the world's wonders was any recognition of the price paid in land and lives—most of all, the enslaved labor on which so much of it turned.

America's raw materials were shown in abundance: piles of ham, barrels of salt, beef, and pork, and "beautiful white lard," as Brown would report. There were cornmeal and peas, rice and tobacco, and hefty bags of cotton. Meanwhile, there was no mention of those who grew or harvested or butchered these products—nothing to indicate that the colorful calico spun on England's brilliant looms had been picked by men, women, and children on the other side of the world who were themselves commodified, bought, and sold. In fact, there were reports that a South Carolinian had considered bringing "half a dozen haughty sinewy negroes" to exhibit, before fearing that the enslaved would try to escape. In the official catalog, the sole reference to slave labor pertained to cotton grown in Africa, not the United States.

The Crystal Palace did include one famous representation of slavery, among the most visited of all the exhibits: a radiant, white marble sculpture called *The Greek Slave*. As the story went, the young woman had been captured by Turks during the Greek Revolution. Her entire family had been decimated, while she alone was "preserved as a treasure too valuable to be thrown away." Naked but for a chain, she stood "exposed to the gaze of the people she abhors." (Anyone suspecting pornography could stand reassured that gazing upon this beautiful nude was no crime, due to the enslaved woman's Christian piety.)

The sculpture was not just one of the most popular objects in the Great Exhibition but also in the wide world beyond. *The Greek Slave* had already traveled much of the United States, from New England down to Charleston. At the Crystal Palace, thousands lined up to peer at her exposed form, discreetly on view in her own red velvet enclosure atop a turning pedestal that put her private area (half masked by her hand and chain) on eye level with a tall man's gaze. The Queen herself would spend a half hour in *The Greek Slave*'s company; slavers and ministers queued up, too, with little sense of irony. The Crafts and Brown, meanwhile, meant to bring these and other ironies home.

A Great Exhibit was required for this Great Exhibition, which was a work of performance art in itself—a "vast panorama," as Brown called it, or "one great theater, with thousands of performers, each playing his own part." Some early proposals were over the top. From overseas, radical White abolitionist Henry C. Wright dreamed of a mock slave auction, with Ellen in her escape suit; Brown with his panorama; Henry Box Brown with his box; and bloodied chains and weapons beside them. But in the end, the trio opted for a subtler approach, one more in line with the Crafts' famed escape and, in its own way, far more subversive. Rather than confront their enemies, as William had in a prior visit, arguing with Southerners about the Fugitive Slave Law, they would simply move through the space of America as openly as they had crossed from South to the North, and from America to overseas. The idea was equal parts radical, simple, and bold. It would be a "walking exhibition" across the world.

They chose a five-shilling day, a Saturday, when there would be fewer visitors overall, but the most powerful classes of visitors would be on the scene. The day being unusually warm, it would soon be hotter inside the palace than out, the greenhouse becoming a hothouse.

Dressed in their weekend best, the Crafts entered the transept with Brown, the Estlins, and other friends, whom they had met at the house of George Thompson, the fiery abolitionist orator, who had been targeted by the "gentleman's mob" in Boston. Thompson was back in America, but his wife and daughters were on hand to show their support for William and Ellen.

By the time of their arrival, the Queen and her retinue had already passed through and were wending their way west through the British galleries. The Crafts and their entourage, meanwhile, would move east, forming their own exhibition within the same glass world.

They moved in twos and threes, arm in arm, four women, four men in all: first, Ellen, with Jenny Thompson (wife of George) and Mr. McDonnell (a leader of the National Reform Association); next, William Wells Brown, alongside Louisa Thompson, the Thompsons' eldest daughter; and finally William Craft, with Amelia, the Thompson's younger daughter, and William Farmer, a journalist. Their destination: the United States of America.

This American pavilion had fallen short. After Americans had made a great fuss about their gallery's small size, and finally landed prime real estate at the end of the eastern wing, they had trouble filling it. A giant fake eagle hovered close to the ceiling, two stories off the ground, presiding over fabric swells of stars and stripes and a wide red banner, but the space below appeared strangely void. A section of a truss bridge held the center, with stairs leading up on either side, so visitors could stand upon it and look over the rails, as if off the side of a train. Resting on the bridge was what appeared from a distance to be a headless vulture, with folded wings: a display of vulcanized rubber, the work of Mr. Charles Goodyear and his eponymous company.

Now, in the shadow of this eagle, beneath the glowing red banner, and under the crystal sky, the three American refugees made straight for the only representation of slavery they would find anywhere in the display of their land of birth: The celebrated *Greek Slave*.

It was said that the artist offered directions for how his figure should be met: not politically, but piously. Naturally, William Wells Brown had his own take. He held up an image from a recent edition of *Punch*, a British satirical weekly, a picture meant as a "companion" to the sculpture, called *The Virginia Slave*. Visibly darker than the stone-white Greek, the Virginian was also exposed to the waist. She wore a scarf around her head; folds of fabric covered her hips. Hands chained, gaze up, she leaned against a pillar with an American flag. The pedestal below her was adorned with whips and chains, and the words "E Pluribus Unum"—or "Out of Many, One"—the motto of the United States.

Visitors were excited and began to crowd. In America, spectators had projected onto *The Greek Slave* what they wished. Many compared the Greeks' quest for freedom to America's during the time of the Revolution, while a minority of abolitionists pointed out that the white marble slave might have represented a light-skinned enslaved woman like Ellen Craft. As she stood between the two representations of slavery, the Greek and the Virginian, Ellen animated both works of art, and ignited conversation.

The trio had previously decided that they would not challenge their enemies directly but rather speak loudly with their group about the evils of slavery, daring their opponents to step out. Their invitation to fight could not have been more clear; the gauntlet, or battle glove, as it was said, thrown down. They were met, however, with silence.

Finally, Brown lay the *Punch* picture inside *The Greek Slave*'s velvet home, declaring: "As an American fugitive slave, I place this Virginia Slave by the side of the Greek Slave, as its most fitting companion."

Still not a word. The procession moved forward. The group was just steps away when they noticed that *The Virginia Slave* was gone. The man who had stolen her (obviously an American) stood with evidence in hand. The trio pivoted and approached, waiting for him to speak, but he chose to keep his lips closed. They continued on, as too, did the silence. They paused at a display of daguerreotypes, a "Gallery of Illustrious Americans," including Henry Clay and John Calhoun, whose faces, flattened and frozen in black and white, stared back mutely.

The one person who paused to notice them was Samuel Colt—the one-time classmate of the Crafts' friend from Philadelphia, Robert Purvis—who had been thrown out of school for exploding a cannon, and whose revolvers had since become world-famous. Next to *The Greek Slave*, Colt's display was one of the most popular American exhibits. Colt was talking over his firearms, the loud clicking sounds that signaled battle, when he suddenly stopped and observed the group. Perhaps he remembered his friend Robert Purvis. Perhaps he smelled war.

For six or seven hours, the walking exhibition continued. The sun changed its angle over the Crystal Palace. The group stopped for refreshments: There were ices, and a fizzy drink from men named Schweppes. There were toilets, too—a revolution in public sanitation, monitored by a sanitation supervisor who tallied every use. In this accounting, all were equal, regardless of status or race; each person counted only for the waste produced and the penny paid to deposit it.

They must have walked miles, passing thousands on their worldwide journey. They went unchecked, unstopped. No one expressed shock or disapproval at the sight of the mixed-race groupings. No one identified them or hunted them down—no one, that is, but the silent slavers, whom the Crafts could recognize at once, and who could only stare back in impotent rage.

In the transparent world of the Crystal Palace, William, Ellen, and William Wells Brown were both visible and invisible—invisible in the way that had so astonished William when he had first arrived in Edinburgh and observed a White man arm in arm with two Black women.

William Farmer, William Craft's partner in the procession, would observe of the silent Southerners: "Probably, for the first time in their lives, they felt themselves thoroughly muzzled. They dared not even bark, much less bite," while the trio, whom they might have hunted in America, spoke and freely moved, and were welcomed by people from all over the world. As Farmer observed: "An artist could not possibly have better models from which to delineate 'Guilt' and 'Innocence' than the slaveholder and the slave, as they appeared in the World's Exhibition."

Here was the ultimate "fugitive slave's triumph." Never mind that they did not want a speaking part: the enslavers were enlisted, despite themselves, to become part of the performance piece that the trio had authored, choreographed, designed. And in this act, the Crafts rewrote their story, as ingeniously, subversively, and boldly as they had authored the narrative of their lives.

Now, posing neither side by side, as master and slave, nor arm in arm, as husband and wife, but together, among friends, the Crafts took their worldwide walk entirely free of the roles that had once defined them, not only in America, but even abroad. The roles they repeatedly evoked on the lecture circuit—roles mixed and matched to inspire shock, tears, and awe—were absent from this final demonstration. In the international crystal transparency that displayed life as it could, might, and perhaps one day would be, in the United States and beyond, William and Ellen, Ellen and William, broke free of all encumbrances as they walked as global citizens: master slave, husband wife, no more.

It was time to take leave. Their London days had been heady ones. In a flutter of days and nights, the Crafts had met a wide circle of abolitionists, including the formidable Bostonian expatriate Maria Weston Chapman (known as "Garrison's lieutenant"), who had been complaining about the Pennington affair all this time from Paris and was finally persuaded to quiet down. They also met William Wells Brown's archnemesis and BFASS secretary, John Scoble, whom Ellen, with her sharp questioning, reduced to stammering. And then it was done. Two days after their "Great Exhibit," the Crafts said good-bye to Brown and journeyed to Ockham with the Estlins.

It must have seemed the far green end of the world. There was an old parish church, a handsome country estate, the school, its farms and fields, and little more. For company there were the Lushingtons: Alice and Frances, two sisters close to Ellen's age, who ran the school, and their father, Stephen, a renowned abolitionist lawyer and reformer, who had a hand in moving the slave trade out of the country. But as William, for one, was unhappy to learn, most of the other people at the school would be children under the age of thirteen. There were about fifty in all—half boys, half girls. The school had been founded to provide such youngsters with practical skills and an education, to keep them out of trouble, and keep potential rebellion at bay.

For the Estlins, it had been tough work persuading their friends to come at all, and, to the end, they would remain in a state of mild panic. Ellen seemed to like it, they thought, but William was unsettled as they circled the grounds. Never mind that the school had its own printing press, globes, and even a "magic lantern," or that the Crafts would have their own cottage and eventually a separate study space. The contrast to the world of the Great Exhibition, with its transparency and vibrant cultures, people of all colors, and mechanical clatter, must have come as a shock. Not even in Georgia had the Crafts lived anywhere so remote.

Couldn't they find something closer to London? William wondered. He did not want to be patronized as a charity case, he told Dr. Estlin, as they discussed the financial arrangements. Personally, William would have preferred to keep speaking through the fall, with Brown and his panorama. But Brown himself had advised the Crafts to choose Ockham. With the lecture season at an end, and Brown's two daughters finally on their way from America, it was time for new beginnings. Estlin, too, made clear that Ockham was the Crafts' best option at this time and that it would be imprudent to turn it down.

Then there was Ellen. Estlin reported that Ellen was in favor of Ockham from the start, and if it is possible to imagine why the Crafts resisted coming here, it is equally possible to understand why they were drawn. For months, the couple had been relentlessly on the move, and together with Brown. Ellen had been physically unwell. In Ockham, they could finally find stillness, safety, and solitude. They could pursue their education and perhaps start a family in freedom—the long-held dreams that had set them in motion in Macon. Here they could pause to make their domestic and educational dreams a reality.

And so they remained in Ockham, while their friends drove back to the metropolis that was thirty miles but another world away. No sooner had their friends arrived in London than they wrote about the Crafts' "happy ending." They spun it joyfully, even as they knew inside that it might not be all it seemed. They were worried about William getting along, and Estlin had given him a warning, saying that if he lost his footing among his new friends here, he would not regain it. About Ellen, he had only the best of things to say. She was, he predicted, "destined for some important missions!"

One such mission became clear in the months to come, as Ellen and William expected a child.

FREEBORN

|||||||||||||||||||||||||||

On an unnamed day in Surrey, a gracious lady, near fifty, lifted the rich folds of her skirts to mount the stairs of a modest cottage. She passed through a narrow hall and paused at the threshold of an upstairs chamber, where a young woman sat by a window, plotting stitches with needle and thread, the tools of her trade. The visitor took note of a spelling book that lay open on the young woman's lap, and newspapers within reach—Garrison's *Liberator* and Douglass's *North Star*—before the young woman, startled, rose to greet her. The visitor was Lady Byron; the young woman, Ellen Craft.

The two ladies would share an hour together over tea, Ellen telling her story once more and bringing her listener to tears. Lady Byron was amazed that Ellen appeared so White, so familiar. She could hardly believe that she was "in the presence of an American slave." Something else about Ellen might have come as a surprise. When she rose to greet her visitor, or to prepare the tea leaves, she might have revealed a belly that swelled, stretching the skirt waist that she would have let out for herself, as she had once done for her enslaver years before.

If so, Lady Byron might have been powerfully reminded of her own pregnancy a long time ago. It was then that this talented woman (nicknamed the "Princess of Parallelograms," due to her gift for math) had discovered that her new husband, the celebrated poet Lord Byron, was both unfaithful and cruel. He had engaged in scandalous affairs—including, reportedly, with his own half sister. Weeks after giving birth, Lady Byron had taken her baby and run. Now her only child, Ada Lovelace (now known as the "first computer programmer" and "first tech visionary"), was ill and soon to die. But there was hope in this child of Ellen's, so long wished for, and—in such contrast to the Byrons' marriage—borne of an enduring love.

The encounter between the two women, which William Wells Brown reported for the *Liberator* (without noting the swelling belly), gives a rare glimpse into the Crafts' lives in Ockham, around which a curtain remains mostly closed. For the couple, it would indeed be a pregnant year, of comings and goings, full of new learning and a new kind of hope—but also cast with shadows, some reaching long from the other side of the world.

A strong, established rhythm marked their days in Ockham, where Ellen and William achieved their lifelong dream of acquiring an education, denied to them in bondage. They spent their mornings at lessons (separate from the schoolchildren) in reading and writing, music, math, and Scripture. Within months, they were reading fluently and taking dictation. In the afternoons, they taught their own skills with needle and lathe, and were both successful and beloved as teachers. On Sundays they attended religious services in the ancient parish church. The couple was popular at school and in the neighborhood: little girls would greet Ellen with nosegays in the mornings, while locals would touch their hats to the Americans as they passed.

But friends acknowledged that the Crafts' situation in Ockham was a "very lonely" one, and that Ellen, in particular, seemed "keenly to feel her isolation from her American friends," as she approached the time when she would give birth. A month into their stay, they had a short holiday in London with William Wells Brown, who reported that they were happy. They were excited to receive a visit from the Estlins, Ellen breaking into a run as soon as she sighted the aged doctor and his daughter coming up the road. Such visits were all too short and rare. Brown was soon on the lecture circuit, where William had wished to be, while they were living in rural exile, with no one near who shared their perspective, no one quite like them.

There were other challenges this year. A rumor had gone around that William Wells Brown was having an affair with Ellen—Ellen, who was so unwell in her early pregnancy that Dr. Estlin had been called out to Ockham, and who would continue to suffer sickness throughout. Dr. Estlin was among those who dismissed the story as nonsense, but it continued to cause so much trouble for Brown that he would sue the man whom he believed had started it: his nemesis John Scoble.

Then there was the news from America. James Smith, Ellen's biological father and her mother's enslaver, had also been sick for some time, and throughout the fall, the Crafts and their abolitionist friends worked "day and night" to free Ellen's mother. Ellen had never stopped worrying about Maria, and if she knew of her father's illness, she would have known, too, that this was likely her last chance, soon gone.

On an early May evening, about halfway through Ellen's pregnancy, as she could feel her baby's kicks and flutters—what midwives
might have called a "quickening"—James Smith breathed his last. At
his death, the *Georgia Telegraph* would sing the praises of this most
"excellent man." As his eulogy read: "All who knew him can bear witness to his incorruptible integrity, and his warmth of heart. The attractive frankness of his manners rendered him universally popular, and
we do not believe he has an enemy behind him. . . ."

"As a sound lawyer, he had few superiors in the state. As a citizen,
he was intelligent and public-spirited—as a friend, reliable and true—
as a neighbor, kind and obliging—as a man, his escutcheon was without spot or blemish."

Swiftly, Smith's property was counted and inventoried. Included
in the listings: a brick mansion in downtown Macon; a plantation in
Houston County; bounteous livestock; and, finally, valued at $17,900,
and tallied above stockholdings, household property, and barnyard
animals: 116 men, women, and children. There was seven-year-old
Ellen ($500). There was sixty-year-old Maria ("000"). And then there
was a forty-year-old Maria, officially appraised at $500, but consid-
ered priceless, both in the eyes of her daughter, Ellen Craft, and—for
very different reasons—in the eyes of her new owner, Eliza Cleveland
Smith.

With James Smith's death, his widow came into possession of his
estate. Mistress Smith had any number of options when it came to
Maria, mother of the child she once gave away. She might have sold
Maria "down the river" or gifted her to a family member. She might
have sold her to the Crafts for any amount of cash. Instead, she chose
to keep Ellen's mother close.

In her last trimester, Ellen received more bad news from the South.
The papers reported that Ellen was so unhappy with her life in freedom that she had deserted her husband and put herself in the hands of
an American gentleman, begging to be returned to her enslavers.

It was as if the Southern authorities, aggrieved at their inability to
control her actions, recover her body, sought to lay claim to her story
instead: to prove that she lacked mastery over living and was a slave
at heart—one who had abandoned her husband and was incapable of
being a wife. Through false news, they would attempt to appropriate

her will, her desire. These reports were so persistent that even Samuel May Jr., the avuncular minister who had guided the Crafts out of Boston, made inquiries, sending a clipping from the *New York Evening Post*.

Ellen tuned into her pregnancy and did not respond at this time. As infuriating as the news might be, she had other priorities. Her baby grew, stretched, reached into her sleep. The weather began to turn crisp. Only then did William Wells Brown write cautiously in a letter to Wendell Phillips that the Crafts were expecting an "increase" to their family.

At last, came that vibrant October evening, forty-six months after she had escaped Georgia, twenty-three months since she had escaped America, at eight o'clock—a soft, dark hour—when her child was ready to be born, and, after a hard labor, Ellen, with William, welcomed into the world their beautiful baby boy.

They named him Charles Estlin Phillips Craft: Charles, the name of William's brother, who had been apprenticed as a blacksmith before he was sold; Estlin, for their English friends, John Bishop and daughter Mary; Phillips, for Wendell Phillips, the golden-tongued orator who had predicted that millions would read their story; and Craft, the name they had known in Georgia, brought North and overseas, never left behind. Through his name, their son would forever carry each phase of their lives and journey up to the moment of his birth.

With her baby in her arms, Ellen's thoughts turned more than ever to Maria, with whom she longed to share the joyful news. Ellen did share one happy moment with another mother, whom she chose to be godmother of her child: Lady Byron. The baroness would return, and at some point, she would present the new mother with large financial gifts—£500 on one occasion, £100 on another, some of it in gold—money all her own.

It was a private fund that Ellen would not touch or disclose for more than twenty years, not even to her husband. James Smith had arranged his will so that his daughters' inheritances—those daughters he acknowledged—would be protected against their husbands' debts; Ellen, in her silence, would arrange her own financial affairs, ultimately protecting herself.

William was deeply moved by the sight of his son, for there was nothing so "consoling to the heart of a fugitive slave," he would write, as to look upon his newborn child, knowing that there would be no "chains and fetters waiting in readiness to grasp and stunt his physical structure, and no hell-born despotism like American slavery hanging over his head, ready to drop, and crush his intellectual faculties to the dust."

Had he been born in the United States of America, this child would have been the legal property of Eliza Collins, and beside her, Robert Collins—who, just as Ellen was giving birth, was publicly debuting his slave-owning manual, in which he boasted of the benefits of living in bondage. Among them, Collins counted the fact that the enslaved need not worry about starvation or illness, knowing that both they and their children would be provided for—"for the money they are soon to be worth."

No more. This child of theirs would not witness what his parents had seen and known and fled. He would not be separated from his mother, as Ellen had been forced from hers. He would not be mortgaged like his father or sold to the highest bidder. This was their "first freeborn child," as William proudly announced, to whom the "blessings of liberty and the pursuits of happiness" belonged. But it was Ellen who truly had the last word.

Four days after her difficult labor, Ellen—still outraged by slavers' efforts to co-opt her story, and finally ready to respond—takes up her pen and fires off a missive. She addresses it to a newspaper editor, also a friend, while aiming for the heart of Georgia. It will be her words, now, that will travel across the seas, over to America, then via railroad and steamers, through magnetic telegraph lines, all over the country, back down the tracks she took to leave the South: from the safety of one cottage to the prison grounds of another, where her journey once began.

Silencing "the erroneous reports" so lately in the American newspapers, and speaking loudly against the claims of her former enslaver, she tells her story in her own written words:

> I have never had the slightest inclination whatever of returning to bondage; And God forbid that I should ever be so false to liberty as to prefer slavery in its stead. In fact, since my escape from slavery, I have got on much better in any respect than I could have

possibly anticipated. Though, had it been to the contrary, my feelings in regard to this would have been just
the same, for I had much rather starve in England, a
free woman, than be a slave for the best man that ever
breathed upon the American continent.

In "these few lines," as she presents them, Ellen shows that she has
accomplished everything she has sought to achieve: freedom, literacy,
and choice. Hers is a published protest, in which she makes the story of
her personal achievement a lesson to the world—her expression of her
own agency an act of communal vindication. She does *not*, however,
mention her newborn. As always, she will tell her story on her own
terms, revealing just as much as she wishes, and nothing more. Her
story and her child belong to her.

She signs off with the name that she has claimed, first and last,
writing it in her own, free hand: "Yours very truly, ELLEN CRAFT."

In a postscript, she adds: "Mr. Craft joins me in kind regards to
your family." For on this day, Ellen Craft, a free woman, a mother, and
a writer, speaks for them both.

CODA

CODA

||||||||||||||||||||||||||||

Every story begins with a question or a quest, and this one ends as Ellen and William meet the goals they set from a darkened cabin in Macon: safety, freedom, literacy, and a family of their own. But Ockham was in its way its own beginning, not a final chord, and there remains one last moment—a reunion—that needs to be told.

"Happily ever after" did not come to the couple in Ockham, though perhaps it might have, had they defined it another way. Perhaps had they stayed on, as friends urged, conforming to others' idea of a success story, more would have known their story, in fulfillment of Wendell Phillips's prophesy that millions would read and know it. Instead, the Crafts would continue to improvise the story of their lives on their own terms.

Once their son, Charles, turned two, they would leave Ockham for London, which would be their home base for nearly twenty years. There they would start new businesses, continue their activism, and have more children: William Ivens (born 1855), Stephen Brougham Dennoce (circa 1857), Alice Isabella Ellen, or Ellen (circa 1863), Mary Elizabeth (born 1868), and Alfred (circa 1869).

The Crafts would also write a book, *Running a Thousand Miles for Freedom*, published in London in 1860 with William named as sole author. Though it went through two editions and received positive reviews, *Running* did not become an enduring best seller like William Wells Brown's or Frederick Douglass's narratives—or novels about slavery such as Brown's *Clotel; or, The President's Daughter* and Harriet Beecher Stowe's *Uncle Tom's Cabin*, both of which featured light-skinned, enslaved heroines fleeing in male clothes. Published after John Brown's raid on Harpers Ferry, in an election year that would make Abraham Lincoln president, the Crafts' book may have come too late to gain the traction of the earlier works. Within the year, the United States would explode in a Civil War.

In America, their friends and fellow activists—including William Wells Brown, Frederick Douglass, Lewis Hayden, William Cooper

Nell—turned their powers to the war effort, lobbying hard to give Black men the right to fight as Union soldiers, and recruiting young men (among them, their own sons) into the Massachusetts Fifty-Fourth and other regiments of the United States Colored Troops. As battles raged, sweeping up the lands and people they had known, William had the impulse to go back to the States "to fight," but in the end, the Crafts decided to fight for justice abroad.

William would journey solo to the west coast of Africa, where his ancestors had been kidnapped into slavery, becoming a teacher, activist, and businessman. He worked to persuade the king of Dahomey (now Benin) to end the slave trade there and to switch to other industries, such as cotton—a substance forever linked to the breaking up of his family and his own sale as a child.

Approaching the kingdom by canoe in 1862, William would come into sights beyond imagining, including an army of two thousand women warriors. He would carry home a belt worn by one of these "Amazons," among other gifts, when he returned to Ellen in England the following year, only to go back—this time for even longer.

Once more, Ellen would not join, remaining in England to raise their four young children. She was "too white to go with him," as she explained to one enquirer, but there was another reason why she chose to stay. The Emancipation Proclamation was issued on New Year's Day 1863, freeing loved ones behind enemy lines—among them, Ellen's mother. Ellen would not rest until she and her mother were reunited.

For more than three years, the Crafts would live with many miles between them, a pattern that would long continue. Critics would question these separations, but this is how the couple would choose to live, both together and apart—or, it might be said, strong enough, together and individually, that they could stand to be apart. Never ones to adhere to scripted roles, they would continue to reinvent their lifelong partnership as husband and wife.

They had separate successes during what would be their longest, transnational separation. William opened a school on the grounds of a onetime slave barracoon in Whydah (Ouidah), and has been credited with helping to end the local slave trade. Yet this epoch would not end happily for him. In 1867 William become physically ill. As he prepared to return home, he requested payment from Dahomey's king, who sent fifty enslaved people instead, chaining them in his yard. William freed the fifty captives, but at great cost. His business partners would hold him responsible for the entire loss.

In England, Ellen continued her activism. She mobilized support for the war; for aid and education for the recently emancipated; and for a girls' school in Sierra Leone—all while parenting alone. She invited fellow activists and fellow refugees from slavery into her home. She raised funds and spoke out, challenging famous writers and politicians. And she made clothes for the newly free. Her family would recall her as an "excellent businesswoman," and, in time, her independent nest egg would exceed $2,000. But her greatest personal success during these years came when she achieved her lifelong dream of reuniting with her mother.

It was a long time coming. Although Lincoln's Proclamation emancipated Maria in 1863, Macon was famously proslavery and pro-Confederate, and she remained locked behind enemy lines. When South Carolina became the first state to secede, Maria must have heard Macon's one-hundred-gun salute, the church bells ringing through city, the rousing cheers. Young men poured out to enlist: among them, a beloved Smith son, Ellen's half brother Bob, who would die leading a charge, sending a parade of mourners down Macon's streets.

Strategically prized because of its railroads, Macon soon took on even greater import as a Confederate arsenal. Not until April 1865 did a very young Union general, James Harrison Wilson, march through the town, with the president of the Confederacy, Jefferson Davis as his prisoner of war. Ellen would enlist General Wilson to find her mother.

From London to Boston, across the country, and down to the South, Ellen mobilized her own army of activists and their friends, to reach General Wilson, on a hot day in July 1865. It took him just one day to locate Maria, who was, as he would report, "living comfortably with some colored friends" only two hundred yards from his own encampment on Mulberry Street in Macon.

The general summoned Maria to his encampment personally, and there, on the very street from which Ellen had escaped, Maria listened as the general read the message from her daughter. Ellen's mother was, the general reported, in "good health . . . very hale, and young-looking for a woman of her age." She answered back at once that she would be delighted to rejoin her daughter overseas if funds could be arranged for her travel.

So it was that on an unforgettable fall day, some four months later, Ellen's mother set off for the train station on her own transatlantic journey, bondswoman no more. She traveled as a nurse to the family of a former Confederate, Lieutenant Colonel James Burton, who ensured safe escort.

As she mounted the train that would carry her away, she was surrounded by the "thousands," as it was reported, who had come to see her off. These were emancipated people, like her, who had heard her daughter's remarkable story, as it was carried in newspapers, into the fury and fear of their enslavers, and finally, to them: a story that helped break down the world as they knew it. A story that led to now.

"Loud were the plaudits of the negro population," the newspapers recounted, "as the cars passed out of the depot from the place where she had been a slave." As Ellen's mother looked out the train window at Macon for the last time, it was not with the fear of who would come after her, as her daughter had, but to the pride of all who cheered.

Over the miles of tracks she went, by riverboat and by carriage, by ocean steamer, and, finally, to London's King's Cross Station, where another crowd awaited, mirroring the scene she had left on the other side of the world. And there was Ellen.

Newspapers would describe how "an anxious trembling pale-faced lady-like woman, with a little boy by her side, having more of the dusky shadow on his brow than his mother, met that parent so dear to them, who seemed like one risen from the dead."

Seventeen years and thousands of miles finally closed as daughter and mother, Ellen and Maria, held each other again. For Ellen, with her child on one side and her mother on the other, past, present, and future met.

———

Whether William, too, was reunited with his mother or other family members is unknown. While he is reported to have "redeemed his mother from slavery," and one brother, Charles, is known to have purchased his freedom and settled in Macon, the paper trail fades for other kin, with the destiny of William's younger sister, Eliza, a particular mystery.

Fewer sources exist to tell of the Crafts' later lives, too, though these years were eventful. After William's return from Africa, with their finances in turmoil and the Civil War over, the Crafts decided to return to the United States to live out an American Dream on their own terms. They went, as they had come, through Liverpool, with some but not all of their family. Two sons, Brougham and William, remained in England to finish school. Maria was not named on the return either, but there was a Mary Elizabeth in Ellen's arms, a toddler whose name echoed those of her grandmother and great-aunt, Mary Eliza Healy. Tragically, young Mary died not long after her family's arrival in Boston. Soon after, her parents would leave the North, for a radical retelling of their former lives, closing a circle with a return to the South.

Although they had planned for Georgia, they settled at a plantation called Hickory Hill in nearby South Carolina. This is where they prepared to write their own happy ending. Combining Northern and transnational capital, with the power of their education, and together with their family, they launched their own agricultural and educational cooperative—an American Ockham. Then, in an act of devastation all too familiar in this era, "night riders" came with their torches, sending up their vision in flames.

The Crafts would try again, now near Savannah, at the Woodville Plantation in Ways Station, Georgia, and here Ellen laid down her strongest roots to date. William was often on the road, lecturing and raising funds, and the site was not promising initially, the "houses miserable holes, dirty and full of rats and snakes," as Ellen recalled, the fields choked with weeds.

But in time, and with help from the children (including the sons who came from abroad), the Crafts succeeded in transforming this once abandoned site of slavery into a farm and school collective, with an active community of workers and students; fields of cotton, rice, and peas; and buildings both newly built and freshly repaired, including a church. At Woodville, the Crafts brought together their lifelong dreams of family, freedom, education, activism, and faith.

The pride of the community was the school, which Ellen declared the "finest for white or colored children in Bryan County." The building was painted white, with glass dormer windows, and stood only a few hundred feet from railroad tracks, where a train hurtled by every day, speeding from Savannah to Florida, a reminder of the past.

Within the sanctuary of this school, as William would report, as many as seventy-five boys and girls—the sons and daughters of the formerly enslaved—learned to write and read. The building doubled as church, and on Sundays, worshippers could be seen putting their shoes on at the door, having walked barefoot from as far as fifteen miles away.

One unnamed woman—106 years old, who had seen most of her fifteen children sold away from her and had once been enslaved on these very grounds—marveled at the transformation: "It used to seem as though the devil was turned loose on this plantation; blood from the backs of the people was made to flow like water, but now, bless the Lord, it has been turned into a temple of the living God."

Beyond their work at Woodville, the Crafts also became active in politics, with William running for state senator on the Republican ticket. (This was an era when both Republican and Democratic parties were very different from what they are today.) He ultimately lost the race to a White Democrat, in an election where "every good citizen who desires purity and honesty in our State administration" was urged to "do his whole duty in approaching the contest." William was even interviewed by President Ulysses S. Grant about an appointment as minister to Liberia. But once more, his and Ellen's dreams exceeded the limits of their world.

Just as the couple had turned their world upside down when they escaped Georgia, with Ellen stepping into a White man's shoes, so they upended the known order upon their return. The astonishment must have gone both ways: for Southerners to see their new Black neighbors dressed in Continental style, speaking with British accents, circulating books, teaching school; and for the Craft children, who had spent their whole lives in England, to start new lives in the state where their parents had been enslaved. But just as the Crafts' trials decades earlier did not end with their leaving the South, so, too, their later turmoil knew no regional bounds. For this time, at Woodville, their opposition came not just from the South, but the North.

The troubles began when one of their Georgian neighbors (threatened, it has been suggested, by the Crafts' successes) began alleging in Boston that the Woodville scheme was a fraud. Later, a Bostonian and former supporter of the Crafts published a letter warning against William in the local papers, causing such damage that William initiated a libel suit in 1878.

Together in court, the Crafts took a powerful stand. In an "easy, straightforward manner," William spoke convincingly for days on end—indeed, one newspaper declared that had the case been judged at the close of his speech, he might have won.

Then Ellen spoke so eloquently and movingly about her work that she was called a "minstering angel among the afflicted." On the stand for hours, Ellen was unfazed by the relentless questioning, including interrogations about her private savings. She had brought these funds from England, "looked upon [them] as sacred," and had never revealed their hiding place, not even to her husband.

But there was enough countertestimony from Georgia, as well as from the North, to undermine the couple's presentation. Most damaging, perhaps, were the statements provided by the Crafts' former friends, including Wendell Phillips (the wealthy abolitionist after whom the couple had named their first son) and Joshua Bowen Smith (the activist caterer), who expressed doubts about the time William spent traveling to raise funds for their school, leaving Ellen to manage Woodville alone.

Why so many turned on them is unclear, though it does appear that what had become a pattern for the Crafts by this time—an independent partnership, where they might work jointly on a cause from long distances apart—made little sense to their contemporaries. Once again, their redrawing of traditional boundaries and subverting of norms was out of step with others in their world.

In the end, William lost the suit, slowly closing the Crafts' American experiment. Although the farm remained operative, the school was shuttered, and the couple's financial hold on Woodville began to deteriorate. But they would stay in Woodville for at least another decade, and this itself was a statement. Theirs has been noted as the "only Black-owned plantation in the county." As Reconstruction gave way to an epoch of terror, with lynchings and vigilante justice, the Crafts would endure. And at least once more, Ellen would tell her story, in a music room in Philadelphia, calling it "an old story, but one worth repeating."

The music room presentation would be Ellen's last public event. Eventually Ellen and William may have lived for some time with their daughter's family in Charleston, but toward the end of her days, possibly around 1891, Ellen would ask to be returned to Woodville for burial under her favorite tree, an oak. How she left the world and when are unknown.

After Ellen's death, William would "devote himself solely to farming," living at Woodville, according to a friend, though he would travel at least once to Boston, where he shared his story. As reported by the son of Dr. Bowditch (the man who had giddily driven William over the Mill Dam): "His return to Boston was sad, for most of those who had befriended him in earlier days had died. . . ."

"During his conversation," the younger Bowditch recalled, "Craft alluded quietly and smilingly to his determination, before leaving Boston, never to return to the South alive and a slave." William would spend his last days in a South of his own choosing, visited by loved ones—including a grandson, Henry Kempton Craft, who remembered how each day, "Grandpa William" would rise to watch the Georgia train as it crossed the boundaries of his property. His wife was gone, but William eventually lived with her namesake, joining his daughter Ellen and her family in Charleston.

There William drew his last breath, at seven o'clock in the morning on January 27, 1900, seventy-six years old, at the dawn of the twentieth century. His death followed paralysis and coma, his movement stilled at last. Sadly, he could not be buried beside his wife. His financial struggles with Woodville were ongoing, and creditors seized the land soon after his death. While Ellen's body remained in Georgia, William was interred at the Friendly Union Society Cemetery in Charleston. Today William and Ellen Craft, together in life, rest apart.

As the Crafts' paper trail fades, others' remain bright, many revealing sudden, tragic ends. Shortly after the Crafts fled Boston, Willis Hughes, the would-be slave catcher, perished after being stabbed through the liver by the brother of his erstwhile partner, John Knight. Meanwhile, William's last enslaver, Ira Taylor, suffered severe depression and took his own life by "station No. 10, on the Central Railroad," after the Civil War.

Dr. Collins would miss this war entirely. Eight days before the combustion of Fort Sumter, after a long illness, he faced a reckoning with his own "master in heaven," accountable to the divine precept with which he closed his essay on slave management: "Masters, give unto your servants that which is just and equal, Knowing that ye also have a master in heaven and ye shall take them as an inheritance for your children. They shall be your bondsmen forever: but thou shalt not rule over them with rigor, but shall fear thy God."

In contrast to the enslaving men, Ellen's "old mistresses" lived long. When Mistress Smith finally died in 1879, at eighty-seven, she was sent off by fellow Methodists with fanfare. Eliza Collins lived even longer, and there is reason to believe that she and Ellen met again. Years later, William would speak of how he and Ellen had "returned to their old home in Georgia," where, by a friend's report, they were "cordially received by their former Masters." Since Robert Collins and James Smith were dead by this time, one of these the "former Masters" might have been Eliza.

William's childhood enslaver, Hugh Craft, died in Holly Springs, Mississippi, in 1867, after being paralyzed for seven years. Craft had built a gigantic mansion and would go down in local histories as a surveyor. But in the end, the person who would put Holly Springs on the map was a seven-year-old girl at the time of her neighbor's death. Her name was Ida B. Wells.

Many activists known to William and Ellen lived notably long, active lives. Among them, Lewis and Harriet Hayden continued their leadership in Boston, where he would become a state legislator, and together they left an endowment: a scholarship at Harvard Medical School that continues in the present. William Wells Brown would spend his later years practicing medicine. He died in 1884 and was buried in an unmarked plot in Cambridge, Massachusetts. Today he finally has a headstone and his own, exhaustive biography—even more massive than his four-hundred-page guidebook—which would surely have made him proud.

The Crafts' surest legacy lived on in their children—the imagined progeny for whom the couple risked all—and the poetic justice they achieved, as they exercised their own mobility and played out variations of Ellen and William's dreams. Two sons would be professionally associated with the rails and mail: Charles Estlin Phillips Craft, the couple's "first freeborn child," became a railway postal clerk, while Brougham worked for the United States Postal Service. A third son, William, would settle in England. Daughter Ellen would be a founding vice president of the National Federation of Afro-American Women (which would become part of the National Association of Colored Women), joining forces with activists such as Ida B. Wells. She would also become an American "first lady" as the wife of William

Demosthenes Crum, United States ambassador to Liberia, who was also a customs collector in Charleston.

Down the generations, more family members would continue to carry on William and Ellen's legacy as teachers and activists, scholars, lawyers, and citizens of the world. One descendant is Peggy Trotter Dammond Preacely, "artist, activist, speaker, community organizer and oral historian," as well as Freedom Rider. On a day near Christmas in 1961, nineteen-year-old Preacely would channel her great-great-grandmother's spirit when, with her younger brother beside her, she journeyed south for a sit-in at a restaurant, where she would face her first arrest. Preacely would recall: "As I sat at the lunch counter in this small back-road town, I was shaking like a leaf, but I also felt brave and strong, as if I were doing something I was destined for."

It might be said that America failed the Crafts. Time and again, they pushed toward some realization of their dreams, only to be cut off, or rather to see the finish line moved. When it finally seemed that the nation would take them back, their chosen homes were destroyed or brought down in court; and they were denied a happy ending even in the ever after.

The absence of a happy ending may partly explain why the Crafts are not better known. Their story eludes easy celebration, resists closure. Yet it is precisely this complexity that remains the source of their enduring power—and why their story needs to be studied and celebrated. Through their audacious escape *and* daring lives, their restless improvisation, persistent innovation, inventive narration, for themselves and for others, the Crafts continually wrote and revised their own American love story.

Their love for each other carried them over state lines and continents, real and imagined markers, and made it possible for them to accomplish together what they might never have achieved apart. They ran for each other, with each other, and as they did, they pushed not only themselves and each other, but also the nation—and the world—to reach for better. In this sense, the lack of a definitive happy ending to their story represents not so much a gap or absence, as, potentially, a space or an opening in the story of America, whose reckonings with the past have the power to transform present and future. This space is ours to enter.

Acknowledgments

An army of curators, archivists, and specialists made my research possible, and my first thanks go to them. Among the many, I wish to call out: Vince Golden, Elizabeth Watts Pope, Nan Wolverton (American Antiquarian Society); Philip Cunningham (Amistad Research Center); Nick Glade, ShanTil Yell (Arlington Public Library); Barrye Brown (formerly Avery Research Center); Christopher Glass (Boston Public Library); Alan Tuten (Central of Georgia Train Organization); Craig Bryce, Donald Wemyss (Glasgow Trades House); Walter R. Holloway (Historical Society of Hartford County); Jay E. Moore (Mariners Museum); Hannah Elder, Dan Hinchen (Massachusetts Historical Society); Muriel Jackson, Alicia Owens (Middle Georgia Regional Library); Amy Reytar, Desiree Wallen, Nathaniel Wiltzen (National Archives); Gentry Holbert, Brett Miller (Spring Hill College); Astrid Drew (Steamship Historical Society); Cory Amsler (Mercer Museum); and Suzanne Inge (Peabody Essex Museum).

Dawn Davis was the reader for whom I wrote. I am grateful to Dawn for making me start over; for sharing the obsession; for working with me past all duty; and for putting the book in Bob Bender's hands. Dawn was right to speculate that Bob must wear a cape, so swiftly and powerfully does he make stories move. My thanks also go to their outstanding associates, especially Johanna Li, Philip Metcalf, Lewelin Polanco, Chelcee Johns, Cat Boyd, Tyanni Niles, and Philip Bashe.

I thank my stars for Julie Barer, whose instincts about stories and their makers make her a creator in the process, and for Brettne Bloom, Nicole Cunningham, and Chloe Knapp of the Book Group. An award from the Whiting Foundation allowed me to tell this story as it needed to be told, and I give special thanks to Daniel Reid, Courtney Hodell, and Adina Applebaum.

I am deeply grateful to the scholars whose work and insights informed my own, especially: Richard Blackett; Erica Armstrong Dunbar; William M. Fowler; Ezra Greenspan, Dean Grodzins; Kathryn Grover; Alicia K. Jackson; Robert O'Meally; Manisha Sinha; David Sutherland;

Harvey Amani Whitfield; and the late Robert Ferguson for his remarks to me on the "mutuality of marriage." For dress history, I'm indebted to the brilliant Lynne Zacek Bassett (who has saved me time and again) and to her fellow specialists: Karin Boehlke, Martha Katz-Hyman, Alden O'Brien, David W. Rickman, and Sara Rivers-Cofield. More thanks go to: Elizabeth Cody, Carl J. Cruz, Kristen Park Hopson, Carol Spinanger Ivins, Sara Kotzin, Frank and Andrea Mirkow, John K. Oh, Dale Plummer, and Larry Smallwood.

Among my kindred readers, I first thank Rachel Kousser for critiquing every beat, logline, and verse, for wrangling every donkey. I'm lucky to have such an amazing creative partner. Lori Harrison-Kahan—Fairy Godwriter—read for me time and again, and conceived the subtitle. Nikiala N'Gail Ridley and Tashi Ridley transformed this book with their page-by-page illuminations. For their responses to chapters and drafts of the manuscript, I also thank: Vivek Bald; Nick Boggs; Lara Freidenfelds; Lisa Gill; Anna Kuchment; Mark Lamster; Wil McKoy; Kym Ragusa; Rachael Rosner; Kara W. Swanson; Conevery Bolton Valencius; Katheryn Viens; and especially Eric Foner, whose generosity as a teacher I can only hope to pay forward, and whose early advice—"Don't let the details overwhelm the story"—became a mantra.

Getting to know Peggy Dammond Trotter Preacely—the Crafts' great-great-granddaughter—has been one of the highlights of this journey. I am grateful to Charles Burnett for bringing us together, and to Ms. Peggy for so generously sharing of her time and stories. I am also grateful to Julia-Ellen Craft Davis for her wisdom about images of her ancestors.

My final thanks go to Anna Kuchment, Allegra Wechsler Lowitt, Meena Ramakrishnan and Allison Zmuda, selected sisters. The Parks, Omonim and Abonim, made trips to Georgia a homecoming. My brother Wonbo and my parents, Jung-Ja Kim and Kyu Sung Woo, have sustained me in every possible way, for which I can never thank them enough. Together, we have learned a language of connection from our chosen kin, Ozzie and Mary Nagler. Kian, Oan, and Nari: Each day with you fills me with wonder. My ultimate thanks goes to Joon, who improved every page of this book with his sharp edits and has shown me what it means not just to write a love story but to live one.

A Note on Sources

The foundational source for this book is the Crafts' narrative *Running a Thousand Miles for Freedom*, a work that bears William's name alone but is now commonly recognized as a joint production by both Ellen and William Craft. Their writing is widely anthologized and taught on college campuses—which is where I first encountered the Crafts, as a graduate student in Robert O'Meally's seminar on the "Literature of Passing."

The Crafts' publication is ripe for literary analysis, with a canny yet confiding voice, narrative and thematic complexity, and powerful deployment of irony and humor. But, like the authors, it defies easy categorization. *Running a Thousand Miles for Freedom* incorporates many genres at once: it is an accurate travelogue, a work of antislavery propaganda, a satire, a picaresque adventure, a faith testimony, and more. Herein lies a central challenge in writing their history today or in using their literary recollections as a primary historical source.

Their book contains a high level of verifiable historical detail, including a few key names—though, notably, not those of Ellen's enslavers, the Smiths and the Collinses, or William's last enslaver, Ira Taylor. While other self-emancipated authors might omit such information in order to protect themselves, their loved ones, any abettors, and escape routes, the Crafts' escape seemed so beyond belief that they were required to prove their "authenticity" to an even greater degree than most, almost as soon as they arrived in the North.

Much of the Crafts' narration can be substantiated by travel accounts, diaries, newspapers, and other sources, down to minute details. The Crafts mention, for instance, that a man fleeing slavery had been captured on the steamship line they planned to take out of Charleston; a local paper confirms this report. The timetables the Crafts describe also match those in guidebooks, while details they provide about their enslavers align with documents such as deeds of sale.

At the same time, there are parts of the narrative that clearly carry the tone of melodrama and where the story itself seems to wear a disguise. A prime example is an interpolated story the Crafts tell about Ellen's aunt's family (called the Slators in the narrative), whose circumstances bear an uncanny resemblance to those of the Healy family, yet also diverge in significant ways. A particular area of challenge lies in the Crafts' recounting of their journey north, with vignettes that cannot be corroborated and, in some cases, are self-consciously literary. In fact, one scholar has gone so far as to suggest that the Crafts sent their draft to William Wells Brown, who "stuff(ed) it" with stories and asides before sending it back. Anyone writing about their travel must decide whether to include all or some or none of these episodes—and how.

In the absence of contradicting evidence, I opted to maintain some representation of each event as the Crafts' described it—first, because this is how they chose to tell their story, and then because, whether or not the episodes unfolded exactly as described (a question that may be asked of any autobiography or historical source), they are emblematic of larger, or what scholars have called "symbolic," truths. In every case, the episode either depicted or typified real dangers particular to that stage of their travel.

For example, the lady from Richmond speaks to the heightened risks the Crafts faced in a city known as the South's slave exporting capital—a site where families were torn apart, such as that of Henry Box Brown. Likewise, the enslaved Pompey represents Africans who were kidnapped into Charleston's harbor despite the international ban on importing slaves. It is because of this trade that enslavers (such as Ellen pretended to be) were required to register at the Custom House, where the enslaved were tallied to ensure compliance with the ban. A similar case can be made for the slave trader on the *General Clinch*, which was often used for slave trafficking. At least two groups of enslaved people were trafficked aboard this vessel during the week of the Crafts' flight, traveling with the kinds of professional traders whom the Crafts described.

All told, these scenes do not change the larger contours of the Crafts' story. I have included some mention of them, with context, with the hope that they will become launching points into further reading, analysis, and discussion. I carry this hope more broadly. Throughout this book, I have tried to expose the seams in my work—or, to use another analogy, provide open source code—so that readers can examine the sources directly and formulate their own conclusions.

This exposure is particularly important for those sections of the story that the Crafts chose not to detail, material comprising more than two-thirds of this book. Their narrative, as they state in the preface to their narrative, is "not a full history" of their lives, but "merely an account of our escape." Consequently, their primary focus is on the northbound journey, with briefer narration of their passage through Canada. They offer little coverage of their experiences before, after, or in between these stories of escape. They make no mention of their travels on the lecture circuit in America and abroad; neither do they describe their experiences in Boston or England. And, though they do name a few friends, such as Robert Purvis and the Estlins, others are entirely omitted—among them, William Wells Brown. This book covers all these gaps and more.

At the same time, the Crafts' note about their book—that it is "not intended as a full history" of their lives—also applies to this one. I have chosen to focus on the story of their mutual self-emancipation against a backdrop of transformation in the United States, both intentionally and in response to the historical materials, which are strongest in the years represented here and demand a focused telling. I have also chosen to write this book as narrative nonfiction, as opposed to a purely academic work, with the goal of evoking, as viscerally as possible, the texture of life in the Crafts' day and age—the places and times through which they moved and lived—while also rendering the epic scope of their enterprise and activism, and finally, as tribute to the couple's own genre-defiant presentation.

To tell the parts of the story that the Crafts did not narrate themselves, I mined newspapers, diaries, letters, narratives, legal documents, and other archival materials. As scholars have discussed, the traditional historical archives are an unstable preserve, particularly where the histories of Black and enslaved people are concerned: full of "scandal and excess," as Saidiya Hartman has described, while also "abysmally thin," to quote Tiya Miles.

Those in power recorded their lives in a bounty of documentation that makes it possible to study their likes and dislikes, choices, actions, and intimacies at close range, even from an immense chronological distance. It is possible to know what one of the Crafts' enslavers ate, or even how he was seen by his children on a given morning. Meanwhile, the destruction of an enslaved family, such as William's, might be represented by a number—if recorded at all.

Yet, as scholars like Hartman, Miles, Barbara McCaskill, and others have powerfully explained and shown, it is possible to extract other meaning from these sources, far beyond the uses for which they were conceived. Even within a diatribe by a proslavery journalist, one can discern the enslaved who read and heard the Crafts' story in Macon, Georgia, in defiance of the law. So, too, can problematic secondary sources be mined. Who kept records then cannot be changed, but how we read and interpret them—what we choose to see, and how we tell the story now—can all transform.

My journey through the archives yielded significant findings, including the pages by which William and Ellen Craft were mortgaged, advertised, sold, or transferred as property. I also uncovered key information about their enslavers, including Robert Collins's business failures and legal trials, which allows for new interpretations of when, how, and why the Crafts escaped bondage. Additional forays beyond the archives—as I retraced the Crafts' itinerary and built vast timelines—enabled me to piece together an unprecedented picture of their lecture travels, crisis in Boston, and international sojourn.

This work builds on the tremendous excavation by previous scholars and the care that others took to preserve the Crafts' history and legacy, beginning with their descendants, who generously shared a trove of correspondences, images, and other records at the Avery Research Center in Charleston, and who keep the story alive to this day. By making their history publicly available, members of the extended Craft family have made a personal treasure a national one.

Generations of scholars have also conducted deep research that I in turn have mined. The sequencing of their discoveries is a story of generous scholarly collaboration across space and time. Florence B. Freedman, Albert Foley, and Dorothy Sterling published the first scholarship, and my telling of this story is particularly indebted to Sterling's. My only regret is that Sterling and Foley provide scant documentation for their painstaking research. I have made it a further goal to locate and annotate their claims wherever possible. In a few cases where I could not verify their findings but consider them plausible, I report them as hearsay.

Richard Blackett's excellent studies provide the most comprehensive historical overview of the Crafts' lives and document their experiences beyond the scope of this book. Barbara McCaskill's detective work and robust literary analysis deliver essential insight into the Crafts' narrative, and her annotated edition of *Running a Thousand Miles for*

Freedom provides a critical foundation for any study about the Crafts. I also benefited from Gail Cima's deep analyses of the Crafts' lecture performances; Jeffrey Green's archival sleuthing; and studies by Stephen Kantrowitz and Gary Collison. Ezra Greenspan's exhaustive research on William Wells Brown strongly informed my understanding and depiction of Brown's character. Finally, new publications by scholars such as Brigitte Fielder and Hannah-Rose Murray have invigorated my readings, while digital mapping sites such as Murray's Frederick Douglass in Britain and Ireland (http://frederickdouglassinbritain.com) represent new frontiers in research.

Digital technologies have made it possible for me to research parts of the history that were not available to early scholars. Foley, for example, knew that a Craft family lived in Macon but could not find evidence of a connection to William. An internet search led me to the proof. Many older texts I reference—including the Crafts' narrative— are viewable on HathiTrust, while articles can be read on the digital library JSTOR. FamilySearch makes genealogical material available for free. Most of the letters I cite from the Boston Public Library's Anti-Slavery Collection are available online. Likewise, many newspapers can be read remotely, thanks to the Library of Congress, Georgia Historic Newspapers, and British Newspaper Archive.

A final note on language: I have endeavored to follow the guidelines recommended by P. Gabrielle Foreman and other senior scholars in "Writing About Slavery," using the terms "enslaved people" and "enslaver" whenever possible, with the purposeful exception of the title and other situations where the point of using terms such as *master* or *mistress*, *slave* or *planter*, was precisely to contest the ideologies they represent. I have also been inspired by Tiya Miles's rich discussion of language at the end of her book *All That She Carried: The Journey of Ashley's Sack, a Black Family Keepsake*. While mindful of current guidelines, I employ established terms like *slave narratives*, and occasionally use alternate terms like *slaver* to avoid repetition.

In the end, I offer one reading of the Crafts' story—an orchestral accompaniment to the melody the couple provide in their narrative, in harmony with a chorus of other voices. My hope is that this telling, together with the sources identified in notes, will spark further conversation about the past that will give new light to both present and future.

Notes

Full citations are given upon first reference for those sources *not* included in the bibliography.

ABBREVIATIONS

ARC Craft and Crum Papers, Avery Research Center, College of Charleston, Charleston, SC.

BAB Blackett, *Beating Against the Barriers*.

BAP Ripley, *Black Abolitionist Papers* (vol. 1, unless noted).

BCC Bibb County Courthouse, Macon, Georgia. Many records, including deeds, wills, and returns, are now viewable at www.familysearch.org.

BDA *Boston Daily Advertiser*.

BF Sterling, *Black Foremothers*.

BP *Boston Post*.

BPL Boston Public Library Anti-Slavery Collection, Boston. Letters cited are digitized.

CFT "Craft, Fort and Thorne Family Papers," Southern Historical Collection, Wilson Library, University of North Carolina at Chapel Hill.

GHS Georgia Historical Society, Savannah, GA.

GT *Georgia Telegraph*, Macon (available through Georgia Historic Newspapers).

HOU Houghton Library, Harvard University, Cambridge, MA.

HvC Willis H. Hughes v. Ellen Craft; Case Files, 1790–1911; Records of District Courts of the United States, Record Group 21; National Archives at Boston, Waltham, MA, https://www.docsteach.org/activities/teacher/oh-freedom-sought-under-the -fugitive-slave-act.

JK "Diary of John Knight, the Slave Pursuer," *TL*, December 6, 1850.

LL McCaskill, *Love, Liberation, and Escaping Slavery*.

MHS Massachusetts Historical Society, Boston.

NARA National Archives, College Park, MD.

NASS *National Anti-Slavery Standard*, New York, NY.

PAS Cima, *Performing Anti-Slavery*.

PDW Webster, *Papers of Daniel Webster*, vol 7.

RTMF Crafts, *Running a Thousand Miles for Freedom*.

SHC Albert S. Foley Jr., SJ Papers, Spring Hill College Library Archives, Mobile, AL.

SHG Sydney Howard Gay Papers, Columbia University, New York, NY.

TL *The Liberator*, Boston.

WH1 "Hughes, the Slave-Hunter's Account of His Mission," *TL*, December 6, 1850.

WH2: "A Card" (with second letter by Willis H. Hughes) *Columbus (GA) Times*, December 17, 1850.

WWB Greenspan, *William Wells Brown*.

OVERTURE

3 **raised torches:** Timothy M. Robert, " 'Revolutions Have Become the Bloody Toy of the Multitude': European Revolutions, the South, and the Crisis of 1850," *Journal of the Early Republic* 25, no. 2 (2005): 261.

3   **"to overspread and to possess"**: Quoted in Julius W. Pratt, "The Origin of 'Manifest Destiny,'" *American Historical Review* 32, no. 4 (1927): 796.

4   **"Declaration of Sentiments"**: "Declaration of Sentiments," National Park Service online, https://www.nps.gov/wori/learn/historyculture/declaration-of-sentiments.htm.

4   **"There is not a nation"**: "Frederick Douglass's 'What to the Slave Is the Fourth of July?,'" EDSITEment, National Endowment for the Humanities online, https://edsitement.neh.gov/launchpad-frederick-douglass-what-slave-fourth-july#02.

4   **find inspiration:** See the preface to *RTMF.*

4   **No Underground Railroad:** See Sinha's definition in *The Slave's Cause*, 400.

5   **"future historians and poets . . ." "Yes!":** "Seventeenth Annual Meeting of the Massachusetts Anti-Slavery Society," *TL*, February 2, 1849.

MACON

7   **Day 1:** In *RTMF*, the Crafts say they depart on Wednesday, December 21, 1848, arriving on Sunday, Christmas Day, but December 25 was a Monday. Early newspaper accounts confirm Wednesday and describe their arrival on the Sabbath. See "Story of Ellen Crafts."

9   **The Cottage:** The Crafts refer to the space as such in *RTMF*, 22. All quotations and thought attributions originate in ibid., 27–28, unless noted. Four o'clock in the morning is observed in *BAP*, 274. On Ellen's size: Robert Collins, "Power of Attorney," HvC; "Tuesday—the Second Lecture," *Nottingham Review* (UK), April 4, 1851. On Smith's height: Fitzgerald and Galloway, *Eminent Methodists*, 10.

9   **"double-story" hat:** "Story of Ellen Crafts," "An Ex Slave's Reminiscences."

10   **thinks of death:** *RTMF*, 28. These observations are ascribed to William, but Ellen may have shared them. Robert Collins articulates his methods in his *Essay.*

10   **borne witness:** Ibid, 68–69.

10   **double vengeance:** Ibid., 28.

12   **William knew:** The Crafts do not detail William's route, but newspaper advertisements, articles such as "Libel Suit," law statutes, and maps indicate the layout of the city and what he needed to avoid. Train schedules in *GT*, December 5, 1848. Sources consulted to portray Macon include: Tubman African American Museum and Catherine Meeks, *Macon's Black Heritage: The Untold Story* (Macon, GA: Tubman African American Museum, 1997); Lane, "Macon"; Eisterhold, "Commercial, Financial"; Dolores Hayden, *Where Poplar Crosses Cotton: Interpreting Urban Landscape in Macon, Georgia* (College Park, MD: Urban Studies and Planning Program, University of Maryland, 2007); O'Toole, *Passing*, especially 11; and "Vincent's New Map of City of Macon, Georgia" (1854) and S. Rose, "Plan of the City of Macon" (1840), both at the Washington Memorial Library, Macon, Georgia.

12   **Where the Collins house stood:** Butler, *Historical Record*, 114. On Nesbit: Stewart D. Bratcher, "Eugenius A. Nisbet (1803–1871)," *New Georgia Encyclopedia*, July 26, 2013.

12   **six feet tall:** *BAB*, 96.

12   **"moderately correct" . . . "a whipping":** Hotchkiss, *Codification*, 814–815; *RTMF*, 10–11.

13   **The pass:** *RTMF*, 22. Duration is unknown: possibly three or four days, as suggested in *BAP*, 274. The special badges are noted in "License Ordinance," *GT*, January 25, 1848.

13   **friends and business partners:** See his early advertisement in *GT*, April 27, 1837.

13   **one night a week:** "Story of Ellen Crafts."

13   **he had seen:** "William Craft to Editor, *London Morning Advertiser*," in *BAP*, 318. On William's vow not to be taken: "Anti-Slavery Meeting in New Bedford" *TL*, February 16, 1849. On the bridge: Jenkins, *Antebellum Macon*, 88.

14   **"Free Sol" . . . said he was careful:** Donald Lee Grant, *The Way It Was in the South: The Black Experience in Georgia* (Athens, GA: UGA Press, 2001), 72; Bellamy, "Macon, Georgia," 309. Free Blacks had a precarious freedom in Georgia, requiring White guardians. See Hayden, *When Poplar Crosses Cotton*, 8; Rogers, "Free Negro Legislation."

15 **Ellen's father:** Dorothy Sterling first introduces his biography in *BF*, 5–6.
15 **Macon had grown up fast:** Sources consulted on Macon listed above ("William knew . . ."). On gambling and lawlessness: Jenkins, *Antebellum Macon*, 113–14. On the hotels: Cunynghame, *Glimpse*, 256. On the theater: Young et al., *History of Macon*, 104. Other services advertised in the *GT*.
15 *the Georgia Telegraph*: "A Young Lady": *GT*, February 15, 1848.
15 **sweet, boyish look:** Joan Severa, *Dressed for the Photographer*, 18.
16 **of all the sites:** *BF*, 13. Scholars give various addresses for the Smiths, including First and Plum (Foley to Craft); and Second and Poplar (Butler, *Historical Record*, 202).
16 **"like a bassoon" . . . "sold his crop":** Fitzgerald and Galloway, *Eminent Methodists*, 110–13; *BF*, 5. On the Smith house: *Old Clinton Historical Society, An Historical Guide to Clinton, Georgia: An Early Nineteenth Century Seat* (Clinton, GA: April 1975), 3 (http://www.oldclinton.org/wp-content/uploads/Historical-Guide-to-Clinton.pdf).
16 **powerful men in Clinton:** See *An Historical Guide*; William Lamar Cawthon Jr., "None So Perfect as Clinton," *Georgia Backroads*, Autumn 2014; William Lamar Cawthon Jr., "Clinton: County Seat of the Georgia Frontier, 1808–1821" (MA thesis, University of Georgia, 1984), especially 170, 174–75; Williams, *History of Jones*, 232–93.
16 **"From Clinton, Georgia":** Calvin Schermerhorn, *Money over Mastery, Family over Freedom: Slavery in the Antebellum Upper South* (Baltimore: Johns Hopkins University Press, 2011), 16.
16 **child of the republic . . . 116 souls:** Foley to Craft; Foley, "Notes"; *BF*, 5; Eddie Tidwell, *Roster of Revolutionary Soldiers in Georgia*, vol. 3 (Baltimore: Clearfield, 1969), 209; Jeannette Holland Austin, *The Georgia Frontier*, vol. 2 (Baltimore: Clearfield, 2005), 320. Smith was known as Major or Colonel; the origin of these titles is unknown. His father's pension papers: Charles Smith, W. 6,122, Revolutionary War Pension and Bounty-Land Warrant Application Files, National Archives and Records Administration, Publication Number M804, Record Group 15, Roll 2207. See also Jenkins, "Antebellum Macon," 403. The names of the enslaved appear in Bibb Court of Ordinary, Record of Returns, 1851–1853, D-481, BCC.
17 **Marquis de Lafayette:** Stephen Frank Miller, *The Bench and Bar of Georgia: Memoirs and Sketches*, vol. 1 (Philadelphia: J.P. Lippincott, 1858), 251–52; Lucian Lamar Knight, *Georgia's Landmarks, Memorials, and Legends* (Atlanta: Printed for the author by Byrd Printing Company, 1919), 576.
17 **"wild, bad boy":** Williams, *History of Jones*, 92; Foley to Craft; Knight, *Georgia's Landmarks*, 826–67; Barber, Elijah, *The State of Georgia vs. Elijah Barber, Alias Jesse L. Bunkley, Cheating and Swindling: True Bill, 1837*, [S.l.: s.n., n.d.], 36–37.
17 **"ring of hair":** Barber, *State of Georgia vs. Elijah Barber*, 59.
18 **lowest rung:** McCaskill, "Very Truly," 510–11.
18 **law required:** "An Ordinance." *GT*, April 25, 1848; Bancroft, *Slave Trading*, 246–47.
18 **"You may have them singly":** Quoted in Cunynghame, *Glimpse*, 254.
18 **first in the world:** Sterling situates Wesleyan in Ellen's view in *BF*, 9. On Wesleyan College (not to be confused with Wesleyan University in Connecticut): Eunice Thomson, "Ladies Can Learn," *Georgia Review* 1, no. 2 (1947): 189–97; Samuel Luttrell Akers, *The First Hundred Years of Wesleyan College* (Macon: Beehive Press, 1976). Smith's role is noted on a historical marker in Clinton.
18 **"Woman can do more":** Thomson, *Ladies Can Learn,* 189–97.
18 **familiarized themselves with the alphabet . . . yearned to learn:** *RTMF*, 53, Bremer, *Homes*, 1:123–24.
19 **mammoth hat:** In advertisement for Belden & Co, GT, August 29, 1848.
19 **"a native Georgian":** See "Death of Mr. Johnston," *Macon Weekly Telegraph*, October 25, 1887. The Crafts spell the name Johnson in *RTMF*, but early reports also say Johnston. "An Escape from Slavery in America," *Chambers Edinburgh Journal*, March 15, 1851.
19 **The outfit:** "Story of Ellen Crafts." On the challenges of corseted movement: Severa, *Dressed*, 15. I owe other clothing details, such as the gravy boat, to Lynne Bassett. She

and David Rickman shared observations on style, and I'm grateful to Rickman for insights into the limitations of Ellen's outfit in his email of October 26, 2020. The boots are recalled in Lyons, "Quaker Family Home." I'm indebted to Sara Rivers-Cofield, who, in an email of October 28, 2020, discussed how the spurs may have enhanced Ellen's disguise, readings I draw from here.

21 **The Station:** Alvarez's *Travel* was indispensable for this chapter, especially his chapters on "The Railroad Passenger Car," "The Perils of the Road," and "The Railroad Station," for details such as the railway car interiors and gravestone pictures between them (55) and description of tickets (118). Other details in Chambers, *Things*, especially 330–35; Henry Benjamin Whipple, *Bishop Whipple's Southern Diary, 1843–1844* (London, MN: H. Milford, Oxford University Press, University of Minnesota Press, 1937), 74. Who, if anyone, shared a car with William is unknown. On Black travelers in this period, see Pryor, *Colored Travelers*; Kornweibel, *Railroads and the African American Experience: A Photographic Journey* (Baltimore: Johns Hopkins University Press, 2010).

21 **pistol . . . kill or be killed:** William notes the gun in "Libel Suit," his mind-set in "Anti-Slavery Meeting in New Bedford," *TL*, February 16, 1849.

22 **her eyes . . . subtle cleft:** Josephine Brown, *Biography*, 76; Robert Collins, "Power of Attorney," HvC; Ellen M. Weinauer, " 'A Most Respectable Looking Gentleman': Passing, Possession, and Transgression in *Running a Thousand Miles for Freedom*, in *Passing and the Fictions of Identity* ed. Elaine K. Ginsburg (Durham: Duke University Press, 1995), 50.

22 **as much as $150:** NC Josephine Brown, *Biography of a Bondman*, 75. See also McCaskill's theories on how the Crafts earned money and prepared in "Ellen Craft," 88.

22 **through ticket:** Samuel Augustus Mitchell, *New Traveller's Guide Through the United States* (Philadelphia: Thomas, Cowperthwait, 1849), 106. Advertised in *GT*, September 5, 1848.

22 **a pair of trunks . . . "Young Master":** "Story of Ellen Crafts."

23 **sculpted mounds . . . Older Georgians still recalled:** Bremer, *Homes*, 1:346. "Ocmulgee Mounds," National Park Service online, https://www.nps.gov/ocmu/index.htm. On Collins and the relics: Ida Young, Julius Gholson, and Clara Nell Hargrove, *History of Macon, Georgia* (Macon, GA: Lyon, Marshall & Brooks, 1950), 80; Butler, *Historical Record*, 160.

23 **The Central Railroad had been plagued . . . fine new ride:** Richard E. Prince, *Central of Georgia Railway and Connecting Lines* (Millard, NE: RE Prince, 1976), 5–7; Dixon, "Building the Central Railroad," 8–13; Alvarez, *Travel*, 18–19; Fraser, *Savannah*, 242, and especially on celebrations, sabotage, and cave-in: Young et al. *History of Macon*, 78–81, 117–118, 242.

24 **"The salvation of Georgia":** Butler, *Historical Record*, 121–22.

24 **race, gender, class, and ability:** Scholars have analyzed these boundary crossings: for example, McCaskill, "Very Truly," 510–11; and Fielder, who adds sexuality in *Relative Races*, 21–22.

24 **paid for by the lives and labor:** See Theodore Kornweibel, "Railroads and Slavery," *Railway & Locomotive Historical Society (R&LHS)*, no. 189 (Fall/Winter 2003), 34–59, and his *Railroads in the African American Experience*; Prince, *Central of Georgia*, 5–6.

24 **what would become of her mother?:** Ellen would voice concerns about retaliatory "cruelty." See John B. Estlin to Samuel May, June 27, 1851, BPL. Further consequences in *RTMF*, 19–20.

24 **another successful passing:** On the significances of Ellen's passing, see Foreman, "Who's Your Mama?," 508.

25 **thinly padded . . . "mad dragon" . . . dozen asthmatic donkeys:** Alvarez, *Travel*, 19, 31, 56.

26 **Scott Cray:** The Crafts identify Cray only by surname, but the 1850 federal census shows his widow, "Mrs. Scott Cray," living with the Collinses. See also the Bank of Darien historical marker at "Site Bank of Darien," The Historical Marker Database

(http://www.hmdb.org/marker.asp?marker=10555); Cray to Joseph M. French, December 24, 1843, East Carolina University Digital Archives, (https://digital.lib.ecu.edu/35482); Bibb Court of Ordinary, Record of Returns, 1856–1858, H-270, BCC; Georgia, *Acts and Resolutions of the General Assembly of the State of Georgia* (Milledgeville, GA: John A. Cuthbert, 1836), 124.

26   **"A reward of ten dollars":** See the advertisement in the *Darien (GA) Gazette*, November 9, 1818.

26   **Kitty, Mary, and Polly:** Thomas R. R. Cobb, *Reports of Cases in Law and Equity, Argued in the Supreme Court of the State of Georgia*, vol. 8 (Athens, GA: T. M. Lamkin, 1850), 153.

27   **action that might have cost her:** *RTMF*, 25.

GEORGIA

31   **Hugh Craft:** The Crafts identify William's enslaver only by surname. Albert Foley wondered about Hugh Craft in a letter addressed to Mrs. De Costa and Mr. Craft, March 1975, ARC. I found proof of the connection and more on Craft in: Franklin L. Riley, *Publications of the Mississippi Historical Society*, vol. 10 (Oxford, MS: Printed for the Society, 1909), 223; Elmo Howell, *Mississippi Back Roads: Notes on Literature and History* (Memphis: Langford & Associates, 1998), 126; Tom Stewart, "From Whence We Came: A Readable Story of Early Holly Springs," *South Reporter* (Holly Springs, MS), April 14, 2005; William S. Spear, *Sketches of Prominent Tennesseans: Containing Biographies and Records of Many of the Families Who Have Attained Prominence in Tennessee* (Baltimore: Genealogical, 2003), 16–17; William Francis and James Monroe Crafts, *The Crafts Family: A Genealogical and Biographical History of the Descendants of Griffin and Alice Craft, of Roxbury, Massachusetts* (Northampton, MA: Gazette, 1893), 734–35. See also Berry, *Princes of Cotton*, 19, 536 n. 29.

31   **might have been Charlescraft:** Crafts, *The Crafts Family*, 734.

31   **William was born to them:** His death certificate, including birth information, appears on Ancestry.com and Find a Grave: https://www.findagrave.com/memorial/63823175/william-craft. On William's family: *RTMF*, 8; Craft to "Dear Father"; "American Slavery," *Bristol Times* (UK), April 12, 1851. Information about Hugh Craft's Bible appeared once on an Ancestry message board.

32   **William's early years:** When William came into Hugh Craft's ownership is unknown. Details in the following chapter, unless noted, are gleaned from CFT, reel 1. See especially Mary to Martha, October 8, 1822; Martha to Mary, October 21, 1823; Hugh Craft to Mary Craft, July 28, 1825.

32   **"Negro clothes":** *Genealogical Abstracts from the Georgia Journal (Milledgeville) Newspaper, 1809–1840* vol. 3 (1824–1828), 163.

33   **"the strangest compound":** Stephen William Berry, *Princes*, 484. Henry Craft's other descriptions of his father appear in a note by him, dated June 14, 1844, Holly Springs, CFT.

33   **Others recalled:** Edward Curtis to "Dear Sister," December 5, 1824, CFT. Craft is listed as an elder in the *Macon (GA) Telegraph and Messenger* June 27, 1876. On his faith: Speer, "Sketches," 16–17. He was called "universally loved" in a pamphlet at CFT: *In Memoriam. Hugh Craft. Elizabeth R. Craft. James Fort. Robert Fort. Lucy Fort. John Y. Craft* (printed at McComb City, MS., ca. 1879), 4.

33   **Damned if you do:** Debby Applegate, *The Most Famous Man in America: The Biography of Henry Ward Beecher* (New York: Doubleday, 2007), 38–39, 121.

33   **loving hearts and spiritual devotion:** *RTMF*, 8–9.

34   **chart from Forsyth:** Tadman, *Speculators and Slaves*, appendix 6, 287.

34   **traders pulled:** Johnson, *Soul by Soul*, 119, 123.

34   **ten years old:** William stated that he worked for one cabinetmaker for fourteen years, dating the start of his apprenticeship (which *RFTF* suggests began after he lost his family) to about 1834 ("American Slavery," *Leeds Mercury* (UK), October 25, 1856).

Records of Henry Craft (born five months before William) show that the Crafts moved when Henry was ten (Speer, *Sketches*, 15).

34   **What astounded William . . . "not for true Christianity":** *RTMF*, 8. Craft's home and property are listed in Bibb County Superior Court, Deed Records 1837–1839, E-5, 396–401, BCC.

35   **fourteen years:** "American Slavery." On boarding: Henry Craft to "Dear Father."

35   **touched by cotton:** Liz Petry, "Chapter Four: The Lash and the Loom," *Hartford Courant*, September 29, 2002. Petry's discussion of the intersections between the cotton industry and the larger national economic picture, and the interconnections between North and South, slave labor and free, inspired mine. See also Eisterhold, "Commercial," 430.

35   **Panic of 1837:** Peter L. Rousseau, "Jacksonian Monetary Policy, Specie Flows, and the Panic of 1837," *Journal of Economic History* 62, no. 2 (2002): 479; "1837: The Hard Times," *Harvard Business School* online, https://www.library.hbs.edu/hc/crises/1837 .html. On failures in Macon: Eisterhold, "Commercial."

36   **his lands were seized . . . a ruined man:** Announcements in *GT*, January 30, 1834, May 21, 1835, July 9, 1838, June 9, 1840; also Berry, *Princes of Cotton*, 536n29.

36   **as one would mortgage a house:** Bonnie Martin, "Slavery's Invisible Engine: Mortgaging Human Property," *Journal of Southern History* 76, no. 4 (2010): 822.

36   **"William a Boy":** The January 10, 1839, deed appears in the Bibb County Superior Court, Deed Records 1837–1839, E-5, 396–401, BCC. If William and his sister were mortgaged together, as stated in *RTMF*, 9, Eliza was the auctioned sister.

36   **shame his son Henry:** Berry, *Princes*, 454–55.

37   **"3 Negroes":** The sale was listed multiple times in *GT* in 1840, through June 2.

38   **Knocked Down:** The Crafts describe the events of this chapter: *RTFM*, 9–10. On snowy cotton fields: Solomon Northrup, *Twelve Years a Slave* (Auburn, NY: Derby and Miller, 1853), 166. On first-time buyers: Reidy, *From Slavery*, 23. On William's family: Henry Craft to "Dear Father."

38   **William may have planned:** The permanent exhibit at the Old Slave Mart Museum in Charleston, South Carolina, notes such methods. Walter Johnson, in *Soul by Soul*, analyzes at greater length the ways in which the enslaved were active players in these sales. On Warren and Charles: Henry Craft to "Dear Father."

39   **eventually sold:** William would describe his buyer as a bank cashier: Ira H. Taylor, as identified by Florence Freedman in the 1969 Arno Press edition of *RTMF*; "Thomas Taylor's Receipt Regarding His Role in the Return of William Craft to Ira H. Taylor," HvC. For average slave prices in Forsyth, North Carolina: Tadman, *Speculators and Slaves*, appendix 6, 287. On William's arrangement with Taylor: "New England Convention," *Anti-Slavery Bugle* (New Lisbon, OH), June 15, 1849; *LL*, 27; "Libel Suit," On Macon's laws, Eisterhold, "Commercial," 438.

40   **halfway toward his prime:** See a related discussion in Johnson, *Soul by Soul*, 151.

40   **questioned the justice . . . decided to run:** *RTMF*, 4, 10; "Proceedings of the British and Foreign Anti-Slavery Society," *North Star* (Rochester, NY), June 22, 1855.

40   **dispersed family members:** Henry Craft to "Dear Father." The Crafts write that William's younger sister lived in Mississippi later (*RTMF*, 9). It is of note that the only known member of William's family whom Henry does not mention is this sister, and that the postscript is addressed to an "Eliza." Two others named in the mortgage, "Sally" and "Allen," appear in this cryptic letter.

42   **The train tore ahead:** See Dickens's description in *American Notes*, 90.

42   **Much of the crew . . . captive labor force:** Whittington B. Johnson, *Black Savannah: 1788–1869* (Fayetteville University of Arkansas Press, 1996), 79; Dixon, "Building the Central Railroad," 12–14.

42   **something to celebrate . . . "Negro brass band" . . . the stations:** Details here originate in Alvarez's *Travel*, 85–89, and his chapter on "The Station," especially 111, 123–25. The "Negro brass band" is Alvarez's description, 86.

43 **people swirled . . . left alone:** Ibid., 127–28, 141–42, 161; Chambers, *Things*, 330–32.

43 **winding course . . . gangs of enslaved workers:** Descriptions paraphrase Carlton Holmes Rogers, *Incidents of Travel in the Southern States and Cuba* (New York: R. Craighead, Printer, 1862), 236, which Alvarez summarizes in *Travel*, 156.

43 **Ellen bore scars:** "Robert Collins Power of Attorney," HvC; *RTMF*, 19.

44 **Her mother's name was Maria . . . African ancestry:** *BF*, 5–7; McCaskill, "Ellen Craft," 83. On "quadroon": *RTMF*, 52.

44 **youthful appearance . . . "gentle Christian woman":** "Ellen Craft and Her Mother," *NASS*, August 12, 1865; "Ellen Craft's Mother," *Newcastle Courant* (UK), December 15, 1865.

44 **house slave:** *BF*, 5–6; Schwartz, *Born in Bondage*, 118–19; McCaskill, "Ellen Craft," 86.

44 **said that James Smith . . . Georgia law book:** *BF*, 6. My presentation closely follows that of Dorothy Sterling, who was the first to notice the timing of the births. On rape as capital offense, see Rogers, "Free Negro Legislation," 33; Hotchkiss, *Codification*, 838.

44 **Maria would be tallied:** Bibb Court of Ordinary, Record of Returns, 1851–1853, D-481, BCC.

44 **paternity of a mixed-race child . . . "the mulattoes":** Chesnut is often quoted in scholarship about the Crafts. See Clinton, *Plantation Mistress*, 199. Schwartz analyzes the complexities in *Born in Bondage*, 44–45, discussing how enslaved mothers were often doubly victimized.

45 **"Devil John":** Cleveland, *Genealogy*, 2084, 2177; Foley, "Notes"; Foley to Craft.

45 **Mistress Smith:** *RTMF*, 3–4. Births in Cleveland, *Genealogy*; obituary in the *Macon (GA) Weekly Telegraph*, March 18, 1879; Fitzgerald and Galloway, *Eminent Methodists*, 112–13. On the mistress's role, including punishment: Schwartz, *Born in Bondage*, 110–11; Clinton, *Plantation Mistress*. I refer to Eliza Cleveland Smith as Mistress Smith to avoid confusion with Eliza Smith Collins.

46 **other family in the area:** *LL*, 27. Foley to Craft; "American Slavery," *Bristol Times* (UK), April 2, 1851; "American Slavery," *Bristol Mercury* (UK), April 12, 1851; Parker, *Trial*, 147.

46 **Much would depend:** See Erica Armstrong Dunbar's discussion of the significance of changed ownership for enslaved women in *Never Caught*, 7, 57–58, 97–98.

46 **"survival pack" . . . emergency kit:** Miles, *All That She Carried*, 36–37, xiv.

46 **struck her as a "horror":** *RTMF*, 19.

47 **invisible forms of training:** *BF*, 6–7; Kirby, *Autobiography*, 302. McCaskill discusses how both Crafts' childhood experiences served as "practice" for their journey in "In Plain Sight."

47 **release from pain:** *RTMF*, 4.

48 **Macon Bound:** On Cooke's 1842 painting *Eliza Cromwell Smith Collins and Collins Lewis Juliet*, see Donald D. Keyes, *George Cooke, 1793–1849* (Athens, GA: Georgia Museum of Art), 68, National Portrait Gallery's "Catalog of Portraits," https://npg.si .edu/object/npg_SSSA0560. On Collins: Cleveland, *Genealogy*, 2177. Harriet Collins's obituary is in *GT*, April 25, 1834.

48 **"Females can never master":** " 'This is where it all began,' presented at Candler Alumnae Center," 2–3 (undated typescript), file 1974, Wesleyan College Archives, Macon, GA.

48 **left the South to study:** Willard L. Rocker, *Marriages and Obituaries*, 53.

49 **Eliza's belly:** Her pregnancy is evidenced by the death of her child in 1838. See "Whose Bones Lie Buried," *Macon (GA) Weekly Telegraph*, February 25, 1891, 7.

49 **Ellen could be called on . . . always on call:** *BF*, 6, 8; McCaskill, "Ellen Craft," 85. Scholars have called attention to the challenges of "house slaves." See, for instance, Annette Gordon-Reed, *The Hemingses of Monticello* (New York: Norton, 2008), 30.

50 **used the enslaved as collateral:** Alicia K. Jackson, *Recovered Life*, 34–36, 166n44, 167n54; Bibb County Georgia Superior Court, Deeds and Mortgages 1839–1842, 6 (G): 272–73, BCC; See also exchanges involving the Collinses and eight enslaved people in Bibb County Georgia Superior Court, Deeds and Mortgages 1848–1853, 9(K), 494.

50   **his brother Charles:** Alicia K. Jackson writes that Robert Collins's frequent business associate (and "likely relative"), Charles Collins, was "well known in Macon as a slave trader." *Recovered Life*, 167 n. 51, 36. While the evidence is limited, her claim is supported by Frederic Bancroft, who identifies Charles Collins, a Macon slave trader and "planter" with bank stock in *Slave Trading*, 246–47. See also Bancroft's journal in his papers at Columbia University, box 9. The federal censuses of 1840, 1850, and 1860 list one Charles Collins in Bibb County; household information indicates that he was Robert Collins's brother. Their family Bible appears in Daughters of the American Revolution, Hawkinsville Chapter, and Cedar Cemetery, *Cedar Hill Cemetery Records, Cochran, Bleckley County, Georgia: Includes Halsey Family Bible Records, Harris-May-Collins Bible Records* (Salt Lake City, UT: filmed by the Genealogical Society of Utah, 1970), 77. Charles Collins's name appears in "ATTENTION PLANTERS! 61 Negroes," GT December 23, 1856. Both the Collinses and Smiths appear as major enslavers in the 1857 Macon tax digests at the Georgia Archives, Morrow, Georgia.

51   **"decidedly more humane":** *RTMF*, 7; McCaskill, "Ellen Craft," 86, 89.

51   **worlds apart . . . "nigger":** *BF*, 9; *TL*, "Anti-Slavery Meeting in New Bedford," February 16, 1849.

51   **"no confidence in white people":** *RTMF*, 52.

51   **Ellen's mother's sister:** Mary Eliza Healy's origins are long debated. Sterling, as well as Foley, identifies her as James Smith's daughter, without sources (*BF*, 7). O'Toole questions such claims in *Passing*, 14, 231n19. Meanwhile, S. T. Pickard reports hearing from Ellen that Mary Eliza was her maternal aunt. See his letter to William H. Siebert in Siebert's papers at HOU (Underground Railroad in Maine, MS Am 2420, 12). Notes kept by descendants (on Caroline DuBose's "From the Shadow of Slavery to Place in History," ARC) support this report. My sketch of the Healys draws from O'Toole's *Passing*, 5–22. See also Albert S. Foley, *Bishop Healy: Beloved Outcaste* (New York: Arno Press, 1969), 9–28; and *Dream of an Outcaste: Patrick F. Healy; the Story of the Slaveborn Georgian Who Became the Second Founder of America's First Great Catholic University, Georgetown* (New Orleans: Portals Press, 1989), 1–11; Foley to Craft.

51   **What set apart the Healys . . . George Washington . . . turned on its head:** O'Toole *Passing*, 14–18. On Healy's legal problems: ibid., 21–22; For the broader history: ibid., 10, 15; Foley, *Bishop Healy*, 18; Rogers, "Free Negro Legislation," 27–37. On George Washington: Dunbar, *Never Caught*, 173–76. On Healy's inability to emancipate: *Passing*. 22. On the "one drop rule," ibid., 2, 15; Clinton, *Plantation Mistress*, 203.

SAVANNAH

55   **"city of shade and silence":** Carlton Holmes Rogers, *Incidents of Travel in the Southern States and Cuba*, 229; Walter Fraser, *Savannah*, 258; Emily P. Burke, *Reminiscences of Georgia* (Oberlin: J. M. Fitch, 1850), 15.

55   **landscape of cotton:** Berry and Harris, *Slavery and Freedom*, 45–47; Fraser, *Savannah*, 246–48; C. G. Parsons, *Inside View of Slavery; Or, a Tour Among the Planters* (Boston: J. P. Jewett, 1855), 23; Cunynghame, *Glimpse*, 260. The railroad is named the city's biggest slaver in the documentary *Steam, Steel and Sweat: The Story of Savannah's Railroad Shops* (Savannah, GA: Coastal Heritage Society, 2003).

55   **"If my great-grandfather":** Quoted in Alvarez, *Travel*, 36.

56   **eight thirty . . . Pulaski House:** The *Savannah (GA) Daily Republican* lists departure times. On the Crafts' stop here: "An Interesting Case," *Savannah (GA) Daily News*, May 28, 1878. Collins's hotel arrivals listed in *Savannah (GA) Daily Republican*, December 15, 1847, *Savannah (GA) Georgian*, January 17, 1849.

56   **"stiff-necked":** Quoted in Malcolm Bell, "Ease and Elegance, Madeira and Murder: The Social Life of Savannah's City Hotel," *Georgia Historical Quarterly* 76, no. 3 (1992): 571. On the menus and ice: ibid., Malcolm Bell, "Savannah's City Hotel," May 1990, City Hotel file, GHS.

56 **moss will not grow:** Karen Wortham shared this story on her "Journey by Faith" tour.

56 **central axis:** The scale of Savannah's slave trade was smaller than what it would become, but its prime coordinates were established. Barry Sheehy, Cindy Wallace, and Vaughnette Goode-Walker call Bay Lane the "Heart of Savannah's Slave-Trading District" (chapter title) in *Savannah: Brokers, Bankers and Bay Lane: Inside the Slave Trade* (Austin: Emerald Book Company, 2012). Daniel Nason describes sales in his *Journal of a Tour from Boston to Savannah* (Cambridge: printed for the author, 1849), 29–32. See also, on the ironies, Clarissa Santos, "Johnson Square," GHS, http://georgiahistory .com/education-outreach/historical-markers/hidden-histories/johnson-square/.

56 **more brothels . . . biggest slave dealer:** Fraser, *Savannah*, 289, 310. On the early bans on rum and slavery: Harris and Berry, *Slavery and Freedom*, 2–4.

56 **"The Weeping Time":** Anne C. Bailey, *The Weeping Time: Memory and the Largest Slave Auction in American History* (NY: Cambridge University Press, 2017).

57 **The Pulaski was known:** Fraser, *Savannah*, 310–11; Byrne, "Burden and Heat," 233; Whittington B. Johnson, *Black Savannah*, 88; Charles Hoskins, *Out of Yamacraw and Beyond: Discovering Black Savannah* (Savannah, GA: Gullah Press, 2002), 112. On the rumors: Jack McQuade: "Flags, Cuspidor, Dungeon Found in Pulaski Wreckage," *Savannah (GA) Evening Press*, January 14, 1957; Beth E. Concepción, "Beneath the Surface," *Savannah*, March 15, 2017.

57 **in order to avoid:** Given that the Central Railroad most likely did not have rest facilities, the Crafts may have had to wait until they boarded the steamer at eight thirty.

57 ***General Clinch . . . wedding cake tiers:*** Eric Heyl, *Early American Steamers*, vol. 6 (Buffalo: Sin, 1953), 126–27. On the area around Bay and the docks: Fraser, *Savannah*, 252–53, 258, 303. Gudmestad's *Steamboats* was critical for this chapter, especially 32–33, 53–77 on steamboat hierarchy. On Savannah as Georgia's main slave port: Byrne, "Burden and Heat," 227; Fraser, *Savannah*, 310.

58 **three-year-old named Sarah:** Captains traveling interstate were required to fill out "Slave Manifests"; Sarah's name appears here. Unfortunately, there is no documentation for the day of the Crafts' travel, possibly because the papers were lost or destroyed. See *Papers of the American Slave Trade*, Series D: Records of the US Customhouses, Part 1: Port of Savannah Slave Manifests, 1790–1860, "Reel 16: Outward, January 1848–September 1850," 141–50, http://www.lexisnexis.com/documents/academic/ upa_cis/100539_AmSlaveTradeSerDPt1.pdf. Thanks to Desiree Wallen at the National Archives in Atlanta for her guidance.

58 **required passengers to be social:** *BF*, 14.

59 **moved to Charleston:** Evidence includes notices for Robert Collins's business with Jesse F. Cleveland (*GT*, October 15, 1839), and his listing in James W. Hagy, *Directories for the City of Charleston, South Carolina . . . 1840–41* (Baltimore: Clearfield, 1997), and Charleston's 1840 census (*not* Macon's). Notably, Eliza's and Ellen's ages match up with those of females in this household. On the Smiths' move to Macon: Foley to Craft.

59 **immense canvas:** George Cooke's 1842 painting, *Eliza Cromwell Smith Collins and Juliet Collins Lewis*. On the son: "Whose Bones Lie Buried," Macon *Weekly Telegraph*, February 25, 1891, 7.

59 **emotional state:** See Dunbar's discussion of Ona Judge's situation in *Never Caught*, 22.

59 **"auction and commission business":** See advertisements in the *Georgia Messenger* (Fort Hawkins, GA), October 10, 1839, unearthed by Alicia K. Jackson, who identifies Robert Collins's partnership in Collins and Cleveland in *Recovered Life*, 34–36. On the family connection: Cleveland, *Genealogy*, 211.

60 **must have taken Ellen . . . Baby Juliet:** On Eliza's inability to spare Ellen: *BAP*, 274. The Smiths' move is noted in *BF*, 9, Foley to Craft. Juliet's birth is dated July 4, 1842, in Cleveland, *Genealogy*, 2177. George Cookes painting dates the birth to 1840.

60 **other memories:** *RTMF*, 7, 23.

60 **back in Macon:** "Dr. Robert Collins of Charleston" appears in Samuel Hazard, *Hazard's United States Commercial and Statistical Register*, vol. 6 (Philadelphia: William

F. Geddes, 1842), 15. He would be back in Macon by 1843, when he had contract for the Central Railroad.

60   **slip of paper:** Unnamed document, box 6, folder 79, ARC.

61   **could not bear . . . exiled:** *RTMF*, 3, 19–20.

61   **Ellen to New Orleans:** Parker raises this possibility in *Trial*, 16.

61   **"cannot live together":** Collins, *Essay*, 12.

62   **not allowed the Christian wedding . . . "jumped the broomstick":** McCaskill, "Ellen Craft," 86.

62   **wax nostalgic . . . "be of service":** Quoted in Caroline Williams, *History of Jones*, 68–69.

63   **Under Watch:** I have relied on Gudmestad's *Steamboats* for details on the culture aboard vessels such as the *General Clinch*, and for other relevant background. See especially "Floating Palaces and High-Pressure Prisons," 60, 68; 64–65 on communal facilities. Scenes in this chapter hew closely to *RTMF* and "An Incident in the South," *Newark Daily Mercury*, January 19, 1849.

64   **one known remedy:** On cholera: Richard J. Evans, "Epidemics and Revolutions: Cholera in Nineteenth-Century Europe," *Past & Present*, no. 120 (1988): 123–46. On opodeldoc: H. B. Skinner, *The Family Doctor, or Guide to Health*, 16th ed. (Boston: published for the author, 1844), 46.

64   **Tybee Island:** I thank Karen Wortham of "Journey by Faith" for her evocation of this island, also described in Byrne, *Burden and Heat*, 217; Berry and Harris, *Slavery and Freedom*, 23.

64   **Through the night:** Charles Lyell, *A Second Visit to the United States of North America* (London: John Murray, 1849), I: 308, Cunynghame, *Glimpse*, 262.

66   **prime season:** Richard McMillan, "Savannah's Coastal Slave Trade: A Quantitative Analysis of Ship Manifests, 1840–1850," *Georgia Historical Quarterly* 78, no. 2, 342.

66   **"State rights":** Fitzgerald and Galloway, *Eminent Methodists*, 110, 113.

67   **New-York Herald:** "Singular Escape" was published here January 17, 1849.

68   **"not by any means the worst":** *RTMF*, 3; Collins, *Essay*, 6.

68   **"slave life in Georgia":** John Brown, *Slave Life in Georgia: A Narrative of the Life, Sufferings, and Escape of John Brown, a Fugitive Slave, Now in England*, ed. Louis A. Chamerovzow (London: W. M. Watts, 1855), 48, 88, 132. On Brown, see F. N. Boney's Beehive Press edition (1972); Fisch, *American Slaves*, 56.

68   **"I have seen slaves":** *RTMF*, 68–69. The Crafts discuss retaliation by slavers in ibid., 20.

69   **publish a statement:** "To the Public," *Savannah (GA) Georgian*, October 30, 1832.

69   **"most trusted":** Collins to Hastings.

69   **mansion was sold:** Smith's purchase of September 4, 1844, and gift to Eliza are documented in: Bibb County Superior Court, Deed Records 1842–1845, H-7, 692–93, BCC. On the house: John C. Butler, *The Life of Elam Alexander* (Macon, GA: J. W. Burke, 1886), 7.

70   **public auction . . . Viney . . . :** "Postponed Bibb Sheriff's Sale," *GT*, September 29, 1846. William dates the wedding to 1846 in "Libel Suit," I did not find conclusive evidence of the sale's execution, but a comparative study of the names listed here against Collins's slave holdings in the 1850 census indicates substantial decreases, especially among the men.

70   **July 1, 1845:** Bibb County Superior Court, Deed Records 1845–1848, I/J-4, BCC. Ellen is described as "one girl . . . about seventeen years of age," younger than her commonly given 1826 birth date.

71   **"negro man":** "Death of Mr. Johnston," *Georgia Weekly Telegraph*, October 25, 1887. More details come from an exhibit on his life at the Johnston-Felton-Hay House Museum; Tommy H. Jones, *The Johnstons, Feltons and Hays—100 Years in the Palace of the South* (Atlanta: Georgia Trust for Historic Preservation, 1993); and related website: http://tomitronics.com/old_buildings/hay%20house/people.html.

71   **"trickery and chicanery" . . . watch his property:** See the case of Johnston v. South

West Rail Road Bank in Strobhart, *Reports*, 359. Griffin's example appears in Jenkins, "Antebellum Macon," 155.

72 **Ellen had given birth to a baby:** McCaskill identifies two sources in "Ellen Craft," 89–90, *LL*, 30; Parker, *Trial*, 147; and James Freeman Clarke, *Anti-Slavery Days: A Sketch of the Struggle Which Ended in the Abolition* (New York: John W. Lovell, 1883), 83–84. Papson and Calarco cite Kirby, *Years* (305–8) in *Secret Lives*, 67. To these I add an unpublished account, "Ellen Craft," from a descendant of Barclay and Mary Ivins, in Lyons, "Quaker Family Home" (thanks to Carol Spinanger Ivins); "Mr. Richards Special Report no. 5, 1891–1892," William Siebert Scrapbooks, Underground Railroad in Massachusetts, vol. 1, HOU, MS AM 2420 (13). Notably, all waited until the Crafts were no longer under direct threat of re-enslavement to tell their stories. Parker was closest to the Crafts: William called him a "great friend" and "the only clergyman in the city in whom he had any confidence." (See his letter to Samuel May, May 29, 1860, BPL; "Libel Suit." Complicating these accounts is the possibility that the child may not have been William's, as discussed in *LL*, 30; Beaulieu, *Writing African American Women*, 228.

72 **"above all . . . the fact that another man":** *RTMF*, 3.

72 **"victim of her master":** See Thomas Wentworth Higginson to Charles Devens, US Marshal, September 29, 1850, Letters and Journals, box 3, Thomas W. Higginson Papers, HOU; McCaskill, *RTMF*, xxii.

73 **descendants would recall:** Albert Foley to Dorothy Sterling, December 27, 1974, Dorothy Sterling Papers, Special Collections and University Archives, University of Oregon. (Note that Foley seems to be confused about the generations.)

73 **"God made of one blood" . . . "God is on our side":** *RTMF*, preface, 21.

73 **Ellen had conceived the plan . . . "Come, William":** McCaskill first credits Ellen in *LL*, 25, citing Josephine Brown's *Biography*, 75–81, quoted here. Others report that William may have saved as much as $220. See "American Slavery," *Leeds Mercury* (UK), October 25, 1856.

74 **Over several days . . . "I think I can make":** *RTMF*, 21–24; "Story of Ellen Crafts; *BAP*, 321; fabrication in ibid., 274. Thanks to Lynne Bassett for the meaning of "green glasses."

75 **privilege and disability:** McCaskill notes how Ellen feigns "deafness, toothache, and snobbery," *RTMF*, x. On the significance of disability in Ellen's passing: Ellen Samuels, " 'A Complication of Complaints': Untangling Disability, Race, and Gender in William and Ellen Craft's *Running a Thousand Miles for Freedom*," *MELUS* 31, no. 3 (2006), especially on "the invalid as 'one who is served,'" 36–38. For a broader discussion: Dea H. Boster, *African American Slavery and Disability: Bodies, Property and Power in the Antebellum South, 1800–1860* (New York: Routledge, 2013).

75 **"eyes, ears, hands, and feet":** Still, *Underground Rail Road*, 369. McCaskill discusses the significance of Philadelphia in "In Plain Sight."

75 **William Johnson, or Johnston:** The Crafts write Johnson in *RTMF*, but elsewhere, Ellen's alias appears as Johnston. See other readings in McCaskill, *LL*, 31–32.

CHARLESTON

79 **Two Houses:** All dialogue and thoughts are from *RTMF*, unless noted. See also "Speech by William Craft" in *BAP*, 246–49. On the telegraph: Butler, *Historical Record*, foreword, 179–81. A plaque and permanent exhibit at the Old Exchange Building (formerly the customhouse) in Charleston describe the largest open-air slave market here.

79 **Sugar House . . . "whipping room":** James Matthews, "Recollections of Slavery by a Runaway Slave," *Emancipator* (New York), August 23, September 13, 20, October 11, 18, 1838. See also Susanna Ashton, "Recollecting Jim," *Common-Place* 15, no. 1 (Fall 2014); Lineberry, *Be Free or Die, The Amazing Story of Robert Small's Escape From Slavery to Union Hero* (New York: St. Martin's Press), 43; Joseph Williams, "Charleston Work House and 'Sugar House'," Discovering Our Past, College of Charleston online, (https://discovering.cofc.edu/items/show/31); Samanthis Smalls, "Behind Workhouse

Walls: The Public Regulation of Slavery in Charleston, 1730–1850" (PhD diss., Duke University, 2015), 35n2 for "little sugar," 55; Miles, *All That She Carried*, 172–73.

80   **"perpetual staircase":** "The Charleston Sugar House," *TL*, June 29, 1849.

80   **police state:** Andrew Delbanco, 26; Ivan D. Steen, "Charleston in the 1850's: As Described by British Travelers," *South Carolina Historical Magazine* 70, no. 1 (1970): 42–44. Population figure from *The Seventh Census of the United States: 1850*.

81   **"It would be difficult to find":** Mackay, *Western World*, 184.

81   **His name was Moses:** "Remarkable Attempt to Escape by A Slave," *Camden (SC) Journal*, November 1, 1848.

82   **Planter's Hotel:** Martha Zierden et al., "The Dock Street Theatre: Archaeological Discovery and Exploration," vol. 42, March 2009. (https://www.charlestonmuseum .org/assets/pdf/ArchaeologyReports/Dock%20Street%20Theatre%202009%20-%20 AC%2042.pdf; Lineberry, *Live Free or Die*, 45.

82   **Crafts passed down . . . buzzards:** The exact route is unknown, but the city's layout is evoked in accounts such as Amelia Murray's (her remarks on buzzards appear in Steen, "Charleston," 41) and maps such as Wellington Williams's "Plan of Charleston" (Philadelphia: W. Williams, 1849).

82   **"America's first theatre":** "Dock Street Theatre: America's First Theatre, Charleston Stage online, https://charlestonstage.com/about-us/dock-street-theatre.

82   **"bawdy, raucous fare":** Joseph Kelly, *America's Longest Siege: Charleston, Slavery, and the Slow March Toward Civil War* (New York: Overlook Press, 2013), 26.

83   **human beings were trafficked:** Beaulieu, *Writing African American Women*, 228.

83   **house slave:** Miles's discussion of badges and Rose's life is meaningful here: *All That She Carried*, 82–87.

83   **in the household:** See Cleveland, *Genealogy*, 2119, and Charleston's 1840 city directory and census.

84   **grandson of the Middle Passage:** *BAP*, 541. Further analysis in *LL*, 19–21.

84   **"little don up buckra":** *RTMF* 35.

85   **"Gentleman Pirate":** Details on the pirate and building are from Ruth M. Miller and Ann Taylor Andrus, *Charleston's Old Exchange Building: A Witness to American History* (Charleston, SC: History Press), especially 14, 47.

86   **tickets straight through:** "Singular escapes," 7; *BAP*, 247. Pricing in William W. Williams, *Appleton's Railroad and Steamboat Companion* (New York: D. Appleton, 1848), 261, 290.

86   **Charlestonians were widely admired:** Walter J. Fraser, Jr., *Charleston! Charleston! The History of a Southern City* (Columbia: University of South Carolina Press, 1989), 225.

88   **three o'clock:** See advertisement in the *Sumter Banner* (Sumterville, SC), November 28, 1849. Compare *RTMF*, 37; a rare nonalignment.

OVERLAND

91   **The Wrong Chap:** This chapter benefits from Cunynghame's vivid depictions of his travels into Wilmington and beyond: *Glimpse*, 264–75. See also Olmstead, *Journey*, 337–40, 368, 374; James Sprunt, *Chronicles of Cape Fear*, 2nd ed. (Raleigh, NC: Edwards & Broughton, 1916), 154, 160; Bryant, *Letters*, 78–79.

91   **"floating volcanoes":** Thomas P. Jones and James J. Mapes, eds., *Journal of the Franklin Institute of the State of Pennsylvania* (Philadelphia: Franklin Institute, 1843), 401.

91   **known for its "irregularities":** James C. Burke, *The Wilmington & Raleigh Rail Road Company, 1833–1854* (Jefferson, NC: McFarland, 2011), 72.)

92   **Charles Dickens had been shaken:** See his *American Notes*, 166.

92   **"Ticket!" . . . "Negro firemen":** Chambers, *Things*, 331–32, Crowe, *With Thackeray*, 143–44.

92   **one comfort . . . "ruined cavaliers":** Cunynghame, *Glimpse*, 269, 276.

93   **single daughters:** Josephine Brown, *Biography of a Bondman*, 78. Other accounts in

Ripley, *BAP*, 246; "An Escape from Slavery in America," *Chambers's Edinburgh Journal* 15 (January–June 1851): 175; "Singular Escapes," 6.

95 **Boxed In:** McInnis's *Slaves Waiting* deeply informed my presentation of Richmond, along with Scott Nesbit, Robert K. Nelson, and Maurie McInnis, "Visualizing the Richmond Slave Trade," Hidden Patterns of the Civil War, University of Richmond online, http://dsl.richmond.edu/civilwar/slavemarket_essay.html. I also drew from Olmstead, *Journey*, 19–24; Mackey, *Western World*, 2:152; Crowe, *With Thackeray*, 130.

95 **"Give me liberty!":** Bryant, *Letters*, 72. On Henry's enslaving practices, see Harlow Giles Unger, *Lion of Liberty: Patrick Henry and the Call to a New Nation* (New York: Da Capo Press, 2010).

95 **"resale center" . . . families were broken:** McInnis, *Slaves Waiting*, 78, 83, 99, 147; Bancroft, *Slave Trading*, 246–47.

95 **"Devil's half acre" . . . "nearly white":** Abigail Tucker, "Digging Up the Past at a Richmond Jail," *Smithsonian Magazine*, March 2009; Sydney Trent, "She Was Raped by the Owner of a Notorious Slave Jail," *Washington Post*, February 1, 2020.

96 **similar routine:** Still, *Underground Rail Road*, 369. See train times advertised in the *Richmond Republican*, May 23, 1849.

96 **"No, that is my boy":** Though this story was likely embellished (as Sanborn writes in "The Plagiarist's Craft"), it is impossible to say if it did not originate in an actual occurrence.

96 **a Richmond man named Henry:** See Jeffrey Ruggles, *Unboxing*; Ernest, ed., *Narrative of the Life of Henry Box Brown.*

98 **The Capital:** On vendors: Bryant, *Letters*, 71; Mackay, *Western World*, 67. On Aquia Landing, see the site marker at "Steamships Stages and Slave Trade—Trail to Freedom," The Historical Marker Database, https://www.hmdb.org/marker.asp?marker=40129.

98 **"two jack-towels" . . . "negro barber":** Dickens, *American Notes*, 2:7, Chambers, *Things*, 268.

99 **pronouncing it "delightful":** Berry, *Princes of Cotton*, 503.

99 **one traveler remembered:** Mackay, *Western World*, 64. Other descriptions in these passages from ibid., 66; Chambers, *Things*, 268; Olmstead, *Journey*, 17–19. On Ona Judge: Dunbar, *Never Caught*. On Alexandria's past as a premier slave export market: McInnis, *Slaves Waiting*, 105.

100 **"dressed like a white man":** *RTMF*, 43.

101 **William and not Ellen:** Marjorie Garber observes the irony that it "is the husband and not the wife who is accused of cross dressing" in *Vested Interests: Cross-Dressing and Cultural Anxiety* (New York: Routledge, 1992), 285.

101 **"single largest known escape attempt":** My discussion draws from Mary Kay Ricks, "Escape on the Pearl," *Washington Post*, August 12, 1998, and her *Escape*, especially 92.

102 **"I know to what this leads":** "Debate in the United States Senate," *GT*, May 9, 1848.

102 **"precisely like droves of horses":** Quoted in Ricks, *Escape*, 96–97. On reports of brisk business: "From Washington," *GT*, January 2, 1849.

102 **"There is nothing wrong" . . . "Jerry":** Quoted in William Dusinberre, *Slavemaster President: The Double Career of James Polk* (Oxford: Oxford University Press, 2007), 18, 20–21, 77–78; Ta-Nehisi Coates, "The Case for Reparations," *Atlantic*, June 2014.

103 **"From Clinton, Georgia":** Calvin Schermerhorn, *Money over Mastery, Family over Freedom: Slavery in the Antebellum Upper South* (Baltimore: Johns Hopkins University Press, 2011), 16.

103 **"Hope Hell Slaughter":** Joseph Henry Allen, ed., *The Unitarian Review*, vol. 36 (Boston, Office of the Unitarian Review, 1891), 197; "Recaptured Fugitives," *NASS*, May 4, 1848.

103 **First-class cars:** Joseph J. Snyder, *Baltimore and Ohio: The Passenger Trains and Services of the First American Common-Carried Railroad, 1827–1971* (Shepherdstown, WV: Juniper House Library Publications, 2012), 45.

104 **Baltimore:** On what they knew: *RTMF*, 44, inspired by Colson Whitehead, *Underground Rail Road* (New York: Doubleday, 2016), 57. Weather reports in the *Baltimore Daily*

Union. William Still in *Underground Rail Road*, 370, says bonds were required, but compare *Laws of and Ordinances Relating to the Baltimore and Susquehanna Railroad Company* (Baltimore: James Lucas, 1850), 69. On praise for William: "Story of Ellen Crafts." Details on spaces and conveyances from: Edward Hungerford, *The Story of the Baltimore and Ohio Railroad, 1827–1927* (New York: G. P. Putnam's Sons, 1928), 1:167; Herbert H. Harwood, *Impossible Challenge, the Baltimore and Ohio Railroad in Maryland* (Baltimore: Barnard Roberts, 1979); James D. Dilts, *The Great Road: The Building of the Baltimore and Ohio, the Nation's First Railroad, 1828–1853* (Stanford, CA: Stanford University Press, 1993), 421n31; Cunynghame, *Glimpse*, 287; Mackay, *Western World*, 104; Anthony J. Bianculli, *Trains and Technology: The American Railroad in the Nineteenth Century* (Newark: University of Delaware Press, 2002), 2:49.

105 **Slatter's old slave pen:** On Slatter, his business, and his tunnels, see Clayton, *Cash for Blood*, 83–91, 667n18; "Cash for Negroes," *Baltimore Sun*, July 18, 1838.

105 **"Where are you going, boy?":** Subsequent quotations, unless noted, from *RTMF*, 44–47.

106 **fight to the death:** "Anti-Slavery Meeting in New Bedford," *TL*, February 16, 1849, 27.

107 **didn't know that it was necessary:** *BAP*, 248–49.

109 **Baggage:** My depiction of the train journey draws from Charles P. Dare, *Philadelphia, Wilmington and Baltimore Railroad Guide* (Philadelphia: Fitzgibbon & Van Ness, 1856), 26–27. On Francis Scott Key: Christopher Wilson, "Where's the Debate on Francis Scott Key's Slaveholding Legacy?," *Smithsonian*, July 1, 2016. On the Negro car: Mackay, *Western World* I: 102–4. All dialogue in this chapter from *RTMF*, 47–50.

110 **"Harbor of Grace" . . . "persons of color":** Jamie Smith Hopkins, "Hidden Gem: Havre de Grace," *Baltimore Sun*, November 8, 2009; Chambers, *Things*, 253. On the transfer and more: *RTMF*, 48; Mackay, *Western World*, 104; Charles Richard Weld, *A Vacation Tour in the United States and Canada* (London: Longman, Brown, Green, and Longmans), 1855), 337; John Disturnell, *A Guide Between Washington, Baltimore, Philadelphia, New York, and Boston* (New York: J. Disturnell, 1846), 20.

113 **Later in the night:** On the lettered stone: Dare, *Philadelphia*, 75. On the horses: Geffen, "Industrial Development," 316; Mackey, *Western World*, II:97.

115 **Christmas Eve Coda:** The Collinses' hesitancy in accepting Ellen's agency appears in Collins to Hastings. See also "Runaway Slaves," *GT*, February 13, 1849. On the cabinetmaker's instinct: *RTMF*, 29.

PENNSYLVANIA

119 **City of Brotherly Love:** The city comes alive in Sam Katz's 2011 documentary *Philadelphia, The Great Experiment*, "Disorder, 1820–1854," available at WPVI-TV online, https://6abc.com/entertainment/philadelphia-the-great-experiment—full-episodes /446858/. Critical sources for this chapter include Elizabeth M. Geffen, "Industrial Development" and "Violence in Philadelphia in the 1840s and 1850s," *Pennsylvania History: A Journey of Mid-Atlantic Studies* 36, no. 4 (October 1969): 381–410; Julie Winch, *Elite of Our People: Joseph Wilson's Sketches of Black Upper-Class Life in Antebellum Philadelphia* (Pennsylvania State University Press, 2000); W. E. B. DuBois, *The Philadelphia Negro: A Social Study* (Philadelphia: published for the university, 1899), 25–45; Daniel R. Biddle and Murray Dubin, *Tasting Freedom: Octavius Catto and the Battle for Equality in Civil War America* (Philadelphia: Temple University Press, 2010).

119 **milliners and mariners:** Daniel Murray Pamphlet Collection (Library of Congress) and Society of Friends, *A Statistical Inquiry into the Condition of the People of Colour, of the City and Districts of Philadelphia* (Philadelphia: printed by Kite & Walton, 1849); Winch, *Elite*, 16–22.

119 **"Pepper pot, smoking hot!":** Winch, *Elite*, 13.

119 **"colored hotel" . . . southern corridor":** "An Ex Slave's Reminiscences"; Winch, *Elite*, 6.

120 **William would recollect:** "Libel Suit."

121 **British travelers:** Ivan D. Steen, "Philadelphia in the 1850's: As Described by British

Travelers," *Pennsylvania History: A Journal of Mid-Atlantic Studies* 33, no. 1 (1966): 33. Geffen vividly evokes the city and its contrasts in "Industrial Development," especially 315–16.

121 **"sisterly affection":** "A Guide to the Stranger, or Pocket Companion for the Fancy: Containing a List of the Gay Houses and Ladies of Pleasure in the City of Brotherly Love and Sisterly Affection" (Philadelphia: s.n., 1849). Coroner's report in Daniel Murray Collection, Society of Friends, "Statistical Inquiry," 34. On the gangs and waste: Geffen, "Violence in Philadelphia," 391, and "Industrial Development," 318.

121 **Vigilance Committee:** Larry Gara, "William Still and the Underground Railroad," *Pennsylvania History* 28, no. 1 (January 1961): 33–44; Joseph A. Boromé et al., "The Vigilant Committee of Philadelphia," *Pennsylvania Magazine of History and Biography* 92, no. 2 (July 1968): 320–51; Janice Sumler-Lewis, "The Forten-Purvis Women of Philadelphia and the American Anti-Slavery Crusade," *Journal of Negro History* 68, no. 4 (Winter 1981–82): 281–88; Nilgun Anadolu Okur, "Underground Railroad in Philadelphia, 1830–1860," *Journal of Black Studies* 25, no. 5 (May 1995): 537–57; Bacon, *But One Race*, 81. On Philadelphia: Richard Newman and James Mueller, *Antislavery and Abolition in Philadelphia* (Baton Rouge: Louisiana State University Press, 2011), 1.

122 **"Philadelphia's best customer":** Geffen, "Violence," 383.

122 **"Carolina Row":** Daniel Kilbride, *An American Aristocracy: Southern Planters in Antebellum Philadelphia* (Columbia: University of South Carolina Press, 2006), 5.

122 **Pennsylvania Hall . . . "those beautiful spires":** Quotations from Ira V. Brown, "Racism and Sexism: The Case of Pennsylvania Hall," *Phylon* 37, no. 2 (2nd quar., 1976): 130, 135. Also see Bacon, *But One Race*, 66–73; Beverly C. Tomek, *Pennsylvania Hall: A "Legal Lynching" in the Shadow of the Liberty Bell* (New York: Oxford University Press, 2013.

122 **Philadelphia had since turned . . . lost its vital force:** Geffen, "Violence," 383; Boromé et al., "Vigilant Committee," 327–28; Larry Gara, "Friends and the Underground Railroad," *Quaker History* 51, no. 1 (1962): 11; Still, *Underground Rail Road*, 611.

123 **"Leave the boys" . . . "in every respect":** Still, *Underground Rail Road*, 5, 370; Gara, "William Still," 33–34. Still comes to life in Laine Drewery's 2012 documentary *Underground Rail Road: The William Still Story*. For more on Still: William Kashatus: *The Underground Rail Road and the Angel at Philadelphia* (Notre Dame, IN: University of Notre Dame Press, 2021).

124 **"good features":** Mifflin Wistar Gibbs, *Shadow and Light: An Autobiography with Reminiscences of the Last and Present Century* (Washington, DC, s.n., 1902), 12.

124 **"tall black man":** The advertisement appears in the *Pennsylvania Freeman*, (Philadelphia), December 21, 1848. Gara discusses the "interrogation" of potential "imposters" in "William Still," 37.

124 **"Scarcely had they arrived":** Still, *Underground Rail Road*, 370.

125 **Charles Dexter Cleveland:** Josephine F. Pacheco, *The Pearl: A Failed Slave Escape on the Potomac* (Chapel Hill: University of North Carolina Press, 2005), 68–69; Cleveland, *Genealogy*, 2:1901.

125 **Crafts' story was unique:** McCaskill, *LL*, 5–6, and *PAS*, 179, 197. Sinha observes the unhappiness of Douglass's and Brown's marriages in *The Slave's Cause*, 285.

125 **Fugitive Slave Act . . . threat of forcible seizure:** Dunbar, *Never Caught*, 105–6; David Smith, *On the Edge of Freedom: The Fugitive Slave Issue in South Central Pennsylvania, 1820–1870* (New York: Fordham University Press, 2013), 96–97. On the dangers of kidnapping: Richard Bell, *Stolen* (New York: 37 Ink, 2019); Berlin, "Slavery, Freedom," 34.

126 **so-called president:** "Robert Purvis Dead," *New York Times*, April 16, 1898.

127 **Purvis:** For this biographical sketch, including details of Purvis's home, his situation in 1848, and all anecdotes, I relied on Margaret Hope Bacon's extensive research in *But One Race*, especially 101–16, and " 'The Double Curse of Sex and Color': Robert Purvis and Human Rights," *Pennsylvania Magazine of History and Biography*, vol. 121,

no. 1/2 (1997): 53–76; and "Robert Purvis at 80," *Pennsylvania Press*, August 3, 1890. Also see Julie Winch, *A Gentleman of Color: The Life of James Forten* (New York: Oxford University Press, 2002), 351–54; and her *Philadelphia's Black Elite* (Philadelphia: Temple University Press, 1993), 152–165. The Crafts' passage through Byberry is noted in Papson and Calarco, *Secret Lives*, 66–67.

127   **passing himself . . . "blooded horses" . . . "intuitive presence in firearms":** All quotations are from "Robert Purvis at 80." Also see Bacon, *But One Race*, 45–47 (includes O'Connell story); Pryor's analysis of Purvis not "passing" but "exposing," *Colored Travelers*, 136–37; Sinha's distinction between colonization and "independent, black-led emigration efforts" in *The Slave's Cause*, 160–71.

128   **"It seemed so natural":** Quoted in Bacon, *But One Race*, 72.

128   *searing August nights . . . "the apathy and inhumanity":* Quoted in Bacon, *But One Race*, 99. See also "Robert Purvis at 80"; Geffen, "Industrial Development," 353; and "Violence," 387. On the challenges of the move to Byberry: Bacon, *But One Race*, 101–2, 105.

129   **true civil rights activist . . . turning point:** This paragraph draws from Bacon, *But One Race*, especially 2, 52–53, 115; "Double Curse," 54. See also Kate Masur's analysis of the antebellum fight for civil rights in *Until Justice Be Done* (New York: Norton, 2021).

130   **His wife, Harriet:** On Harriet Purvis's fund-raising, activism, and more: Bacon, *But One Race*, 96–97; Sumler-Lewis, "The Forten-Purvis Women of Philadelphia," 281–88; Winch, *Gentleman*, 352–53.

131   **two fine paintings . . . "injurious" repercussion:** Bacon, *But One Race*, 39, 84–85. On William and Cinqué: "Anti-Slavery Meetings in New Bedford," *TL*, February 16, 1849. See also Richard J. Powell, "How Cinque Was Painted," *Washington Post*, December 28, 1997; Sinha, *The Slave's Cause*, 411–13. Sinha's analysis of the "interracial and transnational world of abolitionism" shaped my view of these individuals and movements.

131   **"I am in earnest—I will not equivocate":** *TL*, January 1, 1831. On Purvis's differences with Garrison: Bacon, *But One Race*, 114–15.

133   **Tiny Shoes:** On Ellen's illness and dread: Still, *Underground Rail Road*, 370; *RTMF*, 52; "An Ex Slave's Reminiscences." Papson and Calarco observe the Crafts' stay here, as well as Georgiana Bruce Kirby's presence and remarks in *Secret Lives*, 66–67. On Ellen's gentleman's clothes: Lyons, "Quaker Family Home."

133   **"Have you heard?":** Abby Kimber to Elizabeth Gay, December 31, 1848, box 45, SHG.

133   **"I have just come":** James Miller McKim to Sydney Howard Gay, December 26, 1848, box 46, SHG. James A. McGowan, *Station Master on the Underground Rail Road: The Life and Letters of Thomas Garrett* (Moylan, PA: Whimsie Press, 1977).

134   **lost baby . . . "due partially to neglect":** Kirby, *Years*, 305–8. On Kirby: Carolyn Swift and Judith Steen, *Georgiana: Feminist Reformer of the West* (Santa Cruz, CA: Santa Cruz Historical Trust, 1987). Bruce's letters in SGH, box 4, confirm that she was with the Purvises at this time.

134   **reasons to be skeptical:** Lucy Freibert suggests that Kirby may have taken liberties with her reminiscences, and some details in Bruce's story seem far-fetched. See "Kirby, Georgiana Bruce," *American Women Writers: A Critical Reference Guide from Colonial Times to the Present*, online, ed. Carol Hurd Green and Mary Grimely Mason, https://www.encyclopedia.com/arts/news-wires-white-papers-and-books/kirby-georgiana-bruce.

135   **Friends:** William Penn's slave ownership is documented by the Pennsbury Manor museum: "Colonial Americans at Pennsbury: Pennsbury Manor online, http://www.pennsburymanor.org/history/colonial-americans-at-pennsbury/. The following dialogue and scene are from *RTMF*, 52–54. Farrison identifies the Ivinses (spelled "Ivens" in *RTMF*) in *William Wells Brown*, 135. Their property (later owned by Edward Lewis) appears on Thomas Hughes's "Map of Falls Township, Bucks, County, Pennsylvania" (Lith. of Friend & Aub.: Philadelphia, 1858).

136   **if they could read:** On the Crafts' literacy, see also *RTMF*, 53; Bremer, *Homes*, 1:123–24.

137 **For days:** Lyons, "Quaker Family." The Ivinses recalled that visitors came the day after the Crafts' arrival, but the couple felt safer staying with the family. See also Russell Michael McQuay, "Mary Ivins Cunningham (1858–1922) (A Bucks County, PA, Quaker—Born to Paint)" (January 1988), typescript copy from Carol Spinager Ivins. On Barclay Ivins's being held out of unity: U.S., *Encyclopedia of American Quaker Genealogy*, vol. 2, 1005.

137 **"lovely, expensive boots":** Lyons, "Quaker Family"; McQuay, "Mary Ivins Cunningham." On Ellen's correspondence with Elizabeth: "Libel Suit."

138 **William Wells Brown ... "star lecturer" ... copyright:** *WWB*, 150. Greenspan's excellent biography is my major source for Brown in the coming chapters. On the irony of the copyrighting: 150. Other sources include Brown's narratives and Farrison, *William Wells Brown*.

138 **"Erect and graceful" ... "easy." It has been observed:** Quoted in *WWB*, 208, 211. Greenspan describes Brown's ability to listen and his appeal in *WWB*. I draw here on his observation on 69.

138 **the longest year:** Brown, *Narrative of William W. Brown*, 61.

138 **"Fashionable Hair-dresser":** Greenspan, *Reader*, 83; *WWB*, 102–3.

139 **life of an abolitionist lecturer ... "This riding all night is killing me":** Quoted in Blight, *Douglass*, 194. As Blight writes in ibid., 123, "Itinerant anti-slavery activism was a lonely, dangerous, and frustrating vocation." Greenspan details the challenges of itinerancy, Brown's failing marriage, and Henrietta's death in *WWB*, 125–30, 135–38.

139 **move a crowd ... like Brown better:** On the power of fugitive speakers: Larry Gara, "The Professional Fugitive in the Abolition Movement," *Wisconsin Magazine of History*, 48, no. 3 (1965): 196–204. On Brown's "star power" in Pennsylvania: *WWB*, 182–83. On comparisons with Douglass: ibid., 148–49, 208–9; Blackett, *Building an Anti-Slavery Wall*, 134.

139 **learned of the Crafts:** On Brown's interest in the Crafts, his "special" encounter with them, and their immediate connection: *WWB*, 184–86, also Singular Escape," *TL*, January 12, 1849. Brown recounts the mourning garb disguise in *Panoramic Views*, 28.

140 **"white nigger":** Quoted in *WWB*, 39; also Josephine Brown, *Biography of a Bondman*, 12.

140 **"mama's boy" ... scar:** *WWB*, 37, 68.

141 **"first African American man of letters":** William L. Andrews, *From Fugitive Slave to Free Man: The Autobiographies of William Wells Brown* (Columbia: University of Missouri Press, 2003), 1.

141 **"abolitionist baptism":** Sinha, *The Slave's Cause*, 425. Sterling also invokes Harriet Tubman and Sojourner Truth in *BF*, 24–25.

141 **"owed a duty to the cause of humanity":** See his speech in Greenspan, *Reader*, 106–29.

141 **There were other arguments:** Sterling makes the connection to Ellen's mother and raises questions about the Crafts' choices—including names—while citing Brown and Douglass in *BF*, 25–26. Wendell Phillips would report a rumor in the South that "Ellen Crafts is dead." "Speech of Wendell Phillips," *TL*, June 8, 1849. On William as Bill: WH1. See the recurrence of "Ellen" in James Smith's entry: Bibb Court of Ordinary, Record of Returns, 1851–1853, D-481, BCC.

NEW ENGLAND

145 **Singular Escape:** For Brown's bluffing, compare his published plan to advertisements for his solo lectures: "Singular Escape from Slavery," *New York Herald*, January 17, 1849; "Bucks County Meetings," *Pennsylvania Freeman* (Philadelphia), December 28, 1848. The first public account of the Crafts' arrival in New England shows they met Brown in Worcester: "Fugitive Slaves," *Massachusetts Spy*, January 24, 1849.

146 **"grievances of the South":** "Southern Caucus," *New York Herald*, January 17, 1849.

146 **"Congress is doing but little":** Thomas P. Cope, *Philadelphia Merchant: The Diary of Thomas P. Cope, 1800–1851* (South Bend, IN.: Gateway Editions, 1978), 569.

146 **Ringing with bells and whistles:** On Worcester history and its people: *Worcester*

Women's History Heritage Trail: Worcester in the Struggle for Equality in the Mid-Nineteenth Century (Worchester, MA: Worchester Women's History Project, 2002). On Foster: Margaret Hope Bacon, *I Speak for My Slave Sister: The Life of Abby Kelley Foster* (New York: Thomas Y. Crowell Company, 1974), 141, 151.

147   **"former slave"**: On Worcester's Black community: see Daniel Ricciardi, "Census Data of Worcester's People of Color in the 1850s," Worcester and Its People, College of the Holy Cross online, http://college.holycross.edu/projects/worcester/afrcamerican/census_data.htm. On the activists: *Worcester Women's History*, 31–43. On the sons of slavers: O'Toole, *Passing*, 27, 35, 38.

147   **"dioramic spectacle"**: See the broadside "Conflagration of Moscow!" [Worcester, MA: s.n., 1848], American Antiquarian Society, Worcester, MA.

147   **charismatic orator . . . multimedia artist:** Greenspan brings Brown's charisma, style, and techniques as a speaker to life in *WWB*, 124–99. On multimedia: ibid., 289. On becoming literate, 106–8. On Attleboro: "Dear Friends," *Pennsylvania Freeman* (Philadelphia), January 25, 1849. On his suspense: *PAS*, 201, 206.

148   **"Ever since that act"**: William W. Brown, *Narrative*, 106.

148   **dry eye . . . He would tell:** *WWB*, 165. Brown details his life experiences in his *Narrative*.

148   **"a little of the plantation"**: Kantrowitz, *More*, 110; Douglass, *My Bondage and My Freedom*, 362.

148   **"popular" . . . "Friend Brown"**: *WWB*, 189; Samuel May to John B. Estlin, May 21, 1849, BPL; "Dear Friends," 185.

148   **"American Slavery As It Is"**: Greenspan, *Reader*, 108.

149   **on this frigid January evening:** The January 19 event was first reported in "Fugitive Slaves," *Massachusetts Spy*, January 24, 1849, and reprinted in the *Anti-Slavery Bugle* (New Lisbon, OH), February 9, 1849. All quotations are from here, unless noted. In my reading, I especially benefited from Cima's analysis of Ellen's performances in *PAS*, 179–231. On Brown's plot: *BF*, 24–25; *WWB*, 186; *PAS*, 201; Farrison, *William Wells Brown*, 136–37. On credibility, the Crafts' "lie" and its dangers: *PAS*, 214, 241n111. On Ellen's subversion: ibid., 181, 190.

149   **she was almost certainly the first:** Note that Maria Stewart was an earlier public speaker. Cima suggests that "Ellen Craft may have been the first female fugitive to speak from an abolitionist stage" and observes the Crafts' "celebrity magnetism" in *PAS*, 197. On the audience "gasp": *WWB*, 187; *PAS*, 183.

150   **"unfortunate slave" . . . eye to eye:** See *PAS*, 179–81, 191, 202. Cima analyzes how "They were not abject slaves who needed sympathy but resourceful individuals who seemingly needed nothing but the confidence they already exercised—and justice to match."

150   **masters of improvisation . . . performance of her life:** See *PAS*, 179, 185.

151   **exactly the reaction . . . easy to be lulled:** Mayer analyzes what activists like the Crafts were up against and the need to foreground the moral issue in *All On Fire*, especially 364–65, 389–90. See also Delbanco's discussion on the "moral ambiguities of the pre-Civil War years," *War*, 6–14.

151   **forced audiences to confront:** As Delbanco writes: "Fugitives from slavery ripped open the screen behind which America tried to conceal the reality of life for black Americans, most of whom lived in the South, out of sight and out of mind for most people in the North." *War*, 2, 8–9.

152   **shake their hands . . . exit early:** See *PAS*, 203, 196. On early exit: "Correspondence of the *Boston Post*," *BP*, May 2, 1849.

152   **"Jim Crow" . . . other protests:** See Pryor, *Colored Travelers*, 3, 77–78, 90–91, and her chapter on "Criminalizing Black Mobility"; Richard Archer, *Jim Crow North: The Struggle for Equal Rights in Antebellum New England* (New York: Oxford University Press, 2017).

152   **Back Bay:** William A. Newman and Wilfred E. Holton, *Back Bay's Tidal Basin: The Story of America's Greatest Nineteenth-Century Landfill Project* (Lebanon, NH: Northeastern University Press, 2006), 42–43.

153   **Cradle of Liberty:** The picture of the neighborhood to follow draws from Horton and Horton, *Black Bostonians*, especially 1–6; Kendrick and Kendrick, *Sarah's Long Walk*, 21–28; Mayer, *All On Fire*, 108. On *"Nigger Hill"*: Horton and Horton, *Black Bostonians*, 8. On the city's shape: Mayer, *All On Fire*, 45–46.

153   **cadences of many tongues:** These details are from Horton and Horton, *Black Bostonians*, 5–6.

153   **Lewis and Harriet Hayden:** This brief biographical sketch and house description draws from Robboy and Robboy, "Lewis Hayden," especially 596; Kantrowitz, *More*, 92. Thirteen people reported in Austin Bearse, *Reminiscences of Slave Law Days in Boston* (Boston: Warren Richardson, 1880), 8.

154   **"Look upon your mother":** David Walker, *Walker's Appeal, in Four Articles* (Boston: David Walker, 1830). On Walker and his influence: Kantrowitz, *More*, 28–33; Jackson, *Force and Freedom*, 17–20; Kendi, *Stamped*, 165.

154   **"choked with cotton dust":** Quoted in Blackett, *Captive's Quest*, 397. On Nancy Prince: see Kantrowitz, *More*, 188, 467n38.

155   **The Haydens . . . were known to keep firearms:** See Kantrowitz's discussion of Hayden's "pragmatic position" in his chapter on Hayden in *More*, 83–121.

155   **Faneuil Hall:** "The Legend of Faneuil Hall's Golden Grasshopper Weathervane," New England Historical Society online http://www.newenglandhistoricalsociety.com /legend-faneuil-hall-golden-grasshopper-weathervane/. The history of slave sales is acknowledged by the National Park Service: "Faneuil Hall: The Cradle of Liberty," NPS online, https://www.nps.gov/bost/learn/historyculture/fh.htm. See also Robert E. Desrochers, "Slave-for-Sale Advertisements and Slavery in Massachusetts, 1704–1781," *William and Mary Quarterly* 59, no. 3 (2002): 623–64.

155   **If America were a cradle of liberty:** Greenspan, *Reader*, 120.

156   **biggest "Garrisonian" events:** Quarles, *Black Abolitionists*, 62–63.

156   **The founders . . . Massachusetts General Colored Association:** For descriptions of the society's founding and connections to the Massachusetts General Colored Association: William Cooper Nell, *The Colored Patriots of the American Revolution* (Boston: Robert F. Wallcut, 1955), 345; Kantrowitz, *More*, 52–58. Kantrowitz's analysis of the connections between Garrison and Walker are especially significant and have deeply informed my readings.

156   **"Friends, we have met tonight":** Quoted in Mayer, *All on Fire*, 131.

156   **shocked when they met William Lloyd Garrison:** Ibid., 141, 356.

156   **"gentleman's mob":** See "Boston Gentlemen Riot for Slavery," New England Historical Society online, http://www.newenglandhistoricalsociety.com/boston-gentlemen-riot -for-slavery/; Jack Tager, *Boston Riots: Three Centuries of Social Violence; All On Fire*, 203–5.

157   **"No Union With Slaveholders"; core tenets of Garrisonianism:** Mayer, *All On Fire*, 263, 410, Blight, *Douglass*, 104–5. Disputes among abolitionists over Garrisonian tenets had led to a division within the American Anti-Slavery Society a decade earlier, with the American and Foreign Anti-Slavery Society forming in opposition. As Ibrahim Kendi has observed, however, Garrison remained less radical than others, espousing immediate emancipation but gradual equality. See *Stamped*, 168.

157   **"stolen Garrison & Co's thunder" . . . sung to a modified tune:** "Massachusetts Anti-Slavery Society," *Boston Post*, January 26, 1849; Mayer, *All On Fire*, 364–65.

157   **more reasonable path . . . all-or-nothing demands:** See Delbanco, *War*, 7–8, 10, for related questions and complexities. Kantrowitz analyses how Black activists such as Hayden and Douglass resisted Garrisonian extremism, and discusses Free Soil in *More*, 159–67.

158   **a person did not walk slowly:** "To the Public," *TL*, January 1, 1831.

159   **Everlasting Yea:** On Brown's situation, including his marital problems and communication with his enslaver: *WWB*, 167–68, 176–77, 180–81; Farrison, *William Wells Brown*, 120–21. "A's" article was published as: "An Incident at the South," *Newark Daily Mercury*, January 19, 1849, 2.

159   **"Suppose that, by a miracle":** William Lloyd Garrison, *Selections from the Writings and Speeches of William Lloyd Garrison* (Boston: R.F. Wallcut, 1852), 57.

160   **"Ellen Craft":** Samuel May to John B. Estlin, February 2, 1849, BPL.

160   **electric current:** "The Annual Meeting," *TL*, February 2, 1849.

160   **"that they might be answered":** Subsequent quotations from "Seventeenth Annual Meeting of the Massachusetts Anti-Slavery Society," *TL*, February 2, 1849, excepting "Aye!" from "Massachusetts Anti-Slavery Society," *BP*, January 25, 1849.

160   **kinds of songs:** *WWB*, 173–74; Quarles, *Black Abolitionists*, 62; William Wells Brown, *The Anti-Slavery Harp: A Collection of Songs for Anti-Slavery Meetings*, 2nd ed. (Boston: B. Marsh, 1849).

161   **"a very intelligent-looking black man":** Anne Warren Weston to Deborah Weston, January 28, 1849," BPL.

161   **"Union, based on the prostrate bodies":** "Seventeenth Annual Meeting."

162   **"not too proud":** "Massachusetts Anti-Slavery Society," *BP*, January 26, 1849.

162   **lost them both:** These events and related quotations appear in William W. Brown, *Narrative*, 62–77. See also *WWB*, 74–78. On Natchez as a slave-trading hub: *WWB*, 75; Edward Ball, "Retracing Slavery's Trail of Tears," *Smithsonian*, November 2015.

163   **"Future historians and poets":** "Seventeenth Annual Meeting."

163   **George Latimer . . . no guarantees:** Kantrowitz, *More*, 70–76; Scott Gac, "Slave or Free? White or Black? The Representation of George Latimer," *New England Quarterly* 88, no. 1 (2015): especially 79–81; Delbanco, *War*, 180–83. On Lewis Hayden: Kantrowitz, *More*, 114–15.

165   **"A good-looking mulatto man":** "Massachusetts Anti-Slavery Society," *BP*, January 26, 1849; "Runaway Slaves," *GT*, February 13, 1849.

165   **Collins himself would continue to blame:** Collins to Hastings.

165   **"regularity":** Collins, *Essay*, 10. His fears are expressed in Collins to Hastings.

166   ***Address of Southern Delegates*:** Hunter and Democratic Party, *The Address*. Bartlett notes that later versions were watered down in *John C. Calhoun*, 366. After publishing an earlier version, the *GT* featured an edited version on February 13, 1849.

166   **John C. Calhoun:** Biographical details are gleaned from Bartlett, *John C. Calhoun*, especially 366–68; Niven, *John C. Calhoun and the Price of Union: A Biography* (Baton Rouge: Louisiana State University Press, 1988); "Floride Bonneau Colhoun Calhoun," Clemson University online, https://www.clemson.edu/about/history/bios/floride-calhoun.html. Southerners' anxieties are discussed in Bartlett, *John C. Calhoun*, 364–65. On Calhoun and Garrison's shared charge: *TL*, February 9, 1849, 1.

167   **"Abolitionists, with the energy of bloodhounds":** "Extra," *GT*, October 1, 1844. On personal liberty laws: Kantrowitz, *More*, 74; Sinha, *The Slave's Cause*, 391–92.

168   **legal battle:** The appeal was in early 1849; when exactly is unclear. Strobhart, *Reports*, 263–370.

168   **"Ellen has been, from her youth":** Collins to Hastings. A later letter suggests both Ellen and Eliza knew that Eliza was Ellen's enslaver: "Letter from Francis Bishop," *TL*, February 28, 1851.

168   **about to marry:** Jefferson County, State of Georgia, Court of Ordinary, Marriages "White" Book A (1803–1880), 32.

168   **paid a price:** Ellen later expressed her fears of retaliation against her mother, as reported in John B. Estlin's letter to Samuel May, June 27, 1851, BPL.

169   **The Circuit:** My readings in this chapter build on critical analyses by previous scholars, and are indebted especially to Cima's discussion of Ellen's stillness and silence in *PAS*, 196–207. On lectures: Salem Lyceum, *Historical Sketch of the Salem Lyceum* (Salem, MA: Press of the Salem Gazette, 1879), 49–50. On the "Georgia Fugitives": "Interesting Meeting," *TL*, April 27, 1849. On the teaming by Garrisonian organizers: *WWB*, 126–27, Kantrowitz, *More*, 111.

169   **"Hiss it again, my fat friend":** Quoted in Andrea Moore Kerr, *Lucy Stone: Speaking*

Out for Equality (New Brunswick, NJ: Rutgers University Press, 1992), 55. On the response to Stone and Brown: *WWB*, 178–79.

169 **New Bedford, Massachusetts . . . "Sweet Potatoes" . . . community of color:** See these examples and more in Grover, *Fugitive's Gibraltar*, 3, 206. Grover details New Bedford's rich history and diverse population: see especially 56–57 for demographics; also "The Underground Rail Road: New Bedford," National Park Service (https://www.nps .gov/nebe/planyourvisit/brochures.htm).

170 **"sweeten" abolitionist business:** *WWB*, 160. Food listings appear in "Mary J." Polly Johnson, New Bedford Historical Society online (http://nbhistoricalsociety.org/Im portant-Figures/mary-j-polly-johnson/). On the Johnsons, see also Grover, *Fugitive's Gibraltar*, 94, 135.

170 **the girls . . . uneasy reunion:** *WWB*, 160, 176–77.

170 **"white slave":** On all quotations from this event: "Anti-Slavery Meeting in New Bedford," *TL*, February 16, 1849. On winter excitement: *BF*, 24. On William's voice: Bowditch, *Life*, 205.

171 **all across the state:** See "Notices" in *TL*: February 2, 9, 23; March 2, 9, 16, 23; April 6, 20, 26; May 18, 1849, 25. Other sites include the Hopedale community: Daegan Miller, *This Radical Land: A Natural History of American Dissent* (Chicago: University of Chicago Press, 2018), 264n48. On "slave stealer": *The Branded Hand of Captain Walker*, daguerreotype by Southworth & Hawes, 1845, Massachusetts Historical Society online, https://www.masshist.org/database/viewer.php?item_id =154&pid=15. Sterling notes when Brown signals a potential end, and suggests that the Crafts tried to return to Boston, without further evidence: *BF*, 26.

171 **Ride, arrive, greet:** Greenspan discusses the difficulties of itinerant lecturing: *WWB*, 124–26. On the challenges of Black lecturers and "colored travelers," see Pryor, *Colored Travelers*, especially 46–64; Kantrowitz, *More*, 46–50; William Wells Brown, *Three Years*, 167.

172 **"Prejudice against color":** Quoted in Kantrowitz, *More*, 45.

172 **"thrilling account" . . . *I want to hear his wife speak*:** "William and Ellen Craft," *TL*, March 2, 1849.

172 **touch them:** Cima identifies and analyzes the public "press of hands" in *PAS*, 196–98, 203.

172 **"Shrewdly Done":** *Daily Constitutionalist* (Augusta, GA), February 13, 1849. On Southern complaints and anti-abolition: Hunter and Democratic Party, *Address*; "Public Meeting in Regard to the Abolition Movements in Congress," *GT*, February 6, 1840.

173 **worried for their safety:** "William and Ellen Craft," *Anti-Slavery Bugle* (New Lisbon, OH), February 23, 1849.

173 **flexing the fullest muscles:** See Pryor on mobility and citizenship in *Colored Travelers*, 60.

173 **entrance timed a little later:** Cima identifies the delay in *PAS*, 206–7.

173 **working-class enclaves:** Sinha, *The Slave's Cause*, 253–54.

173 **"people's movement":** Thomas Wentworth Higginson, *Cheerful Yesterdays* (Boston: Houghton Mifflin, 1989), 15. On Black activists: Jackson, *Force and Freedom*, 9. When the Crafts met the Remonds is unknown, but Sarah Parker Remond would be their guest in England, as discussed in Zackodnik, *Press*.

173 **they charged admission:** "Welcome to the Fugitives," *TL*, April 6, 1849; Quarles, *Black Abolitionists*, 62.

173 **Court Street meeting house . . . "in simple and artless":** Ellen's speech is recalled in "Interesting Meeting," *TL*, April 27, 1849. On Garrison's history: Mayer, *All On Fire*, 102. See Cima's comparison between Ellen and Henry Ward Beecher in *PAS*, 191.

174 **struck at the prevailing norms . . . popular racist arguments . . . wanted to be White:** My readings are informed by *PAS*, 180–81, 189–90, 201–2; Foreman, "Who's Your

Mama?" 525. On concerns about poverty and the twinning of poor laws and anti-Black laws: Masur, *Until Justice Be Done*.

174 **"silenced" . . . may also have been strategic:** Cima engages critically with readings of Ellen's silence in *PAS*, 180, 231n4. My reading builds on Cima's presentation of stillness and silence as strategy, especially ibid., 179–81; 201–2; 206–7. Cima asserts that Ellen "spoke very loudly through her body language, her onstage positioning, and paradoxically, her stationary silence" (180).

175 **rioting . . . kidnapping:** Eric Foner, *Gateway to Freedom: The Hidden History of the Underground Railroad* (New York: W. W. Norton, 2015), 114–15; *WWB*, 193.

176 **Henry Brown . . . "You are the greatest man in America!":** Ruggles, *Unboxing*, 29, 32–34, appendix B, 134; Henry Box Brown, *Narrative*.

176 **Boston's Melodeon . . . six fugitives:** On the Melodeon's past life as a theater *PAS*, 193. Blight identifies Douglass as "prophet" in his biography. On the six: "N.E. Anti-Slavery Convention," *TL*, June 1, 1849. Watson was likely Henry Watson, who recently published a narrative.

176 **giving in to "ransom":** Blight, *Douglass*, 172; T. Tillery, "The Inevitability of the Douglass-Garrison Conflict," *Phylon* 37, no. 2 (1976): 141–42.

177 **"excited a thrill" . . . "deafening shouts":** "New England Anti-Slavery Convention," *NASS*, June 7, 1849.

177 **"never fit!" . . . "young master":** Quotations are from an article that was first printed in the *Boston Chronotype*, June 30, 1849, later published as "The Story of Ellen Crafts" in other papers.

177 **may not have sat well:** Douglass would write, "The singularly original plan adopted by William and Ellen Crafts perished with the first using, because every slaveholder in the land was apprised of it" (*My Bondage and My Freedom*, 323). On Alfred and Swanky: Ruggles, *Unboxing*, 43–47.

177 **"What an exhibition!":** Douglass's words, Brown's song, and applause all recounted in "New England Anti-Slavery Convention," *NASS*, June 7, 1849. More coverage in *TL*, June 8, 1849.

178 **"It is the slave":** "Speech of Wendell Phillips," *TL*, June 8, 1849.

178 **"Give us the facts":** Douglass, *My Bondage and My Freedom*, 361.

178 **inflammatory rheumatism:** Blight, *Douglass*, 209.

178 **verge of a "breakup":** Ibid., 13. My portrait of Douglass draws from ibid., especially 178–27. On Garrison and Douglass as father and son: 96, 106, 179. On Douglass's anger: 179. On Garrison's being thunderstruck: *Blight, Douglass*, 99–100. See also Kendrick and Kendrick, *Sarah's Long Walk*, 209; Horton and Horton, *Black Bostonians*, 66–68.

179 **"I not only liked":** Douglass, *My Bondage and My Freedom*, 354.

179 **betrayed their own prejudices:** See examples in Kantrowitz, *More*, 61; Grover, *Fugitive's Gibraltar*, 138; Kendrick and Kendrick, *Sarah's Long Walk*, 29.

179 **Soon after his return . . . "slave breaker" . . . value of force:** On the speaking tour: Tillery, "Inevitability," 143; Blight, *Douglass*, 187–88. On the slave breaker: ibid., 59–60. On Douglass's transforming views: Jackson, *Force and Freedom*, 41–44. On Black activists' relationship to the Free Soil Party and other political groups: Kantrowitz, *More*, 159–67; James Oliver Horton and Lois E. Horton, "The Affirmation of Manhood," in *Courage and Conscience*, ed. Jacobs, 127–53.

179 **unhappy marriage . . . nervous breakdown:** Lorraine Boissoneault, "The Hidden History of Anna Murray Douglass," *Smithsonian*, March 5, 2018; Blight, *Douglass*, 209, 213.

179 **ideological collision:** See Robin Lindley, "What You Don't Know About Abolitionism: An Interview with Manisha Sinha on Her Groundbreaking Study," History News Network, February 16, 2018, https://historynewsnetwork.org/article/168091.

180 **a motley crowd of lawyers . . . "crackpots":** Ruggles, *Unboxing*, 48; "The New England A.S. Society," *TL*, June 8, 1849). Hostile men: "Letter from Reverend Mr. Dall" in

TL, June 15, 1849. "Crackpots": Irving H. Bartlett, *Wendell Phillips: Brahmin Radical* (Boston: Beacon Press, 1961), 105.

180 **"Mr. Chairman, Ladies and Gentlemen":** "Speech of Frederick Douglass," *TL*, June 8, 1849.

180 **"great evil to both races" . . . unable to picture:** Henry Clay to Richard Pindall, February 17, 1849, reprinted in Calvin Colton, ed., *The Works of Henry Clay Comprising His Life, Correspondence and Speeches* (New York: G. P. Putnam' Sons, 1904), 346–352. See also Delbanco's analysis of Clay's view in *War*, 229–31.

181 **the Battery in New York:** Blight, *Douglass*, 204–5; "Assault on Frederick Douglass," *TL*, July 5, 1850.

183 **unfinished revolution:** See Barker's *Fugitive Slaves*, especially 14–20.

183 **possibly alerted to a new danger:** *BAB*, 90. The Crafts did attend a Fourth of July celebration in Abington, observed by William Cooper Nell in the *North Star* (Rochester, NY), August 24, 1849.

183 **Luther Holman Hale's:** *LL*, 37–43.

183 **"because the likeness . . .":** *RTMF*, 24. The Crafts note the sale of these pictures in ibid., 10.

184 **"Colored Citizens" . . . prove lucky:** On the party and departure, see *WWB*, 192–93, 198–99; "Farewell Meeting," *TL*, July 27, 1849; the broadside invitation, "Presentation and Farewell Meeting!!," *BPL*, https://www.digitalcommonwealth.org/search /commonwealth:70796c89x; *BAP*, 242; William Wells Brown, *Three Years*, 1–2.

THE UNITED STATES

187 **"city upon a hill":** Many details in this chapter (such as the cheap, green wood) are from Horton and Horton, *Black Bostonians*, 2. Other resources: Kendrick and Kendrick, *Sarah's Long Walk*, 21–28; Kathryn Grover and Janine V. da Silva, "Historic Resource Study for the Boston African American National Historic Site 31," December 2002, https://www.nps.gov/parkhistoryonline_books/bost/hrs.pdf; Mayer, *All On Fire*, 107–8. Self-emancipated authors published in 1849: Henry Bibb, Josiah Henson. On John Winthrop and slavery: C. S. Manegold, *Ten Hills Farm: The Forgotten History of Slavery in the North* (Princeton, NJ: Princeton University Press, 2011).

188 **Peter Custom:** Names appear in the United States Census of 1850 (6th Ward, Boston).

188 **Boston's Black population . . . "Fugitive Slave Church":** Roy E. Finkenbine, "Boston's Black Churches," in *Courage and Conscience*, Jacobs, 182. On the Crafts at Theodore Parker's church: F. B. Sanborn, *Dr. S. G. Howe, the Philanthropist* (New York: Funk & Wagnalls, 1891), 235.

188 **WILLIAM CRAFT:** *TL*, July 27, 1849, and later issues. On Alcott: Jon Matteson, *Eden's Outcasts: The Story of Louisa May Alcott and Her Father* (New York: W. W. Norton, 2007), 196.

188 **prejudice . . . hire another worker:** Sterling contends that no one would hire William (without sources), *BF*, 27. On his business: *Directory of the City of Boston*, 126; Collison, *Shadrack Minkins*, 93; United States Manufacturing Census of 1850 (5th Ward, Boston). See also Horton and Horton, *Black Bostonians*, 6–13.

189 **Miss Dean:** Still, *Underground Rail Road*, 373.

189 **Caroline Healey Dall:** Dall writes that Ellen was "sheltered" at her parents' in *"Alongside:"* (Boston: Thomas Todd, 1900), 93, 100. Also: Helen R. Deese, *Daughter of Boston: The Extraordinary Diary of a Nineteenth-Century Woman* (Boston: Beacon Press, 2005), 126.

189 **grisly murder . . . vice in the slums:** Paul Collins, *Blood & Ivy: The 1849 Murder That Scandalized Harvard* (New York: Norton, 2018). Vice detailed in Horton and Horton, *Black Bostonians*, which draws from crime report, such as Edward H. Savage: *A Chronological History of the Boston Watch and Police: From 1631 to 1865* (Boston, 1865). On "Mount Whoredom": Kendrick and Kendrick, *Sarah's Long Walk*, 26–27.

189 **Sarah Roberts:** Kendrick and Kendrick, *Sarah's Long Walk*, 26–27; J. Morgan Kousser,

"The Supremacy of Equal Rights: The Struggle Against Racial Discrimination in Antebellum Massachusetts and the Foundations of the Fourteenth Amendment," *Northwestern University Law Review* 82 no. 4, 941–1010.

190 **"Wonders of Mental Science"**: "Pathetism, and Its Important Developments," *TL*, December 21, 1849, 3. On Betsy Blakely: "Eighteenth Annual Meeting of the Massachusetts Anti-Slavery Society," *TL*, February 1, 1850.

190 **"appeared to be sincerely happy"**: Bremer, *Homes*, 1:124. She would soon visit Macon, feeling "free and unfettered as a bird" (323). On the Crafts' plans for school: "Singular Escapes," 8.

191 **"hung her head"**: "Longfellow and the Fugitive Slave Act," National Park Service online, https://www.nps.gov/long/learn/historyculture/henry-wadsworth-longfellow-abo litionist.htm.

192 **Compromise:** For details on the tremors: Delbanco, *War*, 215–29; Bordewich, *America's Great Debate*, 106–33. These works have greatly informed this chapter.

192 **"this vexed problem of slavery"**: Bordewich *America's Great Debate*, 122.

192 **considered an "abomination"**: Cong. Globe, 31st Cong., 1st Sess. 144, January 29, 1850, 244–47.

192 **tinderbox . . . "constitutional right"**: Delbanco, *War*, 215; Bordewich, *America's Great Debate*, 121. On the Southern proposals: Bordewich, *America's Great Debate*, 126–27; *War*, 226–28.

193 **"Great Triumvirate"**: Details on the Triumvirs from: Merrill Peterson, *The Great Triumvirate: Webster, Clay and Calhoun* (New York: Oxford University Press, 1997); Bordewich, *America's Great Debate*; Delbanco, *War*, 220–57. See also Remini, *Daniel Webster*; Bartlett, *John C. Calhoun*; and David Stephen Heidler and Jeanne T. Heidler, *Henry Clay: The Essential American.*

193 **"I don't like Clay"**: Neil MacNeil and Richard A. Baker, *The American Senate: An Insider's History* (New York: Oxford University Press, 2013), 281.

193 **Clay has been described:** Peterson, *Great Triumvirate*, 379, 382–83; Bordewich, *America's Great Debate*, 73. Bordewich calls Clay one of Kentucky's "larger slave owners" and describes his "ambivalent" position, a fugitive incident, and views on colonization in ibid., 93–94, 74.

193 **"positive good"**: John C. Calhoun, *Speeches of John C. Calhoun: Delivered in the Congress of the United States from 1811 to the Present Time* (New York: Harper & Brothers, 1843), 225.

194 **"more effectual provision"**: Cong. Globe, 31st Cong., 1st Sess. 144, January 29, 1850, 244–47. See readings of Clay's proposals in Bordewich, *America's Great Debate*, 135; Delbanco, *War*, 232–33; Paul Finkelman, *Millard Fillmore* (New York: Times Books, 2011), 64–69.

194 **"nobody knows where"**: Harriet Beecher Stowe, *A Key to Uncle Tom's Cabin: Presenting the Original Facts and Documents upon Which the Story is Founded* (London: Sampson, Low, Son, 1853), 378–80, Clay would dispute this claim, as discussed in Runyon and Davis, *Delia Webster*, 113–16; Kantrowitz, *More*, 117–18.

195 **"hunt and seize"**: "Petition of Francis Jackson," Massachusetts Anti-Slavery and Anti-Segregation Petitions; House Unpassed Legislation 1850, Docket 2552, SC1/series 230. Massachusetts Archives. Boston, https://iiif.lib.harvard.edu/manifests/view/drs:46 792352$6i.

195 **"cast-iron man"**: Martineau, *Retrospect*, 243. On James Smith's admiration: Fitzgerald and Galloway, *Eminent Methodists*, 110. On Calhoun's appearance in the Senate: Delbanco, *War*, 238; Bordewich, *America's Great Debate*, 156.

195 **"The cry of 'Union, Union'"**: Cong. Globe, 31st Cong., 1st Sess. 144, March 4, 1850, 451–56.

195 **"for no other reason"**: On Calhoun's enslaving practices: Barlett, *John C. Calhoun*, 279–83. For his views on slavery: Peterson, *Great Triumvirate*, 408–11; Delbanco, *War*, 237–48.

196 **"civil war and massacre"**: Quoted in Bordewich, *America's Great Debate*, 164. On

weapons: "Patrick Henry on the Growing Crisis," *New York Herald* reprint, *TL*, March 29, 1850.

196 **Daniel Webster:** Principal sources on Webster, his "Seventh of March" speech," and the fallout include: Remini, *Daniel Webster*, 662–81; Bordewich, *America's Great Debate*, 123–33; 162–72; Peterson, *The Great Triumvirate*, 400; Delbanco, *War*, 248–61.

196 **"Liberty *and* union":** Daniel Webster, "Second Reply to Hayne, January 26 and 27, 1830 (in the Senate), United States Senate online (https://www.senate.gov/artandhis tory/history/resources/pdf/W ebsterReply.pdf).

196 **"I hear the sound" . . . "God-like":** Quoted in Remini, *Daniel Webster*, 183–84.

196 **Monica McCarty:** Fletcher Webster, ed., *The Private Correspondence of Daniel Webster*, vol. 2 (Boston: Little, Brown, 1875), 408; Elizabeth Dowling Taylor, *A Slave in the White House: Paul Jennings and the Madisons* (New York: St. Martin's Press, 2012), 157.

196 **"the best spent money I ever laid out":** Quoted in Remini, *Daniel Webster*, 644.

196 **darker than Ellen Craft:** Parker, *Trial*, 183.

196 **"Puritan" . . . "Cavalier":** Peterson, *The Great Triumvirate*, 406; Bordewich, *America's Great Debate*, 130; "Bosom Buddies: The Surprising Story of America's First Boob Selfie," *Economist*, December 19, 2015. On the journalist Jane Swisshelm and Robert Webster: Marc Wortman, "Why Was Robert Webster, a Slave, Wearing What Looks Like a Confederate Uniform?": *Smithsonian*, October 2014; Remini, *Daniel Webster*, 307.

197 **kinds of choices:** Delbanco's questions in *War* (especially 7, 250–51) led to my own.

198 **"may be the turning point" . . . sick:** Bordewich, *America's Great Debate*, 165; *PDW*, 7:16.

198 **"I wish to speak":** Cong. Globe, 31st Cong., 1st Sess. 144, March 7, 1850, 476–84.

199 **"might have been the moment":** Delbanco, *War*, 253.

199 **"balls of fire":** Samuel P. Lyman, *The Public and Private Life of Daniel Webster* (Philadelphia: J. W. Bradley, 1859), 2:158; Remini, *Daniel Webster*, 672.

200 **"great pleasure":** "Webster and Calhoun," *TL*, April 5, 1850. On other responses: Bordewich, *America's Great Debate*, 170–72; Delbanco, *War*, 255–57; Peterson, *Great Triumvirate*, 464–66; Remini, *Daniel Webster*, 674–80. On Webster's insomnia: Irving H. Barlett, *Daniel Webster* (New York: Norton, 1978), 240.

200 **"If, in the lowest deep":** Quoted in James Brewer Stewart, *Wendell Phillips: Liberty's Hero* (Baton Rouge: Louisiana State University Press, 1986), 146.

201 **"hot pursuit":** Parker, *Trial*, 183.

201 **"black Daniel Webster":** Brenda E. Stevenson, Larry Gara, and Peter C. Ripley, *The Underground Rail Road* (Washington, D.C.: U.S. Department of the Interior, 1998), 68. Reinhard O. Johnson, *The Liberty Party, 1840–1848: Antislavery Third-Party Politics in the United States* (Baton Rouge: Louisiana State University Press, 2009), 1511.

201 **"Northern dough-faces":** "Speech of Rev. Samuel R. Ward" *TL*, May 10, 1850.

201 **urge his fellow "colored citizens":** "Anti-Webster Meeting, *TL*, April 5, 1850. On reports of slave hunters: "Mass Convention at Plymouth," *TL*, April 12, 1850; "Letter from Rev. Calvin Fairbanks," *TL*, April 5, 1850; "A SLAVE-HUNTER IN BOSTON," *TL*, April 19, 1850.

201 **two moneyed gentlemen . . . "self-made man":** "Libel Suit"; *BF*, 28. The timing is uncertain—somewhere before mid-July, when the directory and 1850 census were available. On Charles Craft: Henry Craft to "Dear Father"; Scott, "Diary," 7. On Scott's appearance, see Harney Twiggs Powell's letter of July 21, 1920, in Scott, "Diary." On his being a "self-made man" and pro-Union position, ibid., 4–5. Lords of Loom and Lash in: George Frisbee Hoar, ed., *Charles Sumner: His Complete Works* Vol. 2 (Boston: Lee and Shepard, 1900), 233. See also Joseph Story Fay's biography and letters to Scott, Fay-Mixter Family Papers, MHS; Susan Martin, " 'They belonging to themselves': Minda Campbell Redeems Her Family from Slavery," Massachusetts Historical Society online (http://www.masshist.org/object-of-the-month/2018-february); *PDW*, 421, 427. On connections to the Crafts' enslavers, see Fay's letters to Daniel Webster (November 18, 1850); Seth J. Thomas (November 15, 1850), Attorney General Papers, "Letters Received, 1809–1870," RG60, NARA.

202 **"Attempt to Kidnap!"** . . . **"proved too strong":** *TL*, September 6, 1850.

204 **Octopus Powers:** The phrase is Kendi's, *Stamped*, 189. On this "act without mercy" and canons: Delbanco, *War*, 4, 262; also Frank, *Trial*, xviii.

204 **"This law of barbarism":** Samuel Ringgold Ward, *Autobiography of a Fugitive Negro* (London: John Snow, 1855), 108.

204 **secretary of state:** Irving H. Bartlett, "The Double Character of Daniel Webster," *New England Journal of Public Policy* 3, no. 1 January 1, 1987:47.

204 **"the first fugitive":** "Indictment of Theodore Parker and Wendell Phillips," *TL*, January 19, 1855.

204 **"stretch their tentacles"** . . . **"reasonable force":** Kendi, *Stamped*, 189; United States, *The Fugitive Slave Law* (Hartford: s.n., 1850).

205 **by train, foot, carriage:** Ricks, *Escape*, 227.

205 **"well-armed":** Blackett, *Captive's Quest*, 44.

206 **Theodore Parker reported:** Parker, *Trial*, 146. On the departures, also see Horton and Horton, *Black Bostonians*, 112; Finkenbine, "Boston's Black Churches" in *Courage and Conscience*, Jacobs, ed., 182; Blackett, "Freemen to the Rescue!" in *Passages to Freedom*, David Blight, ed. (Washington, DC: Smithsonian Books, 2004), 137–38.

206 **"exodus":** Blight, *Douglass*, 240. See also Horton and Horton, *Black Bostonians*, 112; Finkenbine, "Boston's Black Churches," in *Courage and Conscience*, ed. Jacobs, 182; Theodore Parker, *The Collected Works of Theodore Parker*, ed. Frances Power Cobbe (London: Trübner, 1863), 187; Blackett, *Captive's Quest*, 398.

206 **choice came to the Hayden house . . . "part-Indian":** Strangis, *Lewis Hayden and the War Against Slavery* (North Haven, CT: Linnet Books), 60; Sinha, *The Slave's Cause*, 397; Runyon and Davis, *Delia Webster*, 120–22. All quotations from Stowe, *Key to Uncle Tom's Cabin*, 378–80, and Robboy and Robboy, "Lewis Hayden," 593–94, except the "fighting Frenchman" from Lin-Manuel Miranda's *Hamilton*.

207 **choice came to William and Ellen:** Cruelties recalled in *RTMF*, 69. On William's business: Collison, *Shadrack Minkins*, 93 and the 1850 United States Manufacturing Census of 1850. On donations: "Collections," *TL*, June 7, 1850. On their home: "Fugitive Slave Excitement in this City," *Boston Post*, October 26, 1850. On school: "Singular Escapes," 8. Eliza Wigham makes her claim in *The Anti-Slavery Cause*, 92.

208 **Revolutionaries:** See related discussions in Sinha, *The Slave's Cause*, 500–42; Barker, *Fugitive Slaves*; and Christopher Bonner, "Runaways, Rescuers and the Politics of Breaking the Law," in *New Perspectives on the Black Intellectual Tradition* ed. Keisha N. Blain, Christopher Cameron, and Ashley D. Farmer, (Evanston, IL: Northwestern University Press, 2018), 209.

208 **"vast concourse":** This and other quotations, unless noted, from: "Declaration of Sentiments of the Colored Citizens of Boston on the Fugitive Slave Bill," *TL*, October 11, 1850. See also "Meeting of the Colored Citizens of Boston," *TL*, October 4, 1850; Dean Grodzins, "'Constitution or No Constitution, Law or No Law': The Boston Vigilance Committees, 1841–1861," in *Massachusetts and the Civil War: The Commonwealth and National Disunion*, ed. Mathew Mason, Katheryn P. Viens, and Conrad Edick Wright (Amherst: University of Massachusetts Press, 2015), 62–66; Kantrowitz, *More*, 180–86. Other vice presidents include Henry Watson and John Telemachus Hilton (obituary in *TL*, March 25, 1864).

208 **own Great Triumvirate . . . "Colored Citizens":** On the three men's different styles: Horton and Horton, *Black Bostonians*, 58–63. Nell was a leader of the battle for school integration. His letter appears in Wesley and Uzelac, *William Cooper Nell*, 278. More on his work in: Francis Jackson, *The Boston Vigilance Committee: Appointed at the Public Meeting in Faneuil Hall October 21st, 1850 to Assist Fugitive Slaves* (Boston: Bostonian Society, 1850). On Morris and his legacy: Kendrick and Kendrick, *Sarah's Long Walk*, 16–60, 207–8; Michael Philip Curran, *The Life of Patrick A. Collins* (Norwood, Mass.: Norwood Press, 1906), 12; Laurel Davis and Mary Sarah Bilder, "The Library of Robert Morris, Antebellum Civil Rights Lawyer and Activist," *Law Library*

Journal, Volume 111:4, 2019. The role of "Colored Citizens" in performing the most vital work is discussed in Kantrowitz, *More*, 183; Collison, *Shadrack Minkins*, 84–5.

209 **genius "Prince of Caterers":** Garrison, *The Letters of William Lloyd Garrison*, Vol. 4 ed. Louis Ruchames (Cambridge, MA: Harvard University Press, 1976), 334; David S. Shields, *The Culinarians: Lives and Careers from the First Age of American Fine Dining* (Chicago: University of Chicago Press, 2017), 145–46; "Bluffed Off," *TL*, October 25, 1850, 91–92.

209 **Robert Johnson:** "Massachusetts Anti-Slavery Society," *TL*, February 4, 1837; Randy J. Sparks, *Africans in the Old South* (Cambridge, MA: Harvard University Press, 2016), 81–102.

210 **singing "Go—go!" "Don't stop!":** Leonard W. Levy, "The 'Abolition Riot': Boston's First Slave Rescue," *New England Quarterly* 25, no. 1 (March 1952): 88.

210 **new era of militancy:** See Jackson, *Force and Freedom*, especially 69.

210 **"bone and the muscle":** Speeches and *reactions* in "Rocking of the Old Cradle of Liberty," *TL*, October 18, 1850; "Fugitive Slave Meeting in Faneuil Hall," *North Star* (Rochester, NY), October 24, 1850. Blackett estimates 3,500 people in *Captives*, 400n6.

211 **"Yes, the laws until repealed":** "Robert Morris, Esq.," *Boston Herald*, October 15, 1850.

212 **"Committee of Safety and Vigilance":** On its relationship to the League of Freedom, see Grodzins, "Constitution or No Constitution," 62–66; Gary L. Collison, "The Boston Vigilance Committee: A Reconsideration," *Historical Journal of Massachusetts*, vol. 12, no 2 (June 1984). Nathaniel Colver would build a school on the site of Lumpkin's jail. See Kantrowitz, *More*, 97.

212 **"CONSTITUTION OR NO CONSTITUTION":** "Fugitive Slave Meeting in Faneuil Hall," *The North Star* (Rochester, NY), October 15, 1850.

213 **Master Slave:** On the weather: Dennis Noble and Truman R. Strobridge, *Captain "Hell Roaring" Mike Healy: From American Slave to Arctic Hero* (Gainesville: University Press of Florida), 28. Details on the Healys, including the property sale and Dunganon in O'Toole, *Passing*, especially 45–50 on the broken heart, the sibling rescue, Margaret's case, and 37 on the paradoxes. See also the fictionalized story of the Slaters, called the family of Ellen's maternal aunt, in *RTMF*, 18.

214 **Unionist . . . celebrated for his justice . . . "romantic":** "Public Meeting," *Georgia Citizen* (Macon), July 5, 1850; Talmadge, "Georgia Tests the Fugitive Slave Law"; "The Macon Mass Meeting and the Georgia Citizen," *Savannah (GA) Morning News*, August 26, 1850; "Mr. Rhett's Speech," *GT*, September 24, 1850. Collins's litigation includes Collins v. Johnson, Thomas R. R. Cobb, *Reports of Cases in Law and Equity Argued and Determined in the Supreme Court of the State of Georgia* (Athens, GA: Reynolds & Bro., 1855), 16:458. On his California venture: "Railroad to California," *Georgia Journal and Messenger* (Macon), July 18, 1849. On the "romantic" escape: Reidy, *From Slavery*, 3; Collins to the attorney general.

214 **"no personal desire":** Subsequent quotations are from Collins to Hastings, though "tempted to follow" is from his letter to the attorney general, which includes similar arguments. On his opposition: "Who Are Our Enemies?," *Georgia Journal and Messenger* (Macon), November 6, 1850; Talmadge, "Georgia Tests the Fugitive Slave Law," 57. On the Union Party ticket and governorship: ibid., 62; "The Next Candidate for Governor," *Georgia Journal and Messenger* (Macon), January 15, 1851. Collins describes the importance of the Crafts' case in his letter to the attorney general.

215 **"very light complexion":** "Robert Collins' Power of Attorney," October 11, 1850, HvC.

215 **"cabinetmaker by trade":** "Ira H. Taylor's Power of Attorney," HvC.

215 **"public Negro whipper":** John Knight Parker, *Trial*, 147; Weiss, *Life*, 95. On the jailer: Jenkins, "Antebellum Macon," 28.

216 **dubbed him a "Sub":** "The Southern Press, South," reprinted in *NASS*, January 2, 1851. On sabotage: "Who Are Our Enemies?"

216   **"large crowd of blacks":** "Meeting on Yesterday," *Georgia Citizen* (Macon), August 23, 1850.

216   **"gentlemen" of wealth and power:** For details about Fay and more: WH1, WH2, JK. The hotel is advertised in *Tremayne's Table of Post-offices in the United States*: (New York: W. H. Burgess, 1850).

217   **Men from Macon:** Knight's and Hughes's letters are major sources here: JK, WH1, WH2.

217   **"short, rowdyish-looking fellow":** "Slave Hunters Arrested."

217   **"cabinet makers":** *Directory of the City of Boston*, 351.

217   **"proper person" . . . "fair specimen":** All descriptions of Hughes's encounters are from WH1 and WH2. One refutation appears in the *Boston Daily Atlas*, December 3, 1850.

218   **"Bill," or "Billy" . . . Horatio Jennings:** Sources for this scene: WH1; WH2; JK; Lydia Maria Child, *The Freedmen's Book*, 195; Bowditch, *Life*, 2:372–73; Weiss, *Life*, 95–96; F. B. Sanborn, preface in Theodore Parker, *The Rights of Man*. Weiss and Sanborn quote from Parker's lost journals, where Parker claims that Knight visited two consecutive days: Tuesday, October 22, and Wednesday the 23rd. However, given that the letter was dated Tuesday the 22nd, this is not possible. See "The Fugitive Slave Law in Boston," *New-York Daily Tribune*, October 29, 1850. On Knight: "Slave Hunters Arrested"; Weiss, *Life*, 95. Neighbors at 51 Cambridge Street are listed in the *Directory of the City of Boston*.

219   **"Boston, Tuesday, Oct 22, 1850":** See the *New-York Daily Tribune*'s reprint of the letter from the *Boston Traveler*, October 29, 1850; also *TL*, November 1, 1850.

219   **"to get Craft":** "No. 3."

219   **"make out his charges in a legal form":** WH1.

220   **"a good deal sick" . . . "wicked and abominable":** Daniel Webster to Millard Fillmore, October 14, 1850, *PDW*, 160. On Webster's preferred amendments to the Fugitive Slave Law: *PDW*, 110–11, 179.

220   **"God knows I detest":** Millard Fillmore to DW, October 23, 1850, *PDW*, 163–164.

221   **"other side of the Neck" . . . charms:** On Seth J. Thomas: *The American Lawyer*, vol. 2 (New York: Stumpf & Stewer, 1894), 79. On Webster: Pamphlet by L. D. Geller, *Daniel Webster: New England Squire*, New England Historical Series Massachusetts, (Cape Cod Publications, 1992).

221   **"lack of educational opportunities" . . . "genial":** See Thomas's entry in American Bar Association, *Report of the Nineteenth Annual Meeting of the American Bar Association*, vol. 19 (Philadelphia: Dando Printing, 1896), 661–64. Thomas recalls Webster's request in *American Lawyer*, 79. Hughes stated that Mr. Thayer made the introduction in "Fugitive Slaves: Case of the Crafts," November 22, 1850, vol. A, 2335, RG 60, National Archives, College Park, MD.

221   **"who could not be intimidated":** "Seth J. Thomas," 663.

221   **"legal pimp of the slave catchers":** Quoted in Leonard W. Levy, "Sims' Case: The Fugitive Slave Law in Boston in 1851," *Journal of Negro History* 35, no. 1 (1950): 44. Thomas was enslavers' counsel in the cases of Shadrack Minkins, Thomas Sims, and Anthony Burns.

221   **"repugnant duty":** "Seth J. Thomas," 663.

221   **"great personal reluctance":** See Thomas's obituary, *Boston Daily Globe*, December 6, 1895.

221   **"They were not pleasant":** *American Lawyer*, 79. On Hughes in the Florida Wars: WH2.

222   **trained for combat:** See testimonies to Hughes's character in *GT*, December 10, 1850.

222   **"alarm the town":** Weiss, *Life*, 95. On Loring and Sewell's visit: "Fugitive Slave Excitement in this City," *Boston Post*, October 26, 1850.

222   **"equivocat(ing) and shuffl(ing)":** WH1.

222   **The "Curtii":** Von Frank, *Trials*, 114–17.

222   **"seized and sent back!":** "Connection of the Curtises with the Recent Cases of Kidnapping in Boston," *TL*, January 19, 1855; Curtis, *Memoir*, ed. Curtis, 121.

222   **As he would explain . . . secret meeting:** "A Fugitive Slave Case," *National Intelligence* (Washington, DC), December 6, 1850, "Indictment of Theodore Parker and Wendell

Phillips," *TL*, January 19, 1855; Levi Woodbury and Nahum Capen, *Writings of Levi Woodbury* (Boston: Little, Brown, 1852), 353. On the case: Erastus B. Bigelow v. Josiah Barber (*BP*, October 25, 1850).

224 **The Commissioner's Wife:** Events recalled in Still, *Underground Rail Road*, 373. On the Hillards: Robert L. Gale, *A Henry Wadsworth Longfellow Companion* (Westport, CT: Greenwood Press, 2003), 106–7; Francis W. Palfrey, "Memoir of the Hon. George Stillman Hillard," *Proceedings of the Massachusetts Historical Society* 20 (June 1882): 339–48.

224 **"ardent Webster Whig" . . . ell of the house:** Siebert, "The Underground Railroad in Massachusetts," 45.

225 **"To the Rescue!":** William's warrant and "Willis H. Hughes' Complaint Against Ellen Craft," both dated October 25, 1850, at HvC. Hughes kept Ellen's warrant, as Riley testifies in "No. 3, Affidavit of Patrick Riley." On Devens: *BAP*, 249; Collison, *Shadrack Minkins*, 97; George Barnes, "Pondering the Complexity of Historical Figures," *Worcester (MA) Telegram and Gazette*, June 27, 2020. On the lawyers' visit: "Boston Slave Hunt and the Vigilance Committee." On Robert Morris: JK; Bearse, *Reminiscences of Slave Law Days in Boston*, 4. For conflicting accounts, compare Hughes's letters (WH1, WH2) to Devens, "No. 2, Affidavit of Charles Devens Jr."

226 **"Negroes and their friends":** Hughes reports this happening when the warrant was released. See WH1; JK; "Fugitive Slave Excitement in this City," *BP*, October 26, 1850.

226 **"TO THE RESCUE!":** "The Fugitive Slave Excitement in Boston," *Portland (ME) Advertiser*, October 29, 1850, reprinted from the *Boston Times*, October 26, 1850.

226 **"general hunt":** "Slave Hunters Arrested."

226 **why the couple resolved to stay:** Collison, *Shadrack Minkins*, 95. On William's mindset: "From Our Boston Correspondent," *NASS*, November 7, 1850; "Slavery in America," *London Times*, December 14, 1850; Parker, *Trial*, 147; *RTMF*, 68–69.

226 **"Spartacus of his race" . . . "Negro population":** "Boston Slave Hunt and the Vigilance Committee."

227 **night watchman . . . "You might as well go":** "No. 3"; "No. 4. Affidavit of James H. Dickson Accompanying Deputy Marshal Riley's Affidavits," November 18, 1850, Attorney General Papers, "Letters Received, 1809–1870," RG60, NARA.

227 **"flatly refus(ing)":** "The Hunt," *NASS*, October 31, 1850.

227 **"the process could only be served":** "Boston Slave Hunt and the Vigilance Committee."

227 **"heroic frenzy":** Archibald Grimke, "Anti-Slavery Boston," *New England*, December 1890, 458. (Note Kantrowitz's skepticism in *More*, 185–56.)

227 **"for his sake":** "Slavery in America," *London Times*, December 14, 1850. See McCaskill's discussion of Ellen's "craft" of a submissive persona in "Ellen Craft," 97. On thoughts of a last good-bye: "Singular Escapes," 8.

228 **"no trouble":** "No. 3, Affidavit of Patrick Riley."

228 **Mary Courzon:** Higginson, "Romance," 47–53. Loring boarded with Courzon's uncle George Searle on New Lane (now Cypress and Washington Streets). Harold Parker Williams, *"Brookline in the Anti-Slavery Movement"* (pamphlet), 80.

228 **"resist unto death":** "Fugitive Slaves in Boston," *Boston Traveler*, November 26, 1850, reprinted in the *New York Daily Tribune*, October 30, 1850. Ellen recalls the pledge in "An Ex Slave's Reminiscences." Jackson discusses such pledges in *Force and Freedom*, 53.

229 **"Slave Hunters in Boston!!!":** *Southern Press* (Washington, DC), October 31, 1850.

229 **"He said his man":** WH1. Devens and Riley would contest this story in "No. 2," Affidavit of Charles Devens Jr. and "No. 3, Affidavit of Patrick Riley."

229 **rogue tier:** Richard Henry Dana to Edmund T. Dana, November 12, 1850, MHS; "The Boston Slave Hunt and the Vigilance Committee." Charles List and John C. Park are among those named. Meanwhile, scholars warn that the role of White activists should not be overemphasized: Kantrowitz, *More*, 182–86; Gary Collison, "The Boston Vigilance Committee: A Reconsideration," *Historical Journal of Massachusetts* (June 1984): 112; Collison, *Shadrack Minkins*, 84–85.

229 **"causing damage to his business and character"**: "The Hunt."

229 **"No!" . . . "towering passion"**: "Slave Hunters Arrested"; *TL*, December 6, 1850. On the Southern style: Manisha Sinha, "The Caning of Charles Sumner: Slavery, Race, and Ideology in the Age of the Civil War," *Journal of the Early Republic* 23, no. 2 (2003): 246.

230 **bail was quickly and secretly met**: Patrick Riley identifies himself and Deputy Sheriff Watson as bailors in "No. 3."

230 **"Negroes in large number"**: JK. Blackett notes the reversal of hunter and prey: *BAB*, 94.

231 **The Coolest Man**: On Joshua Bowen Smith: Weiss, *Life*, 95.

231 **"utmost coolness"**: "Noble Determination of Craft," *GT*, November 6, 1850.

231 **"coolest man" . . . "armed himself"**: "From Our Boston Correspondent," *NASS*, November 7, 1850; Parker, *Trial*, 148.

231 **"send his own brother"**: *RTMF*, 60, also appears in "The Fugitive Slave Act," *Eclectic Review* 1 (January–June 1851): 675.

232 **"His powder had a good kernel"**: Weiss, *Life*, 22.

232 **"submit peaceably" . . . "they would all be at the mercy"**: *RTMF*, 56; Collison, *Shadrack Minkins*, 248n24; Richard Henry Dana to Thomas Stevenson, October 28, 1850, MHS. Webster disregarded Stevenson's advice in his Seventh of March speech, as reported in Bowditch, *Life*, 1:203.

232 **"William does not want"**: "Slavery in America," *London Daily News*, December 14, 1850.

232 **"as a harlot in New Orleans"**: Parker, *Trial*, 16.

232 **"perfect sweetness"**: Higginson "Romance," 50. On Ellen's nightmare: "Slavery in America"; Child, *Freedmen's Book*, 135; Higginson, "Romance."

233 **"He said he would kill. . . ."**: From Wilbur H. Siebert Papers, *Underground Rail Road in Massachusetts*, vol. 2, MS AM 2420 (14), HOU.

233 **the doctor thought it "probable"**: Henry Ingersoll Bowditch, *Bowditch Memorial Cabinet Catalog*, 1877, xxxiv, MS sBd-61, MHS.

233 **"the last meeting"**: Descriptions and quotations from: Bowditch, *Life*, 1:207–8. See also Charles F. Folsom, "Henry Ingersoll Bowditch," *Proceedings of the American Academy of Arts and Sciences* 28 (1892): 310–31. On Bowditch's step outside his comfort zone, and fear: Kantrowitz, *More*, 77–83. On Nat's lesson: Bowditch, *Memorial Cabinet*, xxxix; John T. Cumbler, "A Family Goes to War: Sacrifice and Honor for an Abolitionist Family," *Massachusetts Historical Review* 10 (2008): 57–83.

234 **Mary Courzon . . . Eliza and Samuel Philbrick**: Higginson, "Romance"; Still, *Underground Rail Road*, 373–74; "Slavery in America." Courzon would recall her "Ellen dress" in her letter to Thomas Wentworth Higginson, April 13, 1851, bMS Am 784 (383), HOU. On the Philbricks: Walter S. Burrage, *Proceedings of the Brookline Historical Society at the Annual Meeting, March 20, 1949*, published by the Society, 1949, (http://www.brooklinehistoricalsociety.org/history/proceedings/1949/Philbrick.html).

235 **A World Turned Upside Down**: On the street boys and their cries: Octavius Brooks Frothingham, *Theodore Parker: A Biography* (New York: G. P. Putnam's Sons, 1880), 405; Bowditch, *Life*, 2:372; *LL*, 50; JK. Patrick Riley describes the bailing in "No. 3, Affidavit of Patrick Riley." See also "The Slave Excitement in Boston," *North American* (Philadelphia) October 30, 1850. On Hamilton Willis's connection to the Alcotts and his support of Thomas Sims and Anthony Burns: Von Frank, *Trials*, 81–83; Siebert, "The Underground Railroad in Massachusetts," 84; Pauline Willis, *Willis Records: Or, Records of the Willis Family of Haverhill, Portland, and Boston* (London: printed by St. Vincent's Press), 85–89.

235 **Court Square . . . "negroes" outnumbering Whites**: JK; Kantrowitz, *More*, 186–86. This action sequence intercuts Hughes and Knight's accounts (WH1, WH2, JK) with newspaper reports, paraphrasing: "More Fugitive Slave Excitement," *Boston Daily Times*, October 29, 1850; "Additional Retaliatory Suits in Relation to the Fugitives," *BP*, October 29, 1850; "Slave Excitement in Boston," "From Our Boston Correspondent," *NASS*, November 7, 1850; "Boston Slave Hunt and the Vigilance Committee."

235 **"not without losing"**: "More Fugitive Slave Excitement."

236 **"making sport"**: JK.

236 **"mob of Negroes"**: Richard Henry Dana to Edmund T. Dana, November 12, 1850, MHS.

236 **"colored man"**: "From Our Boston Correspondent." The landscape of cattle markets is recalled in Thomas F. O'Malley, "Old North Cambridge," *The Proceedings of the Cambridge Historical Society*, vol. 20, 1927–929, 131.

237 **passed over the Charles**: Parker has received much of the credit for sheltering the Crafts, but his journals show that they were not with him all this time. They may have stayed at other locations, such as with Mark and Caroline Healey Dall, as Dall noted in "Alongside," 100. I have used multiple sources to piece together a sequence of events, including Parker, *Rights of Man*; Higginson, "Romance"; Bowditch, *Life*, 1:208; Parker's letter to Edna Cheney, in Weiss, *Life*, 308; George Putnam to William Siebert, December 27, 1893, HOU; Siebert, "Underground Railroad in Massachusetts." Collison's discussion of the overlooking of Black activists in this work is also meaningful here ("Boston Vigilance Committee," 111).

237 **"good rifle shot"**: See Parker, preface in *Rights of Man*.

237 **Sheriff Coburn**: Events are recounted in Daniel J. Coburn, "The Boston Slave-Hunt," *NASS* December 12, 1850, WH1; "Boston Slave Hunt and the Vigilance Committee"; JK.

237 **"engaged to go to the theater"**: "No. 3."

238 **"first man to shoot"**: WH1, also "Additional Retaliatory Suits," *BP*, October 29, 1850.

238 **"receive upon his bare back"**: Hotchkiss, *Codification*, 812, 838–40.

239 **The United States Hotel**: The early action in this chapter is recounted in JK, WH1, WH2.

239 **"if it was to apply"**: Parker, preface in *Rights of Man*.

239 **"deprived of the inexpressible pleasure"**: Knight recalls the visits in JK.

239 **"smoking in the streets"**: Richard Henry Dana to Thomas Stevenson, October 28, 1850, MHS. Also WH1; "Boston Slave Hunt and the Vigilance Committee"; "Proceedings of the British and Foreign Anti-Slavery Society," *North Star*, June 22, 1855. On Macon law: Robert S. Davis Jr., *Cotton, Fire, and Dreams: The Robert Findlay Iron Works and Heavy Industry in Macon, Georgia, 1839–1912* (Macon, GA: Mercer University Press, 1998), 101.

239 **"armed to the teeth"**: "Kidnappers in Boston," *Emancipator & Republican* (Boston), October 31, 1850.

240 **"Truly" . . . William, if not Ellen**: "Boston Slave Hunt and the Vigilance Committee." On the serious legal maneuvers: ibid.; Collison, *Shadrack Minkins*, 97; Richard Henry Dana to Edmund T. Dana, November 12, 1850, MHS. Kantrowitz observes the silence on Ellen's agreement in *More*, 188.

240 **Vigilance Committee**: Henry Steele Commager, *Theodore Parker* (Boston: Unitarian Universalist Association, 1982), 214–15.

240 **"Let not dangerous"**: "Rocking the Old Cradle of Liberty," *TL*, October 18, 1850.

240 **"Gentlemen . . ."**: Commager, *Theodore Parker*, 215.

241 **conventional racist views**: Teed, *Revolutionary Conscience*, xvii, 153–57; Chadwick, *Theodore Parker*, 240. Thanks to Dean Grodzins for conversations on Parker and race as well.

241 **"government of the people"**: LL, 28; Clayborne Carson, interview by Melissa Block, "Theodore Parker and the 'Moral Universe,'" *All Things Considered*, PBS, September 2, 2013.

241 **Parker traveled**: The following account of the hotel confrontation, including dialogue (with minor grammatical corrections), draws from Parker's diary, excerpted in Weiss, *Life*, 97–98. See also Parker, preface in *Rights of Man*; Williams, "Brookline," JK, WH1, WH2.

241 **"total depravity incarnate"**: Theodore Parker, *The Collected Works of Theodore Parker*, vol. 5, ed. Frances Power Cobbe (London: Trübner, 1863), 193.

242 **escaped using the same strategy**: "Final Flight of the Slave Hunters—A Precious Confession," *Emancipator & Republican* (Boston), November 7, 1850.

242 **"negroes were secreted":** "A Despatch Received in Macon," *Savannah Morning News*, November 4, 1850.

243 **The Lion's Den:** On Simeon and Betsey Dodge: McCaskill, "Ellen Craft," 95; *LL*, 52; "Sheltered the Fleeing Slave," *Boston Daily Globe*, August 27, 1900. Their activities are described in letters by David Meade, George Putnam, and Simeon Dodge in the Wilbur H. Siebert Papers at HOU.

243 **Lewis Hayden . . . diverse congregations:** Kantrowitz, *More*, 185; Jeremiah and Jane Dunbar Chaplin, *Life of Charles Sumner* (Boston: D. Lothrop, 1874), 157; Calvin Fairbank, *Rev. Calvin Fairbank, During Slavery Times: How He "Fought the Good Fight" to Prepare "the Way"* (Chicago: R. R. McCabe, 1890), 79. On Emerson: Delbanco, *War*, 315–16, 373–76. Sources disagree over the timing and attendance of the meeting, but Thomas's presence suggests it occurred after the Georgians left. On tensions, especially over the use of force: Grodzins, "Constitution or No Constitution," 67–69; also Collison on the work of Black activists, "Boston Vigilance Committee," 109–11.

244 **"telegraphic intelligence":** "Slave-Hunters in Boston!!" *TL*, November 1, 1850.

244 **"his young son":** George Putnam to Wilbur H. Siebert, December 27, 1893, *Underground Railroad in Massachusetts*, vol. 2, MS AM 2420 (14), HOU. On Thompson at Marblehead: Simeon Dodge to Wilbur H. Siebert, January 29, 1894, Wilbur H. Siebert Papers, HOU.

244 **"should any attempt be made to capture":** Bowditch, *Life*, 2:373. This account differs from Archibald Grimke's telling in "Anti-Slavery Boston," where Hayden seems to have stood alone and Ellen is not present.

244 **Theodore Parker's . . . Hannah Stevenson:** I owe the details on Parker's life and home to Dean Grodzins's *American Heretic: Theodore Parker and Transcendentalism* (Chapel Hill: University of North Carolina Press, 2002), and his emails of May 5, 8, 2020. On Ellen's stay: Weiss, *Life*, 102. Grodzins introduced me to Stevenson and her link to Alcott and the Curtii. On J. T. Stevenson: Collison, *Shadrack Minkins*, 248n24; Richard Henry Dana to Thomas Stevenson, October 28, 1850, MHS; "The Boston Post States": *GT*, November 12, 1850.

244 **"the girls":** See Parker's letter to Edna Cheney, published in Weiss, *Life*, 308.

245 **"loaded, ready":** Parker, *Trial*, 187.

245 **"The excitement in Boston":** Frederick Douglass to Amy Post, October 31, 1850, in John R. McKivigan, ed., *The Frederick Douglass Papers*, series 3, vol. 1 (New Haven, CT: Yale University Press, 2009), 434.

245 **"Boston boiled":** George Putnam to Wilbur H. Siebert.

245 **received the telegraph:** "A Despatch Received in Macon" *Savannah (GA) Daily Morning News*, November 4, 1850.

245 **"We had rather have the money":** Collins to the attorney general.

246 **"Your policy":** Collins to Hastings. Collins's letter to Millard Fillmore is referenced in the response penned by W. S. Derrick, the president's acting secretary, published widely in papers such as the *Washington (DC) Daily Union*, November 20, 1850.

247 **Disagreeable Duty:** On the cholera and Taylor's death: Stephen E. Maizlish, "The Cholera Panic in Washington and the Compromise of 1850," *Washington History* 29, no. 1 (2017): 55–64. On this "accidental president": Finkelman: *Millard Fillmore*, especially 72–91.

247 **"Better far for him":** Quoted in John E. Crawford, comp., *Millard Fillmore: A Bibliography* (Westport, CT: Greenwood Press, 2002), xxi. On the threats: Robert J. Rayback, *Millard Fillmore: Biography of a President* (Buffalo: published for the Buffalo Historical Society by H. Stewart, 1959), 268; Elmore Smith, *The Presidencies of Zachary Taylor & Millard Fillmore* (Lawrence: University Press of Kansas, 1988), 195–97.

247 **"dough face":** Garrison, *All On Fire*, 392. On the crises North and South: Smith, *Presidencies of Zachary Taylor & Millard Fillmore*, 211, 217; Rayback, *Millard Fillmore*, 274–75.

247 **"Behind that smiling face":** Smith, *Presidencies of Zachary Taylor & Millard Fillmore*,

162; Frank H. Severance, ed., *Publications of the Buffalo Historical Society, vol. 11: Millard Fillmore Papers*, vol. 2 (Buffalo: Buffalo Historical Society, 1907), 508.

248 **"Any man can perform"**: Curtis, ed. Curtis, *Memoir*, 119.

248 **"THE PRESIDENT"**: *Brooklyn Daily Eagle*, November 5, 1850. On the newspaper reports: "Correspondence of the Baltimore Sun" and "Washington," *Washington (DC) Republic*, November 5, 1850.

248 **"I see the ordering of troops"**: Daniel Webster to Millard Fillmore, November 5, 1850, *PDW*, 178.

249 **England was famed**: On James Somerset: Delbanco, *War*, 90–101; Pryor, *Colored Travelers*, 128–29. Mary Anne Estlin would recount Ellen's surprise at the realities of British abolition, after what she had been led to expect. See Estlin to Miss Weston, May 8, 1851, BPL.

249 **"his wife's account"**: Samuel May Jr. to John Estlin, November 10, 1850, published in Taylor, *British and American Abolitionists*, 353.

249 **"we and our dear little ones"**: *RTMF*, 57. Wigham writes of an "expected child" in *The Anti-Slavery Cause*, 92. On Hayden's special relationship to the Crafts: *Bowditch, Life*, 2:350.

251 **Husband and Wife**: On the new marriage laws: Weiss, *Life*, 99. Their names appear in: "Massachusetts Marriages, 1841–1915," vol. 47, p. 129, Massachusetts State Archives.

251 **("names of parents")**: See McCaskill's reading of the empty space in *LL*, 51.

251 **for the ceremony . . . "peculiar duties"**: Parker recalls the ceremony and his lines in Weiss, *Life*, 99. See also Fairbank, *Rev. Fairbank*, 79–80. Parker's boast to Daniel Webster, December 12, 1850, appears in *PDW*, 189–90.

253 **North**: Sources for the journey: Samuel May Jr.'s letters to John B. Estlin in *RTMF*, 55; Taylor, *British and American Abolitionists*, 352. Unless noted, all dialogue and reflection are from *RTMF*, 55–69. On May: John White Chadwick, "Samuel May of Leicester," *New England* 20, March–August 1899. The Crafts write that Daniel Oliver was their Portland host, but scholars name the Dennetts. See also *BAP*, 478–79. *Mothers of Maine* (Portland, ME: Thurston Print, 1895), 239–41.

254 **all those "Negroes" . . . Knight told his story**: JK.

254 **"Watch the Slave Hunter!"**: Henry Ingersoll Bowditch to Sidney Howard Gay, n.p., November 12, 1850, box 3, SHG.

255 **arrival here had not gone unnoticed**: "Arrival of William and Ellen Crafts in Portland," *Boston Herald*, November 13, 1850; "SUCCESSFUL RESISTANCE," *Savannah (GA) Morning News*, November 22, 1850.

255 **"Every effort should be made"**: "Mr. Fillmore and the Man-Hunt," *NASS*, November 28, 1850.

256 **"law must be executed"**: Webster to Fillmore, October 29, 1850, *PDW*, 173–74. For Webster's demand to Marshal Devens, see his letter to Fillmore, November 15, 1850, *PDW*, 181. The tip is recounted in "The Fugitive Crafts," *BP*, November 14, 1850.

256 **"SUCCESSFUL RESISTANCE"**: *Savannah (GA) Daily Morning News* (November 22, 1850).

256 **"You have whipped Daniel Webster"**: quoted in Collison, *Shadrack Minkins*, 99.

256 **he initially pursued litigation**: Samuel May to John B. Estlin, February 4, 1851, *BPL*; "Attorney General Chittenden and the Boston Marshal," *Boston Atlas*, November 27, 1850; "U.S. Marshal's Return of Writ to Apprehend William Craft," December 9, 1850, HvC.

257 **Georgia Platform**: Talmadge, "Georgia Tests the Fugitive Slave Law"; Richard Harrison Shryock, "Georgia and the Union in 1850" (PhD diss., University of Pennsylvania, Philadelphia, 1926), 313–15.

257 **celebration for George Thompson**: *TL*, November 29, 1850; Blackett, *Captive's Quest*, 24.

257 **"class of foreigners"**: See Curtis, ed., Curtis, *Memoir*, 135–36.

257 **"Noble Determination in Crafts":** *Emancipator & Republican* (Boston), October 31, 1850.

257 **Theodore Parker . . . wrote to Millard Fillmore:** Weiss, *Life*, 100–102. On the victory: Collison, *Shadrack Minkins*, 99.

CANADA

261 **Strangers:** The Crafts were in Canada from November 10 to 29, 1850: "Arrival of the Cambria," *London Morning Chronicle*, December 12, 1850; "Successful Resistance," *Savannah (GA) Daily Morning News*, November 22, 1850. For a fuller treatment of the history, see Harvey Amani Whitfield, *Blacks on the Border: The Black Refugees in British North America, 1815–1860* (Burlington: University of Vermont Press, 2006); D. A. Sutherland, "Race Relations in Halifax, Nova Scotia, During the Mid-Victorian Quest for Reform," *Journal of the Canadian Historical Association* 7, no. 1, 1996: 35–54; *Robin Winks, The Blacks in Canada: A History* (Montreal: McGill-Queen's University Press, 1997); Sharon A. Roger Hepburn, "Following the North Star: Canada as a Haven for Nineteenth-Century American Blacks," *Michigan Historical Review* 25, no. 2 (1999): 91–126.

261 **enslaved in Canada fled to America:** Natasha L. Henry, "Black Enslavement in Canada," *The Canadian Encyclopedia* online (*Historica Canada*), last modified May 8, 2020, https://www.thecanadianencyclopedia.ca/en/article/black-enslavement.

261 **expatriate new emigrants:** Whitfield, *Blacks on the Border*, especially 59–61. On hardships in Canada, ibid., 77–78; *Fugitive Slaves in Canada*, Vol. 1 (MS 2420:1), box 1, Wilbur H. Siebert Papers, HOU; "Visit Among the Refugees in Canada," *Voice of the Fugitive*, February 12, 1851.

261 **extradition was unlikely:** See Winks's analysis of the law in *Blacks in Canada*, 168–74.

262 **"We wish to stop here":** All dialogue and next scenes are recounted in *RTMF*, 63–66.

263 **"sexual kinship":** Here I draw from Brigitte Fielder's analysis of how "Ellen's whiteness depends upon her distance from any assumption of sexual kinship with William" and how "The couple's disguise . . . is not only Ellen's dress and her class/ability/gender presentation, but Ellen and William's relationship to one another." *Relative Races*, 21–22.

264 **roughly 1,700 in the city:** Whitfield, *Blacks on the Border*, 3. On the race riot: Sutherland, "Race Relations."

264 **Reverend Cannady:** McCaskill suggests the minister may have been Reverend Hugh Kennedy of AME Zion Church (*LL*, 99n56). Also see Whitfield, *Blacks on the Border*, 154n128. News of the Crafts appeared previously in the *British Colonist* (Halifax, NS), October 31, 1850.

264 **$250 in total:** Ruggles, *Unboxing*, 115. Other fares in Wellington Williams, *The Traveller's and Tourist's Guide Through the United States of America, Canada, Etc.* (Philadelphia: Lippincott, Granbo, 1851), 16.

264 **Frederick Douglass . . . Samuel Cunard:** Douglass, *My Bondage and My Freedom*, 366; Fox, *Transatlantic*, 200; *LL*, 54. According to Donald Sutherland, William may have given a speech before leaving. See "Race Relations," 50.

266 **the *Cambria*:** Details in this chapter from: Stephen Fox, *Transatlantic: Samuel Cunard, Isambard Brunel, and the Great Atlantic Steamships* (New York: Harper Collins, 2003), especially 107, 113, and "Life on a Steamer" (196–25); William F. Fowler Jr., *Steam Titans: Cunard, Collins, and the Epic Battle for Commerce on the North Atlantic* (New York: Bloomsbury, 2017), 167–82; Isabella Lucy Bird, *The Englishwoman in America*, especially for the menu, 455; Dickens, *American Notes*, 1:1–53, 2:227–49; Philip Sutton, "Maury and the Menu: A Brief History of the Cunard Steamship Company," New York Public Library, online, last modified June 30, 2011, (https://www.nypl.org/blog/2011/06/30/maury-menu-brief-history-cunard-steamship-company), especially on dependability; F. E. Chadwick et al., *Ocean Steamships: A Popular Account of Their Construction, Development* (New York: Charles Scribner's Sons, 1891), 22–23; J. C. Arnell,

"Life on a Cunard Steamer," in *Steam and the North Atlantic Mails* (Toronto: Unitrade Press, 1986), 90–101. Reporting on the gale: *London Standard* and *London Morning Chronicle*, December 12, 1850; *Liverpool Mercury*, December 13, 1850.

266 **"utterly impracticable":** Dickens, *American Notes*, 1:2.

266 **set apart by race and class:** Pryor calls these ships "decidedly raced and classed," and "Transatlantic travel a bastion of white supremacy." See *Colored Travelers*, 130–33, 142–43. Note that in the swift, expensive Cunard ships, steerage was very limited and unlike what was common to large packets. On Josiah Henson: Jeffrey Green, *Black Victorians*, 56.

267 **"graveyard of the North Atlantic" . . . combust into hurricanes:** Fox, *Transatlantic*, x–xi.

267 **comparing the experience to war:** Mackey, *Western World*, 1:19.

268 **"Its howling voice":** Dickens, *American Notes*, I:34.

268 **shipboard tradition:** Fowler, *Steam Titans*, 170–71.

268 **Captain John Leitch:** See his obituary in the *Leeds Mercury*, (UK) July 28, 1883.

268 **Once the slaving capital of England:** Liverpool's International Slavery Museum powerfully exhibits the city's slaving history in a global context; see also *LL*, 56.

OVERSEAS

273 **Man of the World:** William Cullen Bryant describes the sights in *Letters of a Traveller: Or, Notes of Things Seen in Europe and America*, 2nd edition (New York: G. P. Putnam, 1850), 150. On the Crafts' arrival: "William and Ellen Craft," *TL*, January 24, 1851. Sources for William Wells Brown's itinerary and experiences include his *Three Years* and *American Fugitive*; his letter to Frederick Douglass, December 20, 1850, in *BAP*, 239; *WWB*, 203–67; Farrison, *WWB*, 145–96.

274 **"best French":** William Wells Brown, *Three Years*, 72.

274 **twenty gold sovereigns . . . "token of their esteem":** Quarles, *Black Abolitionists*, 127; Josephine Brown, *Biography of an American Bondman*, 64. Brown's efforts on his daughters' behalf are evidenced in his letter to Wendell Phillips, January 24, 1851, MS Am 1953 (327), Wendell Phillips Papers, HOU.

274 **"dark day" . . . "You are the first friend":** William Wells Brown, *Three Years*, 110. On his warnings: "Don't Come to England," *TL*, July 25, 1851; *WWB*, 263. On Betsey: Ibid., 212–14, 232–36.

275 **"A Stray Husband":** *New-York Daily Tribune*, March 12, 1850.

275 **world of abolition here:** Mary Anne Estlin to Miss Weston, May 8, 1851, BPL.

275 **"open war":** *WWB*, 234–35. On Brown's independent stance: William Lloyd Garrison to Elizabeth Pease Nichol, July 17, 1849, BPL. On the BFASS and Garrisonian divide: Blackett, *Building an Anti-Slavery Wall*, 42–45; *BAB*, 48–49, 100; *PAS*, 217; *BAP*, 17.

276 **"smooth as an iceberg":** Elwood H. Jones, "Scoble, John," in *Dictionary of Canadian Biography*, vol. 9 (University of Toronto/Université Laval, 2003); *WWB*, 217, 232–36.

276 **could not have come at a better moment . . . told Douglass:** *WWB*, 248; *BAP*, 242.

276 **"I need not inform":** William Craft to William Wells Brown, December 18, 1850, *BAP*, 241.

276 **Francis Bishop:** "Letter from Francis Bishop," *TL*, March 2, 1851. Household information in: "England and Wales Census, 1851." On Bishop's planned trip, see his letters to William Lloyd Garrison, August 14 and 22, 1852, BPL; William Ingersoll Bowditch, *White Slavery in the United States* (New York: American Anti-Slavery Society, 1855), 8.

278 **Two Williams:** The events in this chapter are recounted in Brown's *Three Years*; the speeches, in newspapers. On Douglass and Edinburgh: Blight, *Douglass*, 163. On the monument at St. Andrew's Square: Darren McCullins, "Charting Edinburgh's Slave Trade History," *BBC News*, October 31, 2018, https://www.bbc.com/news/uk-scotland-edinburgh-east-fife-46030606.

279 **cultural and political scene:** The challenges that Brown faced in England have been well described by other scholars, whose analyses I draw from here, especially: *LL*, 55–75; *BAP*, 1–35; *PAS*, 210–27. On British social unrest and class conflict: Zackodnik,

Press, 49–75. On transatlantic abolitionist politics: Blackett, *Building an Anti-Slavery Wall*, 124–45.

279 **"the genuine black":** Quoted in Fisch, *American Slaves*, 69.

279 **touchiness about money and class:** Zackodnik, *Press*, 57–58; Clytus, "Envisioning Slavery," 211; Fisch, *American Slaves*, 1–4.

279 **"money speculation":** John B. Estlin to Samuel May Jr., April 26, 1849, BPL.

279 **The Crafts would strive:** Contemporaries observed the Crafts' surprise at the animosity against Garrisonians, "the only white people who had ever treated them as friends and equals." Bristol and Clifton Ladies' Anti-Slavery Society, *Special Report of the Bristol and Clifton Ladies' Anti-Slavery Society* (London: John Snow, 1852), 23. Blackett analyzes the conflicts in *BAB*, 100. The trio would steer clear of London, where the anti-Garrisonian British and Foreign Anti-Slavery Society was strong.

279 **"too many of our fugitive brethren":** "Don't Come to England," *TL*, July 25, 1851.

280 **Ellen would be a pioneer:** Zackodnik, *Press*, 58; *BF*, 39.

280 **"respectable audience" . . . newly fired up:** "American Slavery," *TL*, January 24, 1851. On the Crafts' energizing impact: Blackett, *Building an Anti-Slavery Wall*, 126.

281 **"a favourite with the Scotch" . . . "When walking through the streets":** Quotations herein from William Wells Brown, *Three Years*, 164, 171, 173 (with slightly different wording), 167.

283 **Panoramas:** Glasgow history comes alive at the Glasgow Police Museum. On the Father of Glasgow: "Patrick Colquhoun," *The University of Glasgow Story*, University of Glasgow online, https://www.universitystory.gla.ac.uk/biography/?id=WH0206&type=P. On the Grand Hall: "The City Hall," *Glasgow Chamber of Commerce Journal* (February 1858); 155, from Glasgow Scrapbook #23, Michell Library, Glasgow; Frank Worsdall, *Victorian City: A Selection of Glasgow's Architecture* (Glasgow: Richard Drew, 1982), 86.

283 **cries of "Shame!":** Quoted in Russell Jackson, "The Story of Freed Slave Frederick Douglass' Time in 'Beautiful' Scotland," *Scotsman* (Edinburgh), April 1, 2018.

283 **"WHITE SLAVE":** "Illustrated Lectures on American Slavery," *Glasgow Herald*, January 3, 1851. On Ellen's dislike: John B. Estlin to Samuel May, May 2, 1851, BPL.

283 **"American slavery shall one day fall":** "American Fugitive Slave Bill," *TL*, February 14, 1851.

283 **"Fling Out the Anti-Slavery Flag":** Aaron D. McClendon, "Sounds of Sympathy: William Wells Brown's 'Anti-Slavery Harp,' Abolition, and the Culture of Early and Antebellum American Song," *African American Review* 47, no. 1 (2014): 96.

283 **"rapturous":** "American Fugitive Slave Bill."

284 **"one of the loveliest spots":** William Wells Brown, *Three Years*, 175.

284 **"Grand Panorama" . . . truthfulness to nature":** John Banvard, *Description of Banvard's Panorama of the Mississippi River* (Boston: J. Putnam, 1847), 45–46. On Banvard and his "largest painting," see Ried Holien, "John Banvard's Brush with Success" *South Dakota*, September/October 1997.

284 **Brown was also amazed:** William Wells Brown, *A Description of William Wells Brown's Original Panoramic Views of the Scenes in the Life of an American Slave* (London: Charles Gilpin, 1849; repr., Cornell University Library Digital Collections), 2. On being "sold down the river": Edward Ball, "Retracing Slavery's Trail of Tears," *Smithsonian*, November 2015.

284 **"2,000 feet of canvas":** "Illustrated Lectures on American Slavery," *Glasgow Herald*, January 3, 1851. Smaller estimates given in *PAS*, 215; *WWB*, 244, 549n104. For further analysis of the panorama, which survives only in Brown's written descriptions: *WWB*, 240–45; Teresa A. Goddu, "Anti-Slavery's Panoramic Perspective," *MELUS* 39, no. 2, *Visual Culture and Race* (Summer 2014): 12–41; *PAS*, 215–17; Clytus, "Envisioning Slavery," 194–257.

284 **"from representing those disgusting pictures":** William Wells Brown, *Description*, iv.

285 **"minstrel fairies":** Ruggles, *Unboxing*, 117. On Box Brown's panorama and critics:

Fisch, *American Slaves*, 73–83; *PAS*, 215. On the superiority of William Wells Brown's: Joseph Lupton to Samuel May, March 3, 1851, BPL.

285 **("for what purpose"):** William Wells Brown, *Description*, 17.

287 **Soiree:** On the hundreds turned away: "A Great Meeting in Glasgow," *TL*, February 7, 1851. On William Wells Brown's relief: *Three Years*, 177–78. Events to follow are described here and in Brown's *American Fugitive*. On the sixteen hundred: William Wells Brown to Wendell Phillips, January 24, 1851, MS Am 1953 (327), Wendell Phillips Papers, HOU WWB, 249.

287 **"I ken nae":** On Dick: William J. Astore, *Observing God: Thomas Dick, Evangelicalism, and Popular Science in Victorian Britain and America* (New York: Routledge, 2017), 16, 22; John A. Brashear, "A Visit to the Home of Dr. Thomas Dick, *Journal of the Royal Astronomical Society of Canada* 7 (February 1913): 19.

287 **"How I wished":** William Wells Brown, *Three Years*, 181.

288 **continued in Aberdeen:** Ibid., 306; Blackett, *BAB*, 98.

288 **Williams dominated . . . Why her public silence?:** See *PAS*, 180–81; McCaskill, "Yours Very Truly," 523; Kenneth Salzer, "Great Exhibitions: Ellen Craft on the British Abolitionists Stage," in *Transatlantic Women: Nineteenth-Century American Women Writers and Great Britain*, ed. Beth Lynne Lueck, Brigitte Bailey, and Lucinda L. Damon-Bach (Durham: University of New Hampshire Press, 2012), 138–39; Zackodnik, *Press*, 70–71. On the stigma against women speaking: Ibid., 56–57; Fisch, *American Slaves*, 84. On Ellen's sitting: *Nottingham Review*, April 4, 1851.

288 **"only ensure more cruelty":** John B. Estlin to Samuel May, June 27, 1851, BPL.

288 **"rather liked":** Ibid., May 2, 1851, BPL.

288 **identify with the black community:** Cima shows how Ellen "performed her allegiance to the black community" and "self-identified as black or improvised past racial categories": *PAS*, 189, 201.

288 **"At present":** "The *Anti-Slavery Advocate*," *TL*, March 23, 1853; *PAS*, 224.

289 **"The night was a glorious one":** Next descriptions also from William Wells Brown, *Three Years*, 307.

289 **George Combe:** William Wells Brown, *American Fugitive*, 267; Cameron A. Grant, "George Combe and American Slavery," *Journal of Negro History* 45, no. 4 (1960): 259–69. Combe writes about the royals in diaries at the George Combe Collection, National Library of Scotland, Edinburgh.

289 **Fanny Kemble:** Catherine Clinton, *Fanny Kemble's Civil Wars* (Oxford: Oxford University Press, 2000), 33, 63, 201; Irving H. Bartlett, *Wendell Phillips: Brahmin Radical* (Boston: Beacon Press, 1961), 28.

290 **"majestic overhanging brow":** "Cecelia Combe Diary," Journal in the US, 1842, MS 7459, George Combe Collection. On Van Buren: "Miscellaneous Personal Papers of Cecelia Combe," MS 7460, George Combe Collection. On her table: "Menus of Cecelia Combe," MS 7467, George Combe Collection. Thanks to Caroline Sloat for her consultation on British cuisine.

290 **Dr. James W. C. Pennington:** On the politics of Pennington, British Garrisonianism, and the Crafts: Blackett, *Building an Anti-Slavery Wall*, especially 124–35; *BAB*, 1–87; William Wells Brown to Wendell Phillips, January 24, 1851, MS Am 1953 (327), Wendell Phillips Papers, HOU. See also Pennington's *The Fugitive Blacksmith* (London: C. Gilpin, 1850). The Crafts did not wish to take sides, as analyzed in *BAB*, 100. Also see "Anti-Slavery Meeting," *TL*, February 28, 1851.

291 **"scolded them":** Mary Ann Estlin to Miss Weston, May 8, 1851, BPL.

291 **Ellen, however, chose to laugh:** See Cima's analysis in *PAS*, 218–19. On Ellen's realizations about abolition: Mary Anne Estlin to Miss Weston, May 8, 1851. *BAB*, 97–101. On warnings: Lupton to May, BPL. On the Crafts' finances and Brown's "liberal terms": Taylor, *British and American Abolitionists*, 377; John B. Estlin to "My Dear Mrs. Chapman": May 26, 1851, BPL; *WWB*, 248–49. On the Crafts' mothers: McCaskill, "Profits," 76–77; "American Slavery," *York Herald and General Advertiser* (UK), March 29, 1851.

292   **Harriet Martineau:** Much of the action of this chapter comes from William Wells Brown, *Three Years*, 185–207.

292   **sailed for New York:** Martineau describes her travels in these three sources, which this segment follows closely: *Harriet Martineau's Autobiography*, vol. 2, ed. Maria Weston Chapman (London: Smith, Elder, 1877); *Views of Slavery & Emancipation: From Society in America* (New York: Piercy & Reed, 1837); *Retrospect*, vol. 1. Deborah A. Logan's scholarship has also informed this chapter, including *Collected Letters*; "The Redemption of a Heretic: Harriet Martineau and Anglo-American Abolition in Pre–Civil War America," in *Proceedings of the Third Annual Gilder Lehrman Center International Conference at Yale University*, October 25–28, 2001; *The Hour and the Woman: Harriet Martineau's "Somewhat Remarkable" Life* (DeKalb: Northern Illinois University Press, 2002).

293   **antislavery reputation . . . proslavery heat:** Logan, "Redemption," 2; Linda K. Kerber, "Abolitionists and Amalgamators: The New York City Race Riots of 1834," *New York History* 48, no. 1 (1967): 28–39.

293   **marry a Black person . . . "amalgamation":** Martineau, *Autobiography*, 2:14–19.

293   **"piece of Indian work" . . . "mulatto":** Martineau, *Retrospect*, 225–27.

294   **"You know my theory":** ibid., 235; Martineau, *Autobiography*, 2:21.

294   **"young heiress's first ball":** Martineau, *Retrospect*, 238.

295   **"Whatever I learned":** Martineau, *Views of Slavery*, 32.

295   **"come and see how . . ." "You will be lynched" . . . first thoughts . . . receive threats:** Martineau, *Autobiography*, 2:46, 48, 55–57.

295   **"oppression of the negroes" . . . "The voice of a white":** Martineau, *Views of Slavery*, 7, 11.

296   **once recalled as "disgusting":** Martineau, *Retrospect*: 217–18. See Miles's reading of Martineau's "negative stereotyping" in *All That She Carried*, 142.

296   **"Mrs. Martineau":** Logan, *Hour and the Woman*, 273n4.

296   **"Amazons," she called them:** Harriet Martineau, "Year at Ambleside: February," *Sartain's Union Magazine of Literature and Art*, Vol. 6, January–June 1850, ed. Mrs. C. M. Kirkland and Professor John S. Hart (Philadelphia: John Sartain, 1850), 139; Alexis Easley, "The Woman of Letters at Home: Harriet Martineau and the Lake District," *Victorian Literature and Culture* 34, no. 1 (2006): 297.

296   **hilltop home, the Knoll:** The scenes of their encounter are based on William Wells Brown, *Three Years*, 196–207; Harriet Martineau to "Dear Lucy (Aiken)," April 5, 1851, in Logan, *Collected Letters*, 3:190, 196. Subsequent quotations, unless noted, are from Brown.

297   **Martineau would later tell friends:** Mary R. Courzon to Thomas Wentworth Higginson, April 13, 1851, MS 784, Thomas Wentworth Higginson Papers, HOU.

297   **"I found them sensible":** Martineau to "Dear Lucy."

297   **"she did not find him so agreeable":** Courzon to Higginson.

297   **"finest spots on the valley":** Martineau to "Dear Lucy."

298   **Through mesmerism . . . raced desert bandits:** Easley, "Woman of Letters," 293; Logan, *Collected Letters*, vi–vii.

298   **"mischief" in a woman:** Quoted in Easley, "Woman of Letters," 300. For lore on boots and cigars: Jules Brown, *The Rough Guide to the Lakes District* (London: Rough Guides, 2002), 60; Sarah Perry, "Essex Girls," The 2019 Harriet Martineau Lecture, National Centre for Writing online, last modified June 20, 2019, https://nationalcentreforwriting.org.uk/article/sarah-perrys-harriet-martineau-lecture/.

298   **enchanted landscape:** William Wells Brown, *Three Years*, 206. See also Harriet Martineau *Complete Guide to the English Lakes* (Windermere, UK: John Garnett, 1855).

298   **"The negroes carried away":** Martineau to "Dear Lucy." On Martineau's curiosity: Courzon to Higginson.

300   **"The thing can be done":** Harriet Martineau to William Wells Brown, March 14, 1851, in Logan, *Collected Letters*, 290.

301   **They told this story . . . "white slave":** "Anti-Slavery Meeting in Newcastle," *Newcastle*

Guardian and Tyne Mercury (UK), March 15, 1851. Wilson Armistead listed the Crafts in his Leeds household: "Fugitives from Slavery—Remarkable," *Illustrated London News*, April 19, 1851. On working-class crowds: Lupton to May, BPL; Zackodnik, *Press*, 65–66. See Zackodnik's analysis of how Ellen, as the "White Slave," represented the "American slave and the pauperized British mother" (69).

301 **"the poorest man":** "American Slavery," *York Herald and General Advertiser* (UK), March 29, 1851.

301 **come into his own:** Blackett, *Building an Anti-Slavery Wall*, 125; *BAP*, 271; *PAS*, 215; "American Slavery." On family: "American Slavery," McCaskill, "Profits," 76–77.

302 **Ellen's part:** When Ellen did tell the story decades later, she did not credit William with the idea, but rather spoke of "we." See "An Ex Slave's Reminiscences"; Murray, *Advocates*, 212–13.

302 **"white woman":** "Three Fugitive Slaves in Nottingham," *Nottingham Review* (UK), April 4, 1851.

302 **John Bishop Estlin:** On his close bond with Brown: *WWB*, 236–39. For a critical reading of Estlin's "paternalistic vision": Fisch, *American Slaves*, 1–4. On his turn to antislavery: William James, *Memoir of John Bishop Estlin* (London: printed by Charles Green, 1855), 236.

302 **"If the Crafts do not find ready friends":** "A Good Man Gone," reprinted in *TL*, July 6, 1855.

302 **the Crafts were reminded:** *RTMF*, 67. The Estlins express their warm feelings and conversations with Ellen in letters, e.g., John B. Estlin to May, May 2, 6, 1851, BPL.

303 **"Craft has none of Brown's energy":** John B. Estlin to May, May 2, 1851, BPL.

303 **"showman-like" . . . low class:** John B. Estlin to Eliza Wigham, May 3, 1851, BPL; critical readings in Zackodnik, *Press*, 66; *PAS*, 217.

303 **"They are quite like the family" . . . "home":** Emma Michell to Miss Weston, May 9, 1851, BPL; John B. Estlin to May, May 2, 1851, BPL.

303 **"painting" . . . "great delight":** John B. Estlin to Samuel May, May 2, 1851, BPL. On the children: "The Panorama of American Slavery," *Bristol Mercury* (UK), April 12, 1851.

303 **"score a higher position":** John B. Estlin to Wigham, BPL.

303 **"a most respectable audience":** "American Slavery," *Bristol (UK) Mercury*, April 12, 1851.

303 **mobilized committee meetings . . . expert navigator:** Mary Anne Estlin to Caroline Weston, June 6, 1851, BPL.

303 **answered "wrenching" questions:** Michell to Miss Weston, May 9, 1851, BPL. Blackett shows how the Crafts helped Garrisonianism, despite complications and later "cooling": *BAB*, 98–101.

304 **"a little alarmed":** Michell to Miss Weston, BPL.

304 **tidings from Samuel May Jr.:** John B. Estlin to May, May 2, 1851, BPL.

304 **Thomas Sims . . . "Sims, preach Liberty to the Slaves!":** Levy, "Sims' Case," 71.

305 **"great curiosity":** "The Boston Fugitive Slave Case," *Daily Constitutionalist* (August, GA), April 12, 1851.

305 **exchange of letters . . . "The enforcement of the law":** The letters appear in *BP*, June 9, 1851.

305 **emancipation was not possible:** O'Toole, *Passing*, 10, 42–43. On the Crafts' refusing purchase: William Craft to Theodore Parker, January 24, 1851, Theodore Parker Collection, MHS.

306 **the holdout on Ockham . . . "unusual good temper":** John B. Estlin to May, June 27, 1851, BPL.

306 **"Oh, how I should like . . ." "I am a slave no more":** Emphasis mine. Michell to Miss Weston, BPL.

308 **The Great Exhibition:** For my evocation of the World's Fair, I relied on Michael Leapman's lively *The World for a Shilling* (London: Headline Book, 2001). Details include the story of the Chinese junk captain, discussion of "shilling days," list of

machines, and gemstone cages: 121, 190, 146–50, 170. See also Julia Baird, *Victoria the Queen: An Intimate Biography of the Woman Who Ruled an Empire* (New York: Random House, 2017), 243–57; Liza Picard, "The Great Exhibition," British Library online, last modified October 14, 2009, https://www.bl.uk/victorian-britain/articles/the-great-exhibition#. On the printing press: Ibid., "Ellen Craft," *Illustrated London News*, April 19, 1851, 316. On Eliza Collins: "Needle Work," *Southern Cultivator*, vol. 10, no. 11 (November 1852), 325, 85. On Enoch Price, *WWB*, 262–63.

309   **"I am never so happy":** Mary Anne Estlin to Caroline Weston, May 16, 1851, BPL.

309   **Charles Dickens:** John B. Estlin, to May, June 27, 1851, BPL.

309   **six million souls . . . sixty-five thousand daily visitors:** Picard, "The Great Exhibition," "The Great Exhibition," *Sussex Advertiser* (UK), June 24, 1851.

310   **"Great Britain and Her Dependencies":** Great Exhibition, *Official Catalogue of the Great Exhibition of the Works of Industry of All Nations* (London: Spicer Brothers, 1851), 2.

310   **"the greatest building":** William Wells Brown, *Three Years*, 210. Brown makes these observances in a letter about a later visit. On languages: Green, *Black Americans*, 20; "Incidental Paragraphs," *Bristol Mercury* (UK), June 21, 1851. On 100,000 items: Leapman, *World*, 10. On repeat visits: William Wells Brown, *American Fugitive*, 204; William Farmer, "Fugitive Slaves at the Great Exhibition," *TL*, July 18, 1851.

310   **"emblem of the capitalist fetishism of commodities":** Quoted in Catherine Golden, *Posting It: The Victorian Revolution in Letter Writing* (Gainesville: University Press of Florida, 2009), 129.

311   **"beautiful white lard":** William Wells, *Three Years*, 215. See also Farmer, "Fugitive Slaves."

311   **"half a dozen haughty sinewy Negroes":** Quoted in Green, *Black Americans*, 22.

311   *The Greek Slave:* See readings in Vivien Green Fryd, "Reflections on Hiram Powers's Greek Slave," and Lisa Volpe, "Embodying the Octoroon: Abolitionist Performance at the London Crystal Palace, 1851," both in *Nineteenth-Century Art Worldwide* 15, no. 2 (Summer 2016); Charmaine Nelson, *The Color of Stone: Sculpting the Black Female Subject in Nineteenth-Century America* (Minneapolis: University of Minnesota Press, 2007), 75–86; McInnis, *Slaves Waiting*, 181–88; Lisa Merrill, "Exhibiting Race 'Under the World's Huge Glass Case': William and Ellen Craft and William Wells Brown at the Great Exhibition in Crystal Palace, London, 1851," *Slavery & Abolition*, 33 no. 2 (2012): 321–36; Joy S. Kasson, "Mind in Matter in History: Viewing the Greek Slave," *Yale Journal of Criticism* 11, no. 1 (Spring 1998): 79–83.

311   **"preserved as a treasure":** Quoted in Henry T. Tuckerman, *Book of the Artists: American Artist Life* (New York: G. P. Putnam & Son, 1867), 285; *PAS*, 220.

311   **suspected pornography:** Merrill, "Exhibiting Race," 328. On the sculpture's travel route and the Queen's viewing: Nelson, *The Color of Stone*, 78.

311   **"vast panorama":** William Wells Brown, *American Fugitive*, 204, 206; see also Merrill's discussion of performance in "Exhibiting Race," 322.

311   **mock slave auction:** "American Slavery in the World's Fair in London," *TL*, February 28, 1851.

312   **prior visit . . . "walking exhibition":** This scene is based on Farmer, "Fugitive Slaves." Weather and other details are from daily press reports on the exhibition, including the *London Morning Chronicle*, June 23, 1851; *London Daily News*, June 24, 1851; *Liverpool Mercury* (UK), June 24, 1851.

312   **American pavilion . . . *Greek Slave*:** Volpe, "Embodying." On the artist's directions: *PAS*, 221; Kasson, "Mind in Matter." On the "companion" picture: John Tenniel, "The Virginian Slave, Intended as a Companion to Power's [*sic*] 'Greek Slave,'" *Punch* 20, June 7, 1851, 236.

313   **spectators had projected:** McInnis, *Slaves Waiting*, 183–84; Volpe, "Embodying."

314   **Samuel Colt:** Bacon, *But One Race*, 22. I am not the first to notice that the only person to take note of the procession was—significantly—a maker of explosives.

314 **There were toilets:** Documentary of the "Great Exhibition" in the Furniture gallery at the Victoria and Albert Museum was useful on this topic. The penny price appears in Baird, *Victoria*, 247.

314 **"Probably, for the first time":** Farmer, "Fugitive Slaves"; *PAS*, 222. See Merrill's reading of "choreography" and the group's implication of spectators in "Exhibiting Race," 325.

315 **reduced to stammering:** Mary Estlin to Anne Warren Weston, June 27, 1851, Wendell Phillips Papers, HOU.

315 **unhappy to learn:** See John B. Estlin to May, June 27, 1851, BPL.

315 **school had been founded:** Blackett, *BAB*, 102–3; *BF*, 42–43. On the Lushingtons: Green, *Black Americans*, 18; "Stephen Lushington and Fugitive Slaves in Ockham," Exploring Surrey's Past, https://www.exploringsurreyspast.org.uk/themes/subjects/black_history/abolitionists/lushington/. John B. Estlin estimates the numbers in his letter to May, June 27, 1851, BPL.

316 **"magic lantern":** Items are listed in *BF*, 42. Source: W. A. C. Stewart and W. P. McCann, *The Educational Innovators, 1750–1880* (London: Macmillan, 1967), 213.

316 **financial arrangements . . . Ellen was in favor:** See John B. Estlin, letters to May, June 27 and December 12, 1851, BPL. Estlin guaranteed tuition for a year. The Crafts contributed by teaching and working, and others such as Lady Byron also donated funds. On Ellen's illness: Mary Estlin to Caroline Weston, May 16, 1851, BPL.

316 **"destined for some important missions!":** John B. Estlin to May, June 27, 1851, BPL.

317 **Freeborn:** The opening scene follows Brown's letter (signed "Leander"), *TL*, September 3, 1851 (also *American Fugitive*, 300). The meeting supposedly occurred "some months" before the date of the letter (August 6), so Ellen might well have been pregnant, as has elsewhere been noted.

317 **"Princess of Parallelograms" . . . "first computer programmer":** Miranda Seymour, *In Byron's Wake: The Turbulent Lives of Lord Byron's Wife and Daughter: Annabella Milbanke and Ada Lovelace* (New York: Pegasus Books, 2018), 40; Betsy Morais, "Ada Lovelace: The First Tech Visionary," *New Yorker*, October 15, 2013.

318 **days in Ockham:** *BAB*, 103; *PAS*, 222–23; John B. Estlin to May, August 15, 1851, BPL; Sheila Brown, "Ockham School," in *Root and Branch: A Publication of the West Surrey Family Historical Society* 37, no. 2 (September 2010): 73. On the Crafts' popularity: John B. Estlin to May, December 12 and August 15, 1851, BPL. On locals: Harriet Beecher Stowe, *Sunny Memories of Foreign Lands*, vol. 2 (New York: J. C. Darby, 1854), 107.

318 **"keenly to feel her isolation":** John B. Estlin to May, September 2, 1852, BPL.

318 **having an affair:** *WWB*, 265; Farrison, *William Wells Brown*, 201; John B. Estlin to William Lloyd Garrison, June 7, 1852, BPL. On Ellen's illness: John B. Estlin to Mrs. Chapman, April 3, 1852, BPL. "William and Ellen Craft," *TL*, December 17, 1852.

318 **"day and night":** See John B. Estlin's letter to the editor in the *Bristol Mercury* (UK) October 4, 1851.

319 **"excellent man":** "The Late James Smith," *GT*, May 18, 1852.

319 **his property was counted:** Bibb Court of Ordinary, Record of Returns, 1851–1853, D-481, BCC.

320 **reports were so persistent:** May to John B. Estlin, September 1, 1852, BPL; "Ellen Craft," *Georgia Journal and Messenger* (Macon), August 25, 1852.

320 **an "increase" to their family:** William Wells Brown to Wendell Phillips, September 1, 1852, HOU.

320 **Charles Estlin Phillips Craft:** "Foreign and Domestic," *Bristol Mercury* (UK), October 30, 1852. The Crafts do not specify the link to William's brother.

320 **Ellen's thoughts turned:** "Ellen Craft," *TL*, April 1, 1853.

320 **large financial gifts:** Sterling claims (without sources) that Byron gave Ellen £100 in gold sovereigns, in *BF*, 52. Other amounts in: "The Craft Libel Suit," *BDA*, June 12, 1878; "Craft v. Schlesinger," *Boston Journal*, June 1, 1878.

320 **arranged his will:** See Bibb Court of Ordinary, Record of Wills, 1851, B-17, BCC.

320 **"consoling to the heart . . .":** "William and Ellen Craft," *TL*, December 17, 1852.
321 **"for the money":** Collins, "Essay." The first edition was published by B. F. Griffin in Macon and written for the Macon Fair of 1852 (October 19–23), which offered $100 for the best essay on the subject. *De Bow's Review* 3 (1852): 103. (Collins lost.) Charles was born October 22.
321 **"first freeborn child":** "William and Ellen Craft," *TL*, December 17, 1852.
321 **"I have never had the slightest":** "Letter from Ellen Craft" (dated October 26, 1852), *Anti-Slavery Advocate*, December 1852. John Bishop Estlin and Richard Webb edited the paper, as noted in *BAP*, 330–31; see also McCaskill's reading in "Very Truly," 512–14.

CODA

325 **Coda:** This sketch of the Crafts' later years draws largely from *BAB*, 103–37; McCaskill, "Profits"; *BF*, 43–59; *PAS*, 219–30, and reporting on William's 1878 libel suit. On the Crafts' British experiences, see especially Green, *Black Americans*, 18–27; Murray, *Advocates*, 211. Children's dates (with some discrepancies) are from *LL*, 39–40; Green, *Black Americans*, 19, 27.
325 *Running a Thousand Miles for Freedom*: On the publication history: *BAB*, 105, *LL*, 58–70.
326 **go back to the States "to fight":** *BF*, 45; source in "The Commonwealth, Boston," October 2, 1869, folder 1:79, Dorothy Sterling Papers, Amistad Research Center, Tulane University, New Orleans, LA.
326 **west coast of Africa:** *BAB*, 108–13, 118–21, especially on the barracoon (119), on William's work helping to end the local slave trade (137), and on the fifty enslaved (120), whom William discusses in "Crafts v. Schlesinger," *Boston Journal*, June 7, 1878. There is further evidence of children similarly given to William. See *BAB*, 113 and Charles Craft's letter on Ellen's behalf, "An Appeal from Africa," *Freed-Man* (UK) July 1, 1866. Also on Africa: Green, *Black Americans*, 22–24; McCaskill, "Profits," "Libel Suit"; Robin Law, *Ouidah: The Social History of a West African Slaving "Port," 1727–1892* (Athens: Ohio University Press, 2004), 241.
326 **two thousand women warriors . . . "too white to go with him":** Child, *Freedmen's Book*, 203–4. For a later, unconfirmed report that Ellen was to "sail shortly for the African Coast": "Special Meeting," *Freed-Man* (UK), March 1, 1867.
326 **Critics would question:** *BAB*, 132.
327 **Ellen continued her activism:** *BAB*, 122; *BF*, 47; *PAS* 229; Murray, *Advocates*, 211.
327 **"excellent businesswoman":** "Craft, Ellen," in *Notable American Women (1607–1950): A Biographical Dictionary*, ed. Edward T. James, Janet Wilson James, and Paul S. Boyer. (Cambridge, MA: Harvard University Press, 1971), 2:397. On her nest egg: "Libel Suit,"
327 **famously proslavery:** Robert Scott Davis, "A Cotton Kingdom Retooled for War: The Macon Arsenal and the Confederate Ordinance Establishment," *Georgia Historical Quarterly* 91, no. 3 (Fall 2007): 268–69. On "Bob": Fitzgerald and Galloway, *Eminent Methodists*; obituary in the *Macon (GA) Telegraph* July 29, 1862.
327 **"living comfortably":** "Ellen Craft and Her Mother," *TL*, August 4, 1865.
327 **Ellen's mother . . . she was surrounded by the "thousands":** "Ellen Craft's Mother," *Freed-Man*, December 1, 1865. Little is known about Maria beyond her appearances with Ellen in 1866, noted in Green, *Black Americans*, 26–27, and reported in the *Freed-Man*, July 1, 1866.
328 **"redeemed his mother" . . . a particular mystery:** On William's mother: "Slavery," *Newcastle Courant* (UK), December 4, 1857; *RTMF*, 10; McCaskill, "Profits," 76–77. On his brother: "Diary of Isaac Scott," 7, 83; "Libel Suit," Charles Craft settled with his wife, Sarah, in Macon, where census records show them in possession of $5,000 each—an astonishing sum in 1870.

329   **return to the United States . . . Mary Elizabeth:** Green, *Black Americans*, 27; *LL*, 29.

329   **an American Ockham . . . "night riders":** *BAB*, 103, 125; also see "Libel Suit," "Prof-its," 88.

329   **"houses miserable holes":** "Craft Libel Suit," *BDA*, June 12, 1878. On its transformed appearance: "Georgia," *BDA*, July 30, 1875.

329   **"finest for white or colored":** "Craft v. Schlesinger," *Boston Journal*, June 11, 1878.

330   **"It used to seem":** "Georgia," *BDA*, July 30, 1875.

330   **"every good citizen":** "Radical Trickery: A Ticket for the Legislature in the Field," *Savannah (GA) Morning News*, October 6, 1874. On William's interview with President Grant: "Libel Suit,"

330   **turned their world upside down . . . British accents:** On the culture clash and threat posed by the Crafts' success: *BAB*, 132–33, *LL*, 80–83. On their accents: Bowditch, *Life*, 2:372; *BF*, 49.

330   **a libel suit:** The case file at the Massachusetts State Archives in Boston is thin (#1752 SJC/8u CRAFT v. Schelsinger et al., April 1878, Rec. 180). For further analysis: *BAB*, 130–33; McCaskill, "Profits," 89–90; *LL*, 75–86.

330   **"easy, straightforward manner":** "Craft Libel Suit," *BDA*, July 16, 1878.

331   **"ministering angel":** "The Craft Libel Suit," *BDA* June 12, 1878.

331   **"looked upon [them] as sacred":** "Craft v. Schlesinger."

331   **statements provided by the Crafts' former friends:** *BAB*, 133; *BF*, 57. Blackett has noted how, facing high fees even to process witnesses in Georgia, the Crafts had few testimonies, and discusses the doubts of Phillips, Smith, and William Still (*BAB*, 131–33). McCaskill reveals support from Robert Morris and others (*LL*, 81–86; "Profits," 90). See also "Craft Libel Suit," *BDA*, June 14, 1878; "Craft v. Schlesinger."

331   **William lost the suit . . . epoch of terror:** *BAB*, 133–36.

331   **"only Black-owned plantation":** "Craft, Ellen, (1826–C. 1891)" *Women in World History Encyclopedia*, September 23, 2021, https://www.encyclopedia.com/women/encyclopedias-almanacs-transcripts-and-maps/craft-ellen-1826-c-1891; *BF*, 55.

331   **"an old story":** "An Ex Slave's Reminiscences"; Murray, *Advocates*, 212–13.

331   **her favorite tree, an oak:** *BAB*, 135. Most scholars give 1891 as Ellen's death date, though some family members recall the year as 1897. See Fradin and Fradin, *5,000 Miles*, 90. As Blackett notes, little can be ascertained about this period. One source suggests (without references) that Ellen moved to Charleston without William. See *Notable American Women*, 2:397.

332   **"devote himself solely to farming" . . . "During his conversation":** Bowditch, *Life*, 2:373.

332   **"Grandpa William":** Florence B. Freedman, *Two Tickets to Freedom: The True Story of William and Ellen Craft, Fugitive Slaves* (New York: Scholastic, 1993), 96.

332   **drew his last breath . . . rest apart:** His death certificate is available at "South Carolina, Death Records, 1821–1968" (database online) Provo, UT, USA: Ancestry.com Operations, 2008. The Crafts' separation is replicated in images: Foreman, in "Who's Your Mama?," 523–26, observes that the Crafts never occupy the same picture.

332   **sudden, tragic ends:** On Willis Hughes: "Fatal Rencounter," *Baltimore Sun*, January 13, 1851; Parker, *Collected Works*, 5:193. On Ira Taylor: Reidy, *from Slavery to Agrarian Capitalism*, 4; "Melancholy Event," *Charleston (SC) Daily News*, May 16, 1867. On Robert Collins: Rocker, *Marriages and Obituaries*, 271.

333   **"old mistresses":** See Fitzgerald and Galloway, *Eminent Methodists*, 113; Eliza Cleveland Smith's obituary in the *Macon (GA) Weekly Telegraph*, March 18, 1879; Eliza Collins's 1889 testament in Wills, Bibb County, Georgia, book C (1870–1891), 456.

333   **"returned to their old home":** Bowditch, *Life*, 2:373.

333   **Hugh Craft:** Berry, *Princes of Cotton*, 536n.9.

333   **Lewis and Harriet Hayden:** On the Haydens' ongoing trials: Kantrowitz, *More*, 413–19. They also helped found the Museum of Fine Arts and fund the Massachusetts Historical Society (Robboy and Robboy, "Lewis Hayden"). See Alvin Powell, "Legacy

of Resolve," *Harvard Gazette* online, February 23, 2015, news.harvard.edu/gazette /story/2015/02/legacy-of-resolve/.

333   **lived on in their children:** *BF*, 59, 97; *LL*, 87–88; Green, *Black Americans*, 27, 143; Fradin and Fradin, *5,000 Miles*, 89–91; "Inventory of the Craft and Crum Families, 1780–2007," ARC, https://avery.cofc.edu/archives/Craft_and_Crum.html; Christopher McKeon, "Ockham Unveils Tribute to Escaped Slaves Who Settled in Surrey Village," Surrey Live, last modified September 16, 2018, getsurrey.co.uk/news/surrey =news/ockham=unveils=tribute=escaped=slaves=15138622.

334   **"artist, activist" . . . "As I sat":** See Preacely's website: Peggy Trotter Dammond Preacely, www.peggytrotterdammondpreacely.com; Faith S. Holsaert et al., eds., *Hands on the Freedom Plow: Personal Accounts by Women in SNCC* (Champaign: University of Illinois Press, 2010), 163–71.

334   **America failed the Crafts:** See McCaskill on how the Crafts' work "carefully places responsibility on the entire United States" ("Profits," 82); and on second acts and the Crafts' reinvention and legacy in *LL*, 88–92.

A NOTE ON SOURCES

339   **defies easy categorization:** See McCaskill on "reclaiming the Crafts' narrative as both literature and history in her introduction to *RTMF*, viii.

339   **Ellen's enslavers:** Florence Freedman revealed them in the 1960 Arno Press edition of *RTMF.*

339   **prove their "authenticity":** *BF*, 25. On authentication, see also Heglar, *Rethinking*, 84.

340   **"stuff(ed) it" with stories:** Sanborn presents Brown as a possible coauthor in "Plagiarist's Craft," 908. Zackodnik gestures at a more organic influence in *Press*, 67. Brown's influence is clear, but it worth noting that he is absent from *RTMF*, as Heglar does in *Rethinking*, 108n5.

340   **"symbolic" truths:** Miles, *All That She Carried*, 17; Johnson, *Soul by Soul*, 11.

341   **"scandal and excess" . . . "abysmally thin":** Saidiya Hartman, "Venus in Two Acts," *Small Axe* 12, no. 2 (2008): 5; Miles, *All That She Carried*, 301. See also ibid., 16–19, 300–302; Marisa J. Fuentes, *Dispossessed Lives: Enslaved Women, Violence, and the Archive* (Philadelphia: University of Pennsylvania Press); Murray, *Advocates*, 27–29; McCaskill, *LL*, 10–12.

342   **Generations of scholars:** See also Mary and Albert K. Cocke's letters to Albert Foley, SHC.

343   **follow the guidelines:** P. Gabrielle Foreman et al., "Writing about Slavery/Teaching About Slavery: This Might Help," community-sourced document, accessed January 28, 2022, (https://docs.google.com/document/d/1A4TEdDgYs1X-h1KezLodMIM 71My3KTN0zxRv0IQTOQs/mobilebasic?usp=gmail). See also Miles, *All That She Carried*, 287–89.

Selected Bibliography

Includes frequently cited sources. Full citations for other sources included on first reference in Notes.

Alvarez, Eugene. *Travel on Southern Antebellum Railroads, 1828–1860*. Tuscaloosa: University of Alabama Press, 1974.

Bacon, Margaret Hope. *But One Race: The Life of Robert Purvis*. Albany: State University of New York Press, 2007.

Bancroft, Frederic. *Slave Trading in the Old South*. Columbia: University of South Carolina Press, 1996.

Barker, Gordon S. *Fugitive Slaves and the Unfinished American Revolution: Eight Cases, 1848–1856*. Jefferson, NC: McFarland, 2013.

Bartlett, Irving H. *John C. Calhoun: A Biography*. New York: W. W. Norton, 1993.

Beaulieu, Elizabeth Ann, ed. *Writing African American Women: An Encyclopedia of Literature*. Westport, CT: Greenwood Press, 2006.

Berry, Daina Ramey, and Leslie Maria Harris, eds. *Slavery and Freedom in Savannah*. Athens: University of Georgia Press, 2014.

Berry, Stephen William, ed. *Princes of Cotton: Four Diaries of Young Men in the South, 1848–1860*. Athens: University of Georgia Press, 2007.

Blackett, R. J. M. *Beating Against the Barriers: The Lives of Six Nineteenth-Century Afro-Americans*. Ithaca, NY: Cornell University Press, 1986.

———. *Building an Anti-Slavery Wall: Black Americans in the Atlantic Abolitionist Movement, 1830–1860*. Baton Rouge: Louisiana State University Press, 1983.

Blassingame, John W. *Slave Testimony*. Baton Rouge: Louisiana State University Press, 1977.

Bordewich, Fergus. *America's Great Debate: Henry Clay, Stephen A. Douglas, and the Compromise That Preserved the Union*. New York: Simon & Schuster, 2012.

"The Boston Slave Hunt and the Vigilance Committee," *New-York Daily Tribune*, November 2, 1850.

Bowditch, Vincent Yardley. *Life and Correspondence of Henry Ingersoll Bowditch*. Boston: Houghton, Mifflin, 1902.

Bremer, Frederika. *The Homes of the New World: Impressions of America*. New York: Harper & Brothers, 1853.

Brown, Henry Box. *Narrative of the Life of Henry Box Brown, Written by Himself*. Edited by John Ernest. Chapel Hill: University of North Carolina Press, 2008.

Brown, Josephine. *Biography of an American Bondsman by His Daughter*. Boston: R. F. Walcutt, 1856.

Brown, William Wells: *American Fugitive in Europe*. New York: Sheldon, Lamport & Blakeman, 1855.

———. *Narrative of William W. Brown, a Fugitive Slave*. 2nd ed., enlarged. Boston: Anti-Slavery Office, 1848.

———. *Three Years in Europe: Or, Places I Have Seen and People I Have Met*. London: Charles Gilpin, 1852.

Butler, John C. *Historical Record of Macon and Central Georgia*. Macon, GA: J. W. Burke, 1879.

Byrne, William A. "The Burden and Heat of the Day: Slavery and Servitude in Savannah, 1733–1865." PhD diss., Florida State University, 1979.

Chambers, William. *Things as They Are in America.* London: W. and R. Chambers, 1854.

Child, Lydia Maria. *The Freedmen's Book.* Boston: Ticknor and Fields, 1865.

Cima, Gay Gibson. *Performing Anti-Slavery: Activist Women on Antebellum Stages.* Cambridge, MA: Cambridge University Press, 2014.

Cleveland, Edmund Janes, and Horace Gilette. *The Genealogy of the Cleveland and Cleaveland Families.* Vol. 3. Hartford, CT: Case, Lockwood & Brainard, 1899.

Clinton, Catherine. *Plantation Mistress.* Columbia: University of Missouri Press, 1982.

Clytus, Radiclani. "Envisioning Slavery: American Abolitionism and the Primacy of the Visual." PhD diss., Yale University, 2007.

Collins, Robert. *Essay on the Treatment and Management of Slaves.* Boston: Eastburn's Press, 1853.

———. Letter to the Attorney General of the United States, November 1, 1850. Attorney General Papers, "Letters Received from GA Private Citizens, 1809–1870," RG60, NARA.

———. Letter to J. S. Hastings. *BP*, June 9, 1851.

Collison, Gary. *Shadrack Minkins: From Fugitive Slave to Citizen.* Cambridge, MA: Harvard University Press, 1997.

Craft, William, and Ellen. *Running a Thousand Miles for Freedom: The Escape of William and Ellen Craft from Slavery*, ed. Barbara McCaskill. Athens: University of Georgia Press, 1999.

Craft, Henry, to "Dear Father." April 1, 1844, CFT; Craft/Fort Family Letters (MUM00091). Department of Archives and Special Collections. J. D. Williams Library, University of Mississippi. https://libraries.olemiss.edu/cedar-archives/finding_aids/MUM00091.html.

Crowe, Eyre. *With Thackeray in America.* London: Cassell, 1893.

Curtis, George Ticknor. *A Memoir of Benjamin Robbins Curtis*, LL.D Edited by Benjamin R. Curtis. Boston: Little, Brown, 1879.

Cunynghame, Arthur Augustus Thurlow. *A Glimpse at the Great Western Republic.* London: R. Bentley, 1851.

Dall, Caroline Healey. *"Alongside": Being Notes Suggested by "A New England Boyhood" of Doctor Edward Everett Hale.* Boston: Thomas Todd, 1900.

Delbanco, Andrew. *The War Before the War: Fugitive Slaves and the Struggle for America's Soul from the Revolution to the Civil War.* New York: Penguin Press, 2018.

Dickens, Charles. *American Notes.* London: Chapman and Hall, 1842.

The Directory of the City of Boston. Boston: George Adams, 1850.

Dixon, Max. "Building the Central Railroad of Georgia." *Georgia Historical Quarterly* 45, no. 1 (March 1961): 1–21.

Douglass, Frederick. *My Bondage and My Freedom.* New York: Miller, Orton & Mulligan, 1855.

Dunbar, Erica Armstrong. *Never Caught: The Washingtons' Relentless Pursuit of Their Runaway Slave, Ona Judge.* New York: 37 Ink, 2017.

Eisterhold, John A. "Commercial, Financial, and Industrial Macon, Georgia, During the 1840's." *Georgia Historical Quarterly* 53, no. 4: 424–41.

"An Ex Slave's Reminiscence." *Greencastle (IN) Banner*, January 19, 1882.

Fairbank, Calvin. *Rev. Calvin Fairbank During Slavery Times: How He "Fought the Good Fight" to Prepare "the Way."* Chicago: R. R. McCabe, 1890.

Farrison, William Edward. *William Wells Brown: Author and Reformer.* Chicago: University of Chicago Press, 1969.

Fielder, Brigitte. *Relative Races: Genealogies of Interracial Kinship in Nineteenth-Century America.* Durham, NC: Duke University Press, 2020.

Finkelman, Paul. *Millard Fillmore.* New York: Times Books, 2011.

Fisch, Audrey. *American Slaves in Victorian England: Abolitionist Politics in Popular Literature and Culture.* Cambridge: Cambridge University Press, 2000.

Fitzgerald, O. P., and Charles B. Galloway. *Eminent Methodists*. Nashville: M. E. Church, South, 1898.

Foley, Albert S. to Henry K. Craft, May 7, 1958, ARC.

_____. "Notes from Mrs. Daly Smith," box 9, folder 68, SHC.

Foreman, P. Gabrielle. "Who's Your Mama? 'White' Mulatta Genealogies, Early Photography, and Anti-Passing Narratives of Slavery and Freedom." *American Literary History* 14, no. 3 (2002): 505–39.

Fradin, Dennis B., and Judith Fradin. *5,000 Miles: Ellen and William Craft's Flight from Slavery*. Washington, DC: National Geographic Children's Books, 2006.

Fraser, Walter. *Savannah in the Old South*. Athens: University of Georgia Press, 2005.

Geffen, Elizabeth M. "Industrial Development and Social Crisis 1841–1854." In *Philadelphia: A 300-Year History*. Edited by Russell F. Weigley. New York: W. W. Norton, 1982.

Green, Jeffrey. *Black Victorians in Victorian England*. Barnsley, UK: Pen and Sword History, 2018.

Greenspan, Ezra. *William Wells Brown: An African American Life*. New York: W. W. Norton, 2014.

_____. *William Wells Brown: A Reader*. Athens: University of Georgia Press, 2008.

Gudmestad, Robert H. *Steamboats and the Rise of the Cotton Kingdom*. Baton Rouge: Louisiana State University Press, 2011.

Grover, Kathryn. *Fugitive's Gibraltar: Escaping Slaves and Abolitionism in New Bedford, Massachusetts*. Amherst: University of Massachusetts Press, 2001.

Harris, Leslie M., and Daina Ramey Berry. *Slavery and Freedom in Savannah*. Athens University of Georgia Press, 2014.

Higginson, Thomas Wentworth. "Romance of History." In *The Liberty Bell*. Boston: Prentiss and Sawyer, 1858.

Horton, James Oliver, and Lois E. Horton. *Black Bostonians: Family Life and Community Struggle in the Antebellum North*. Revised 20th anniversary ed. New York: Holmes & Meier, 1999.

Hotchkiss, William A. *A Codification of the Statute Law of Georgia*. 2nd ed. Augusta, GA: C. E. Grenville, 1848.

Hunter, Robert Mercer Taliaferro, and Democratic Party (US). *The Address of Southern Delegates in Congress, to Their Constituents* (Washington, DC: Towers, Printer, 1849).

Jackson, Alicia K. *The Recovered Life of Isaac Anderson*. Jackson: University Press of Mississippi, 2021.

Jackson, Kellie Carter. *Force and Freedom: Black Abolitionists and the Politics of Violence*. Philadelphia: University of Pennsylvania Press, 2019.

Jacobs, Donald M., ed. *Courage and Conscience: Black and White Abolitionists in Boston*. Bloomington: Indiana University Press, 1993.

Jenkins, William Thomas. "Antebellum Macon and Bibb County." PhD diss., University of Georgia, 1967.

Johnson, Walter. *Soul by Soul: Life Inside the Antebellum Slave Market*. Cambridge, MA: Harvard University Press, 1999.

Kantrowitz, Stephen. *More Than Freedom: Fighting for Black Citizenship in a White Republic, 1829–1889*. New York: Penguin, 2012.

Kendrick, Paul and Stephen. *Sarah's Long Walk: The Free Blacks of Boston and How Their Struggle for Equality Changed America*. Boston: Beacon Press, 2004.

Kendi, Ibram X. *Stamped from the Beginning: The Definitive History of Racist Ideas in America*. New York: Nation Books, 2016.

Kirby, Georgianna Bruce. *Years of Experience: An Autobiographical Narrative*. New York: G. P. Putnam's Sons, 1887.

Lane, Macon. "Macon: An Historical Retrospect." *Georgia Historical Quarterly* 5, no. 3 (1921): 20–34.

"The Libel Suit. The Romantic Story of a Runaway Slave." *BDA*, June 7, 1878.

Logan, Deborah, ed. *The Collected Letters of Harriet Martineau*. London: Pickering & Chatto, 2007.

Lyons, Joan P. "Quaker Family Home Became Stop on Underground Railroad," *Zionsville (IN) Times Sentinel*, August 25, 2004.

Mackey, Alexander. *The Western World; or, Travels in the United States in 1846–47*. London: R. Bentley, 1849.

Martineau, Harriet. *Retrospect of Western Travel*. Vol. 1. London: Saunders and Otley, 1838.

Mayer, Henry. *All On Fire: William Lloyd Garrison and the Abolition of Slavery*. New York: St. Martin's Press, 1998.

McInnis, Maurie D. *Slaves Waiting for Sale: Abolitionist Art and the Southern Slave Trade*. Chicago: University of Chicago Press, 2011.

McCaskill, Barbara. "Ellen Craft: The Fugitive Who Fled as a Planter." In *Georgia Women: Their Lives and Times*. Vol. 1. Edited by Ann Short Chirhart and Betty Woods. Athens: University of Georgia Press, 2009.

———. Interview with Phoebe Judge. "In Plain Sight." *Criminal*, no. 59. Podcast audio. January 20, 2017, https://thisiscriminal.com/episode-59-in-plain-sight-1-20-2017/.

———. *Love, Liberation, and Escaping Slavery: William and Ellen Craft in Cultural Memory*. Athens: University of Georgia Press, 2015.

———. "The Profits and the Perils of Partnership in the 'Thrilling' Saga of William and Ellen Craft." *MELUS* 38, no. 1 (2013): 76–97.

———. "'Yours Very Truly': Ellen Craft—The Fugitive as Text and Artifact." *African American Review* 28, no. 4 (1994): 509–29.

Miles, Tiya. *All That She Carried: The Journey of Ashley's Sack, a Black Family Keepsake*. New York: Random House, 2021.

Murray, Hannah-Rose. *Advocates of Freedom: African American Transatlantic Abolitionism in the British Isles*. Cambridge: Cambridge University Press, 2021.

Nell, William C. *William Cooper Nell, Nineteenth-Century African American Abolitionist, Historian, Integrationist: Selected Writings from 1832–1874*. Edited by Dorothy Porter Wesley and Constance Porter Uzelac. Baltimore: Black Classic Press, 2002.

"No. 2, Affidavit of Charles Devens Jr. US. Marshal of Mass—on the subject of Wm. Craft a Fugitive Slave, November 1850." Attorney General Papers, "Letters Received, 1809–1870," RG60, NARA.

"No. 3, Affidavit of Patrick Riley," November 18, 1850. Attorney General Papers, "Letters Received, 1809–1870," RG60, NARA.

O'Toole, James M. *Passing for White: Race, Religion, and the Healy Family, 1820–1920*. Amherst: University of Massachusetts Press, 2002.

Papson, Don, and Tom Calarco. *Secret Lives of the Underground Railroad in New York City: Sydney Howard Gay, Louis Napoleon and the Record of Fugitives*. Jefferson, NC: McFarland, 2015.

Parker, Theodore. *The Trial of Theodore Parker for the "Misdemeanor" or a Speech at Faneuil Hall Against Kidnapping Before the Circuit Court of the United States, at Boston, April 3, 1855*. Published for the author, 1855.

Parker, Theodore. *The Rights of Man in America*. Edited by F. B. Sanborn. Boston: American Unitarian Association, 1911.

Pryor, Elizabeth Stordeur. *Colored Travelers: Mobility and the Fight for Citizenship Before the Civil War*. Chapel Hill: University of North Carolina Press, 2016.

Quarles, Benjamin. *Black Abolitionists*. New York: Oxford University Press, 1969.

Reidy, Joseph P. *From Slavery to Agrarian Capitalism in the Cotton Plantation South*. Chapel Hill: University of North Carolina Press, 1995.

Ricks, Mary Kay. *Escape on the Pearl*. New York: HarperCollins, 2007.

Ripley, C. Peter. *The Black Abolitionist Papers*. Vol. 1, *The British Isles, 1830–1865*. Chapel Hill: University of North Carolina Press, 1985.

Robboy, Stanley J., and Anita W. Robboy. "Lewis Hayden: From Fugitive Slave to Statesman." *New England Quarterly* 46, no. 4 (1973): 591–613.

Rocker, Willard L. *Marriages and Obituaries from the Macon Messenger, 1818–1865.* Easley, SC: Southern Historical Press, 1988.

Rogers, W. McDowell. "Free Negro Legislation in Georgia Before 1865." *Georgia Historical Quarterly* 16, no. 1 (1932): 27–37.

Ruggles, Jeffrey. *The Unboxing of Henry Box Brown.* Richmond: Library of Virginia, 2003.

Runyon, Randolph, and William Albert Davis. *Delia Webster and the Underground Railroad.* Lexington: University of Kentucky Press, 1996.

Sanborn, Geoffrey. "The Plagiarist's Craft: Fugitivity and Theatricality in *Running a Thousand Miles for Freedom.*" *PMLA* (Journal of the Modern Language Association of America), 128 no. 4 (2013): 907–22.

Scott, Isaac. "The Diary of Isaac Scott, 1859–1864." Copied from the original by Peyton Sagendorf Moncure, 1980 (http://dlg.galileo.usg.edu/gac/isd/pdfs/gac-03-03-02-01. pdf).

Severa, Joan. *Dressed for the Photographer: Ordinary Americans and Fashion, 1840–1900.* Kent, OH: Kent State University Press, 1995.

Siebert, Wilbur H. "The Underground Railroad in Massachusetts." *Proceedings of the American Antiquarian Society*, April 1935, 25–100.

"Singular Escapes from Slavery." *Leeds Antislavery Series* 35, 8. Printed in Wilson Armistead, *Five Hundred Thousand Strokes for Freedom: A Series of Anti-Slavery Tracts.* London: W. & F. Cash, 1853.

Sinha, Manisha. *The Slave's Cause: A History of Abolition.* New Haven, CT: Yale University Press, 2016.

"Slave Hunters Arrested." *Boston Daily Chronotype*, October 28, 1850; *GT*, November 6, 1850.

Sterling, Dorothy. *Black Foremothers: Three Lives.* 2nd ed. New York: Feminist Press, 1988.

Still, William. *Still's Underground Rail Road Records: With a Life of the Author.* Philadelphia: William Still, 1886.

"The Story of Ellen Crafts." *Anti-Slavery Bugle* (New Lisbon, OH), July 14, 1849.

Strobhart, Albert. *Reports of Cases in Equity, Argued and Determined in the Court of Appeals, by Court of Errors During the Year 1849.* Vol. 3. Columbia, SC: A. S. Johnston, 1850.

Tadman, Michael. *Speculators and Slaves: Masters, Traders, and Slaves in the Old South.* Madison: University of Wisconsin Press, 1996.

Talmadge, John E. "Georgia Tests the Fugitive Slave Law." *Georgia Historical Quarterly* 49, no. 1 (1965): 57–64.

Taylor, Clare. *British and American Abolitionists.* Edinburgh: Edinburgh University Press, 1974.

Von Frank, Albert J. *The Trials of Anthony Burns: Freedom and Slavery in Emerson's Boston.* Cambridge, MA: Harvard University Press, 1998.

Webster, Daniel. *The Papers of Daniel Webster: Correspondence.* Vol. 7, 1850–1852. Edited by Charles M. Wiltse and Michael J. Birkner. Hanover, NH: University Press of New England, 1986.

Weiss, John. *Life and Correspondence of Theodore Parker.* Vol. 2. New York: D. Appleton, 1864.

Wigham, Eliza. *The Anti-Slavery Cause in America and Its Martyrs.* London: A. W. Bennett, 1863.

Williams, Carolyn White. *History of Jones County, Georgia, for One Hundred Years, Specifically 1807–907.* Macon, GA: J. W. Burke, 1957.

Williams, Harold Parker. "Brookline in the Anti-Slavery Movement." *Brookline Historical Publications*, no. 18. Brookline, MA: Riverdale Press, 1900.

Zackodnik, Teresa C. *Press, Platform, Pulpit: Black Feminist Publics in the Era of Reform.* Knoxville: University of Tennessee Press, 2011.

Image Credits

Insert: **1** Courtesy of the Middle Georgia Archives, Washington Memorial Library, Macon, Georgia **2** New York Public Library (NYPL) **3** Courtesy of Carol Spinanger Ivins **4** Schomburg Center for Research in Black Culture, Manuscripts, Archives and Rare Books Division (SCR) **5** Boston Public Library (BPL) **6** National Portrait Gallery, Smithsonian Institution (NPG) **7** Metropolitan Museum of Art (MMA) **8** Social Law Library, Boston, Massachusetts (SLL) **9** MS A M 2420(14), Houghton Library, Harvard University **10** Division of Political and Military History, National Museum of American History, Smithsonian Institution (NMAH) **11** BPL **12** MMA **13** NYPL **14** "General view of the exterior of the building" by Henry Vizetelly, from Dickinson's Comprehensive Pictures of the Great Exhibition of 1851, Paul Mellon Collection, Yale Center for British Art **15** Avery Research Center at the College of Charleston

Endpaper, left to right, top to bottom: **Charles Sumner** (MMA); **Samuel Ringgold Ward** (SCR); **Henry Ingersoll Bowditch** (MHS); **Lady Byron** (NYPL); **Henry Box Brown**, at center (Library of Congress, hereafter LOC); **Calvin Fairbank** (Boston Athenaeum); **Simeon Dodge** (State Library of Massachusetts); **Charity Still** (SCR); **William Wells Brown** (SCR); **Richard Henry Dana Jr.** (National Park Service, Longfellow House-Washington's Headquarters National Historic Site); **Ellen Craft** (Courtesy of Carol Spinanger Ivins); **Eliza Wigham, Mary A. Estlin, Jane Wigham** (BPL); **Harriet Bell Hayden** (NMAH); **Sarah Parker Remond** (Peabody Essex Museum); **Lucy Stone** (LOC); **William Craft** (SCR); **Frederick Douglass** (NPG); **Robert Purvis** (BPL), **Harriet Martineau** (NYPL); **Abby Kelley Foster** (LOC); **John Bishop Estlin** (Courtesy of Fran Aitkens); **Mifflin Wistar Gibbs** (SCR); **Lewis Hayden** (SCR); **Francis Jackson** (LOC); **Robert Morris** (SLL); **Samuel May Jr.** (MHS); **Georgianna Bruce Kirby** (Courtesy of The Society of California Pioneers); **Theodore Parker** (NPG);

Index

96 INDEX

Garrisonians in, 156–57, 169, 175, 176, 179, 180, 233, 253, 254, 275
in Great Britain, 275–76, 279, 290–91, 302, 303, 306, 312, 315
lecture circuit in, *see* abolitionist lecture circuit
militant resistance and, 154, 155, 156, 179, 182–83, 201, 209, 210, 211–12, 226, 227–28, 233–34, 236, 238, 243, 250, 251–52
"non-resistance" approach in, 32, 155, 156, 179, 210, 233, 240
in Philadelphia, 121–23, 125, 130
racism in, 179, 241, 295–96
women in, 121, 122, 129, 130, 133, 146–47, 148–49, 155, 169, 170, 173, 207, 209–10, 224, 239, 254, 275, 280, 290, 293, 295–96, 297, 302, 303, 306, 312, 315
see also abolitionists; *specific antislavery organizations*
Appeal . . . to the Colored Citizens of the World (Walker), 154

Baltimore, Md., 16, 100, 101, 103, 104, 105, 111, 176, 280
Baltimore Sun, 172, 248
Bishop, Francis and Lavinia, 276–77
Black people, Black community, 99, 147, 170, 173, 180, 181, 189, 216, 264, 289, 328
in antislavery movement, *see* abolitionists; antislavery movement
in Boston, 126, 147, 154, 187–88, 189, 190, 205–6, 210, 217, 226–27, 230; *see also* Boston, Mass., antislavery activism in
laws and restrictions on, 12, 80, 154, 238, 239, 257
in mass exodus to Canada, 205–6
"one drop rule" and, 52
in Philadelphia, 119–20, 121, 122, 123
racial segregation and, *see* segregation
as soldiers in Civil War, 326
violence against, 119, 122, 128–29, 139, 181
voting rights and, 129
see also free Blacks; fugitive slaves (self-emancipated people); enslaved people, enslavement
Boston, Mass., 5, 60, 126, 132, 137, 141, 145, 153–55, 159, 165, 170, 173, 178, 181, 182, 187, 189, 194, 200, 208,

210, 211, 214, 217, 220, 221, 231, 233, 243, 244, 248, 249, 251, 254, 276, 279, 284, 290, 304, 330, 332
anti-abolitionist mob violence in, 131, 243, 257, 295, 312
Black community in, 126, 147, 155, 187–88, 189, 190, 205–6, 210, 217, 226–27, 230; *see also* Boston, Mass., antislavery activism in
Boston Common in, 153, 156, 188, 189, 204, 216, 217, 228, 231, 245
Crafts in, 152, 153–54, 155, 188–89, 201, 202, 207, 216, 218, 219, 226–27
failed school integration case in, 189–90
Faneuil Hall in, *see* Faneuil Hall
Harvard homicide in, 189, 190
Hayden safe house in, 188, 190, 194, 206, 218, 227, 231–32, 244, 249, 250, 251
Melodeon in, 176, 188, 212
United States Hotel in, 216, 219, 236, 237, 239, 241–42
Boston, Mass., antislavery activism in, 5, 126, 153, 154, 163, 167, 190, 207, 209, 214, 247, 257–58, 291, 318, 333
African Meeting House gatherings and, 156, 208–10, 216, 219, 228
anti-slave catcher protests and mobs in, 155, 226, 230, 235–36, 237–38, 239, 241, 242, 254, 257
divisions and opposing strategies in, 156, 157–58, 212
Douglass's fiery Faneuil Hall speech and, 5, 179–83
Faneuil Hall meetings in, 5, 179–83, 200–201, 222, 240
firearms and explosives in, 155, 227, 236, 238, 239, 244, 251
and freeing of recaptured fugitive slaves, 155, 210, 301, 304
legal obstacles for slave catchers constructed by, 222, 225, 229, 235, 237, 239, 240
Massachusetts Anti-Slavery Society convention and, 155, 156–58, 159–64
militant resistance and, 154, 155, 156, 201, 209, 210, 211–12, 226, 227–28, 233–34, 236, 238, 239, 240, 243, 251–52
New England Anti-Slavery Society convention and, 176–78